WALL STREET

HARPER'S WEEKLY.

JOURNAL OF CIVILIZATION

Vol. XVII.—No. 877.]   NEW YORK, SATURDAY, OCTOBER 18, 1873.   [WITH A SUPPLEMENT. PRICE TEN CENTS.

Entered according to Act of Congress, in the Year 1873, by Harper & Brothers, in the Office of the Librarian of Congress, at Washington.

WALL STREET

A HISTORY

FROM ITS BEGINNINGS TO THE FALL OF ENRON

Charles R. Geisst

OXFORD
UNIVERSITY PRESS
2004

OXFORD

UNIVERSITY PRESS

Oxford   New York
Athens   Bangkok   Buenos Aires
Cape Town   Chennai   Dar es Salaam   Delhi   Hong Kong   Istanbul
Karachi   Kolkata   Kuala Lumpur   Madrid   Melbourne   Mexico City   Mumbai
Nairobi   São Paulo   Shanghai   Taipei   Tokyo   Toronto

Copyright © 1997 by Charles R. Geisst

First published by Oxford University Press, Inc., 1997
First issued as an Oxford University Press paperback, 1999
Reissued in cloth & paperback by Oxford University Press, Inc., 2004
198 Madison Avenue, New York, New York 10016

www. oup.com

Oxford is a registered trademark of Oxford University Press

The Library of Congress has cataloged the hardcover edition as follows:
Geisst, Charles R.
Wall Street : a history / by Charles Geisst.
p.   cm.   Includes bibliographical references and index.
ISBN 0-19-511512-0 (cloth)
ISBN 0-19-513086-3 (pbk.)
1. Wall Street—History.   I. Title.
HG4572.G4   1997   332.64'273—dc21   97-6096

ISBN 0-19-517061-x (reissued, cloth)
ISBN 0-19-517060-1 (reissued, pbk.)

1 3 5 7 9 10 8 6 4 2

Printed in the United States of America
on acid-free paper

For Margaret and Meg

Contents

Preface

Since the first edition of this book appeared almost seven years ago, Wall Street has added a substantial chapter to its history. The events that began to unfold after 1998 were as unanticipated as the events leading to the Crash in 1929. The full effects will take more time to be felt but it is clear that the market collapse beginning after the new millennium changed many investors' opinions of Wall Street and its role in the economy. It does not substantially alter Wall Street's history, however.

Throughout the last two centuries, Wall Street has been in a constant tug-of-war with Washington over the role finance played in the nation's affairs. Since the War of 1812, private sources of capital have contributed to the country's finances. Throughout the nineteenth century, Wall Street developed its own unique personality and institutions based upon the simple premise that outside interference was mostly lacking. The New York Stock Exchange and others developed as self-regulating institutions for lack of any other meaningful regulator. But as the economy became broader and more developed, this status quo would begin to be challenged by government, leading to the momentous events of the New Deal and the changes it brought to the world's largest financial marketplace.

When Wall Street overstepped its bounds by causing havoc among investors and other societal institutions, Washington had to intervene. After the 1930s, it was thought, incorrectly, that scandals in which investors were bilked of billions of dollars and many financial institutions seriously compromised would not occur again. Except for the odd scandal occurring over the years, the assumption remained fundamentally intact until 2001. Events developing since that time only prove that the centuries-old conflict between Washington and Wall Street will continue.

CRG

Oradell, New Jersey
November 2003

WALL STREET

Introduction

This is the first history of Wall Street. From the Street's earliest beginnings, it has never had its own complete history chronicling the major events in finance and government that changed the way securities were created and traded. Despite its tradition of self-reliance, it has not developed without outside influence. Over the years, government has had a great deal to do with Wall Street's development, more than financiers would like to admit.

Like the society it reflects, Wall Street has grown extraordinarily complicated over the last two centuries. New markets have sprung up, functions have been divided, and the sheer size of trading volume has expanded dramatically. But the core of the Street's business would still be recognized by a nineteenth-century trader. Daniel Drew and Jacob Little would still recognize many trading techniques and basic financial instruments. Fortunately, their philosophies for taking advantage of others have been replaced with investor protections and a bevy of securities laws designed to keep the poachers out of the henhouse, where they had comfortably resided for almost 150 years.

Bull markets and bear markets are the stuff that Wall Street is made of. The boom and bust cycle began early, when the Street was just an outdoor market in lower Manhattan. The first major trauma that shook the market was a bubble brought on by rampant land speculation that shook the very heart of New York's infant financial community. In the intervening two hundred years, much has changed, but the Street still has not shaken off the boom and bust mentality. The bear market of the 1970s and the recession of 1982 were followed by a bull market that lasted longer than any other bull market except the one that began in the late 1950s.

Wall Street history has undergone several phases, which will be found here in four distinct periods. The first is the early years, from 1790 to the beginning of the Civil War. During this time, trading techniques were developed and fortunes made that fueled the fires of legend and lore. The second period, from the Civil War to 1929, encompassed the development of the railways and the trusts, the robber barons, and most notably the money trust. It was not until 1929 that the money trust actually lost its grip on the financial system and became highly regulated four years later. Only when the grip was broken did the country enter the modern period of regulation and public accountability. The third period was relatively brief but intense. Between 1929 and 1954 the markets felt the vise of regulation as well as the effects of depression and war. The fourth and final period began with the great bull market of the Eisenhower years that gave new vitality to the markets and the economy.

Stock and bond financing began early, almost as soon as the new Republic was born. During the early period, from the 1790s to the Civil War, investors were a hardy breed. With no protection from sharp practices, they were the victims of predators whose names have become legends in Wall Street folklore. But the days of Drew, Little, and Vanderbilt were limited. The second-generation robber barons who succeeded them found a government more interested in developing regulations to restrain their activities rather than looking the other way.

The latter part of the nineteenth and the early twentieth century saw a consolidation of American industry and, with it, Wall Street. The great industrialists and bankers emerged during this time to create the leviathan industrial trusts that dominated economic life for nearly half a century. Although the oldest Wall Street firms were only about fifty years old at the turn of the century, they were treated as aristocracy. The great banking houses of Morgan, Lazard, and Belmont were relatively young but came to occupy a central place in American life, eclipsing the influence of the robber barons such as Jay Gould and Jim Fisk. Although the robber barons were consolidators and builders in their own right, their market tactics outlived their industrial prowess in the annals of the Street.

The modern era in the financial world began in 1934 when New Deal legislation severely shackled trading practices. Investor protection became the new watchword as stern new faces replaced the old guard that had allowed the excesses of the past under the banner of free enterprise. The new regulators were trustbusters whose particular targets were the financial community and the large utility holding companies. No longer would nineteenth-century homespun philosophies espousing social Darwinism be permitted to rule the Street. Big fish would no longer be able to gobble up small ones. Small fish now had rights and were protected by the new federal securities laws.

The fourth phase of Wall Street's history came in the late 1950s, when the small investor became acquainted with the market. Many securities firms began catering to retail customers in addition to their more traditional institutional clients such as insurance companies and pension funds. With this new emphasis, the Street began to change its shape. Large, originally retail-oriented firms emerged as the dominant houses. The result was all-purpose securities firms catering to all sorts of clients, replacing the white-shoe partnership firms of the past.

Since the Great Depression, the major theme that has dominated the Street has been the relationship between banking and the securities business. The two have been purposely separated since 1934 in order to protect the banking system from market catastrophes such as the 1929 stock market crash. But as the world becomes more complex and communications technology improves, the old protections are quickly falling by the wayside in favor of integrating all sorts of banking activities under one roof. While this is the most recent concern on the Street, it certainly has not been the only one.

Throughout its history, the personalities on Wall Street have always loved a good anecdote. Perhaps no other segment of American business has such a fondness for glib phrases and hero worship. Many of these anecdotes have become part and parcel of Wall Street lore and are included in this volume. They were particularly rampant in the nineteenth century, when "great man" theories of history were in vogue. Prominent figures steered the course of history while the less significant simply went along for the ride. As time passed, such notions receded as society became more complex and institutions grew and developed. But originally, the markets and industrial society were dominated by towering figures such as Andrew Carnegie, John D. Rockefeller, and J. P. Morgan. Even the more typical robber barons such as Commodore Vanderbilt and Jay Gould also were legends in their own time. Jay Gould became known as "Mephistopheles," Jay Cooke the "Modern Midas," and J. P. Morgan the "financial gorgon." Much of early Wall Street history involves the interplay between these individuals and the markets. One of the great puzzles of American history is just how long Wall Street and its dominant personalities were allowed to remain totally independent from any meaningful source of outside interference despite growing concern over their power and influence.

Several startling facts emerge from the Street's two-hundred-year existence. When the Street was dominated by individuals and the banking aristocracies, it was usually its own worst enemy. Fortunes were made and lavishly spent, capturing the headlines. Some of the profits were given back to the public, but often the major impression was that market raiding tactics were acts of collusion designed to outwit the smaller investors at every turn. The major market falls and many banking crises were correctly called "panics." They were the results of investors and traders reacting poorly to economic trends that beset the country. The major fear was that money would be lost both to circumstance and to unscrupulous traders more than willing to take advantage of every market weakness.

The crash of 1929 was the last old-fashioned panic. It was a crucible in American history because, while more nineteenth- than twentieth-century in flavor, it had no easy remedy. The major figures of the past such as Pierpont Morgan were not there to help prop up the banking system with their self-aggrandizing sense of public duty. The economy and the markets had become too large for any individual or individuals to save. The concerted effort of the Wall Street banking community to rescue the market in the aftermath of the crash proved to be too little too late. Investors had been ruined and frightened away from a professional traders' market. No one group possessed the resources to put the economy on the right track. America entered October 1929 very much still in the nineteenth century. By 1933, when banking and securities legislation was finally passed, it had finally entered the twentieth century. From that time on, the public demanded to be protected from investment bankers, who became public enemy number one during the 1930s.

Throughout its two-hundred-year history, Wall Street has come to embrace all of the financial markets, not just those in New York City. In its earliest days Wall Street was a thoroughfare built alongside a wall designed to protect lower Manhattan from unfriendly Indians. The predecessor of the New York Stock Exchange was founded shortly thereafter to bring stock and bond trading indoors and make it more orderly. But Wall Street today encompasses more than just the stock exchange. It is divided into stock markets, bond markets of various sizes and shapes, as well as commodity futures markets and other derivatives markets in Chicago, Philadelphia, and Kansas City increasingly known for their complexity. In the intervening years, other walls have been created to protect the public from a "hostile" securities business. The sometimes uneasy relationship between finance and government is the theme of Wall Street's history.

CHAPTER ONE

The Early Years
(1790–1840)

Remember, time is money.

Benjamin Franklin

America in 1790 was a diverse place and a land of unparalleled opportunity. The existing merchant class, mostly British and Dutch by origin, had already carved out lucrative careers as merchant traders. They made their livings in countless ways, but most revolved around trading essential commodities that Europeans coveted, such as furs, natural resources, and tobacco. Land speculation was another area that drew attention because the Americans had an abundance of land and the Europeans desired it probably more than any other type of property. In these endeavors the great American fortunes—those of Girard, Astor, Biddle, and others—would be made, and occasionally broken.

Most of America's riches were based upon an abundance of land. The New World provided more than just space for the land-starved Europeans. The millions of undeveloped acres west of the Alleghenies provided tangible proof that the extremely pessimistic demographic theories of Thomas Malthus had a distinctly American antidote. "Population, when unchecked, increases in a geometric ratio. Subsistence only increases in an arithmetic ratio," Malthus wrote in his 1798 *Essay on the Principle of Population* suggesting that the population was growing faster than food supplies. But the abundance of North America was proof that pessimistic theories of doom were misguided. The United States was the savior of overcrowded Europe. Horace Greeley later wrote, "If you have no family or friends to aid you, and no prospect open to you . . . turn your face to the great West and there build up your fortune and your home." By the time he wrote this in 1846, at least two generations had already done so.

With the abundance of land, food, furs, and minerals, the only constraint on accumulating wealth was self-imposed. Success was limited only by lack of imagination. Trading with the Europeans and with the Indians, manufacturing basic staples, and ship transportation all had been pursued successfully by some of the country's oldest, and newest, entrepreneurs. The businessman providing these services was adding value to other goods and services for a society that was hardly self-sufficient at the time. Making money was smiled upon, almost expected, as long as some basic rules of the game were followed. Others had to benefit as well from entrepreneurship. A popular form of utilitarian philosophy was in vogue, and America was proving to be its best laboratory. The Protestant ethic had not yet disappeared, but leverage was not well accepted. Borrowing money to become successful in business was becoming popular because it was recognized as the only way that capitalism could be practiced in some cases. But the practice was still not socially acceptable and also had a weak institutional underpinning.

Between independence and the Civil War, land played the pivotal role in American investments and dreams. The vast areas of the country and its seemingly never-ending territories provided untold opportunities for Americans and Europeans alike. They represented everything the Old World could no longer offer—opportunity, space to grow, and investment possibilities. The idea certainly never lost its allure. When early entrepreneurs borrowed large sums of money, it was often to purchase land in the hope of selling it to someone else at a profit. Even after much land was titled in the nineteenth century, its central role in American ideology was never forgotten. Its role as the pivotal part of the American Dream is still often used to describe the American experience on an individual level.

At the time of American independence, land was viewed less for homeownership than for productive purposes. England had already been stripped bare of many natural resources, and new lands were sought to provide a new supply. The oak tree was already extinct in Britain, and many hardwoods had to be imported. The sight of the vast Appalachian forests proved tempting for the overcrowded and overtaxed Europeans who coveted the timber, furs, and minerals that these vast expanses could provide. Much land was also needed to provide the new addictive crop craved by both Europeans and Americans—tobacco.

The desire to own property had also been deeply ingrained in the European, and particularly English, imagination. In the previous century, after Britain's civil war, John Locke had argued forcefully for property as an extension of man's self. To deprive a man of property was to deprive him of a basic right, as the framers of the American Constitution knew well. Arguing persuasively in *The Federalist Papers*, James Madison stated, "Government is instituted no less for protection of the property than of the persons of individuals."[1] This constitutional principle would help make property a central issue in American politics. But in the 1790s it was still something of a novel concept that nevertheless presented opportunities for vast wealth. No sooner had the ink on the Constitution dried than European investments in the new country increased substantially. Within a few years, land speculation would cause the first financial crash on Wall Street.

Despite the promise, doing business in colonial America in the middle and late eighteenth century was not an easy matter. Each colony had its own currency and jealously protected its own economic position, even when the federal government was formed after independence. The Constitution prohibited the states from coining their own money after 1789, but the chartered banks that would soon be established within the states took up that task. In the early years of the new Republic, many of the same problems persisted. The country was not the homogeneous place that it was later to become. Business between merchant traders, the lifeline of the early economy, could be conducted in British pounds, French francs, or Spanish doubloons, as well as the new American dollars. When transactions proved especially risky, payment was often requested in specie—gold or silver bullion. In the absence of state or federal taxes or high labor costs, great fortunes were amassed by the American merchant class. But the marketplace was hardly as efficient as those of the mother countries, Britain and Holland. Basic institutions were still lacking. The new U.S. Treasury Department was not instituted until six months after George Washington was sworn in as president in 1789.

Another institution the new country lacked was an organized stock exchange, a place where shares in trading companies and early manufacturers could change hands. Without an organized exchange, commerce in the new country would not develop quickly or well. Exchanges were needed so that investors could become familiar with companies and their products. Only when the merchants began turning their attention to providing money for new ventures did the idea of trading shares and bonds become more attractive. A market for these sorts of intangible assets had already existed in Europe for about a hundred years, but the idea was slow in crossing the Atlantic.

The European stock exchanges, or *bourses*, as they were called, were established in the seventeenth century as places where governments could sell their own loans (bonds) and the large mercantile trading companies could raise fresh cash for their overseas adventures. The Dutch developed their bourses first, as early as 1611, with the English following about seventy-five years later. Besides trading commodities vital to the developing mercantilist trade, both bourses began to actively trade new concepts in financing—shares and loans or bonds. Governments and the early trading companies began to look upon private investors as sources of capital. Borrowing from investors was preferable to raising taxes and certainly much safer, for more than one British government had run into trouble by over-taxing its citizens. Investors warmed to the idea of share ownership be-cause it limited their risk in an enterprise to the amount actually invested in it. Although the partnership form of control was far from outdated, the new corporate concept began to take hold.

After the Revolutionary War, the new American federal government immediately found itself in delicate financial straits, complicating matters considerably. The first Congress met in New York City in 1789 and 1790. The war debts of the former colonies and the Continental Congress were all assumed by the new government. Unfortunately, it had little actual rev-enues to pay for them. If the new Republic did not honor its existing debts, progress would be difficult for new creditors would not be found easily. As a result, the U.S. government borrowed $80 million in New York by issu-ing federal government bonds. Necessity became the mother of invention, and the American capital markets, however humble, were born. But as Ben Franklin was fond of saying, "Necessity never made a good bargain."

The major competition for money came from basic industries and fi-nancial institutions that were quickly establishing themselves in the new country. Most of these institutions were American versions of British trad-ing companies and financial institutions well-known in the colonies before the war. Merchants, traders, and investors trusted these companies much more than they did governments. As a result, the rate of interest paid by the new government had to be fairly high to compensate, but buyers still did not provide strong demand for the new bonds. After having shaken off the yoke of British colonial domination, the entrepreneurs and merchants in New York, Boston, and Philadelphia were not particularly keen to loan money to another government, especially one as untested as the new fed-eral government, which did not yet even have a permanent home. As a re-sult, many of the new government bond issues were only partly sold.

The three major East Coast cities were the home of American capital-ism in its infancy. Philadelphia had the distinction of being the home of the first actual stock exchange, Boston continued as a shipping and bank-ing center, and New York was the rapidly emerging center for financial services such as insurance and banking. Although the government bonds were sold in all three places and other major cities such as Baltimore and Charleston as well, New York developed the first active market for the bonds and the shares of emerging companies.

Local merchants and traders would gather at various locations in lower Manhattan, around Wall Street, along a barricade built by Peter Stuyvesant in 1653 to protect the early Dutch settlers from the local Indi-ans. There they congregated to buy and sell shares and loans (bonds). As the nascent securities business quickly grew, the traders divided them-selves into two classes—auctioneers and dealers. Auctioneers set the prices, while dealers traded among themselves and with the auctioneers. This early form of trading set a precedent that would become embedded in American market practice for the next two hundred years. The only problem was that the auctioneers were in the habit of rigging the price of the securities.

The new market, conducted at the side of the street and in coffee-houses, was a crude approximation of the European stock exchanges that had existed for some time. The London and Antwerp stock exchanges were quite advanced in raising capital and trading shares and bonds for governments and the early mercantilist trading companies. The exchanges developed primarily because both countries were the birthplaces of modern mercantilism and industrial capitalism. Equally, the British and the Dutch exported much capital abroad, in hope of reaping profits from overseas ventures. This was possible, and necessary, because both had excess domestic capacity and money and were anxious to find new areas of profit. And many years before the American Revolution, both had already had their share of financial scandal, the South Sea bubble and tulip speculation being two of the more noteworthy. These early scandals had proved that sharp dealings and rampant speculation could seriously diminish the enthusiasm of private investors, who were vital for the development of industrial capitalism. The same situation prevailed in New York, where the antics of an early speculator made raising money difficult in the middle and late 1790s.

"Fifteen Different Sorts of Wine at Dinner"

In March 1792 a local New York merchant speculator named William Duer became overextended in his curbside dealings, and many of his speculative positions collapsed. Having financed them with borrowed money, he was quickly prosecuted and sent to debtors' prison. Duer was not, however, just another merchant intent on making a few dollars in the marketplace. An immigrant from Britain before the Revolution, he had been educated at Eton and was a member of a prominent English family with extensive holdings in the West Indies. Duer permanently settled in his adopted country in 1773, becoming sympathetic with the colonists' grievances against Britain. Well acquainted with New York society, he quickly began to hold positions of importance. He was a member of the Continental Congress, a New York judge, and a signer of the Articles of Confederation. He was also secretary to the Board of the Treasury, a position that made him privy to the inner workings of American finance in the late 1780s. Having developed a keen knowledge of international finance, he was intent upon opening a New York bank capable of rivaling the great British and Dutch merchant banking houses of the time.

Duer was especially well versed in the amounts of money invested in the former colonies by the Dutch and English. Many of his real estate and curbside speculative positions were assumed in anticipation of the inflow of money from abroad. In 1787 he was closely involved in the Scioto speculation, in which he and some colleagues were granted rights to large tracts of western lands that they intended to sell to foreign interests. Unfortunately, the Treasury brought charges against him for malfeasance that it claimed occurred when he was still occupying government office. When the charges were brought, Duer was almost broke, having fully margined himself to engage in his various securities undertakings. When he became bankrupt, the entire curbside market quickly collapsed, and the shock waves reverberated for several years while he languished in debtors' prison.

Alexander Hamilton intervened on Duer's behalf in 1797 but was able to obtain only a short reprieve. Duer had been instrumental in helping Hamilton establish the Bank of New York a decade earlier, but even the intercession of his powerful friend was not enough to save him. This was the first case of a mighty financier having fallen. During his heyday, Duer often regaled his friends and associates at dinner at his home on Broadway, not far from Wall Street, where Trinity Church is still located. He had married Catherine Alexander, better known as "Lady Kitty," the daughter of British officer Lord Stirling; at the wedding, the bride had been given away by George Washington. Duer's dinner parties were popular, especially with Lady Kitty acting as hostess. As one contemporary said, "Duer lives in the style of a nobleman. I presume that he had not less than fifteen different sorts of wine at dinner and after the cloth was removed."[2] Perhaps it was his regal style that annoyed his prosecutors. After the brief interlude arranged by Hamilton, Duer was returned to debtors' prison, where he eventually died in 1799.

The new marketplace took some time to recover from the unwinding of his positions, and the banks recoiled at having lost money at a time when the new federal government was pressing them for funds. Duer had the distinction of being the first individual to use knowledge gained from his official position to become entangled in speculative trading; in effect, he was the first inside trader. What his inauspicious downfall displayed would have a serious impact upon the marketplace throughout its history. Duer joined the land-based speculation bandwagon like many of his contemporaries, but in doing so he violated one of premises of eighteenth-century trading. America was still a conservative place where the Protestant ethic was in full bloom. Ostentatious displays of wealth were considered vulgar or evidence of dishonesty. Duer's crimes were as much those of taste as they were felonious. His British background and his wife's family connections did not help matters at a time when anti-English sympathies were particularly high. New York laws concerning property of foreigners and debts owed to them were among the harshest in the country prior to the Constitution. After the British fled the city during the war, the New York legislature passed the Confiscation Act in 1779, allowing British loyalist interests to be seized. Several other laws were also passed that illustrated New York's distaste for its former colonial masters. While Duer did not fall into that camp, he was suspect, as was George Washington in some quarters, of being too pro-British. And his debts were considered exorbitant, especially when frugality was being preached by Alexander Hamilton, the first secretary of the Treasury. Even Thomas Paine, the American pamphleteer who espoused many radical causes of the day, was writing in favor of fiscal conservatism in the new Republic. The prison sentence was remarkable for its severity, especially in light of Duer's role in New York society and his high political positions.

Within a month of Duer's collapse and the crash that followed, the auctioneers and dealers resolved to move themselves in from the street and the coffeehouses and to find a more permanent location. Only the previous summer, curbside dealings had become organized and auctions were conducted twice per day. Now it became apparent that the marketplace needed a central location so that dealings could be better controlled and better records kept. The New York state legislature helped matters considerably by making the sale of federal or New York securities issues illegal at auctions as they were currently conducted in order to provide some integrity to the market. In the early years of the market, it was apparent that auctioneers were rigging prices to suit themselves rather than provide fair prices for investors.

Recognizing the need to clean up their operations, the dealers and auctioneers entered the Buttonwood Agreement in May 1792. Meeting under a buttonwood tree, today the location of 68 Wall Street, the traders agreed to establish a formal exchange for the buying and selling of shares and loans. The new market would be more structured, conducted without the manipulative auctions. This market would be continual throughout the prescribed trading period, and a commission structure would be established. All of those signing the agreement would charge each other a standard commission for dealing. Those not signing but still intending to trade would be charged a higher commission. Nonmembers either could not afford the membership fee or refused to pay, preferring to keep their curbside activities alfresco.

Purchases and sales of securities could be made in specie (gold or silver) or for cash, usually New York dollars issued by the banks. Obligations of the new government had to be made in U.S. dollars. Government bonds dominated trading in the 1790s, and it was not until 1798 that the first new issue of a commercial enterprise appeared. The New York Insurance

Company finally came to market in 1798, having the distinction of being the first new commercial issue after the market collapse caused by Duer. During the period leading to the War of 1812, the only issues that joined government bonds in the market were those of New York banks and insurance companies. The first chartered American bank—the Bank of North America, founded by Robert Morris and located in Philadelphia— was followed by the Bank of New York in 1784.

Founded by Alexander Hamilton, the Bank of New York received its state charter in 1791 and modeled itself closely upon Morris's bank, which had proved highly successful. It would soon become a favorite of investors, partly because of the reputation of Hamilton himself. As secretary of the Treasury, he had proposed full payment of the national debt and tariffs to pay for government spending. He was renowned for his conservative fiscal policies. Most of the new banks that opened were incorporated and had to become state-chartered as a result. State charters ranged from difficult to very easy to obtain, depending upon the locale. The only banks that did not require a charter were private banks—institutions that performed most of the functions of chartered banks but did not issue their own currencies. New York was slowing eroding Philadelphia's position as banking center of the country. Pennsylvania passed a law making private banks illegal, so in the future private bankers looked toward New York as their home. One notable early example of a private bank was Alexander Brown and Sons in New York, later to become Brown Brothers Harriman, one of the few banks to remain private until the present day. One of the chartered banks' major functions soon would become lending money to market speculators and investors in addition to the usual loans made to merchants. That link would provide a close tie to the securities markets that would never be effectively severed.

The bond influence was stronger than that of stocks. Issues of both stocks and bonds were quoted on a premium, or discount, basis. Regardless of the type of issue, a par value was always established when the security was first sold. Dealers would quote premiums or discounts from par rather than simply the day's actual price as compared with the previous day's price. Most deals were for cash, but some forward contracts, called *time bargains*, also could be arranged. Under this arrangement, delivery was for some time in the near future at a price arranged on the day the deal was struck. But this sort of dealing was highly risky because it depended almost entirely upon a verbal agreement between interested parties.

The First Central Bank

When the first Congress met, one of its original orders of business was to establish the Bank of the United States, which was incorporated in 1791.

The main office was located in Philadelphia, with branch offices in New York and other major East Coast cities. Unlike many of the chartered commercial banks of the period, the central bank was provided with branches in other states, a practice that annoyed many state bankers, who felt they were held at a comparative disadvantage since they were confined to their home states. In fact, the branches crystallized the opposition to the bank more so than its role as the central bank. Local merchants, many of whom were in the process of setting up state-chartered banks, did not want any competition or regulation from a federal entity.[3] When the central bank was dissolved in 1811 after its charter was allowed to lapse, over 120 state banks were already chartered. Many had begun their own note issuance, and within a few years many had flooded the market with paper, prompting the government to resort to specie payments in 1817. The ability to print notes was a power that many new banks and their owners were loathe to surrender to a strong central bank.

Originally, the Bank of the United States was one of the first hot stock issues in American history, but its own short but troubled history reflected the divisions still rampant in the new country. Even though it proved highly profitable to its shareholders, profits were not enough to save it in the long run. The issue was well subscribed, but it was not the sort to be traded by the auctioneers and dealers on Wall Street and in Tontine's Coffee House, the favorite watering hole of the merchant traders. The original capital of the bank was set at $10 million, with the federal government subscribing to $2 million. In return, the bank loaned $2 million to the government at 6 percent interest, to be repaid in ten equal installments. The bank also served as the government's fiscal agent. The public was allowed to subscribe to the remaining $8 million. However, in contemporary terms, most of the public subscriptions went into institutional hands. Unfortunately for the bank, those institutional investors were mostly foreign. The more substantial domestic merchants of the time subscribed to the balance.

While the structure of the Bank of the United States was relatively simple and its capital was readily supplied by investors, it fell into the greater ideological controversy concerning the role of the federal government in the new Republic. In 1791 Thomas Jefferson had expressed his own reservations about the ability of the federal government to charter a private company, which the bank remained throughout its brief history. Although part of that particular controversy would be settled in 1819, there was also the fear that the bank would evolve into a strong central institution fashioned after the Bank of England—the oldest central bank, dating from 1694. The "Old Lady of Threadneedle Street," as it became known, acquired a monopoly over the issuance of bank notes that would certainly not have been readily accepted in the United States at the time.

Tontine's Coffee House, 1793.

At the same time, other banks began depositing money with it, using it as a clearinghouse for their transactions, meaning it could dictate the type of currency it would accept. The sort of centralized power that the Old Lady was acquiring did not please those in the United States who were more interested in states rights than federal prerogatives.

Part of Bank of the United States' problems could be traced to its private investors. Of the $8 million available for public subscription, over $7 million was subscribed by foreigners, mostly British. Many British investments in the United States were represented by the banking house of Baring, later Baring Brothers. As early as 1803, Barings had been appointed official agents of the U.S. government and would represent British interests for years to come. The company had helped finance the Louisiana Purchase. Along with Treasury bonds, financial institutions in general were favorite investments of Britons in the immediate postcolonial period. But the idea of having the bank, effectively the central bank of the country, in foreign hands proved too much of a risk for many. Naturally, the ownership question played into the political hands. A Mr. Desha, congressman from Kentucky, feared that George III was a major shareholder. Given the king's mental state at the time (reputedly on the verge of madness), Desha claimed it was not wise to be held ransom by such investors, although he conceded that George would probably pay millions for the renewal of the charter in 1811.[4]

The bank was liquidated after Congress refused to renew its charter in 1811. In the twenty years in which it operated, it yielded investors about 8 percent per year in dividends and netted them about 57 percent in capital gains. The federal government netted over $600,000 on its initial investment.[5] Yet feelings were so strong about the bank's role in the developing national government that it could not find enough support, and its charter expired. The British investors had their subscriptions returned just before the outbreak of the War of 1812. The return of their funds became an important chapter in American finance because it showed that the government was willing to do business on an impartial basis, and that would influence future British investments for decades to come. One of the largest domestic investors at the time of liquidation was Stephen Girard of Philadelphia.

Immediately after the hostilities, British and other foreign interests in federal government debt began to wane. The reduction was to prove temporary, however. British and Dutch holdings of Treasury securities

Wall Street 1832 with branch of the Bank of the United States in center.

amounted to over one-half of the amount outstanding in 1803, although
they declined to about 25 percent by 1818. Other foreign investors
came from the mercantilist economies in Europe but were fairly insignificant.[6] Despite what proved to be a temporary lack of interest,
the tradition of British and Dutch investments, established in the early
days of the markets, would be reestablished and continue for well over a
century.

Between 1790 and 1817 a permanent central location for the New
York stock exchange was never established, although auctions were abandoned. Dealers operated in over-the-counter fashion, buying and selling
among themselves without officially congregating to set a price for a security. Government bonds became more popular and accounted for about
one-third of all securities traded in this period. When the War of 1812 intervened, causing speculative activity to grind to a halt, the government issued bonds to pay for the war effort. The image of the British setting
Washington, D.C., and the White House afire in 1814 did not boost investors' confidence. And many British investments in the United States
were prudently liquidated so as not to appear to be financing the enemy.
Many of these investments were also needed for the war effort against
Napoleon. When some of these sales occurred, it became publicly apparent for the first time that many investments in the United States originated from British investors, a phenomenon to be seen again and again
throughout the nineteenth century.

During the war a spate of new issues also appeared for commercial enterprises in addition to those of the government. In 1812, four new bank
stocks appeared for the Franklin Bank, City Bank, Phoenix Bank, and the
Bank of America. New York City also entered the market with a new bond
issue. Shortly thereafter, stocks appeared for nonfinancial companies.
Canal stocks became investor favorites, with those of the Erie Canal proving especially popular in New York City. The first life insurance company
in the country—the Philadelphia Company for Insurance on Lives and
Granting Annuities—was chartered in Philadelphia in 1812 as well. The
insurance companies that had proved popular in the markets prior to that
time were mostly maritime and casualty companies.

The government's offering of war bonds did not fare well initially, although it did eventually net several "underwriters" a fair profit. In February the Treasury attempted to raise $16 million to finance the war but was
able to sell only about $6 million. As a result, it sold the balance to three
individuals—John Jacob Astor of New York, Stephen Girard, and David
Parish, representing Barings. The three behaved in a manner similar to
underwriting syndicates that would appear later in the history of Wall
Street: they bought the bonds with their own and borrowed money and
then sold them for a profit to business contacts.[7] This was possible because

Astor and Girard were two of the most successful merchants in the country, each with an extensive list of business connections.

The underwriting proved to be enormously lucrative. The $10-million block was bought for about forty cents on the dollar and sold for eighty-two cents, netting the underwriters a profit of some $4.2 million, equal to one-quarter of what the government intended to raise. While the Treasury had little choice but to seek the assistance of merchants, a clear trend was being set that would raise the ire of future politicians, including Andrew Jackson. The commercial cum banking sector was making enormous profits at the expense of a hard-put government—a lesson that would be learned the hard way and would be resurrected some twenty years later by Jackson himself.

By the beginning of the war, such profits were not uncommon among the elite of the merchant class. Astor, a German who had emigrated to America from his home in Walldorf, Baden, in 1784 with $200 in his pocket, was worth about $250,000 at the turn of the century and a reputed $20 million at his death in 1848. Originally, he had intended to join his brother, who owned a butcher's shop in New York. He had some experience in making wooden flutes and had entertained ideas of doing the same in New York. But the ship bringing him to the United States was forced to take harbor in Chesapeake Bay because of bad weather, then became frozen in the bay and had to wait two months for a thaw. In that time Astor learned much about the fur trading business from a fellow passenger who had experience trapping in the American West. By the time spring approached and before he ever set foot in the country, he knew what his new profession would be. He had decided to become a fur trader.

His wealth came from a variety of enterprises that included mercantilist trading activities in commodities, real estate speculation, and, most significantly, the fur business. Fur trading remained his primary interest in his early years. Astor became the major fur trader operating in the Pacific Northwest, selling furs in both the United States and the Orient. He was also one of the first truly diversified American capitalists, using much of his revenue to purchase large tracts of land in and around New York City. The numerous landmarks and neighborhoods in New York still bearing his name give testimony to the extent of his holdings. Unlike Stephen Girard, Astor had little use for formal learning. Horace Greeley's *Tribune* described him as an aggressive man who "wrote a wretched scrawl, setting spelling and grammar equally at defiance." His business techniques were often questioned but were almost always successful. While openly advocating plying the Northwest Indians with liquor in order to make them more amenable to doing business, he was also a renowned philanthropist who actively sought to put forward a kinder image of himself in his later years.

Stephen Girard, a French emigrant, had similar humble origins. He worked his way through shipping companies to become a ship's captain at the age of twenty-five. He then quickly branched out and became a successful trader and owner of several merchant ships, all named after French Enlightenment philosophers. Like Astor, he was short of formal education, but he had a keener appreciation of learning, which accounted for his interest in banking in addition to trading. When the 1812 war loan went poorly as it was first announced by the Treasury, he and Astor arranged with Secretary of the Treasury Gallatin to buy the unsold portion and dispose of it among business contacts. Although they were well compensated for their efforts, the success of the loan helped to calm the marketplace and restore confidence in the federal government, which was at a low ebb. Andrew Jackson would later characterize the rich merchants as a monopoly that used the banking system for their own ends, but the war loan was one example of their providing a stable political influence in a period of great political and military uncertainty.

This was the first time a securities syndication of any sort had been successfully organized. The profits made by the three provided an example to other merchants of how the same sort of method could be used for new issues of commercial enterprises. Afterward, the Treasury quickly moved to open government bonds to competitive bidding to remove any hint of impropriety so that critics could no longer claim that the government and the wealthy acted in concert to ensure huge profits for the merchant bankers.

New York Exchange Develops

The turmoil caused by the War of 1812 prompted the dealers who had signed the Buttonwood Agreement to organize themselves further to retain their business. They met several times in 1817, eventually to establish the New York Stock and Exchange Board, the first organized stock exchange in the country.[8] The name derived from the board room at Tontine's Coffee House, where members would gather daily and state their bids and offers on securities. Trading was restricted to members only.

The new organization elected Nathan Prime as president and John Benson as secretary. Both were longtime Buttonwood members. The exchange acted quickly to establish minimum commissions that members would charge each other for trades. Nonmembers could trade with members but at higher commission rates. This quickly established the tradition whereby brokers on the exchange had a more privileged position than outsiders who simply dealt with or for the public. But the new system was far from ideal. The prices at which deals were struck were not made public. Although recorded on a daily basis, they were not always made available to the press. In fact, prices were not uniformly available in the New York newspapers for years. Customers had to rely upon brokers for advice and simple price reporting. Such lack of information meant that the prices and frequency of trading by nonmembers would be only as good as the brokers who transmitted information among themselves.

The lack of information on early stock prices can be attributed partly to the relatively small number of securities that were actually traded on a regular basis. In 1818 the exchange listed only five U.S. government issues, one New York State issue, ten bank issues, thirteen insurance companies, and several foreign exchange deals.[9] Most of the deals listed were from local companies, so while the new market was better organized than in the past, it was still far from being national in any sense. In fact, part of the problem in developing markets beyond the local level was the matter of speculation and stock manipulation, which occurred on a wide scale.

Not all stock trading was conducted on the new exchange. The "members only" designation precluded many from engaging in trading, and the twenty-five-dollar fee charged to become a member kept others from joining. But the possibility of profits still provided a great lure to many nonmember brokers, who were still numerous. They congregated outside the exchange, weather permitting, and traded among themselves along the curb of Wall Street. These *curbstone brokers* specialized in stocks not traded on the exchange and quickly developed a tradition that would lead to the organization of the New York Curb Market, the forerunner of the American Stock Exchange, which itself did not move indoors into permanent facilities until the early 1920s. The lack of a central location made the curb market the forerunner of the over-the-counter market as well.

Despite the improvements made by the exchange, its image was still somewhat tawdry. Those who were able to accumulate sizable fortunes on the stock exchange (and manage to hold onto them) were not considered among New York City's rich unless their assets were turned into real property assets. Trading was a means of achieving wealth only if it could be translated into what people of the time considered wealth. Real property reigned supreme. The United States was still not considered an absolute certainty to survive, and paper assets continued to be frowned upon in many quarters.

One of the exchange's major competitors for funds in the early years was a purely domestic form of financing that did not depend upon foreign investors and did not require any particular knowledge or sophistication. Lotteries had been a popular method of financing projects since before independence. After the War of 1812 they became more sophisticated as lottery ticket dealers began to spring up in order to sell tickets to as wide a population as possible. The first major dealer in lottery tickets of all sorts was S. and M. Allen Company, originally of Albany, New York.

Solomon and Moses Allen were the sons of an itinerant preacher in upstate New York. Solomon, originally a printer, saw the lottery business from the purely practical side. If he could sell what he printed, his prospects would be brighter. Lottery tickets themselves were very popular. Harvard College, Thomas Jefferson's Monticello, and the Washington Monument all benefited from funds raised in various lotteries. When the Bank of the United States closed in 1812, a speculative fever gripped the country and the lottery business directly benefited.

The Allens originally began their business in Albany around 1808. By 1828 they had established thirteen offices along the East Coast from Boston to Mobile. Through these branches they bought and sold tickets both to the public and for their own account. They handled most of the major lotteries of the time, although Solomon astutely detected a trend away from lotteries and decided to shift his business to the securities business. After the New York Stock and Exchange Board was established, the Allens became active members. In the early 1820s, the business shifted completely to stocks, bonds, and the different note issues of the states. It dealt with little if any foreign exchange, preferring to leave that aspect of the merchant banking business to those with more expertise and better overseas connections.

The Allens continued to prosper but were forced to contract their business in the late 1820s because of a series of losses. S. and M. Allen was a respected member of the New York exchange but became heavily leveraged to some southern banking clients. The company ran into trouble following the closing of the Second Bank of the United States in 1832 and became one of the subsequent depression's most notable casualties; its creditors finally forced a liquidation. Yet what it was able to accomplish paved the way for many more successful securities firms in the future. The Allens developed one of the first branch networks for selling paper assets to the public. Their success proved that distribution would be vital to the survival of the securities business. The wider the contacts of a firm, the better its chances of selling securities to a wide range of clients. It is significant to note that when the Allens became involved with the sort of stocks that appealed to British investors, their business began to unwind. Within a short time, other merchant bankers would follow their lead and develop similar distribution networks. One of their other legacies was an employee who later would found his own firm, Enoch Clark.

Biddle's Bank

Proponents of a nationwide bank pressured Congress to create the Second Bank of the United States in 1816, five years after the first bank's charter was allowed to lapse. Pressure to create the second bank was brought by Stephen Girard and John Jacob Astor. Girard was a firm believer in the central banking concept. When the first bank ceased to exist, he bought its premises in Philadelphia and named it the Bank of Stephen Girard. Whether he hoped to cash in on the demise of the first bank or merely wait for the second bank to become established is not clear, but once the second bank was proposed he was one of its most avid supporters. He also became the largest shareholder in the second bank, subscribing to $3 million of its capital stock. The second bank was larger than its predecessor but had a similar organizational structure. Capital was set at $35 million, and the federal government again subscribed to 20 percent of the bank's capital. Under the new charter, the president could name five of the bank's twenty-five directors. Its new head was William Jones, who was succeeded in 1819 by Langlon Cheves; neither was particularly popular. Jones presided over a bank lending spree that helped create inflation, giving much indirect political support to central banking detractors. Cheves actually foreclosed on some loans made to commercial banks, incurring the wrath of the banks and their customers as a result.

Because of the first bank's failure to survive, the second offering of stock was weak. The British investors returned for the second offering because they had been well compensated the first time around. But opposition to the central banking idea was now more developed, and investors would have to be enticed to subscribe to the new issue despite the relative financial success of the first bank. As an incentive, investors were allowed to pay for shares with government bonds. Many of the state-chartered banks opposed the second institution for the same reasons they had opposed the first. It could establish branches across state lines branch but they could not. Second, the matter of note issuance by the state-chartered banks was still a contentious issue. The state banks complained that the central bank accumulated their notes and coin and then presented them for redemption in specie.[10] While central bankers would argue that this practice was necessary to prevent inflation and debasement of currencies, the state banks saw it as poaching on their ability to make, and indeed manufacture, money. Their opposition to the second bank in a sense underlined the reason so many merchants were turning to banking after the War of 1812. State banks were capable of coining their own money, and as long as specie payments were not required they could achieve significant financial control over the states that chartered them.

What the second bank lacked in investor confidence was quickly erased by a landmark judicial decision. The new bank was aided immeasurably by Chief Justice John Marshall in the landmark 1819 Supreme Court case *McCulloch v. Maryland*. Maryland had attempted to tax all banks and bank branches in that state that were not chartered by the state legislature. This policy was aimed directly at the Bank of the United States, which had a branch in Baltimore. McCulloch, the chief cashier of the bank, failed to pay a $15,000 annual fee required by the state, resulting in the lawsuit. The Maryland courts had ruled against McCulloch, and the case eventually found its way to the Supreme Court.

John Marshall ruled in favor of Congress to establish a corporation, although he recognized that the word *bank* was not found in the Constitution. However, he noted that if Maryland were allowed to tax the bank branch then it would assume for itself powers to alter the Constitution. If he allowed Maryland's ruling to stand, he would be forced to admit that the states were more powerful than the federal government. The result, therefore, was that the Bank of the United States was lawful and free of tax burdens imposed by any of the states in which it was located. He argued that "The result is a conviction that the states have no power, by taxation or otherwise, to retard, impede, burden, or in any manner control, the operations of the constitutional laws enacted by Congress to carry into execution the powers vested in the general government."[11] This was a crucial ruling both for the bank itself and for the states' rights debate that would arise over the next forty years. It would also resurface a hundred years later in the debate over the federal taxation of municipal bond interest payments.

The bank was also helped immeasurably when Nicholas Biddle became its president in 1823. The short tenures of Jones and Cheves had left the bank with no direction and with new enemies in many quarters. Biddle was perhaps the best-known American financier of the day. Prior to his banking career, he had established himself as a historian and something of a literary lion. He wrote a history of the Lewis and Clark expedition (which he had to relinquish to others before its completion) and was the editor of the country's first literary magazine, *Port Folio*. Because of his eclectic interests, he had arguably the best reputation of any American in international financial circles, which were vital to the ultimate commercial success of the country. For the balance of its life, the bank was known as "Biddle's Bank" because of the strong influence he exercised over it.

But one of Biddle's major shortcomings was aligning himself against Andrew Jackson, the popular president from the Tennessee frontier. Biddle was the archetypal dilettante of his day, dabbling in many enterprises, usually with success. He was from a leading Quaker family in Philadelphia, had graduated from the University of Pennsylvania at the precocious age of thirteen, and later studied at the College of New Jersey (now Princeton). He served in various diplomatic posts early in his career before becoming a director of the Bank of the United States. When the bank opponents united under Jackson, following the victory over Adams in 1828, Biddle cast his lot with the anti-Jackson forces. Accusations quickly followed that funds of the bank were being diverted to support Jackson's political opposition. Although the rumors were never substantiated, they nevertheless provoked the ire of the president, who for ideological reasons also had been a detractor of the central banking idea for some years.

The fate of the bank rested upon the personal animosity between Jackson and Henry Clay, his Whig opponent in the 1824 presidential election and a strong bank supporter. Biddle had cast his lot with Clay against Jackson in the late 1820s. Jackson's detractors claimed from the start that he was not fit for high office. One wrote, "In General Jackson, there is no want of ambition, whatever there may be of ability. That he is the tool of others, every passing day brings new and indubitable evidence and the nation is subjected to the action of two powerful causes of evil."[12] The great fear was that the Jacksonian forces represented a new breed of politicians whose main desire was "booty" from political office. The election was the only presidential contest decided in the House of Representatives because Jackson had failed to garner the necessary number of electoral votes. Clay, also lacking a majority and sensing that he could not prevail, cast his votes for John Quincy Adams, who then was declared the winner.

Jackson was furious after his loss, but he gained his revenge in the 1828 election by defeating Adams. The 1824 loss would leave him with an abiding dislike of those who opposed him. Biddle then made his alliance with Clay, knowing that Jackson was opposed in principle to the central bank. By doing so, he had ineptly allied himself with Jackson's strongest political foe. The fate of the second bank was effectively sealed well before Jackson nullified its charter four years later. Other opponents had already taken sides in the dispute as well. Senator Thomas Hart Benton of Missouri stated in 1831, "I object to the renewal of the charter of the Bank of the United States because I look upon the bank as an institution too great and powerful to be tolerated in a Government of free and equal laws. Its power is that of a purse; a power more potent than the sword."[13] When the bank's charter was scheduled for a premature renewal in the Bank Bill of 1832 (requested by Biddle), Jackson vetoed it with a fair assurance that the veto would not be overridden. In his veto, Jackson claimed that the bank was under the executive branch of government, not under the auspices of Congress, which had created both institutions. He as president saw little actual use for it. He wrote, "It is to be regretted that the rich and powerful too often bend the acts of government to their selfish purposes. . . . many of our rich men have not been content with equal protection and equal benefits but have besought us to make them richer by act of Congress."[14]

Jackson's opposition to the bank was personal as much as philosophical. Unlike many politicians and merchants of his day, he was neither well-to-do nor particularly well educated. He had been forced to withdraw twice from public life—once as senator from Tennessee and once as a state judge—for lack of personal funds. Both times, he retired temporarily to the Hermitage, his recently built family home in Tennessee. It was not until he took command of the Tennessee militia through an elected office, thought to be mostly titular, and began to fight the Creek Indians in Georgia and Alabama that he rose to national prominence. When he successfully repelled the British invasion of New Orleans in 1815, his star rose even higher and he began to be mentioned as a potential presidential contender. His background was far different from the backgrounds of those who supported the Bank of the United States, notably Girard and Biddle.

On the darker side, many advocates of the bank claimed that Jackson was nothing more than a dupe for powerful commercial forces opposed to the bank for reasons of greed. But the recriminations did not forestall the end of the bank. After his reelection in 1833, he ordered all federal deposits withdrawn from the bank as a sign of his lack of support. Since the bank acted as depository for the Treasury, this immediately caused a liquidity crisis that forced many small banks out of business and dissuaded many foreign investors from further stock purchases. After these measures, the bank was doomed to failure. Although congressional support for the bank was strong in some quarters, Jackson's veto could not be overridden. Jackson portrayed the bank as a rich man's toy that had no place in his scheme of popular representation known as Jacksonian democracy. The implications for the country's finances and commerce were rapidly becoming clear. Senator Clayton of Delaware starkly stated that within four years of the veto, "Bankruptcies and ruin, at the anticipation of which the heart sickens, must follow in the long train of evils which are assuredly before us."[15] He was correct, but the time span was even shorter. Within a year, a banking collapse and recession had begun. Within four years the full implications set in when the panic of 1837 occurred, proving Clayton's remarks correct.

What became known as the panic of 1837 proved to be one of the worst depressions of the nineteenth century. The suspension of specie payments had forced many banks out of business and with them many small businesses that depended on them for their economic lifelines. The farming business was especially hard hit, and many farmers were forced into liquidation. Business failures became numerous as the banks began to fail. Wall Street witnessed several bank closings in May 1837, and the militia once had to be called in to preserve order at Broad and Wall Streets. George Templeton Strong, an observer, wrote in his diary that on May 2 matters became "worse and worse in Wall Street as far as I can learn. Everyone discouraged; prospect of universal ruin and general insolvency of the banks . . . workman thrown out of employ by the hundred daily. Business at a stand; the coal mines in Pennsylvania stopped, and no fuel in prospect for next winter—delightful prospects these."

Jackson's veto had even broader implications for the development of the securities business and commercial banking than simply nullifying the charter of the second bank. By curtailing the development of a central bank, the commercial banking institutions of the day were given more *de facto* power over their own states' banking systems than otherwise might have been the case. At the same time, they were given an opportunity to delve into the securities business, as elementary as it may have been. Jackson had followed through on his principles but failed to replace the useful functions of the bank, and the nation was again left financially rudderless. Banks were given a clear message that would last for the remainder of the century: Do what you wish to make money without upsetting anyone or causing financial scandal and you will most likely be left alone.

After its charter expired, the bank continued to operate as a Pennsylvania bank for several more years before winding up its operations permanently by declaring bankruptcy in 1841. Biddle retained an active interest but, frustrated, resigned in 1839. Within two years the bank was defunct. For the next twenty-five years the country's banking system was fragmented, with the chartering of banks remaining a state matter. Not until federal banking legislation was passed during the Civil War did the nation's banking system receive some necessary definition, although it was far from the sort of discipline that could be provided by a central bank. Jackson's actions and the lack of a political force capable of overriding them had created the beginnings of an oligopoly that would dictate American economic life for the next century.

Although Jackson's opposition to the second bank provided its death knell, part of his argument against it would ring loud for the next century and have a profound impact upon the country's economic development. Jackson maintained that the bank was a monopoly, being used by the rich to become even richer. Allowing the Bank of the United States interstate powers only enabled the rich merchant bankers who were its supporters to increase their influence and wealth. During the first quarter of the nineteenth century, criticisms against the government's relations with wealthy merchants and bankers had been raised many times. The commercial class operated without much government interference and many times flouted its power in the face of authority. A government agent wrote to Secretary of War Lewis Cass in 1831 about the behavior of Astor's fur trading employees in Missouri. His letter described them as those who "entertain, as I know to be a fact, no sort of respect for our citizens, agents, officers or the Government or its laws or general policy."[16] Commercial practices were not accustomed to outside intervention. American business would agree with Thoreau's dictum, stated shortly thereafter, "that government is best which governs least." During the first half of the nineteenth century, business in general was developing much more quickly than government, leaving Washington to constantly play catch-up with commerce and industry. While trying to change that attitude, Jackson had only reinforced it by failing to provide adequate guidelines for bankers.

This tension between business and government was destined to play a significant role in the development of the securities markets and investment banking as well over the course of the century. Never particularly amicable, government and business tolerated each other well, but it was becoming clear that business was practicing a new social and economic philosophy that was oriented toward the future and the accumulation of wealth. Government, on the other hand, was caught up in ideological matters concerning states' rights, slavery, and manifest destiny, and could not turn its full attention to business practices until much later in the century. In the interim, American business and its financiers operated free of any meaningful regulation.

Turnpikes and Canals

Before the development of railroads, shipping was the only viable way of moving people and goods in the United States, especially over long distances. Because of the large number of merchant ships in existence, the costs involved were relatively low. Almost all of the successful merchant traders who made up the wealth of the country were, or had been, involved in shipping at one time or another in their careers. When Robert Fulton's first significant steam-powered boat, the *Clermont*, proved successful in 1807, it sparked even greater support of devotees of shipping because it represented the most significant advance in that form of transportation in centuries. But new forms of transportation would develop in the United States that would challenge shipping within a few decades.

The largest growth sector in the American economy in the period following the War of 1812 was transportation, namely, those companies building roadways and canals. Many of these new companies organized as corporations in order to finance themselves for the effort. Corporations were still not common at the time but were becoming more popular as the need for capital became stronger. Potential investors were attracted to the fact that they were not liable for more than the amount they invested in one of these new companies. The potential gains could be astronomical, although experience would prove that, in the long term, these investments provided only an average return.

Roadway companies developed first. The Lancaster Pike, completed in 1794, was the first privately built roadway in the country, extending between Philadelphia and Lancaster, Pennsylvania. Many new German immigrants used it to penetrate the interior of Pennsylvania and beyond to the Midwest. The turnpike authority had the right to collect tolls and declare eminent domain when charting its course through the countryside. The publicity attached to the Lancaster Pike led other states to begin granting charters for turnpike construction. New York and Pennsylvania led the way in this respect, authorizing companies that eventually built over four thousand miles of roadways.

Turnpikes usually sold their stock and bonds to investors on the local markets. In this respect, more capital could be raised in Philadelphia, Boston, and New York than anywhere else. Yet, as many economic historians have noted, the roads were rarely profitable in the long run. Individuals used them and were happy to pay the tolls to travel on paved roads, but using them to send freight was a much more expensive matter. For most shippers it was cheaper to send commodities such as wheat and other grains down the Mississippi by barge through New Orleans and up along the east coast than it was to send the same goods the short distance from Lancaster to Baltimore by turnpike. Despite their contribution to the American infrastructure, the new roadways would take a relatively long time to develop as a means of freight transport. Shipping remained supreme.

Because of the popularity of boat transport, it is not surprising that canals flourished in the early nineteenth century despite the fact that they were much more difficult to build than roadways. The first significant canal proposed in the country ran between Albany, New York, and Lake Erie, a distance of about 350 miles; it was called the Erie Canal. Although they stimulated the public imagination, canals were extremely capital-intensive, and bond offerings alone would not pay their development costs. As a result, many had to be funded with state monies as well because they were risky ventures as well as new concepts in the United States. However, as work on the Erie Canal progressed, it became apparent that it would succeed and foreign investors were attracted. By 1829, more than half of the Erie's debt was held by foreign investors, again mostly British and Dutch.[17] While many turnpike companies were building roads in the East, there were only a handful of canal companies, which generally remained linked financially to the states in which they were located.

Railways also began to appear about the same time as the canals. The first American railway companies—both hauling mostly freight—were found in Massachusetts and Pennsylvania. The first passenger company was the Baltimore and Ohio Railroad. All appeared between 1826 and 1830. However, they were not the railways of the future because they used either sails or cables as their means of power. Only when the first steam locomotive produced in the United States appeared—the Tom Thumb, constructed for the Baltimore and Ohio—did the industry begin to grow exponentially. By 1840 the United States claimed three thousand miles of rail, more than twice the amount of track in Europe. Soon the canals would be obsolete.

As a result, the transportation companies became the first growth sector of the early capital markets, which otherwise still specialized in bank stocks, insurance companies, and bonds of the federal government and (increasingly) municipalities. The exchanges (especially New York) were developing reputations that began to attract sharp operators as the number of stocks they traded increased. For all of the genuine issues listed on the early exchanges, there were also those that had never quite lived up to expectations, and they would also become part of the legend of the early nineteenth century for somewhat different reasons. While many companies were the victims of poor management or poor business judgment, their stocks still benefited from the relative lack of sophistication of investors other than professionals

Early Market Practices

In the first century following independence, the United States was a debtor country that relied to a great extent on foreign investment. Without it, many of the new enterprises would not have been able to develop because the number of wealthy domestic individuals was limited, although rapidly growing. In addition to the bonds of the federal government, foreign investors were also drawn to those of the states and the larger municipalities, especially those with long-standing foreign connections such as Boston and New York City. But sharp practices on the rudimentary stock exchanges would dissuade others, as well as many potential domestic investors.

In 1825 the country experienced one of its frequent and severe economic slowdowns. State banks were issuing an excessive amount of notes, and the Bank of the United States was attempting to come to grips with the inflationary and liquidity problems that followed. The Franklin Bank in New York failed, and the stock exchange in New York collapsed on its back. The effect was so severe that the exchange lost 75 percent of its volume (from about four hundred thousand shares turnover in 1824) and did not recover until 1831. On March 6, 1830, the exchange witnessed the dullest day in its history, trading only thirty-one shares. This was particularly significant because earlier in the decade the exchange had reached its first thousand-share day. Despite the slack activity at this and other periods in the stock exchange's brief history, sharp traders were still out to make a buck by hook or by crook, or sometimes by a combination of the two.

Early in the history of the New York Stock Exchange, the tempting link between speculative finance and politics proved strong. When one of New York's early railroads, the Harlem Railroad, began trading publicly, a Senator Kimble of the New York legislature publicly opposed its enlargement. Railroad stocks were quickly becoming favorites of investors, representing the expansion of the country and the best that technology could offer. By opposing the company's expansion through additional stock issues, it would have appeared that the stock would have been done irreparable harm when in fact the opposite occurred. The current price was benefiting from an "inflation," to use a popular term of the time. Kimble and others took the occasion to begin "cornering" the stock, selling it to other investors who thought the company had more potential in a limited number of shares. They did not actually own the stock but were selling it short, betting upon the price eventually dropping rather than rising.[18]

In order to ensure a price drop, Kimble then pushed a bill through the legislature calling for the enlargement of the railroad, causing its stock to fall on the exchange as investors realized that enlargement meant being diluted of their current shareholdings. When the price fell, the short sales were covered and profits realized. This sort of cornering occurred many times on the exchange. Basically, it meant controlling the supply of the stock available for trading, then manipulating news on the stock for the benefit of the traders. Even the stock of the Second Bank of the United States was cornered in the 1830s before it became apparent that its fate was sealed by Jackson's political opposition.

Although stock prices were not regularly reported to the press during the first century of the stock exchange's history, news articles on many of the new companies coming to market were common, and often less than correct. Placing flattering or unflattering articles in the press was a favorite technique of manipulators seeking a public reaction. Unfavorable news could help them corner shares cheaply as the price fell, to be sold later at a higher price. Or it could be used to force down the price with the assistance of the public, or "outsiders," as they became known. Conversely, favorable news could be used for the same two ends as well. Because of the machinations of the speculators, it was difficult to tell what forces were influencing a stock, causing more than a few fainthearted investors to avoid stock investments in favor of other less volatile investment alternatives.

Stock cornering was only one practice in the bag of tricks that characterized early trading. An early investor's guide, desribing the tricks and motives of the traders, was published in 1848 based upon the anonymous author's years of trading experience on the New York exchange. It also demonstrated that members of the exchange itself were not insulated from predatory practices by other traders. One novice trader was reputed to have bought himself a seat for the standard $25 fee and in a short time accumulated a fortune of $150,000—a considerable sum at the time that would have made him one of the richer members of New York society. However, quickly thereafter he lost the entire amount and more in an equally short period as the other traders turned against him. Such experi-

ences only helped the New York Curb Market develop as an alternative to
the New York Stock and Exchange Board.

One of the dubious practices of the period was arranging for deals to
be done on a "time-delivery" basis, a technique that has since become
known as *forward trading*. Traders would buy a stock at an arranged price
and then have the delivery of their cash for the transaction delayed for
perhaps a month or two. In the intervening period, they would hope for
the stock to rise so when it came time to purchase it, they could simply
finish the deal and then sell quickly at a higher price, making an instant
profit. If the transaction was for a shorter time, no cash would be necessary in order to make the profit. This practice was quite prevalent during
the stock exchange's early years, although such sales were not legally
binding. If a trader failed to honor his part of the contract, there was no
legal recourse.[19]

But this fact did not stop time deliveries. Traders were assumed to be
gentlemen who would honor contracts as required, except in those instances where it did not suit them. Anyone injured by such activities might
sue if a deposit or collateral for such a trade was lost, but reverting to the
courts was usually fruitless and was frowned upon as dishonorable. Duer's
experience was not far from the minds of many traders. Gentlemen dealt
with other gentlemen on their honor, without fear of legal actions. This
had the net effect of making the New York Stock and Exchange Board an
insider's group whose members frequently preyed upon each other and
outsiders as well. Stories abound of members who left the exchange floor
for relatively short periods for vacations or business trips only to find their
time-delivery positions worthless upon returning, even after being assured
by other members that they would be well looked after in their absence.

Traders on the exchange were divided into two groups—bulls and
bears. Bulls anticipated rising prices; bears were short sellers. The stocks
both dabbled in the most were labeled "fancy stocks," those of "no particular or known value, which represent worthless or embarrassed corporations which have failed in the undertakings for which capital was
contributed. . . . their real worth, or rather worthlessness, is so little
known, that it seldom interferes with an unlimited expansion or contraction in prices."[20] In short, these were stocks of companies with no real
prospects, which traders recognized as purely speculative: "bubble" companies whose value would soon erode. In a period when information traveled slowly, it was safe to assume that these stocks would never be worth
anything again in the long run so they became means whereby traders
could occupy themselves without fear of actually harming the companies'
prospects.

One of the more subtle methods of price manipulation was engaging
in *wash sales*. Today, wash sales are best understood as purchases and sales

at the same price by the same investor or groups of investors seeking to establish tax losses. In the early years of the stock exchange, they meant the same but without income tax. If two traders wanted to depress the price of a stock in order to accumulate it, they would conspire to buy and then immediately sell stock to each other at a price lower than the existing price. The net effect was no gain or loss by either party. However, those witnessing the sale on the floor of the exchange would think the stock was weakening and would sell in anticipation of further price drops. As selling intensified, the original parties would then buy up whatever number of shares were offered by the sellers, establishing cheap prices for themselves. Conversely, those wishing to sell might arrange wash sales to give the impression that the stock was on the rise in order to sell at a higher price than the market currently quoted.[21]

These sorts of activities probably cast more light than any other upon the economic role of the early stock exchange. Admitted manipulation of many stocks by one of the two established camps—bulls and bears—proved that economic development would in a sense be slow without the aid of foreign investors. Large domestic merchants, such as Astor and Girard, who played such a large role in the development of the early banking system and the government securities market, did not speculate on the exchange. The New York market was still too small and clubby to provide more than a gambling arena for traders who had accumulated enough capital and leisure time to speculate on stocks. As the anonymous author of the early investor's guide said of a trader who had been victimized by his fellow floor brokers: "It had one good effect . . . that such an insight into the business disgusted him . . . and induced him to seek an honorable independence, which he has since acquired in a more respectable employment."[22]

The early years of Wall Street provided a foundation for trading techniques, commissions, trading rules, and underwriting. However, the gaming atmosphere and the predatory practices helped show that the marketplace was still very much in its infancy and would need years to mature. Although America needed a stock exchange from the earliest years of the Republic, it would take several decades more for the exchanges to develop to the point where they would be treated as different from gaming places. The major factor influencing American business expansion in 1840, as in the colonial period, was foreign capital. Without it, American economic growth would have been seriously impaired. Over the course of the nineteenth century, domestic capital would find its way to Wall Street in increasing amounts, but it would take another century before the United States was standing firmly on its own financial feet. Capital would continue to flow into the country despite the shoddy treatment that some foreign investors received from the brokerage community and bankers.

Even in the early years, Wall Street showed that it was evolving into a
curious amalgam of utilitarian philosophy and social Darwinism. Jeremy
Bentham's 1789 treatise, *Introduction to the Principles of Morals and Legislation*, paved the way for the early manufacturing age by espousing the idea
of social utility. The general notion of utility would become the American
ideal, although Bentham himself probably would not have recognized its
new application. All activities could be measured by the amount of good
they produced for the greatest number of people. New products and industries created new wealth, employment, and a sense of the common
good. Wall Street would quickly adopt this attitude, claiming time and
again that it was highly utilitarian by producing capital for expansion while
allowing traders to determine the day-to-day values of companies. From
its earliest years, it would claim to be aiding in the developing process of
industrial capitalism. For the most part, it accomplished those ends, but
the marketplace and the financial system had many flaws that would take
years to work out. In the interim, the economy produced many winners
and losers on a cyclical basis. Periods of economic slowdown or depression
were referred to as *panics*, indicating that the larger economic issues surrounding them were ignored while the psychological side of bullishness or
bearishness was emphasized. When the economy turned nasty, Darwin
could always be invoked. Only the fittest survived in a constantly changing
world. Since most significant American thinking up to that time—the theories of *The Federalist Papers*, Thomas Jefferson, Tom Paine, and James
Fenimore Cooper—had taken place within political economy and constitutional theory, these new, overly simplified ideas had great appeal. They
were not intellectual, and they were easy to comprehend. They reduced
social and economic factors to a simple, almost crude, basis but would nevertheless set the stage for a century of unparalleled growth. America had
the pop ideology it needed to succeed, and Wall Street was becoming its
best-known example. But the markets were far from well developed. Over
the next thirty years they would continue to experience cycles that would
spell success and ruin, sometimes with astonishing speed.

The Railroad and Civil War Eras (1840–70)

He that sells what isn't hisn
Must buy it back or go to prison.

Daniel Drew

Within forty years of being established, Wall Street was known as the playground of those who had set their sights upon becoming rich and powerful. Between the 1830s and the Civil War, a new generation of trader-speculator appeared who made his predecessors look tame by comparison. A great deal of this phenomenon could be attributed to the fact that Wall Street operated in an environment entirely free of regulation. Without constraints, it was only natural that trading would become more predatory while American industry grew larger year by year.

After the Second Bank of the United States officially closed its doors, a new era was about to dawn on American society. The one institution capable of preventing future financial crashes had been dismantled in favor of ideological arguments that were persuasive but had no sound financial basis. But at the time, those responsible for the demise of the central banking idea viewed it quite differently. They saw the end of the central bank as a victory for the common man against the rich. The states also welcomed the decision to close the bank since they claimed that an interstate institution chartered by the federal government infringed upon states' rights. The victorious side, however, had no viable alternative for the central bank, and economic swings between prosperity and downturn became much more frequent.

The closing of the second bank threw the country into turmoil again, causing serious financial distortions in the banking system and the markets. From the outside looking in, it appeared that the country lacked the political will to develop a stable banking system, relying instead upon a patchwork of state and local regulations and traditions in place of a centrally regulated system. Since the War of 1812, there had been no fewer than four severe recessions within a twenty-five-year period, accompanied by at least a half dozen smaller cyclical downturns. The American economy was on an upward pattern but was occasionally interrupted by hiccups that led to serious economic problems for all but the fittest.

During the 1840s the stock market seemed to be the perfect example of the growing popularity of the theory of evolution, first proposed in the 1790s by the English naturalist Erasmus Darwin but made universally popular by his grandson Charles Darwin. The ideas of natural selection and survival of the fittest became the language of the market, where traders constantly tried to better each other in cornering operations. The results were often bankruptcy and personal ruin. The New York exchange and the other regional exchanges become the personal battlegrounds of that undeniably American class of capitalists, the robber barons. After fifty years of development, Wall Street was still very much the personal fiefdom of a few influential traders.

The notion of survival of the fittest was strongly reinforced by the role of war in American society during the nineteenth century. The War of 1812 had forced the Treasury to borrow and had introduced the wealthy merchants to the bond business. The Mexican war of 1846–48 and the Civil War would also play pivotal roles in American financing and would help develop the financial markets. Most of the emerging companies coming to market were local: their appeal usually was found in the regions in which they operated. The New York Stock and Exchange Board traded only those that had New York interest or those with broader appeal. The marketplace still was not national in the true sense. But selling war bonds during both conflicts would force the market and its selling methods to become more national. So, ironically, war helped the American marketplace and economy develop, despite the fact that foreign investors, upon whom the Americans depended, usually were scared away by armed conflict. However, in at least one of these two wars, they were avid investors in American Treasury bonds.

Despite the problems, many traditions had begun which would become mainstays of American economic life. Astor and Girard had proved that merchants from outside the financial world could aid the U.S. Treasury by underwriting government bonds, making a profit in the process. Banking had become a lure for many entrepreneurs. The most successful were those who provided an array of merchant and commercial services to their customers. Municipal governments were successful in selling their bonds—many of them to foreign investors—so they could continue to build infrastructures and provide the services the Industrial Revolution required. Canals and roadways had also proved especially popular (although expensive), and the railroads were on the verge of being challenged by communications as one of the largest growth industries in the country.

The possibilities that the new types of transportation afforded investors drew more merchants into the financial services business. Many came from humble origins, even humbler than those of Astor. More than one had begun his career as an itinerant merchant, selling hardware and household goods from the back of a horse-drawn carriage. Usually these merchants would borrow money to buy their inventories and would repay the loan when they returned from their travels (the origin of the term *working capital*, which has endured to the present). Many merchants quickly realized that the individuals or small banks loaning them money worked less hard than they did selling their wares on the road. That prompted many of them to try their hand at the banking business, and many small merchant bankers set up shop, especially during the travails of the Second Bank of the United States.

The banking profession that many entered was still a far cry from the investment banking business as it is understood today. Prior to the Civil War, anyone who loaned money to a company by buying its bonds was considered a financier to the company. The same was true of stockholders. Many of the new bankers simply bought bonds from a company when they were first issued and either held them as investments or arranged to sell them to other financial institutions for a small fee. This was a crude form of underwriting but not the same type that would emerge later in the century, when syndicates of investment banks would pool funds and buy entire issues from companies with the intention of reselling to other investors. New securities before the Civil War had dozens of initial investors, most of whom were financial institutions ranging from the larger New York and Philadelphia banks down to the small two-man operations that remained in business for only a short time.

Early Investment Bankers

In the 1830s, many new investment houses emerged to help investors trade shares and foreign exchange and raise capital for new companies and entrepreneurs. Nathaniel Prime, one of the early members of the stock exchange in New York, established Prime, Ward and King in 1826 as a private bank. About the same time, John Eliot Thayer established a similar operation in Boston, which later would become Kidder, Peabody and Company. Although Thayer's firm was well diversified, it became increasingly involved in railway finance prior to the Civil War, joining other merchants-turned-bankers such as Thomas Biddle and Company of

Philadelphia and Alexander Brown and Company of Baltimore. While all performed essentially the same operations, the merchants turned bankers were very similar to their British merchant banking counterparts since they became bankers in order to serve themselves and other merchants. The brokers and other finance people who turned to banking forged strong connections between what is known today as commercial banking (taking deposits and making loans) and investment banking (underwriting securities), especially by loaning depositors' funds to the early securities markets.

The Allen firm was liquidated in 1836 and succeeded by E. W. Clark and Company. Clark was a distant relative of the Allens who had worked for them on occasion before deciding to open his own firm in Philadelphia. Like his predecessors, Clark was fond of branching and opened several offices based upon the Allens' model. And neither was he dependent upon foreign capital, preferring to keep most of his business domestic. E. W. Clark became a prime distributor of American Treasury bonds during the Mexican war. The firm's New York office eventually spun off on its own as Clark, Dodge and Company, a name that would be familiar on Wall Street until the Civil War. But the firm will probably remain most famous for an employee it hired in 1839, who became a partner in 1843: Jay Cooke, who would take the Allen and Clark branching concept to new heights during the Civil War and become a major financier to Pennsylvania and the U.S. Treasury.

Many merchant bankers also appeared in New York, migrating from other areas where they had initially found some success. Merchant bankers had a distinct edge over commercial bankers that would play an important role in American economic history for the next hundred years. Private merchant bankers, using their own capital as a base for their operations, were not required to have a state charter and as a result did not have to make their financial positions public. Successful private bankers would be able to develop considerable financial power without outside scrutiny since they were not accountable to anyone other than their clients. In the early days of American finance this helped them keep above the states' rights arguments that surrounded much of the banking industry and also kept them out of the money printing controversy since private bankers did not issue their own notes.

The nature of private banking attracted foreign firms eager to do business in the United States. In the late 1830s, the already legendary N. M. Rothschild (originally a German firm) of London established an American connection through an agent, August Belmont, who in turn established August Belmont and Company in order to represent the Rothschilds in North America. The Rothschilds already had considerable interests in the United States, but the economic problems in the country in the 1820s had

August Belmont. (Collection of the New-York Historical Society)

dissuaded them from further direct connections until Belmont convinced them to send him as a potential agent. Belmont, originally named August Schonberg, was a twenty-year-old employee who had worked at a Rothschild outpost in Italy advising the Vatican on its financial affairs. He changed his name to Belmont, a French variation of Schonberg, upon arriving in the United States. The new house began to rival Barings for American business, within several years becoming the major creditor of the U.S. government, mostly because of Belmont's shrewd assessments of New York society and finances. The Rothschilds had already established a legendary reputation for shrewdness. Most of the financial world already knew of their acumen in using carrier pigeons to inform them of Wellington's victory at Waterloo. They then quickly sold government bonds in the market, only adding to London's pessimism. Then by buying British government bonds before anyone else knew of the victory, the firm made handsome profits after the news of victory reached London, lifting depressed bond and stock prices. The Rothschilds' coup helped make them a legendary banking name, rivaling the Medici in the annals of European finance. In astute hands, the carrier pigeon became the nineteenth century's first example of speedy financial communications. But not everyone in the United States would be happy with the growing foreign influence in finance, especially during the crises of the late 1830s and early 1840s.

Despite the presence and influence of foreign capital, the large majority of new merchant banks and private banks that opened in the 1830s and 1840s were American in origin. Corcoran and Riggs opened for business in Washington in 1837, E. W. Clark in Philadelphia in the same year, and Lee, Higginson and Company in Boston in 1848. Of the three, Lee, Higginson would become the most influential and would survive well into the next century, although Clark's Jay Cooke was perhaps the most famous apprentice of the period. At the time of the founding of the Federal Reserve in 1912, Lee Higginson would be named as one of the most influential investment banks in the country, a backhanded compliment at the time. All three firms specialized in securities and foreign exchange dealing, and also served the local wealthy client bases of their respective cities.

One of the major financiers to the railways was Winslow, Lanier and Company, founded in New York City in 1849 by James F. Lanier. It acted as paying agent and transfer agent for many companies, especially the railroads, something of a novel practice at the time since most merchant bankers simply took positions in securities and acted as passive investors or short-term traders. One innovation that the company introduced to railway bonds was selling by sealed bids,[1] a technique that had been used by the Treasury for the previous twenty years, partly in response to criticisms about being too close to the large merchants who had helped sell the War of 1812 issues. But perhaps one of the most important firms of all to appear before the Civil War was that of George Peabody and Company, founded by an American living in London in 1851. The firm was better known for Peabody's partner, Junius Spencer Morgan, who was recruited by Peabody from Boston. Junius's son, John Pierpont Morgan, or J. P., who would become probably the best-known banker of the early twentieth century, was just a schoolboy when his father worked for the London firm. Junius changed the name of the firm to J. S. Morgan and Company when Peabody retired, marking the beginning of the extraordinary influence that Morgan, his son, and grandson would hold over American finance for the next ninety years. The Morgan firm, later to become a full-fledged domestic American bank, would continue to specialize in funneling foreign capital to the United States for well over a century.

Although American in origin, the Peabody and (later) Morgan firms were still considered foreign because of their locations but were nevertheless responsible for directing a considerable amount of foreign capital from Europe to the United States. By the 1840s, foreign capital was heavily invested in American Treasury bonds, municipal bonds, and the stock and bonds of the rapidly expanding railways. But not all of the newly established houses were quintessentially American. Many were established by German Jewish merchants and quickly became embedded as major forces in the merchant banking business.

Many of the houses established by German immigrants were associated with one central paternalistic figure, usually the founder of the firm. Joseph Seligman, a Bavarian Jew who came to the United States in 1837, rapidly established J. and W. Seligman and Company along with several of his brothers. They followed the same pattern as the Allens and established branch offices for dealing in securities and gold. They would become one of New York's premier banking families, with a long and colorful list of clients. Perhaps their most famous client of the century was Jay Gould, the robber baron later referred to as "Mephistopheles."[2] In similar fashion, the Lazard brothers of New Orleans formed Lazard Freres in 1832 and quickly used their European connections to establish a base outside the United States as well. Marcus Goldman, another Bavarian Jew, established Goldman Sachs and Company in 1869. One of the firm's specialties was trading in commercial paper, a market the United States sorely lacked in the period prior to the Civil War. The absence of such a market had contributed to the many business downturns and panics that occurred before the war. Goldman came to dominate the commercial paper market and is still a major force in the money market today.

Abraham Kuhn and Solomon Loeb established Kuhn Loeb and Company in New York in 1867, a company that is best known for a later chief executive, Jacob Schiff, who married into the firm in 1885. Schiff directed the firm's fortunes, making it one of the premier private banks in the country by the end of the century. The Jewish firms specialized in the usual merchant banking business, and many opened branch operations in Germany and sold large numbers of American Treasury bonds to German and other European investors. By doing so, they changed the complexion of American creditors, who for many years had been predominantly British. They were also cliquish, keeping to themselves socially. Usually, the top job at a firm was passed on only to a relative or to a son-in-law, ensuring a line of succession when the patriarch died or retired.[3] But despite their separation from the purely "Yankee" houses in the securities business, these firms became central members of New York society by virtue of their influence and far-reaching business connections.

The Jewish banking houses shared an essential element with the Yankee houses that proved indispensable on Wall Street. All were enthusiastically bullish on the economic prospects for the United States and sold that bullishness to foreign and domestic investors alike. Long before securities analysis became popular, they touted the relative safety of the United States from invasion and stressed the vast resources of the country, many of which were still being uncovered, as their own success demonstrated.

None of the Jewish or Yankee firms had pre-dated the Revolutionary War; all were successful products of the nineteenth century. Foreign investors in particular recognized their youth, but they were not always pleased with the results of their American investments. But for the most part, no one argued with the motives of the early American merchant bankers; to use a later phrase, they were all bullish on America.

"A Nation of Swindlers"

Prior to the Civil War, municipal bonds were among the most popular investments of foreigners. Many East Coast cities had large immigrant populations and were well known to overseas investors as entry points into the country. Along with Treasury bonds, municipals were heavily purchased by British investors especially. Barings actively sought quality municipal bonds for its clients, investing British surplus capital into what many considered to be a promising and politically safe haven for capital. The municipal bond market rivaled the Treasury market for investors' attentions, especially before the Mexican war, when the states and cities required capital more urgently than the federal government.

The heavy foreign interest prompted the Treasury to begin surveying the amount of foreign investment in the United States, a phenomenon that would surface periodically over the next century. By 1853 it was assumed that over half the bonds issued by Jersey City and Boston were held by foreigners and that over 25 percent of those issued by New York City were in foreign hands.[4] In dollar terms, this meant somewhere between $150 and $200 million of outstanding bonds, an astonishing number given that a major crisis had occurred only ten years before that cast serious doubt on the integrity of American investments in general.

When the Second Bank of the United States went out of business in 1836, many states quickly began to feel the economic pinch. Within two years, two separate economic crises emerged, proving Senator Clayton of Delaware somewhat prescient in predicting economic ruin to follow the bank's demise. Many states had regularly used the Bank of the United States to support their bond issues. When it failed, they were no longer able to borrow from the bank to pay their interest, and eight states went into default (Arkansas, Indiana, Illinois, Louisiana, Maryland, Michigan, Mississippi, and Pennsylvania, in addition to the Florida territory). Dislike of foreigners and fear of foreign influence became a familiar excuse for not paying interest. Part of the excuse had to do with the Rothschilds, a banking house that was feared partly because of the nefarious reputation of August Belmont as a suave but dark foreigner. Rumors constantly spread throughout Wall Street that Belmont was actually an illegitimate Rothschild offspring sent to the United States to avoid embarrassment for the family. Small and stocky, he was reputed to be popular with women and had an imposing business presence. A hundred years later, a Walt Disney animator confessed that he had used a nineteenth-century likeness of Belmont as his model for the evil coachman in the movie *Pinocchio*.[5] The governor of Mississippi declared that the state would not pay interest so that the Rothschilds could not "make serfs of our children"—one of the earliest recorded remarks to reveal fears of the Jewish and foreign banking cabal that would play such a prominent role in American jingoism, especially in the South, for years to come.

On the other side, the states' refusal to pay brought opprobrium down on the entire country. Unfortunately, the United States as a whole was achieving the same sort of reputation abroad. Its image became so tarnished that the British dubbed their former subjects "a nation of swindlers."[6] Many Britons, misunderstanding the evolving nature of American federalism and the slowly developing enmity between the states and Washington, hoped the federal government would come to the aid of the states. The popularity of American investments had sunk to a low not seen since the War of 1812, but for very different reasons. The United States' popularity as a safe haven for money, somewhat exaggerated prior to the Civil War, had sunk considerably, and it would take some extraordinary salesmanship to convince substantial foreign investors to continue investing as in the past.

One positive note did emerge when the country's first business credit rating agency was established in New York in 1841 during the uproar over the states' default. The Mercantile Agency was established by Lewis Tappan, a New York merchant who recognized the need for providing credit analysis of the ever-growing number of companies doing business. Tappan's agency was renamed Dun and Bradstreet in 1933. Another credit agency was established in the late 1850s by Samuel C. Thompson, a private banker who had gone bust in the panic of 1857. His agency distributed a list, "The Bank Note Detector," describing bogus bank notes being passed around New York at the time. This newsletter became required reading for bankers because of the large number of state bank notes in existence that were sometimes difficult to verify. Slowly, firms that made a living as watchdogs over the financial business were beginning to emerge in their own right.

Jacob Little and Short Selling

Not long after the states' default, one of the New York Stock and Exchange Board's most influential speculators scored a coup unlike any previously seen on Wall Street. Jacob Little had developed a sharp reputation in the late 1830s as a speculator with few equals. He founded his own firm,

Jacob Little and Company, in 1835 and made sizable amounts of money selling short in the panic in 1837. He was the archetypal bear of his day. But he showed his real trading acumen by recognizing structural market differences that others had ignored. The Rothschild lesson of twenty-odd years before had not been lost.

Little was a dour-looking man who would not immediately bring to mind the image of a swashbuckling short seller. A contemporary remarked that "the only thing remarkable about this gentleman is his extraordinary appetite . . . for he has been known to gorge and digest more stock in one day than the weight of his whole body in certificates."[7] Most of Little's fortunes (he accumulated and lost several) were made by being a short seller, a perpetual bear. He was one of the relatively new breed of audacious traders who took the counterposition to bulls in the marketplace, especially when the bullish sentiment came from overly optimistic foreign investors.

During the states' default crisis, Little observed that the British were continuing to conduct a market for American securities in London because of their vast number of investments in the United States. Among the many securities traded in London were those of the Erie Railroad, an early British investment favorite. About the same time that Little began selling short Erie, a group of bulls successfully cornered the stock, apparently having Little at their mercy. Many of his deals were done on a time-delivery basis, so it appeared that when it came time for him to settle, the price of the stock would be high and he would face imminent ruin. But when settlement came, Little delivered convertible Erie bonds that he bought in London to cover his positions, netting him a handsome profit while the American price was otherwise unrealistically high.

Little's coup so infuriated the exchange that it passed new trading rules limiting time deliveries to only 60 days, down from the 180 or 360 days then in practice. But Little did not learn prudence from his adept trading of Erie. In 1856 he again assumed a large short position in the stock worth about $10 million. Unfortunately, he became entangled in the panic of 1857 and the market began to fall precipitously, only adding to his desire to continue selling. But the market unexpectedly turned around abruptly and began to rise. The bears gave way to the bulls, and Little's sense of timing proved ill advised. He lost over $1 million by the time he finally covered his shorts. His adversaries delighted in the fact that it was the largest trading loss recorded until that time.

Little was only one of many traders who made a living by selling short those securities that appeared most appealing to foreign investors. Yet by the beginning of the 1850s, foreign investment had resurrected and continued unabated until the outbreak of the Civil War. Barings had again begun recommending American investments, including municipal bonds, to its clients. Some of the nicknames adopted by traders give an indication of how foreign investors, especially the British, were often treated. One favorite stock of British investors was the Morris Canal and Banking Company, a New Jersey banking and canal company with some well-heeled connections. Since the late 1830s the company had had substantial Rothschild interest and had been heavily sold in London. The Biddle family also had a substantial holding. British investors referred to the company as the Morrison KEN-il, preferring their characteristic flat pronunciation to the more French-sounding. The American stock traders seized upon that quickly, dubbing the stock the Morrison "Kennel," giving an excellent indication of what they thought of the company's prospects. That was only one of a number of stocks, including the Erie Railroad, that the traders liked to corner. Time eventually proved the traders correct when the company was forced into bankruptcy in 1841 in particularly messy court proceedings.

Despite the poor record of the states in paying interest, the growth possibilities offered by American infrastructure investments proved too enticing to be overlooked. During the debt payment crisis in 1841, widespread rumors hinted that Britain would declare war in order to retrieve its investments. However, the British rancor over the states' default subsided after a couple of years. Of more immediate importance were the periodic bouts of unrest witnessed in Europe. In 1848 alone, revolutions had occurred in Austria, Italy, France, and Prussia. The same year saw the publication of *The Communist Manifesto* by Marx and Engels. For those of the capitalist class, the notion that surplus value was immoral theft was repugnant, but it was certainly spreading throughout Europe. In 1840 the French anarchist P.-J. Proudhon had argued that property was theft in his classic book *What Is Property?* Such questions challenged the commonly accepted premise that capital was to be invested to make more money. The European intellectual tide was swinging radically left. These factors made European investors look westward, and much European capital would escape between the 1840s and the beginning of the Civil War. Although the United States had its periods of uncertainty, such as the Mexican war, it was considered safe from invasion and had a population not subject to radical notions of property.

The country had grown immeasurably in stature within a twenty-five-year period. Within a relatively short time, political and economic confidence was restored after the War of 1812 and the economic crises that followed. Technological advances led the way. The telegraph, introduced by Samuel Morse in 1844, was in widespread use within four years. It enticed more investors, including foreigners, than any other single technological development since the railroads and would quickly revolutionize communications in the same way that railroads had revolutionized transportation. Unfortunately for the markets and banking, the telegraph would bring news from California that would eventually shake the foundations of Wall Street once again in a pattern that was becoming all too familiar. The telegraph would have a profound impact upon the financial services business and helped put an entire generation of carrier pigeons out of work. Trading and speculation were on the verge of a new information era. By 1850 more than ten thousand miles of wire had already been laid in the United States, while barely any had been laid in Britain outside of London. British investors recognized the investment opportunities almost immediately. *The Economist* reported that "the owners of the magnetic telegraphs throughout the Union are said to obtain from 10 to 14 per cent on their outlay."[8] That was double the amount of return earned on a Treasury bond at the time.

The war with Mexico cast a cloud over the political horizon. But the Mexican conflict also posed significant opportunities for both investors and merchant bankers that would mark a distinct period of intense banking development prior to the Civil War. Ironically, the war would open a new era in securities distribution that would involve selling war bonds to retail investors.

By the mid-1840s the United States was developing rapidly. The New York Stock and Exchange Board moved to new quarters at the corner of Wall and William Streets in the newly constructed Merchant's Building, today known as the Old Customs House. The exchange rented the largest hall in the building, and by this time was holding two boards (sessions) per day, one in the morning and one in the afternoon. The initiation fee was raised to $400 in order to restrict membership to a better class of trader. In 1845 the *New York Sun* published a list of the wealthiest people in New York City, meaning those with assets of at least $100,000 in actual property, not simply paper assets acquired on the stock exchange. Topping the list was John Jacob Astor, whose wealth was estimated at between $5 and $20 million. Other prominent Wall Street personalities were August Belmont and Nicholas Prime (the most successful member of the exchange at the time), although most of the eighty-six individuals on the list were merchants rather than Wall Street figures. Familiar names included Commodore Vanderbilt, the Roosevelts, and the Lorillards.

Despite the steady growth registered in the economy, the 1840s were quiet for the market. New listings included some mining companies and additional railways. One factor that changed the complexion of American society immensely and added more emphasis to the securities markets was the discovery of large amounts of gold in California, initially found at Sutter's Mill in 1848. Within a year, $10 million had been produced from the mines. For the next ten years production grew geometrically, and within ten years over $500 million would be mined. The gold rush set off another bout of speculative fever, much more intense than earlier ones. Any stocks directly or indirectly affected by gold became investor favorites. The railroads were the immediate favorites, followed by the new banks that opened in the West. Gold would provide what many banking institutions lacked in reality—hard assets. Unfortunately, the banking boom came crashing to a halt in the panic of 1857.

Relations between the Americans and Britain also improved substantially during the 1850s until the Civil War intervened. In the summer of 1851 sailors from both countries engaged in the first of many races when the yacht *America* beat all British challengers in a race that became known as the America's Cup. By this time the British were becoming accustomed to being outmaneuvered by their former colonies on the high seas. Recognizing that the United States was poised to surpass the mother country in accomplishments on many fronts, *The Economist* acknowledged, "The *America*, by beating the very best of our craft, has at once alarmed and convinced us. . . . We rejoice in the success of the *America* because we believe it is likely to ensure us against defeat on matters of much greater moment than yacht sailing."[9]

The "Western Blizzard"

All of the new developments in technology and manufacturing continued to lead investors to the marketplace. For all of the successes, many found the experience less than pleasant. In 1839 the New York Stock and Exchange Board listed 144 stocks, almost half of which were banking institutions. Twenty years later, the number had actually declined by some thirty companies. Those that remained were stronger financially than they had been earlier, but the decline is striking in a period that would suggest even greater growth. The reasons for this odd phenomenon can be attributed to Wall Street's by now familiar three old bogeys—panic, inflation, and fraud.

Greed surfaced egregiously in the early 1850s with some of the first examples of stock certificate fraud on a large scale. In 1854 Robert Schuyler, the president of the New York and New Haven Railroad, issued almost $2 million worth of fraudulent stock in his own company. He had been the president of the Illinois Central only a year before and had taken the new job under allegations of fraud at his old firm, which eventually proved to be true. The idea was simple. The proceeds of the false sale would go straight into the pockets of the conspirators who drew up the ideas to begin with. What could not be anticipated was the astute purchase of Illinois Central stock by British investors. Many Americans sold the Illinois, assuming that Schuyler's tenure there probably also was tainted with fraud. The securities of Illinois Central dropped precipitously in the market.

Then British investors, prompted by their American advisers, moved in to
make large purchases.[10] They made a fair profit after the fact. Shortly
thereafter, another scandal was unveiled when Alexander Kyle, president
of the New York and Harlem Railroad, issued three thousand shares of bogus certificates in his own company. The reasons for fraud on this level
were simple: railroad stocks were favorites of foreign investors, and the
great distances between them and the companies the stocks represented
made fraud a tempting option. Who would notice if a few extra shares
were missing?

In the later 1850s the United States became a victim of its own success.
The West became more explored and developed and the gold rush continued. As the population moved westward, so too did banks, and the western
territories became overpopulated with small chartered banks, many of
which naturally issued their own bank notes. By 1857 the enormous
amount of gold mined in California caused many of the banks to issue an
excessive number of notes. Prosperity was beginning to cause money inflation, which created the appearance of even more prosperity.

The boom atmosphere caused imports to increase. Building projects
mushroomed all over the country, many financed with borrowed money. A
relatively large bubble was expanding that would burst in 1857. The actual
panic began in August when the Ohio Insurance and Trust Company
failed, causing widespread confusion. About $5 million of liabilities were
left unpaid. The effects spread far beyond Cincinnati, the company headquarters, and soon were felt by insurance companies in New York, the nation's insurance capital. As they made cash demands on their banks, the
banks reacted to cover their own positions. In October, eighteen banks in
New York City suspended specie payments. As many as twenty thousand
New York workers lost their jobs as a result.

The panic that blew into New York was called the "western blizzard"
because of its western origins. But contrary to common sense, Wall Street
enjoyed the blizzard. Many short sellers prospered. Little and others, long
accustomed to making money at the expense of others, continued to do so
by anticipating the panic. Then after the banks suspended specie payments, the marketplace surprisingly turned around and began to rise. The
bulls then had their day in the sun as a result. The resilience of the marketplace and the traders' ability to make money under such confusing circumstances surprised many commentators of the day. One noted that
"nothing but *the* final conflagration will put an end to Wall Street speculations and Wall Street swindles. An ordinary earthquake does not trouble
the operators at all."[11]

Many suspected that the banks' reaction to the insurance failures was a
bit overdone, but that by refusing specie payments they quickly restored
confidence in the financial system. The shakeout in New York caused a

number of bankruptcies among traders and dealers. This was certainly not the first time the phenomenon had occurred; other panics in the 1830s had also caused marginal dealers to close their operations. But by 1857 an ideological current was beginning to develop on Wall Street that would prevail for decades. The undertone was distinctly predatory. Reflecting the prevailing social philosophies of the day, Henry Clews, a prominent trader who began his career on Wall Street in 1857, later wrote in his memoirs that the panic was "a fine exemplification of the survival of the fittest and proved that there was a law of natural selection in financial affairs."[12] Clews proved to be only a few years out of step with the best example of that comment yet to be found on Wall Street. The career of Jay Cooke best typified survival of the fittest of a major financier witnessed until that time.

The Rise of Jay Cooke

Jay Cooke was the son of two upstate New Yorkers who departed for the Illinois Territory after the War of 1812. His family traced its ancestry back to the Massachusetts Bay Colony in 1630, although it had not gained a great deal of wealth in the intervening period. The family eventually settled in Ohio, in what was later to be Sandusky, where Jay was born in 1821. Over the next twelve years his father, a lawyer, served both in the Ohio legislature and for a term in the U.S. House of Representatives. The Cookes were not the typical frontier family, and it would not be long before their son looked eastward to make his own fortune.

After working briefly in St. Louis, he made his way to Philadelphia to work for his brother-in-law in a shipping firm. In 1839 he took a job as a clerk with E. W. Clark and Company, where he began to learn the trade of marketing securities to customers, displaying some of the keen business sense and autocratic personality that were to mark his later success. Clark was the major Philadelphia firm other than Girard's bank, but it employed different marketing techniques. Clark would often take out advertisements in local newspapers touting securities it wanted to sell. In addition to selling local securities on behalf of Pennsylvania and its various municipalities, Clark also reached farther afield, selling railway stocks and bonds. The firm also provided daily market commentary for the local newspapers in Philadelphia. In the mid-1840s it opened an office in New York that was devoted exclusively to the securities business without some of the other merchant banking trappings.

Despite the success of Cooke himself in later years on the retail side of the securities business, Clark's first major coup occurred when it helped sell Texas bonds to the public just before the Mexican war. Texas issued many bonds before the war, realizing that if the United States was victorious it would be annexed. This possibility provided a strong marketing incentive, and investors flocked to purchase the obligations, assuming the bonds would increase in price when the Mexicans were defeated. Many of the buyers turned out to be officials of the U.S. government who knew a good thing when they saw it. Although the northern states were originally opposed to war, Cooke later acknowledged in his memoirs that "the opposition from the North was undoubtedly overcome through the cohesive power of public plunder."[13] The Clark firm learned relatively early on that its greatest profits would be found during times of war. The lesson was not lost on Cooke either.

But even more money was to be made from the Mexican war bonds issued by the Treasury to help pay for the conflict. The Treasury was required by law to have the proceeds of the bond deposited in one of the sub-treasuries, or Treasury branches, of the United States, which were located at various points throughout the country. Clark's St. Louis office floated the funds it raised for the Treasury by depositing the money in its New York office by mail. While waiting for the delivery of the draft it had mailed itself, the firm had the use of the Treasury's funds, which earned it a few extra dollars. Then the funds had to be transferred back to St. Louis, which did not have a sub-Treasury. The Clark firm then arranged for a bond drawn on itself to be delivered to the Treasury, saying that it was good for the funds. When the smoke cleared from the transaction, the firm had netted itself about 8 percent of the money it had helped raise without incurring any risk. The Treasury got its money, and Clark made unusual profits because of the slow delivery of the mails and the nature of the Treasury depository system. Everyone familiar with the complicated transfer operation learned that the Treasury was quite amenable to being manipulated when it urgently needed funds. The lesson would not be lost when the Civil War began.

The Clark firm did not survive the panic of 1857. By that time, it was operating in a fashion similar to modern investment banks. Many of the securities it purchased were for its own account, to be sold to investors later at higher prices. Much of the money invested in these securities was borrowed from banks, and when the panic began and the banks closed, the firm was forced into liquidation because it lost its lines of credit. Enoch Clark himself died at about the same time, and unlike many of the Jewish firms, assured of a line of succession, Clark's firm could not be maintained. Its offices closed, leaving Jay Cooke without a job, but not for long.

For a couple of years after the panic, Cooke busied himself with various independent financing ventures. He had accumulated a small fortune while working for Clark but was too conservative to rush into a new venture on his own until the effects of the panic had finally subsided. He organized several companies that bought individual canal companies from their sponsor states and dabbled in a few railroad companies. Finally in

January 1861 he opened Jay Cooke and Company in Philadelphia—organized as a private bank and located literally in the shadow of Girard's bank. Pennsylvania had begun to allow private banks to operate again, and Cooke's was one of over thirty in the city.

At the time Cooke was opening his bank, the country's financial health again deteriorated. Anticipating an armed conflict, foreign investors had been selling their American securities and taking cash out of the country, causing a flight of gold. The stock market plunged to lows not seen even in the panic of 1857. The cotton exporting business collapsed, and many Southern banks suspended specie payments, causing problems in other parts of the country. The U.S. Treasury could cover only 25 percent of its expenditures and was desperate for cash. The Treasury, led by Salmon Chase, committed itself to a sound money policy that caused the large banks to abandon efforts to help it finance itself. As a result, the Treasury resorted to the issue of the dreaded "greenbacks," paper money with no metallic backing. This about-face dismayed the banks even more, and many became reluctant to help the Treasury in its financings at the onset of the war.

When the firm began, Cooke was worth an estimated $150,000, a respectable sum but not enough to put him into the ranks of Philadelphia's wealthiest. The new bank was operated as a partnership but was dwarfed by older, more established institutions in the city. The largest and most influential of the private banks was Drexel and Company, followed by Girard. All were involved in essentially the same sort of business—dealing in discounted commercial paper, government bonds and notes, stocks, and bills of exchange. They all also took in deposits from wealthy individuals. But size and influence were not to be Cooke's forte. His influence would be built around political connections and the lessons he had learned at Clark.

The turning point for Cooke's career as a private banker came because of his brother's association with Salmon Chase, Abraham Lincoln's secretary of the Treasury and a former senator from Ohio. Chase was a man of high principle; in addition to being a fervent abolitionist, he also kept a tight rein on the Treasury's finances by requiring competitive bidding by bankers for new issues of Treasury bonds. The lessons of the past were not forgotten, and Chase would not sell bonds to bankers at just any price. The coup that Astor, Girard and Parish had pulled several decades earlier had been used time and again by various populist politicians, and the new Republican party that had assumed the White House wanted to remain above criticisms that it helped the rich get richer at the government's expense. The opportunity to abide by these principles would not be long in coming after the first shots of the Civil War were fired at Fort Sumter.

When the war began, the State of Pennsylvania decided to issue a bond for $3 million to provide for the state's defense against potential attack by the Confederacy. The job of selling the issue to investors was substantial, for many remembered Pennsylvania's default during the 1841 crisis. But Cooke spotted an opportunity for his fledgling firm if he could manage to distribute a major portion of the debt. The normal method of distribution would have been to obtain the best price available for the bonds, which might have meant a substantial discount from par to the participating banks. Cooke, on the other hand, tried to convince Pennsylvania officials to sell the bonds using patriotism as a sales tool. That would mean obtaining full face value, or par, for the bonds rather than selling at a discount.

Because of his novel approach, Pennsylvania appointed Cooke and Drexel and Company as the agents for the sale. This was a personal coup for Cooke, who had been in business for only a short time. Drexel had at least ten times as much capital as Cooke and frowned upon its upstart partner. But none of this deterred Cooke, who took out advertisements in the local newspapers touting the bonds' merits. The ads played upon the patriotism of the potential investors but emphasized the financial side as well: "But independent of any motives of patriotism, there are considerations of self-interest which may be considered in reference to this Loan. It is a six per cent loan free from any taxation."[14]

All of this meant there was little profit in the transaction for Cooke and Drexel. They would make only pennies on the sale of each bond. While this was the hook that Cooke had used to persuade Pennsylvania to use his bank in the first place, it would not provide a good long-term strategy for his new firm. Cooke had something else in mind that the bonds were able to accomplish for him.

As a private banker, Cooke was somewhat short of working capital. Banks make their money by having large amounts of working capital, that is, deposits from customers that can be loaned to others or used to purchase bonds or securities. When he was named agent for the transaction, he ensured himself of a large inflow of deposits from customers who deposited funds with him in order to make their purchases. Additionally, he persuaded the state to name his bank as an official state depository, which solved his working capital needs in a moment; other depositors would now be more inclined to use his bank since he was no longer short of working capital.

The sale was a huge success. Institutions of all sorts bought the bonds. Individual investors also flocked to the issue, partly because of the patriotic theme, as well as the fact that it was denominated in amounts as small as fifty dollars. Building upon his earlier experiences with Clark, Cooke had scored his own personal success with a government without actually preying upon structural weaknesses in the financial system that allowed him to take undue advantage. Filled with pride, he made certain that everyone remotely interested in the issue heard of his success. As one of his biographers noted, claiming that Cooke was promoting the Northern cause in the war, he sent a list of the bond subscribers to Secretary Salmon Chase, Jefferson Davis, and the *Times* of London.[15] No one recorded what the subscribers thought of having their names in the hands of the president of the Confederacy.

Civil War Financing

By 1864, newspapers were referring to Cooke as "our modern Midas." Cooke's performance in the Pennsylvania issue made him closer to Salmon Chase. After the Civil War began in earnest in 1861, Cooke participated in several Treasury financings along with the other major Northern banks in Boston, New York, and Philadelphia. But sentiment began to turn against the Union late in 1861 and early in 1862. In 1862 the Union navy physically removed some Confederate agents from the British ship *Trent*, provoking what became known as the Trent affair. Again, many predicted war between the North and Britain as a result, although strained diplomatic relations were the only result. British investments began to decline rapidly. Adding insult to injury, at least in the eyes of the Union, was the fact that the British appeared to be favoring the Confederacy, using the same sort of arguments in its favor that it had previously used to justify the American Revolution. *The Economist* argued that the South had as much right to secede as the colonies did in 1776: "Instead of one vast state, we shall have two with different objects and interests, and by no means always disposed to act in concert or in cordiality."[16] The North had been disposed to act arrogantly in the past, in the opinion of the newspaper, although it indirectly admitted that cheap cotton exports from the free-trading South were paramount in Britain's mind. The Northern states always favored tariffs, much to Britain's dismay. More to the point was the fact that since the Revolution the North had been much more anti-British than the South. Restitution laws, such as those in New York, were more apt to be found north of the Mason-Dixon line.

Against this sort of background, Salmon Chase attempted to raise a huge war bond issue. The Union had just lost the battle of Bull Run, and the North's finances needed shoring up if it was to use its considerable financial muscle to defeat the rebels. But specie payments had been suspended at the beginning of the war, and investors did not warm to the prospect of loaning the government money. Again, the problem arose of how to sell the bonds and at what price. The Treasury decided to issue a huge $500-million issue dubbed the 5-20s—one of the most famous financings in American history until that time. The bonds paid 6 percent interest and matured in twenty years but were callable after five years, hence the nickname 5-20s. Interest was to be paid in gold. Chase offered these bonds for sale in 1862 at par, but the issue was far from successful. Because he refused to take less for them, he called directly upon Cooke, who had had such success with the Pennsylvania issue and other previous, smaller Treasury offerings.

Cooke entered the 5-20 picture in the autumn of 1862 at the request of Chase. Since the usual investors, namely, the bankers and merchants, were not proving viable, other avenues needed to be explored. Obviously, the British investors were also absent from the financing, as were the Dutch and Germans. Nothing short of a massive effort to sell the largest bond issue in American history would be needed if the financing was to be successful. Cooke plunged into the deal with a fervor rarely seen in the banking business. His efforts contributed in no small way to the outcome of the war.

The selling strategy was simple. Cooke enlisted agents from most of the major Northern cities and states and from all business ranks. While many of the large bankers were absent from his distribution group, there was no shortage of small-town bankers, insurance salesmen, and real estate dealers. At their height the agents numbered more than twenty-five hundred. Having opened a Washington office at the beginning of the war, Cooke coordinated sales throughout the country via the telegraph. This made Jay Cooke and Company the first "wire house," a firm that sold securities throughout the country using the telegraph wires to confirm purchases and sales. It allowed the sales to be coordinated from a central point rather than continue haphazardly as in the past.

Newspapers and billboard advertisements were also employed extensively to market the bonds. Patriotism was the key ingredient in the sales pitch, especially since most of the demand was from the retail sector. No investor was too small for the effort. The advertising itself was distinctly unsophisticated. The issue was portrayed as suitable for widows and orphans. Divine Providence was invoked on the Union's side, as well as the prospect of lower taxes in the future if the Union war effort, and the bonds, succeeded. Connecting bankers to a divine mission certainly did not hurt the image of the profession. Other aspects of the advertising, for the more sophisticated investor, emphasized the return and stressed the safety of U.S. government obligations. The result was enormously successful. As the *Philadelphia Press* described Cooke, he had "succeeded in popularizing the great five-twenty loan, and now finds the people so anxious to convert their currency into bonds that it is only with difficulty he can meet the sudden and increasing demand."[17]

Cooke's success in the marketing of the 5-20s was significant for the selling of securities in general. Although accomplished away from Wall Street, it proved that modern forms of communication could be used successfully to sell securities to those who previously had been unreachable. Modern underwriting had not yet appeared on Wall Street, but when it did, the principle of diversifying risk that Cooke had shown through his wide distribution network would not be forgotten. Although most new corporate issues of stocks and bonds were still distributed by local bankers, this new method introduced the greater public to securities for the first time. Treasury bonds were much safer than the banks in which many people kept their savings. The Philadelphia banker, originally from Ohio, had developed a method of selling that was to be openly embraced by the New York firms in the years ahead.

Cooke did not make a fortune selling the 5-20s. He eventually sold an estimated $360 million of the issue, for a total commission of around $200,000. The commission did not compensate him for the risks he faced, but the exposure he gained made Jay Cooke and Company the best-known merchant or investment bank in the country. But one of the by-products of his success was more competition. New investment banking houses began to open west of the Mississippi, lured by the success Cooke had enjoyed with his ad hoc sales network. The number of banks in Chicago proliferated after the Civil War. Several New York banks also made great inroads in the business because of their association with Cooke, especially Fisk and Hatch, and Livermore and Clews. Cooke had done more than develop retail sales via the wire. He also gave many new banks the impetus to expand.

But then allegations arose concerning Cooke's conduct. Chase was criticized for employing such a small Philadelphia banker as Treasury agent. Cooke's success was much envied and he had many detractors, many of whom wanted to see him disassociated from the Treasury. Both the House of Representatives and the Senate studied Cooke's relations with the Treasury, looking for potential fraud or graft. What they found instead was that Cooke had assumed enormous risks for little real compensation, and the inquiries promptly ended. Apparently, Cooke was every inch the patriot and bull that he appeared, and Congress thought it unwise to pursue him. Both he and Chase were fervent abolitionists, so it was easy to see why Chase took a liking to him in the first place. Wall Street was certainly less enthusiastic about him because his undaunted bullishness ran counter to the way in which many floor traders on the exchange made their livings.

Despite Cooke's clean bill of health, Chase did not employ him in the next sale of Treasury offerings. As a result, the very next issue went poorly. Realizing his mistake, Chase invited Cooke back to sell what became known as the 7-30s: three-year notes paying 7.30 percent interest. Interest rates had risen because of the war and the overall decline in securities prices. Chase offered Cooke better commission terms than those he had received on the 5-20s. However, he protected himself and the Treasury by insisting that no notes would be delivered until payment had been received and that he could terminate Cooke's contract as Treasury agent at any time during the offering. This latter stipulation was required in order to avoid any float management by Cooke on the issue, allowing him to reap gains similar to those realized by Enoch Clark on the Mexican war issues. Cooke's reaction was predictably furious. After reading Chase's terms, he remarked, "Some passages of this letter are more fit for the instructions to a fool or a dishonest agent than one deserving confidence & tried & trusted heretofore to millions."[18] He did, however, begin to organize for the sale of the notes in January 1865. Politics made him angry but did not dampen his patriotism.

Cooke's techniques for selling the 7-30s were much the same as those for the original issue. However, around the country he opened what were called "working men's savings banks," which were actually evening sales offices at which working people could buy bonds after hours. The addresses of the banks were listed in advertising that he took out in newspapers throughout the country. The bonds could be bought in denominations as small as fifty dollars. Agents were even instructed to sell bonds to soldiers on the days they received their pay. No potential marketing target escaped Cooke's attentions, and no investor was too small. This additional marketing strategy made the 7-30s even more widely distributed than the 5-20s. Praise for Cooke was now even more profuse than it had been two years earlier. Apparently, he had the true Midas touch.

The war ended in April 1865, but money was still needed, more desperately than during the war itself. Cooke managed to sell $500 million of the issue, which finally totaled over $800 million, making it the largest bond issue in American history. During the sale, some of the agents took to discounting the bonds to customers in order to sell them more easily, a practice that infuriated Salmon Chase and Cooke. Cooke asked for, and received, permission to organize a stabilization fund whereby he would buy up those bonds being offered at a discount in order to keep their offering price steady. This practice had never been seen before in the United States, although it would become part and parcel of securities underwriting thereafter, continuing to the present day. Ineffective underwriters could damage a new securities issue by cutting its price, and this sort of technique was designed to ensure that the damage was minimal.

After the war, Cooke and his partners had time to tally their fortunes. There was still a suspicion that Cooke was a war profiteer despite all the praise that had been lavished upon him by the press. Even several Confederate newspapers openly admired his ability to fund the Union cause. However, there was little reason to suspect the firm of having profited unduly from the war. If anything, the opposite appears to have been true. After four years of operation, Jay Cooke and Company of Philadelphia had profits of $1.1 million, two-thirds of which went to Cooke and one-third to his partner, William Moorhead. Some of the profits were found in the Washington branch, which showed profits of about $750,000, split among the partners.[19] Summing up, Jay Cooke personally made slightly more than $1 million for his efforts in selling over $1 billion of Treasury war bonds in the most successful marketing effort to date. That amounted to about one-tenth of 1 percent for the endeavor.

Most of his funds were kept in the banking business. Not having made enough money to feel particularly comfortable and being too young to retire, Cooke and his bank sought new areas to dabble in, which he hoped would be more profitable than the bond efforts. The railway business proved to be a great lure, and by the end of the 1860s he was heavily involved in railroad finance, which would eventually prove to be his undoing. But his contributions to the annals of American finance and a blue-chip reputation had already been made. He was, however, slightly out of step with the other great financiers of the period, who were emerging in large numbers from various parts of the country. While Cooke was more than willing to work out of a sense of patriotic duty, the newer breed of speculator was not blessed with the same compunction. Like Cooke, they recognized structural deficiencies in the American financial system and were more quick to exploit them for personal profit, regardless of the costs. One of them, unknown to Cooke at the end of the Civil War, would prove to be instrumental in putting him out of business shortly thereafter.

Even before the 7-30s, the development of the bond market had been a huge boost for the country's finances. New York became the official capital of American finance in 1863 when Congress passed the National Bank Act. This first significant piece of financial legislation passed in the country allowed only "national" banks to issue notes, depriving the state banks of that ability and seriously curtailing their activities.[20] Afterward, their numbers began to decline sharply nationwide. The banking act made state-chartered banking far less lucrative than it had been in the earlier part of the century because the small banks could no longer literally coin their own money. The publishers of "The Bank Note Detector" suddenly began to lose a great deal of business. These newly designated national banks had the exclusive right to issue notes that in turn were backed by government bonds. Jay Cooke had been instrumental in backing the bill when it was before Congress, and his efforts led to the development of the Treasury bond market, located primarily in New York. While not the most popular figure on Wall Street, Cooke nevertheless bequeathed it what would become one of its most profitable businesses. The business, and the lessons to be learned from it, would be picked up by others who were still emerging on Wall Street. Within a short time, aiding the U.S. Treasury in various endeavors would become one of the specialties of J. P. Morgan, among others.

Mephistopheles Appears

Despite Jay Cooke's success, he was not destined to be the most famous financier of his era, only of the Civil War period. That distinction would belong to others whose antics and audacity made them both envied and hated at the same time. The stock exchange, with which Cooke had little direct contact or interest prior to the Civil War, would become the hunting ground of this breed of financiers, who were more akin to William Duer and Jacob Little than to August Belmont or Cooke. The new breed later became known as the *robber barons*.[21] At the time, the name would have been a euphemism. This breed would change the face of American business and give added credence to the idea that only the fittest survived.

About the same time that Jay Cooke was entering the banking business, a schoolboy at a private academy in New York State was having dreams of making money. Jason "Jay" Gould was born in 1836, the son of a farmer whose ancestors were English and Scots. Described as sickly or tubercular, the young boy had few interests other than learning how to make money. One of his rebellious qualities was displayed when he refused to learn by rote at school, displaying an independence that would serve him well in finance years later. But he displayed a literary grasp nevertheless. Like Nicholas Biddle before him, he showed some literary flare by writing *A History of Delaware County* (New York, his birthplace) while still in his teens before turning his attention to finance.

Although Gould's family dated back to mid-seventeenth-century New England, the unfounded suspicion was that his real name was Gold and that he added the extra *u* so his name would sound less Jewish. Such stories abounded, especially when he became more famous and his detractors were looking for "flaws" in his personality. After school he landed a job in surveying in Ulster County and was able to save five hundred dollars. Shortly afterward, he raised five thousand dollars by selling his maps and history and went into the tanning business with a considerably older man named Zadoc Pratt. Together, as equal partners, they opened a tannery near Stroudsburg, Pennsylvania, that was soon to become the nation's largest. The tannery was so successful that Pratt named the town where it was located Gouldsboro. But the success soon turned to disaster for Pratt. Gould had been discovered cooking the books at the tannery, which he managed, and siphoning off funds for some use unknown to his elder partner. Furious, Pratt did not prosecute but allowed Gould to buy him out for one-half of what he originally invested in the firm. Gould obtained the

money from a New York source. He had been secretly learning and playing the futures market for leather hides in the New York futures market.

Gould began his career in New York by persuading Charles Leupp, a
successful leather merchant, to become his partner and buy into the Pennsylvania tannery. Leupp happily obliged, although he did not know of a
small but secret private bank that Gould had established in Stroudsburg
that he had originally used to siphon off Pratt's funds. Within a short time,
Gould continued to use the firm's profits to play the hide futures markets
without his new partner's knowledge. By 1857 he effectively had cornered
the hide market and was worth $1 million on paper. He had not yet turned
twenty-one.

When the panic of 1857 occurred, the hide market collapsed and
Gould lost nearly everything. Word of the collapse soon reached Leupp,
who hastily traveled to Stroudsburg to confront Gould. The younger man
simply shrugged off the loss, which had bankrupted both of them, as bad
luck. Like Pratt before him, Leupp was so astonished by Gould's machinations that he was not sure how to proceed against his erstwhile partner.
Leupp was stunned at his bad fortune and Gould's apparent lack of business ethics. He returned home to New York to his mansion on the East
Side, where he committed suicide shortly thereafter. He had the sad distinction of becoming the first fatality in Jay Gould's long and infamous
business career.

By 1869 Gould was the president of the Erie Railroad. James "Jubilee
Jim" Fisk was the managing director. The railroad had been one of the
most pitiful stocks on the exchange and had been the object of numerous
bear raids, the most dramatic led by speculator Daniel Drew, who forced
its price down from sixty to thirty dollars before moving in to offer a loan
to its embattled management. Under Gould and Fisk, who had gained
control after a long and nasty battle, the company was suspected of being
slowly looted by its senior management. Shareholders suffered while the
management treated themselves like royalty. The company had its executive offices in an opulent building on Broadway in New York City that became something of a tourist attraction. While Gould remained somewhat
affable and reserved, Fisk maintained a flamboyant lifestyle that reflected
the decadence of the times. He always had at least one female executive assistant on the payroll. One was actually discovered being paid one thousand dollars per month for "services rendered" to the managing director.[22]

The two men treated the railroad as if it was their personal baronial
fief. The style of the railroad management reflected the decadence of the
immediate postwar period in general. The venality at the Erie was not dissimilar from that of the Grant administration occupying the White
House. Carpetbaggers roamed the defeated South, plundering it as if it
were a bottomless source of wealth, and speculators were rampant on the

stock exchange. But in 1869 Gould conceived a plot that was grandiose even for the age and has been kindly described as Napoleonic in stature. He decided to corner the gold market in the United States.

Gould maintained vast political connections. His most immediate were with Boss Tweed and the Tammany Hall gang that controlled New York City politics. With some of the Tammany crowd he controlled the Tenth National Bank, an institution supported more by favorable public relations than by actual deposits. But in order to control the gold market, his connections would have to be higher and better placed. The U.S. Treasury held $100 million in gold at Fort Knox that it frequently used to stabilize the gold market. Any attempt to corner the price depended upon the Treasury remaining away from the market. If it decided to intervene, or was tipped off about Gould's intentions, the cornering operation would come undone. What Gould needed was nothing less than the ear of a compliant Ulysses S. Grant. Most of Gould's biographers assumed that Gould knew Grant was not particularly quick with details and might be manipulated into believing that the price of gold would rise purely through normal market forces. In order to get within shouting distance, he decided to employ the Seligmans and their long-standing Washington connections.

Gould started accumulating about $7 million worth of gold and forced the price to a premium of over 140 percent. He was joined in the operation by Fisk and Daniel Drew, another well-known speculator and railway financier. Then with the aid of rumor and traditional cornering techniques, he helped force the price to a high slightly in excess of 160 percent. This forced the bears to begin covering their short positions, and the price remained firm at slightly over 160. Among the bears was Cooke's New York office of Dodge and Company. The Tenth National Bank was used to support Gould by certifying that he had the funds to finance himself. The terrifying prospect of losing everything forced many bankers, including Cooke, to implore Grant to intervene in the market. They finally convinced him that the price rise was nothing more than a ploy by speculators.

The Treasury entered the market in several days, adding to the gold supply. Within an hour the price fell 30 percent. Brown Brothers in New York coordinated the sale of gold, and finally the price stabilized, but the next day the financial community was in chaos. Several large and respected Wall Street firms had failed, the most notable being Lockwood and Company. Cooke's Dodge office did not fare well; It lost a reputed $76,000 on the affair, a sizable amount in those days. The fiasco had a sobering effect on the entire Cooke firm, which quickly became extremely conservative and refused all deals except those thought to be most sound. But as it cast about looking for new financing opportunities, it could no longer rely upon selling Treasury bonds. Fatally, it turned instead to financing railroads to gain greater returns than it had received in the past.

Gould made a killing from the cornering operation. He sold most of his gold positions at the top of the market and made an estimated $10 million for his efforts. The Seligmans joined him in this stroke of exquisite market timing. For years it has been assumed that they were tipped off before the Treasury entered the market, and most fingers have pointed at Grant himself. But no evidence has ever surfaced that the president forewarned his old friends of the impending stabilization operation, although he has been suspect ever since. Others involved in the stabilization operation could easily have informed him. But Gould would not escape the operation totally unscathed. He had angered too many people. He had not warned his partner Fisk in time, and Fisk did not profit from the operation as did Gould and the Seligmans. When news of the gold corner was finally made public, Gould was attacked by an angry crowd in New York and barely escaped with his life. Thereafter, he always traveled with a bodyguard, even when taking an evening walk from his home on Fifth Avenue. He was eventually removed from the presidency of Erie in 1872.

The fallout on Wall Street was predictable. The stock market collapsed on September 24, 1869, a day that became known as "Black Friday." Dozens of brokers failed as a result. This proved to be particularly inauspicious for the New York Stock Exchange (NYSE), which had formally changed its name during the Civil War in 1863. In January 1869 it had moved to require its listed companies to register their shares with it in order to prevent companies like Schuyler's and Kyle's from overissuing common shares. Many of the stronger bankers, including Jay Cooke, mounted rescue operations to save others who were tottering on the brink. The shakeout did nothing to enhance the reputation of the exchange, which had been in the forefront of Gould's manipulations for some time. But the wrenching changes it caused for Wall Street in general and Cooke in particular would force Cooke ultimately to make decisions that would lead to the bankruptcy of his firm within several years.

The Fall of the House of Cooke

All of the financial travails of the late 1860s convinced Jay Cooke that he should turn his attention away from government bonds and concentrate instead on railways. The margins for profit on bonds and stocks were certainly greater, and there were opportunities for merchant bankers to take positions in the roads for themselves. Railways were still the lifeline of the nation and in a sense appeared as good a bet as government bonds as long as the likes of the Erie could be avoided. But the railroad companies had proved fertile ground for the robber barons, and the temptation to make a killing seems to have overtaken Cooke after the Civil War.

Early in 1870, Cooke became the exclusive agent for bond issues of the

Northern Pacific Railroad. He also became the company's fiscal agent and had the authority to appoint some of its board members. His compensation was about three-quarters of the company's stock, effectively making him both owner and investment banker. Cooke's plan was to aggressively market the bonds for the company among both domestic and international investors, but he ran into opposition on both counts. Domestic investors did not warm to the idea of buying railroad stocks or bonds. Memories of Gould, the gold corner, and his connection with the Erie and other railroads he had dabbled in were still fresh in many minds. Domestic investors would not buy bonds from the king of bond salesmen, and Cooke had a difficult time marketing issues. Foreign investors also showed little interest. William Moorhead failed in an attempt to persuade substantial foreign interests to invest. As a result, Cooke's holdings in the railroad were not substantially decreased, and he found himself in the position of paying most of its operating expenses.

The atmosphere on Wall Street had become extremely tense as a result of Jay Gould's presence. He and Russell Sage had been rampantly speculating in the stock of another transportation company, the Pacific Mail Steamship Company, which had already been plundered by Commodore Vanderbilt before Gould bought a substantial stake. The stock market was becoming jittery, as was the New York press corps. As late as September 1, 1873, the *New York World* warned, "There is one man in Wall Street today whom men watch, and whose name, built upon ruins, carries with it a certain whisper of ruin. . . . They that curse him do not do it blindly, but as cursing one who massacres after victory."[23] The very presence of Gould made the market poised for a severe panic.

As his inventory of Northern Pacific holdings became well known, Cooke's depositors began to abandon him by withdrawing funds from his bank. The feared that his position might endanger their deposits. As a result, Jay Cooke and Company found itself short of working capital and finally had to close its doors on September 18, 1873. After only a dozen years in business, the firm had fallen prey to the same forces it had been able to avoid in the first years of its existence during the Civil War. The stock market subsequently collapsed and more firms on the street failed, among them Fisk and Hatch, Clark, and Henry Clews. The results were more dismal than those in 1869. Wall Street was again in ruins, and it would take several years to regain its footing.

Two crashes within a four-year period demonstrated that Wall Street still had a long distance to travel before it would be free of individual influences, which had plagued it throughout its eighty-year history. Securities dealing and banking still operated in a remarkably loose atmosphere. There were no regulators, nor was there much will to regulate the activities of speculators. The dependence upon foreign capital was still strong.

The failure of Jay Cooke, overwhelmingly a domestic financier, proved that firms without strong foreign connections were still at risk to turns in the domestic economy. Although these circumstances suggested that controls should have been introduced, the opposite occurred. The post–Civil War period became the heyday of those individual financiers known as the robber barons. American financial history was becoming more colorful and more hostile. And the atmosphere was turning even more predatory than before. The fifty-year period in which the robber barons ruled the roost was a time of many Pyrrhic victories, when the victorious took no prisoners, as the *New York World* had suggested. This was best symbolized after the 1873 crash when Jay Gould bought the *New York World* and became a newspaperman.

CHAPTER THREE

The Robber Barons (1870–90)

You have undertaken to cheat me. I will not sue you,
for law takes too long. I will ruin you.

Cornelius Vanderbilt

After the Civil War, the American economy began to expand again, more dramatically than before. The population grew, aided by an influx of European immigrants, providing fresh labor for the new industries springing up all around the country. The actual size of the country had trebled since independence, with new territory being added through expansion and conquest. Railroad expansion began again after the hiatus during the war, with more miles added to existing roadways every year. The first transatlantic telegraph cable was laid in 1866, and the first transcontinental railroad was officially opened in 1869, despite the revelations and public outcry following the Crédit Mobilier affair after 1867. All of the promise the United States had offered its European investors and new arrivals began to reach greater fruition than at any other time in American history.

Accompanying this promise was the continuing lure of great riches. The great American fortunes were to be established during this era that encouraged extravagant wealth and provided few barriers to its accumulation. The earlier examples of John Jacob Astor and others had led many ambitious men, many with no formal education to speak of, to achieve notoriety and fame that would have been inconceivable in Europe. Within a generation, even the coarsest of these early industrialists such as Drew or Vanderbilt would be considered part and parcel of the social fabric. Ironically, though, many of those who actually accumulated the vast fortunes were considered social pariahs in their own time.

The familiar foreign investors also returned after the war but were temporarily diverted by the panic of 1873, when Jay Cooke and Company closed its doors. British investments again began to increase steadily. The overwhelming favorite of British investors was Treasury bonds, by some estimates accounting for over two-thirds of all foreign investment in 1870. In the commercial sector, railroad stocks remained the favorites. Almost all of the stock and most of the bonds of the Atlantic and Great Western Railroad were owned by foreigners. Railroads had proved to be highly resilient choices despite the treatment some American traders had meted out to the British in the past. Although the manufacturing and shipping industries were growing rapidly, foreign investors remained devoted to the railroads. Much of that interest was far from blind. Railroads were among the few American industries that had collateral behind their securities obligations. Their rolling stock provided some real value for investors. This was especially important in the years immediately following the war because the United States had suspended specie payments in favor of the greenbacks during the war. Railroads had better backing than most industrial obligations and, in the eyes of some, the U.S. government as well.

This fact was not lost on many of the industrialists and speculators who dominated the economic scene before and after the Civil War. Railroads had proved to be their personal hunting grounds and had netted many of them great fortunes before the war broke out. Trading in the stocks of the Erie and the Harlem Railroads had made both lines infamous by 1865, and they would remain so for the next several decades. Many traders had already turned their attention to railroads in the West, but the major roads in the East, especially in and around New York, remained favorite targets until the panic of 1873. In the preceding twenty years, the New York legislature and the municipalities had poured more than $40 million into railroad subsidies in much the same way that many states had done for the turnpikes and canals of previous generations, ranking it among the highest spenders in the country.[1] But many of the new roads were mainly short rail lines, which did not connect with each other, remaining only trunk lines with no greater ambitions than to connect two not-too-distant cities or towns. After they had been built, their usefulness as potential pieces in a larger chess game of consolidation became apparent to a few budding industrialists.

Speculative fever remained strong, with good reason. The money economy had changed, with a great deal of wealth in the South destroyed and paper money with no metallic backing dominating the North. Specie payments eventually were resumed in 1879, four years after Congress passed the Specie Resumption Act, which limited the amount of greenbacks in circulation to 30 percent. When resumption began, greenbacks were worth their face value in gold. But the interim between the end of the war and the depression that followed the panic of 1873 was unsettling. Gambling and investing became more popular than in the past, especially in light of the view that money was perceived to be worth less. Almost all of the gains made by raids accomplished on the stock exchange were free of tax, despite income taxes imposed during the war. Declaring income was not a high priority among the wealthy. The market atmosphere was still free of any meaningful government influence.

In 1868 the population was around thirty-eight million, an amount that would double by the end of the century. Of that total, only a quarter of a million tax returns were filed. In 1870, a total of 9,500 returns were filed that actually admitted annual incomes of five thousand dollars or more.[2] While these were sizable figures for the time, they paled in comparison with the amounts purportedly made by the highest earners. Tax avoidance became so endemic that the temporary income tax was abandoned in 1872 when the government was desperately in need of funds. The American population felt no compunction at paying tax. This occurred at a time when great windfalls were being made on the stock exchanges, and the raiders and traders who accomplished them were hailed as savvy investors in the press. Apparently the Treasury could not convert what was found in the newspapers into revenue for itself. As in the past, government was still playing catch-up with industry and Wall Street and had a long way to travel before coming within sight of the commercial sector in general.

Speculative fever did not discriminate. Even members of Congress became involved in the hot stocks of the day. One broker recalled how a young congressman named William McKinley came to his office and stated, "I want to buy 50 shares of Erie. I am told that it will some day be worth more money. Here is $500, and if you want more at any time let me know. In the meantime, do not bother me by telephoning. I will pay no attention to its fluctuations." The broker agreed, not necessarily needing a nervous client. But within ten minutes of leaving the office, the future president was on the phone, inquiring, "How is Erie now?"[3]

Ransacking the Treasury

The developments in rail transportation were not made without an extraordinarily high cost. The opening of the transcontinental railroad was hailed as a major engineering feat, full of promise for the country as a whole. In reality, it occurred under a cloud of graft and corruption that quickly emerged as the largest scandal in American history to date. Astute opportunists seized the desire to link the country by rail with the bedlam caused by the Civil War to advance their own pockets at government expense.

Pressure for a transcontinental link had been mounting for some years before the war began. The Northern politicians accused their Southern counterparts of wanting to finance the link so they could extend slavery into the West. The Southerners, in turn, replied that the North was home to most of the major railroad swindlers and speculators who had severely hurt economic development in the South with their rapacious behavior. But during the war the Congress passed legislation that gave the Union Pacific Railroad the land and right-of-way to build the line west of Nebraska, with various other roads converging from the east to that point. The federal government would supervise the building of the road and help finance it since it did involve confiscating land in some cases. While the congressional grant was generous, the real money was to be made in actually constructing the road. In order to do so, private interests formed the Crédit Mobilier Company, incorporated in Pennsylvania for the occasion.

Crédit Mobilier was the brainchild of Oakes Ames, a member of Congress who set himself up as head of the company. He sought outside investors who would invest a few thousand dollars with the intent of doing all the actual construction of the Union Pacific. He attracted a fair number of bankers, among them William E. Dodge, William H. Macy, and Morton, Bliss and Company (a partner of the latter, Levi Morton, later became vice president under Rutherford Hayes). Other investors included Cyrus McCormick and George Pullman. The company then bid for projects, bribed various officials, and was granted the bulk of the work for building the road. Since the company had no employees to speak of, the work was subcontracted. Many of the subcontractors used immigrant labor, especially Chinese workers, and became widely known for the practice for generations thereafter.

Ames and his partners charged the government twice what the construction actually cost. The total bill for the Union Pacific was about $100 million, half of which went into the pockets of the shareholders of Crédit Mobilier. The scandal that emerged prompted Congress to set up an investigatory commission to probe the construction company. The hearings revealed that many more members of Congress were involved in the scandal as investors or as recipients of bribes from the construction company itself. The Senate committee recommended expelling Ames from his seat, and the government sued Crédit Mobilier for fraud and expropriation of funds. The case eventually reached the U.S. Supreme Court but was decided in favor of the company, claiming that the government could not sue until the company's debt finally matured in 1895. That effectively ended the case and allowed most of the directors and investors off the hook with almost $50 million in compensation for their efforts. The episode left the Union Pacific itself under a heavy debt burden. Investors decided that the company's future was clouded, and the stock underwent a wave of short selling as a result.

Despite the tumultuous events, Wall Street made several reforms in order to keep up with the changing times. Stock tickers were first introduced in 1867, made possible by the advent of the telegraph. Prices were now available shortly after trades were made. Seats, or memberships, on the exchange also were allowed to be sold to others. Originally, seats were held for life and were not transferable. Members also had to pay their annual dues and engage in some exchange activity for the seats to remain active. After 1868, members were able to sell them to others or pass them to other members of the family when they decided to retire. The return on a seat for the early members who were still active was quite healthy. In 1868 the price for a seat ranged between seven and eight thousand dollars. But the New York Stock Exchange still had a problem that would remain embedded in its reputation for years. It was the home of the railroad and bank speculator. The Boston Stock Exchange had more shares of industrial companies listed than did New York and was considered a safer place to invest, although traders there practiced many of the same techniques as did those on the NYSE. But the New York remained the best-known exchange and home to many of the legendary predators of the era.

Throughout the post–Civil War period, the term *panic* was still used to describe economic downturns. The press and economists of the day attributed falling prices, bankruptcies, and business failures to a loss of public confidence. At first glance this appears to have been nothing more than a bad choice of words to characterize poor economic conditions, but it would become more important as time passed.[4] In many cases these losses were attributed to individuals and the institutions they operated, giving a personal touch to recessions, if not a totally accurate one in economic terms. But in the case of the great speculators cum industrialists, subsequently named the *robber barons*, the term *panic* was highly appropriate in describing the aftermath of their actions. Despite the growing economy, these individuals were capable of causing economic ruin in their wake as they worked relentlessly to accumulate vast fortunes in an unregulated economy.

A significant change was occurring in the way in which companies were managed. The stock form of organization had come of age since the turn of the century, and while many of the Wall Street firms were partnerships, many large companies were now stock companies rather than sole proprietorships or partnerships. This was the dawn of what is known as the age of managerial capitalism. Companies were now being run by a class of managers who were not necessarily related to the founder of the company or married to one of his offspring. Once this change occurred, Wall Street became the direct beneficiary. These expanding companies needed new infusions of capital, and these capital needs put pressure on the investment community to grow along with them.

But the panic of 1873 produced a long period of economic stagnation that saw over three hundred banks fail and thousands of businesses accompany them into oblivion. The susceptibility of so many banks and companies to downturns in the economic cycle only added to the popularity of stock companies, where the liability was limited for shareholders. It also made many companies that did survive the depression very cheap to outside bids and vulnerable to takeovers. There was no shortage of speculators ready to take advantage of these circumstances. But not all of them were necessarily interested in companies for their intrinsic values. Many saw the period as an opportunity for cornering operations, while others seized opportunities to pounce upon distressed companies to forge larger ones in order to dominate the marketplace. The robber barons and their bankers were beginning to re-create corporate America, consolidating many smaller companies into large industrial combines.

Daniel Drew's Trick

One of the best-known railroad speculators before and after the Civil War was Daniel Drew, whose antics became something of a legend by the time he was middle-aged. He was an illiterate curmudgeon with strong religious leanings whose name drew gasps of envy and fear from traders on the exchange as well as from railroad executives who feared they might be his next quarry. A tall, gaunt man who had little use for learning, he ironically showed the most financial acumen of any trader of his time, although a company's financial statements had a different meaning for him than for other investors. By the time the Civil War ended, Drew already had made a sizable fortune in his favorite activity, short selling. He was one of a predatory breed of speculator who hid behind a corporate insignia. As a bear trader he had no equal, and the sheer audacity of some of his favorite tricks delighted even his adversaries. One of the best known was his renowned handkerchief trick.

Drew was born in Putnam County, New York, and had an eclectic career before entering the stock market. In each vocation he developed a shoddy reputation and usually found it to his advantage to move into another line of work. He was at various times a cattle driver, tavern owner, moneylender, steamboat owner, and finally a broker. He eventually found his way to New York, where he became a partner in the Wall Street firm of Drew, Robinson and Company. There he was able to engage legally in what he had done many times since being a cattle driver: selling things he did not own to others. His original business stake was provided by John Jacob Astor's son. When he did actually deliver the goods he had promised, there was no guarantee of their condition. He reportedly would transport cattle over great distances in upstate New York by rail without feeding them or giving them water. When they neared their purchaser's destination, he allowed them to drink. The cattle became known as his "watered stock." On Wall Street this term meant something quite different, and it would be an interesting coincidence that Drew's greatest coup on the stock market would have to do with the financial version of watered stock.

Henry Clews was later to give the standard definition of watered stock that would characterize so much of nineteenth-century railroad financing. Most of the rails were financed with bonds, actually for more than the construction projects usually cost. The bondholders took all the risks of the projects; if the projects went bust, the reorganizations that usually followed occurred at their expense. The stockholders, usually including the directors of the company, held the stocks, which had little risk attached to them and had the potential to rise sharply in the market as the directors helped "talk up" the stock in the press and in advertising. However, if a bear raid occurred, the stock was highly vulnerable because it was worth much more on paper than in reality. Clews recognized the risk in this sort of financing: "The Socialistic seductions which have captivated such large masses of the working population of Europe will all the more readily find acceptance among our millions of laborers because they have before their eyes such conspicuous instances of the unequal division of wealth and the overwhelming power of organized capital."[5] Even one of Wall Street's own took Marx's exhortations to the working class seriously.

Drew's bear activities eventually brought him into contact with the notorious Erie Railroad stock, which had already been well picked over by many traders for years. In 1854 he loaned the Erie, desperate for funds, $1.5 million, receiving a mortgage on its engines and rolling stock in return. He became a director of the company and after the 1857 panic also became treasurer. On the face of it, it appeared that Drew had done what many other speculators had done before him—become legitimate. But as a true predator, he was interested in the stock of the Erie for other reasons. It gave him a steady supply of shares to sell short. The assets of the railroad were worth ten times the amount he loaned it, although it had a terrible reputation in the marketplace. Erie's stock became known as the "Scarlet Woman of Wall Street," a nickname that remained with it for years afterward. Its rolling stock was unreliable and its rails were in deplorable condition, having caused many crashes. Drew managed to buy into a company with the sort of stock that is every short seller's dream—a poorly run company with dubious assets, worth more on paper than in reality. One of the better-known bits of Wall Street doggerel at the time went as follows:

> When Uncle Dan'l says "Up"
> Erie goes up.
> When Uncle Dan'l says "Down"
> Erie goes down.
> When Uncle Dan'l says "Wiggle waggle"
> Erie bobs both ways.

Drew then proceeded to sell short Erie shares to the extent that he sold more shares than actually existed. Ordinarily, such a practice would bring ruin, but he had a reserve of stock unbeknownst to the rest of the market. Like Jacob Little, he had purchased convertible bonds and used them to cover his shorts, making a fortune in the process. In order to get the price of the stock as high as possible before beginning to sell it short, he visited a New York City club where stock traders congregated. Sitting down on a particularly hot day, he pulled a handkerchief out of his pocket to mop his brow. As he did so, a small piece of paper fell onto the floor, but no one bothered to tell him. After he left, the other traders pounced on the paper, which just happened to contain a "bullish" piece of news on the Erie. They then proceeded to frantically buy the stock, pushing it to new highs in the market. It was only then that Drew began selling it short, wiping many of them out in the process as the stock price dropped precipitously.

Such operations made Drew a legend in his own time. During the latter part of his career he attracted two protégés who would effectively take over the railroad after his death in 1867: Jim Fisk and Jay Gould. Drew taught them that speculation and looting of one's own corporation were preferable to adding value to business enterprises in a true economic sense. The trading behavior that had developed in the stock market prior to the Civil War would have repercussions for several generations. Although the Erie survived well into the twentieth century, it only managed to pay investors a dividend during World War II. Other investors in companies that appealed to the robber barons would not be even that lucky. When the Boston investment firm of Kidder, Peabody became intimately involved with the Atchison, Topeka and Santa Fe Railroad in 1870, a long relationship began that would benefit both companies. The railroad was reorganized, and Kidder became its major shareholder and financial consultant along with Barings. As the railroad was being reorganized, Jay Gould began to show some interest. The king of the Erie was now turning his attentions westward. Francis Peabody, a partner in the firm, wrote to another partner suggesting a reorganization that would keep Gould from attempting a takeover. "If he should do so," he wrote, "it would not only be a great disaster to the property but a terrible mortification for K. P. & Co., who practically would have cooked the goose for him to eat."[6]

Although Kidder's intervention saved the railroad from predators, it did not mean that the company would have an easy time of it in the future. The road had grown to be a full-fledged continental carrier with a huge appetite for funds. A bond floated in 1881 was subsequently refinanced by two hundred-year issues that floundered in subsequent years. It was not until 1995 that the two issues were finally settled, when the successor company Santa Fe Pacific Corporation agreed to be acquired by Burlington

Northern, ending Santa Fe's century of independence. Burlington agreed
to compensate the bondholders of record.

Fisk and Gould proved worthy successors to the master and Gould
would move to even greater triumphs than the gold corner and the looting
of the Erie. Fisk departed more abruptly. In 1872 he was sued by a former
mistress, one of his favorite divas employed at the New York opera house
adjacent to Erie's headquarters. She claimed that he failed to continue to
pay her sums of money they had agreed upon earlier that later had
amounted to blackmail. When Fisk began to lose interest in her and took
her off the payroll, she threatened to expose what she knew of his dealings
at the Erie and elsewhere. The trial itself became a popular attraction of
the day, for it promised to expose the management of the Erie and some of
the Tammany Hall crowd in the process. One afternoon as Fisk left the
courtroom he was followed and shot several times by the woman's current
lover for reasons that were not particularly clear. He died shortly thereafter, effectively ending the suit and any potential embarrassment to the
establishment. Wall Street had witnessed a drama suitable for the stage,
and many New Yorkers openly lamented Fisk's passing despite the reputation of the Erie board of directors. Thomas Nast, the reigning political
cartoonist of the day, depicted the funeral in *Harper's* with Boss Tweed and
Jay Gould hovering over the grave of Fisk above the caption "Dead Men
Tell No Tales." The accompanying editorial stated, "Now that he is dead
they seek to make him the scapegoat for all their sins."[7]

Early Underwriting

The expansion of the securities business made profits for the commercial
banks as well as the brokers. Since the days of Duer, the New York banks
had been loaning money to brokers to finance their positions. After the
Civil War, this business became more intense because of the way in which
NYSE member brokers settled their accounts. New York brokers settled
their accounts every day, which required the use of borrowed money. The
funds, technically called *call money*, were readily supplied by the New York
money center banks, which naturally assumed the brokers would pay back
the amounts extended to them. But as the stock market became more and
more volatile, it was possible that some of these brokers would not be able
to cover the loans. When they failed, the banks would also be placed in
jeopardy, as was the case in several panics.

As American industry grew larger over the years, requiring more capital for expansion, the investment community devised several methods of
raising large amounts of money. Some were new, while others were varia-
tions on older methods. The stock exchanges were still fairly disparate
places, trading in shares of companies within their immediate geographic

FEBRUARY 24, 1872.]   HARPER'S WEEKLY.   165

"Dead Men Tell No Tales." (Collection of the New-York Historical Society)

areas. New issues of stocks and bonds were still sold by private bankers, securities dealers, and commercial banks within their local areas as well.
These methods worked well when the amounts of money required were
small to moderate. But when the amounts became large, local sales and
distribution were inadequate, as Jay Cooke had proved during the Civil
War. Wall Street needed to find new means of raising substantial pools of
investment cash.

During the years following the war, investment banking began to
emerge to take up this challenge. The first standard form of underwriting

appeared in 1870 when Jay Cooke and Company put up $2 million of its own funds to underwrite Pennsylvania Railroad bonds. The firm bought the bonds from the company, thereby guaranteeing it the funds it needed, and then undertook to sell the bonds to investors. The technique was certainly not new. Astor, Girard, and the American representative of Barings had done the same with the War of 1812 bonds on a onetime basis. Underwriting insurance risk had been practiced for some time by Lloyd's of London for maritime insurance, but the Pennsylvania bonds were the first underwriting attempt for a commercial company. Once the method proved successful, it became common in the last quarter of the nineteenth century. It was welcomed by companies because of the guarantees of funds it provided in what could be frantic economic conditions. The frequent panics and periods of slow economic activity did not help companies raise funds on a regular basis because they frightened away investors. The emerging underwriters were performing a valuable function in marketing securities on a regional and national basis. They assumed the risks of buying the securities and then reselling them to investors. In return, they received liberal fees that proved to be a magnet for many commercial banks that soon got into the business, augmenting their deposit and loan business. Many were more trusted by their clients than the companies whose shares and bonds they sold.

More Sharp Practices

The so-called robber barons came from a variety of social and economic backgrounds and affected very different sectors of American life. Despite their uncanny ability to spot structural deficiencies in companies, and indeed in the financial system as a whole, they were for the most part uneducated. Like John Jacob Astor before them, most had little use, if not contempt, for formal learning. Cornelius Vanderbilt, Fisk, Gould, Drew, and Russell Sage were all prime examples. They would be followed by John Rockefeller and Andrew Carnegie, both of whom possessed little formal education. They were all able to amass vast fortunes because of structural conditions within the economy, and all owed a significant debt to their bankers, without whom many would not have been able to finance their ventures. And once these ventures had begun, the investment bankers helped them consolidate their holdings into large industrial combines that began to threaten the status quo of American society later in the century. American capitalism was poised to venture into unknown territory.

The other great industrialists of the nineteenth century would probably not like to be included in the same category as Jay Gould, the "most hated man in America" during his lifetime. The death of Charles Leupp was never forgotten by the public, and his name arose more than once

Panic of 1869. (Collection of the New-York Historical Society)

when Gould was discussed. During the gold corner of 1869, crowds in New York City were heard to openly chant, "Who killed Leupp?" as they sought Gould, bent upon revenge for the strife he had left in the wake of the gold corner.

The career of Russell Sage is a prime example of chicanery combined with financial acuity, which resulted in a large fortune for the former wholesale grocer from Troy, New York. New York State was destined to be the birthplace of many of the robber barons because of the numerous small, trunk line railroads that dotted its landscape. Many saw the deficiencies in the small lines firsthand and heard about the antics of others in the business firsthand as well. Born in 1816 in Oneida County, Sage entered the wholesale grocery business in Troy, where he eventually became a town alderman and treasurer. While serving in local government, he was instrumental in seizing control of a local trunk railroad that the town had helped finance. He paid around $200,000 for it and sold it to the New York Central for slightly less than $1 million. The apparently astute transaction was full of chicanery and bribery, traits for which Sage became well known during his long career, but on the surface it made him appear as a clever businessman, and he was soon elected to Congress in 1854.

The period prior to the Civil War saw Sage engaged in many railroad deals, usually using his insider's knowledge gained in Congress to move in

on deals at the appropriate time. After several successful railroad deals in
the Midwest, Sage had the good fortune to meet Jay Gould in Troy. Soon
after, he moved to New York City and set himself up in the banking business, not unlike Daniel Drew before him. During the war he loaned
money to the call money market using a method that would later become
very popular in finance. When market conditions were tight, he would exact high rates of interest, amounting to perhaps 1 to 2 percent overnight,
or would call the money in immediately if the borrower objected.[8] The
latter technique gave the impression that he was sympathetic to investors
desirous of repaying loans early when in fact it was not particularly profitable to allow the loans to remain outstanding. He also became known as
the "put and call" king by becoming one of the early speculators to use options to buy and sell stocks.

Sage had engaged in numerous business deals that made him a sizable
fortune during the war. Among them was an investment in the Pacific Mail
Steamship Company, once pillaged by Commodore Vanderbilt. The company received heavy government subsidies for hauling mail in California
and in the Pacific. These subsidies made the company ripe for the occasional sale of securities, which its directors could then make good use of as
they saw fit. Other than Sage, notable investors during and after the Civil
War were Brown Brothers and Company of New York and Henry Clews,
the stock exchange trader who headed a securities house of the same name.
A congressional committee that investigated the company in 1873 discovered that its monopoly was granted by Congress only after a series of
bribes and manipulations. Sage claimed innocence of any wrongdoing because he apparently used front men to acquire his shares and could therefore claim that he acquired his personal interest on a purely neutral basis.[9]

Sage remained probably the most clever of the robber barons involved
in finance because he was somewhat out of the public view for most of his
career. But his alliance with Gould brought both of them a vast fortune
when they teamed up to seize control of the Union Pacific Railroad.
Shortly thereafter, their immediate target became the Kansas and Pacific
Railroad, which held a virtual monopoly on land grants and right-of-way
in its area. They claimed they were about to open a competitive line in
Colorado, which forced down the price of the Kansas and Pacific on the
stock exchange. Secretly, they began to buy up the shares in a cornering
operation when the stock became extremely depressed. They then sold the
Kansas and Pacific to the Union Pacific for an enormous profit of almost
$40 million. The competing line was abandoned as soon as it had served its
purpose. Gould did the same to the Union Pacific in 1883. After stripping
it of its assets, he sold off his interests when the press and Congress again
began to show undue interest in his actions.

The main antagonist of Drew and Gould both before and after the

Civil War was Cornelius "Commodore" Vanderbilt, who obtained his nautical nickname because of his business ventures in shipping, which earned him a reputation not unlike Drew's in the railroad business. Vanderbilt was the archetypal first-generation robber baron and an acknowledged legend in his own time. His stock market tactics were markedly different from those of Drew and Jacob Little, but they often achieved the same ends. In a Darwinist age, Vanderbilt developed a reputation as a plunderer who took no prisoners. The railroad industry soon became his focus of attention when it became clear that shipping could not achieve the growth potential of the rails.

The Commodore had the most dour reputation of the early industrialists. Born in 1794 in Staten Island to poor Dutch farmers, he was a plainspoken man of few words who developed a legendary reputation for being parsimonious. Even after accumulating a vast fortune, he still managed to keep his wife of many years on a short financial string before finally having her committed to an asylum in later life. He appears to have had little use for any of his nine children either, keeping them at arm's length from his business ventures during his lifetime. His son William, who eventually inherited the bulk of his empire, was relegated to a family farm on Staten Island until he was in his midforties.

Having no formal education, Cornelius Vanderbilt borrowed a small amount of money from his parents and began a ferry service from Staten Island to New York City. During the War of 1812, he transported provisions for the army in and around New York. Within six years he worked for a ship owner who competed with Robert Fulton for passenger and freight service between New York and Philadelphia. Within ten years his own company dominated shipping on the Hudson River. One of his most common business tactics was to underbid his competition in order to win customers' business. Then, having a captive group of clients, he would increase the rates back to a competitive level, forcing many of his competitors to ruin while irritating many of his customers in the process. His tactics were so deplored that many of his competitors actually paid him to stay away from certain parts of the shipping business, earning him an estimated monthly income of over $60,000 for simply not competing with them.

Throughout his life, Vanderbilt kept the accounts of his businesses in his head, entrusting them to no one. Despite this lack of trust, the lack of paperwork never seemed to hurt his strategies. Vanderbilt came to the railroads rather late in life. In 1862, at the age of sixty-eight, he began buying shares of the New York and Harlem Railroad and mounted a successful corner on the stock. The acquisition of the Harlem stock in particular was a particularly messy affair. Vanderbilt was forced to entice many members of the New York legislature to part with their personal holdings of stock at fairly high prices in order to complete the acquisition, forcing the stock up from $25 per share to over $150. Then Daniel Drew suddenly began a bear raid on the stock, aided by rumors that some of the legislators had reconsidered their positions, in a clear attempt to force down the value of the stock and ruin the Commodore in the process. The takeover had turned into a typical stock exchange raid and counterraid between the two most notorious manipulators of their day, Drew, the great bear raider, and Vanderbilt, the master of the cornering operation. Vanderbilt prevailed, having wiped out many of his adversaries when the stock reached $285 per share. Drew suffered substantial losses and admitted defeat. Within a year Vanderbilt controlled the road and began a bid to control New York City streetcar service as well. He paid for the streetcar service by bribing the Tweed ring, reputedly paying more for the bribe than the trolley line itself was worth. Public opinion began to turn against him because of the publicity surrounding the deal. It was becoming clear that Vanderbilt wanted to control rail service from the Canadian border to the Great Lakes and south as far as the Battery in New York City. In this respect he was successful. Over the next several years he acquired several New York state railroads, namely, the Hudson River, the New York Central, and the Lake Shore, as well as the Michigan Southern and the Canadian Southern, totaling over forty-five hundred miles of track. In 1868 he made an attempt to gain control of the Erie but was foiled by the combination of Drew, Fisk, and Gould, who gained a measure of victory following the Harlem fiasco.

Despite his unsavory reputation, he scored a major public relations coup in 1873 by beginning construction on the Grand Central Terminal in New York. The panic of 1873 had created severe economic woes for New York City, but the massive construction project put thousands of men to work. Added to that was the generally bad publicity generated by the Crédit Mobilier scandal that was just emerging from Congress, adding to the unsavory reputation of railroad finance in general. Rumor had it that Vanderbilt built the station simply so he would have a suitable place from which to embark to his many personal properties. Regardless of the reason, the project elevated his public image during a time of economic crisis. But more important, his consolidation of the railroads, many of which formerly were poorly run and notoriously treated, began a trend that was to dominate the next fifty years of American life.

The ventures in shipping and the railroads made Vanderbilt an extraordinarily rich man. At his death in 1877 he was worth a reputed $100 million, making him the richest man in the country. His fortune certainly benefited his heirs more than himself. Despite his money, he was always considered a social pariah because of his coarse manners and, unlike his successors, was never admitted into New York society. He never lost his sailor's foul language and never developed a fondness for anything but the most simple of clothes. But his legacy to American business would be in his skills of consolidation. Whatever the reasons for his collection of railroads, the industry became more efficient as a result and would play a vital role in the growth of other sectors of American industry over the next twenty-five years. But personal rivalries would continue to affect the expansion of the rails, many times to their detriment, especially when new industries such as steel production came to take advantage of the railroads' divisiveness. But without the nationwide distribution network provided by the railroads, the other major smokestack industries would have had a much more difficult time developing.

The railroads also enabled budding entrepreneurs in other businesses to make their fortunes. In Chicago, Philip Armour had set himself up in the meatpacking business during the Civil War, making a good living by selling pork to the Union army. Criticisms were frequently heard about the quality of the pork, which often made soldiers sick. These stories coincided with Vanderbilt's reputed largesse in supplying a well-traveled ship to the Union army that was used to transport troops despite its appalling, rusty condition. One commentator remarked that it had made the journey despite its condition and that the soldiers stood better chances of survival on the battlefield. Although Armour's pork was of a wide range in quality, the army's appetite for it kept the price unusually high while belligerencies continued. But Armour, who had been at various times a miner, grocer, and farmer before entering the meat business, anticipated Lee's surrender at Appomattox and rushed by train to New York, the home of the commodities futures markets at the time. He began selling pork short on the local futures exchanges at prices ranging as high as forty dollars per barrel. Then, as Grant's final victory was announced, he began covering as the price dropped precipitously in a fashion that evoked memories of the Rothschild coup after the battle of Waterloo. When the smoke cleared, Armour had made about $2 million. He then returned to Chicago and invested the profit in his meatpacking company. Soon it was exporting canned beef to Europe from its headquarters in Chicago, which was well served by rail links. By the turn of the century, Armour and Company was well on its way to becoming the largest meat packer in the world. It would also become the indirect object of Upton Sinclair's attention in his monumental exposé of the meatpacking industry in *The Jungle*, published in 1906.

Assuming extraordinary business risks became the forte of the early industrialists, who quickly became known by the sobriquet "captains of industry." The nickname was appropriate whether it was interpreted as a shipping or military term. As Vanderbilt and Gould had proved, collecting and patching up rickety industries could be enormously profitable, and useful as well, because it provided economies of scale that would help them become more efficient and even more profitable. But rarely were the savings passed along to the consumer. What amounted to kickbacks were kept as profits. The new breed of industrialist would be making his fortune by consolidating businesses, relying less upon stock market raids and more upon relentless pressure in business to achieve his ends. His investment banker would play a major role in these enterprises, collecting enormous fees by financing and restructuring new companies.

Consolidators of Industry

Andrew Carnegie was perhaps the best illustration of an obscure immigrant who, with uncanny insight, would do more to shape American industry than anyone of his period except perhaps John D. Rockefeller. Born in 1837 in Scotland, Carnegie emigrated to Pennsylvania with his family when he was thirteen. After he took a job in a telegraph office, it was soon discovered that he was one of the first people who could decipher telegraph messages by ear, an ability that helped him find a job with the Pennsylvania Railroad as an assistant to the superintendent of the line. When the superintendent, Thomas Scott, was made president, Carnegie also rose quickly through the ranks, and by the time the Civil War erupted he had a senior management job. The railroad was the best proving ground a budding industrialist could have hoped for because it controlled the Pennsylvania state legislature in much the same way that the Harlem Railroad was closely tucked in with members of the New York legislature. They practiced the sort of patronage for which the era was renowned.

But being restless and believing that the telegraph business was by then passé for someone with ambition, Carnegie started his own business, the Keystone Bridge Works. The company built iron and steel bridges for the railways, replacing the older wooden bridges of the past. Soon Carnegie expanded into making rails. During the war the demand for steel increased and the price soared to $130 per ton. And the need for railways was pressing. As Carnegie recalled, "The railway lines of America were fast becoming dangerous for want of new rails and this state of affairs led me to organize in 1864 a rail-making concern at Pittsburgh. There was no difficulty in obtaining partners and capital."[10] The lessons he learned at the Pennsylvania would serve him well in later years; in addition, the business introduced him to the intricacies of the steel industry. By the time of the panic of 1873, he had decided that steel was the industry of the future and he forged ahead exclusively in that direction. Unlike the railroad barons who used the dangerous state of the rails to pounce upon cheap stocks, Carnegie saw an opportunity to supply new materials so that they, and he, could continue expanding.[11]

Within several years of entering the steel business, Carnegie's Pittsburgh-based operations became the largest steel producers in the United States. The second half of the nineteenth century became the era of steel and iron as well as railroads. The profits from Carnegie's steel operations were around $1.5 million a year. But Carnegie himself was a steel man with little desire to become occupied with the day-to-day operations of the industry, which he left for others to manage. Despite his relentless exhortations to his employees to work harder and produce more and more, he nevertheless attracted fiercely loyal workers who, like him, recognized the potential of the new industry. Two of them came from very different backgrounds, but both would leave their own marks upon American industry and finance—Henry Clay Frick and Charles Schwab.

By the early 1870s Carnegie had found his way to New York, leaving his Pittsburgh business for others to run. In the city he became acquainted with other captains of industry and became familiar, if not enamored, with the mechanics of the New York Stock Exchange. Although always entranced with money for its own sake, he never warmed to market speculation. He gave occasional speeches at the American Art Galleries on topics such as the "Aristocracy of the Dollar" but, unlike his major rivals and colleagues, never owned many stocks. Shortly after arriving in the city, he was swamped with offers for various financings from people he did not know who were attracted to him because of his reputation and wealth. Many were for deals to actually buy up whole industries, using his money to a large extent; such offers amused the industrialist, but he declined them all. As he noted in his autobiography, "The most notable offer of this kind I ever received was one morning in the Windsor Hotel. Jay Gould, then in the height of his career, approached me and said he had heard of me and he would purchase control of the Pennsylvania Railroad Company and give me one half of all profits if I would agree to devote myself to its management."[12] Gould's generosity was the result of personal animosity between himself and Thomas Scott, the president of the railroad. Carnegie declined the offer, citing his loyalty to Scott, his former mentor. There is no record of Gould's reply to such a display of loyalty.

During his career, Carnegie had only one speculative common stock holding, in the Pennsylvania Railroad. That position was carried on 100 percent margin, with the funds being supplied by banks. The other cash positions he held were small, but he still felt they took too much of his time. He later recalled, "I found that when I opened the paper in the morning I was tempted to look first at the quotations in the stock market. As I had determined to sell all my interests in every outside concern and concentrate my attention upon our manufacturing concerns in Pittsburgh, I further resolved not even to own any stock that was bought and sold on the stock exchange." The exchange was by then reporting the prices of some stocks to the newspapers on a regular basis because of the introduction of the ticker tape. Carnegie believed that the mind of a trader focused "upon the stock quotations and not upon the points that require calm thought. Speculation is a parasite feeding upon values, creating none."[13]

The face of American capitalism was beginning to change slowly, at least at the very top. Bear raids and corners were still the stuff of avaricious floor traders but would be used less and less to accumulate fortunes at the expense of others à la Drew and Vanderbilt. Attitudes did not undergo a radical transformation, but at least industrialists began to have some contacts outside the world of business. Whether that changed their attitudes is probably moot because Carnegie, like Vanderbilt, was always known for obtaining customers through vicious price undercutting at his competitors' expense. But he was able to move in better social circles than Vanderbilt or Gould, as can be seen in Carnegie's friendly personal relationship with the English writer and philosopher Herbert Spencer. Spencer was one of the group of social thinkers known popularly as social Darwinists because of his attempt to fuse Darwin's biological principles with his own views on society and social development. Prior to devoting himself to scientific inquiries and philosophical writing, Spencer had been editor of *The Economist* and was partially responsible for that newspaper's many favorable views on American society prior to the Civil War. His scientific and philosophical writings, best seen in his *First Principles* (1862) and *Principles of Ethics* (1879–1893), claimed that men possessed two types of knowledge: intuition and individual knowledge. Individual achievement was best accomplished by those who built upon their intuition, which was common to all men. The most successful distanced themselves from others by applying their acquired knowledge. The friendship was a natural because Carnegie, like many of his contemporaries, also believed in that crude form of evolution in business that was vaguely translated as "survival of the fittest," where some men were able to build their individual knowledge and success more adeptly than others. However, unlike Henry Clews and other Wall Street personalities, he clearly did not believe such principles could be applied to stock exchange floor trading techniques, producing the greatest good for the greatest number. Carnegie also numbered other prominent men of the period as his friends, including Matthew Arnold, George Bernard Shaw, the Earl of Elgin, and William Gladstone.

Although Carnegie had no taste for common stocks, he did prove to be an effective raiser of capital in his own right. In 1869 he obtained a bid for his Keystone Bridge Works to build a bridge over the Mississippi River at St. Louis. He also helped the local planners obtain funding so they would be able to pay him. Four million dollars was needed for the project. Significantly, Carnegie traveled to London, not New York, to find the funds. He intended to sell bonds to raise the money, and he wanted to employ Junius Spencer Morgan and his London bank in the enterprise. In something of a major coup, Carnegie persuaded Morgan to buy the bonds from him, but Morgan insisted on dozens of changes in the wording of the bond certificates themselves before they could be sold. The banker encouraged the industrialist to send the request for the changes home to the bridge authority via the mails and to take a vacation in Scotland while waiting for a reply. Not being that patient, or trustful, Carnegie sent a transatlantic telegram instead.

Within twenty-four hours Carnegie had permission for the necessary changes, but he still was not finished with the new bond issue. He had arranged to meet the financial editor of the *Times* in Morgan's office, "well knowing that a few words from him would go far in lifting the price of the bonds on the [London] Exchange. American securities had recently been fiercely attacked, owing to the proceedings of Fisk and Gould in connection with the Erie Railway Company . . . and I knew this would be handed out as an objection and therefore I met it at once."[14] Carnegie was totally successful. The editor agreed to write a favorable article on the bridge and its role in expanding American transportation. "When he left the office, Mr. Morgan clapped me on the shoulder and said: 'Thank you young man; you have raised the price of those bonds five per cent this morning.' To which Carnegie replied, 'All right, Mr. Morgan, now show me how I can raise them five per cent more for you.'"[15]

Despite Carnegie's protests to the contrary, he had learned the press relations tricks of securities manipulators well and the bond issue was a great success. His avoidance of the New York capital market was significant on two counts. It showed the continued reliance upon British investors that had dominated American finance since the early days of the century and also displayed a distrust of the predators that still roamed Wall Street. However, many commentators saw through some of his ideological stances. Later professing himself to be a champion of workers' causes, almost a budding socialist, Carnegie was caught in a characteristic ideological cross fire one day when *The Economist* reported, "Mr. Carnegie has publicly announced himself a socialist, and a keen sympathiser with wage earners in one breath and, to the amazement of his men, ordered a reduction of from 10 to 33 per cent in wages throughout his works. An inquisitive reporter asked him if he were ready to divide up his wealth in conformity with his profession and the iron and steel millionaire said 'No.'"[16]

Carnegie's career was paralleled by that of John Davison Rockefeller, another product of upstate New York who was destined to change American industry and the way it was financed. He was the son of an itinerant trader who sometimes sold quack cancer medicines. In 1853, when John was sixteen, his family migrated to Ohio, settling in Cleveland, where the young man began to look for a job. Eschewing work in small shops, he instead sought employment in one of the major industries, intent upon learning how the infrastructure of the country worked rather than simply working for a living.

At the age of nineteen, Rockefeller and a friend, Maurice Clark, opened a trading firm in Cleveland under the name Clark and Rockefeller, using their savings and borrowed money to finance it. They became commission merchants for commodities such as grains, pork, and breadstuffs and quickly began to prosper. When the Civil War provided a ready customer in the Union army, they, like Armour, began to prosper by supplying it with foodstuffs and other basic commodities and materials. But while their turnover was high, their profits were relatively small and in their first year they netted only about five thousand dollars between them, a return of about 1 percent of turnover.

While Clark provided the trading expertise, Rockefeller became the brains of the business and busied himself with management and relations with bankers. Within a couple of years, the young firm prospered, making the two young men wealthy by contemporary standards. Then in 1864 their fortunes began to change. Oil had been discovered in Titusville, Pennsylvania, in 1859, and within a few years Clark and Rockefeller was dealing in barrels of oil in addition to its usual commodities. It soon became apparent that there were two sides to the oil business. The speculative side was in its production—drilling and bringing the oil out of the ground; the less speculative side was in refining it and selling it to customers. Rockefeller could see both sides from his natural vantage point in Cleveland, which quickly became dotted with refineries for the Pennsylvania crude.

When Rockefeller spotted this opportunity, American industry and industrial organization was on the verge of a major revolution. In 1863 he bid $72,000 for a Cleveland refinery and quickly made the transition from the commodities procurement business to oil refining. He sold his interest in the commodities firm. His new firm, Rockefeller and Andrews, was one of the largest in Cleveland. Only several years before, a new rail line had opened the city to the rest of the country, and within a short time it was a major oil refining and export center. The railroads themselves clamored for the new oil business. Since the railroads were still in their growth period, the astute businessman could not fail to notice that they could be played against each other in order to drive down shipping costs. Commodore Vanderbilt's old ploy from the shipping business was about to be turned on its head by customers who would use the railroad's eagerness to drive down haulage prices for themselves.

In his early years Rockefeller had borrowed considerable sums from banks to finance the company's expansion. He obtained significant new funding for his refinery when the firm entered new business arrangements with Henry Flagler, a trading partner who was particularly friendly with Rockefeller. Flagler brought in both cash and an entrepreneurial sense that the firm needed, for it was he who became mainly responsible for negotiating discount rates with the railways, always eager to do continuing business with the oil refiners. The railways continued to expand into the western United States and were willing to discount haulage prices to the oil industry to keep their customers from being poached by other lines. Flagler was able to negotiate what amounted to cutthroat rate discounts because of the size of the Rockefeller company, and he used this ability to full advantage. However, the oil industry had recently fallen upon hard times. By 1869, supply far exceeded demand and the oil production industry was in a full-blown depression. Only the large firms survived because they were able to control the costs of doing business, shipping being one of them. Many smaller firms were not able to respond and went out of business or were absorbed by others.

As American society continued to develop and industrialization proceeded at what appeared to be a breathtaking pace, several economic facts of life began to change, signifying a change for business itself. For over seventy years after the Constitution was ratified, economic growth had constantly increased despite the pauses created by the various panics. The influx of new immigrants and the growing domestic population consumed increasing amounts of goods and services. Business provided the perfect example of a simple sort of equation that was characteristic of the Manchester school of economics, the dominant school of economic thought at the time. Originating in Britain with Adam Smith's writings at the time of the American Revolution, the predominant theme in this classical school of thought was that both business and the individual prospered economically when the heavy hand of government was far removed. Adam Smith believed that a guiding hand controlled man economically and that "invisible hand" was his own self-interest. Economic self-aggrandizement was best realized when governments remained in the background. No one in American business would have argued with such propositions, for they also dovetailed nicely with the crude form of social Darwinism that characterized so much of American business thought. But one of the Manchester school's basic tenets was under attack as society became larger and more complicated.

One of the cornerstones of the Manchester school's influence was found in the writings of a French economist, Jean-Baptiste Say. Say held that increases in the production and supply of goods necessarily meant an increase in the demand as well. There was no such thing as excessive production in his ideas (known as Say's law or Say's theory of the market), which was a perfectly valid interpretation of the early years of industrialization but became less timely as industrial society expanded. At some point it needed to slow down to catch its collective breath. Consumers could not continue consuming without retrenching, nor could bulls continue to buy stocks, especially in the presence of bear raiders. In 1869 the oil producers were experiencing just that sort of phenomenon as demand for their crude oil declined sharply.

Rockefeller clearly recognized the trend and responded by seizing the opportunity presented by the oil recession to expand his firm. In 1870 he was approached by some potential New York investors, but he rejected them for fear of losing control of the firm. Instead, he and his partners created a joint-stock company. Shares were distributed only among the existing partners and new shareholders would be admitted only when the need for fresh capital was pressing. This would keep the firm safe from predatory investors and bankers who could seize control by offering capital for expansion and then demanding large blocks of stock in return. In January 1870 the new company was established in Ohio as the Standard Oil Company. The original shareholders were John and William Rockefeller, Andrews, Flagler, and his relative by marriage Stephen Harkness. The original capital of Standard Oil was $1 million. John D. Rockefeller was the largest shareholder, holding twice as much stock as any of his former partners. Most important, by that time the company was the largest oil refiner in the United States, accounting for 10 percent of all refining capacity.

Rockefeller's reputation to that point was that of a brilliant organizer who paid considerable attention to detail, almost to the point of pedantry. But in 1872 a drastic change occurred, tarnishing his reputation, that had its direct origins in the oil depression of 1869–70. The railroads serving the Pennsylvania and Ohio area and the local oil refiners together formed an organization dedicated to pooling their interests, ostensibly to prevent further losses in both industries. Refineries in certain areas would be served only by certain rail lines, which would determine the fees to be paid for hauling the oil. Rates were effectively doubled, and nonmembers would be charged the same standard rates, but one-half of what they paid would be returned to members, effectively lowering the members' haulage costs.

This was one of the first American cartels. The organization, the South Improvement Company, was in effect providing kickbacks for members at the expense of nonmembers while rigging prices in the process. The public outcry was predictably shrill. A clerk in one of the Ohio railway offices put the new, collusive rates in effect before they were properly announced to the public. The news immediately went out on the telegraph, and within hours oil producers and refiners were clamoring to discover why the haulage rates had doubled without any apparent reason. When they discovered the reason, the oil refiners came under immediate and harsh attack. The petroleum producers quickly united against the refineries, and hordes of oil workers roamed the streets of Cleveland bent upon revenge on the collaborators. Yet Rockefeller remained steadfast in his belief that the cartel was a just, equitable arrangement. He remarked, "I had our plan clearly in mind. It was right. I knew it as a matter of conscience. It was right between me and my God. If I had to do it tomorrow I would do it again the same way—do it a hundred times."[17]

The tensions that developed between the organizers of the trusts and those who opposed them for business or moral reasons became one of the great political and economic battles of the nineteenth century. Contained within it were conflicting notions of fair play, competition, and a general distrust of railroad tycoons. When news leaked of the freight rigging concocted by the South Improvement Corporation at the behest of Rockefeller in 1868, battle lines were quickly drawn. In a larger context, the problem was not uniquely American but one of industrial society in general. The same sort of industrial strife was waged between coal miners and management in France and was chronicled in Émile Zola's novel *Germinal*, published in France in 1885. The two sides in that fictional dispute would lock horns in a battle that neither would win. Zola's title refers to the seventh month of the French revolutionary calendar of 1793, the period commonly known as the third week of March through the third week in April. Coincidentally, it was in the third week of March 1868, that the oil producers of Pennsylvania met in New York with Commodore Vanderbilt to enlist his help against the price-rigging cartel and Standard Oil, hoping to dissuade him from signing the New York Central to a similar agreement.

Despite the protests of the oil producers and the lukewarm cooperation offered them by the railroads, the oil depression set in and forced many producers to the wall. The strategy worked phenomenally well. Within a short time, Rockefeller had single-handedly consolidated the oil refinery business in Cleveland. Competitors were offered a simple alternative: sell out to Rockefeller or be forced out of business by the South Improvement Company. Most took the easier alternative. Within a few months of the cartel's announcement, Rockefeller and Standard Oil controlled all of Cleveland's refining capacity, and with it about 20 percent of oil refining in the country.

The consolidation of the refining business was followed closely by Congress in an 1876 investigation. Clearly the nature of American business had been changed by the relentless pressure put upon the smaller companies that eventually succumbed. Despite the philanthropy, which he had practiced from the earliest days of his professional life and would continue to practice on an even grander scale later when he began to withdraw from active participation in his business, in the public's opinion Rockefeller's support of the cartel put him squarely in the robber baron's camp.[18]

Equally important was the nature of the South Improvement Company itself. Chartered in Pennsylvania, it was one of the first examples of a trust company in American corporate history. Essentially, it was owned by other companies, which is not uncommon in American business today, but at the time the concept was revolutionary. Many states actually prohibited one company from holding stock in another. This kept monopolies in check and also prevented banks from crossing state lines, a method used by local state bankers to keep the larger out-of-state banks from encroaching upon them. But after the establishment of trust companies, the antimonopoly idea would require further refinements because trusts, and quickly thereafter holding companies, exploded on the American corporate scene. They became the natural organizational forms by which American industry grew into large corporations in the post–Civil war period. They were as important during their time as stock companies had been earlier in the century when they were first used on a relatively wide scale.

Baronial Finances

In the early 1880s the banking and securities industries began to recover from the panic of 1873. The number of banks, commercial and private, began to grow again as banking lured entrepreneurs after the severe depression. Banking itself was also making great inroads. Americans were settling about 70 percent of all financial transactions by check after the Civil War, and these deposits proved irresistible to bankers. The flow of money into the banks increased substantially. Bond yields declined, encouraging companies to borrow. Foreign investment also increased again, displaying British and now French interest in American investments. But Wall Street as such was not the direct beneficiary. The securities industry prospered, but the New York part did not prove a magnet to all investors. The success of the Boston banking firms, notably Kidder, Peabody and Lee Higginson, was due in no small part to their connections with London. Having been burned by numerous bear and bull traders on the New York Stock Exchange, many English investors still were attracted to American investments but with some understandable trepidation.

Many foreign investors, especially the British, were increasing their direct investments (in real property assets) in the country, and such investments did not require the services of brokers. But they did require investment bankers with access to large pools of funds. The Morgan banking business in London had risen to become the preeminent Anglo-American investment firm, and by the Civil War Junius Spencer Morgan was considered to be at the apex of his profession. Being located in London from midcentury was a distinct advantage, for the British were the main exporters of capital to the rest of the world throughout the period.

Many British investors who bought directly into American property investments sought to establish some sort of control lest their investments go awry. Many companies were established solely to control British property in the United States, with offices in both London and New York or some other American city. Dozens of these enterprises were established to oversee the American holdings. Much of this business was welcomed, although it had little effect upon the securities business. But substantial amounts of funds were still being directed to the United States by the firms with established European contacts, especially J. S. Morgan and Company.

When Junius Spencer Morgan left Boston for London in 1854, his son John Pierpont Morgan was only a teenager. Junius Spencer sent his son to the University of Göttingen for several years to study mathematics before being sent to New York as a clerk for the firm's American representative. That was during the panic of 1857, which was proving to be a fertile training ground for many future financiers. Within three years he left to establish J. Pierpont Morgan and Company in New York. The new firm became the American agent of J. S. Morgan. By 1870 the younger Morgan had already established a sizable fortune dealing in gold and exchange and selling securities. Pierpont, already contemplating retirement in his midthirties, then was persuaded to join forces in Philadelphia to form Drexel, Morgan and Company, making that old-line firm even stronger with Morgan's New York presence under its corporate umbrella. It was one of Philadelphia's oldest banking houses but was second to Jay Cooke and Company in reputation because of Cooke's success during the Civil War.

Railroads provided a major opportunity for the Drexel, Morgan firm. The death of Commodore Vanderbilt had left his son William with the bulk of New York Central stock in 1879. William had inherited over $90 million of his father's estate, an amount that inspired fear both in the public and in government circles. Prime Minister Gladstone of Britain, upon hearing of the size of the inheritance, the first great American industrial fortune, remarked to the Vanderbilt family lawyer: "I understand you have a man in your country who is worth $100 million. . . . The government ought to take it away from him, as it is too dangerous a power for any one man to have. Suppose he should take his money and lock it up, it would make a panic in America which would extend to this country and every other part of the world, and be a great injury to a large number of innocent people."[19] William's succinct response upon hearing the remark has managed to linger over the years: "The public be damned."

Two years earlier, railroad workers on many of the major lines had called a general strike against many of the roads, including the New York Central. The lines began to lower railway workers' wages at the same

The Modern Colossus of Roads. (Collection of the New-York Historical Society)

time they were cutting prices to the oil refiners. Some of the techniques used by the railroad management, including burning their own rolling stock and then blaming it upon the strikers, set public opinion against the roads and their managements. The New York state legislature was contemplating punitive taxes against railroads in general and the New York Central in particular. Vanderbilt's divestiture seemed auspiciously well timed for financial as well as political reasons. Although the Commodore had never trusted his son, considering him somewhat dull, William proved to be astute by approaching Pierpont Morgan and asking for help in divesting some of the stock in order to reduce his holding in the line. Morgan agreed but realized that the New York Stock Exchange was not the best place to sell the shares, especially since the Commodore's reputation, and that of the New York Central itself, was far from forgotten. Pierpont instead decided to sell the shares in London on the quiet, using a syndicate composed of Drexel, Morgan and J. S. Morgan. The syndicate bought the shares and sold them successfully to domestic and foreign (mostly British) investors, netting Vanderbilt over $30 million and Morgan an unheard-of $3 million commission. The deal enhanced the reputation of the Morgans, especially Pierpont, who had managed to bring some sanity to railroad financings, and he was well lauded in the press. The *Commercial and Financial Chronicle*, the most prestigious financial newspaper of its day, cited Morgan as one of the country's preeminent financiers. The size of the commission also gave an insight into the size of the fees investment bankers were charging their clients, apparently without much fuss. Ten percent fees for corporate business became a standard that would last for decades.

William Vanderbilt showed some acumen by investing his proceeds in U.S. Treasury bonds rather than in other railroads, opting for safety of return rather than more speculative investments.[20] That would have made it difficult for the government to expropriate it from him, taking Gladstone's advice, if he was one of its major creditors, by holding its Treasury bonds. But at the end of the day there was a higher price to pay. Pierpont quietly began to acquire shares from all the disparate subscribers, including Jay Gould and Russell Sage, and soon would come to control the railway himself.

The deal, one of the early acquisitions made by Morgan using his banker's vantage point, would be followed by many more over the next thirty years. Morgan and some of the other investment banking houses used their inside tracks to involve themselves in the structuring of the new corporate America and became consolidators in their own right. Within twenty to thirty years, many of the famous American corporations would be constructed by investment banking firms that took a large stake of the operations for themselves. The official public reaction to such consolidation would come before World War I. However, in the latter part of the nineteenth century, public indignation was not yet aroused by the firms within the investment community. With the exception of a few well-publicized trips to the public well through Treasury financings, bankers remained out of the limelight and, for the most part, safe from public criticism.

Those who did bear the brunt of public opprobrium were the industrialists who violated the basic premise of the American ethos. When private greed overtook the public good, the shenanigans of the robber barons would not be tolerated. In the nineteenth century the United States still adhered to many of the principles that had characterized it at the end of the eighteenth. Enterprise was encouraged, especially on a local scale, and government interference was not appreciated. The virtues that caught the attention of Alexis de Tocqueville, recorded in his *Democracy in America*, published in 1835, were still very much in evidence. But smallness remained a virtue, in government as much as in business. Tocqueville admired America for its New England form of local democracy, and Americans still admired individual, local efforts in making money, which until the Civil War meant in relatively small business enterprises. But once the age of managerial capitalism began to emerge and the captains of industry turned small enterprises into pawns on their grandiose chessboards, public attitudes would begin to change. Many Americans had little idea of what Jay Gould did, but many hated him for it nevertheless. Soon public opprobrium would turn on the other industrialists of the period. The turn of the financiers would come later, in the twentieth century, when many of their corporate creations became too large to be comprehensible.

After the demise of Jay Cooke and Company, Treasury bond financings took a turn for the worse. In 1877 the Treasury issued $260 million worth of new bonds. Without a war to worry about and without a scrupulous public watching its every financing move, the Treasury employed a syndicate of investment bankers to underwrite the issue. The bonds were bought by a syndicate of Drexel, Morgan and Company in conjunction with J. S. Morgan, August Belmont, and J. & W. Seligman. The bonds were bought from the Treasury at a discount of 4 percent from par and resold to the public at par, netting the underwriters a profit of around $10 million. Half of that went to Drexel, Morgan alone. The U.S. Treasury had not allowed underwriters such a massive profit since the War of 1812. The public outcry was shrill.

In the absence of Salmon P. Chase, long since retired from the cabinet, the Treasury was in different hands in 1877. John Sherman was Rutherford Hayes's secretary of the Treasury. An able administrator, former senator from Ohio, and younger brother of William Tecumseh Sherman, he was primarily self-taught but demonstrated unusual financial acumen in his political career. He served as chairman of the Senate Finance Committee and was a supporter of the Specie Resumption Act. He later returned to the Senate, where he helped forge several important pieces of legislation bearing his name, notably the Sherman Anti-Trust Act, passed in 1890. But during his two-year tenure as Treasury secretary, his preoccupation with the greenback question and specie resumption led him to ignore the bond financing, allowing the investment bankers to slip into the deal for such huge profits. As a result of the bond issue, the Senate held hearings in 1879 and called upon Sherman to provide details to justify his actions. But the damage had already been done, and the syndicate had its profits for perhaps the easiest of any underwritings undertaken to date.

A corporate bond underwriting in 1880 showed the great leaps made by underwriting syndicates for corporate issues and earned Drexel, Morgan even more profits. Since the fall of Jay Cooke, the Northern Pacific Railroad was still in need of funds, and it approached Drexel, Morgan for advice on issuing $40 million of bonds. There was an element of sweet revenge in the deal since Cooke had beaten Drexel, Morgan into second place in Philadelphia investment banking during the Civil War. The syndicate—composed of Drexel, Morgan; August Belmont; and Winslow, Lanier and Company—was to become the largest underwritten offering of railroad bonds until that time. Belmont's interest in both the Treasury and Northern Pacific issues was on behalf of foreign interests, including the Rothschilds. Drexel, Morgan's profits on the two deals exceeded the amount Jay Cooke made on all of his war bond issues six times over.

Investment banking had finally come into the spotlight as companies continuously needed new capital to expand. By the mid-1880s, American capitalism had entered a more mature phase. More common stocks were being issued than ever before and a good number of bonds were maturing, being replaced with new borrowings by the same companies. In 1885 the total appetite for new funds was slightly over $250 million, with almost 80 percent being satisfied through bond borrowings.[21] The fees generally averaged around 10 percent of the proceeds, so it can be seen that Wall Street and the select underwriters around the country were making good profits simply by collecting fees. But underwriting fees were only part of the potential profits that could be made by acting for companies. Investment bankers were already taking sizable stakes in companies they served as financial advisers, giving them an inside track on the firms' prospects.

Mephistopheles Strikes Again

Never tiring of using his time-proven methods of acquisition, Jay Gould decided in the early 1880s that he should own a telegraph company, under the pretext that telegraphy and the railroads went hand in hand in devel-

"Song of the Street." (Collection of the New-York Historical Society)

Jay Gould Fleeing. (Collection of the New-York Historical Society)

oping the country. The most developed and influential telegraph company in the country at the time was Western Union, controlled by William Vanderbilt. In order to wrest control of the company, despite the looming presence of Vanderbilt, Gould opened a multiple attack. He announced that he was going to open a competing company while at the same time mounting a bear raid on Western Union stock. Having owned the *New York World* since 1873, it would be relatively easy to have the paper publish articles questioning the value of the company and its management in order to help force its price down.

Using the newspaper to cry monopoly at Western Union, Gould began to short its stock using select friends on the floor of the New York Stock Exchange. He then announced that he was launching the Atlantic and Pacific Company to challenge the monopoly. This was an ingenious ploy because it indicated a slight shift in his familiar strategy. By emphasizing competition over monopoly, he was sounding a battle cry that would be heard again and again in the latter part of the century. The stock of Western Union began to fall, and Gould and his short-selling colleagues reputedly made a million dollars each when they covered their positions. That he was able to employ the newspaper to his own ends is

"Drowning in His Own Pool," *Puck*, 1884. (Collection of the New-York Historical Society)

somewhat remarkable since it had already acquired a reputation as Gould's mouthpiece. Its readership had fallen as a result, and it was losing money. But those who read the paper apparently believed what they saw and joined in the selling spree.

The directors of Western Union were in a quandary. The stock was down and their business was declining, probably because the public feared Gould more than it took him seriously about establishing a competing company. Regardless, they bought out the Atlantic and Pacific for about $10 million, leaving Gould with a handsome profit. He persisted, however, not yet finished with the battle. The paper again attacked Western Union, and another bear raid was mounted. The members of the pool that Gould had organized were all experienced bear raiders, but as they were happily shorting the stock an anonymous buyer appeared and forced many of them to cover their shorts at a loss as the price began to rise. The buyer was no one other than Gould himself, who had now mounted a corner in order to gain control of Western Union. His buying activities forced many of his pool into large losses. Henry Clews relates that Gould was encountered by a member of the unsuccessful bear pool on Exchange Place who proceeded to pick him up by his lapels and drop him in front of a barbershop. Gould suffered the indignity and quietly returned to his office, making certain the trader lost $15,000 before the day was finished.[22]

In what proved to be one of the most copycat of all robber baron operations, Gould mounted one of his last plundering operations in 1881. New York City was in the throes of developing a rapid transit system using overhead trolleys. Like Commodore Vanderbilt before him, Gould was intent upon dominating this new form of transit and would stoop to any level to attain it. He employed the same two methods of intimidation he had used to gain control of Western Union. He sued one of the two companies engaged in the development, charging that it was a monopoly. At the same time, he used the newspaper to mount a barrage against the company and its management.

The stock price promptly fell by 50 percent, whereupon Gould and Russell Sage aggressively began acquiring it. Using their majority holdings, they then prematurely filed for bankruptcy, and the stock price continued to collapse. But the company appeared to make a miraculous recovery, and within a few months the price had rebounded. It obviously was not in as bad shape as Gould and Sage had maintained. Once they had total control, they issued new stock, raised prices, and enjoyed enhanced earnings. But the fiasco did not go unnoticed in the press. The *New York Times* took them to task in no uncertain language: "There is no more disgraceful chapter in the history of stockjobbing than that which records the operations of Jay Gould, Russell Sage and Cyrus Field and their associates in securing control of the system of elevated railroads in New York City."[23]

When Gould's interest in the *New York World* subsequently waned, he found a willing buyer in Joseph Pulitzer, who purchased it in 1883 for about $350,000. Only after Pulitzer had signed the papers making the purchase official did Gould inform him that his son George had a small interest in the paper that he would like him to keep, if Pulitzer had no objections. "Not," replied Pulitzer sharply, "if you do not object to seeing it stated each morning in the year that the Gould family has no control or influence in the property."[24] Only then did Gould acquiesce to the buyer's demands by relinquishing all control and influence over the newspaper.

The period immediately following the Civil War was a crucible in American history. The practices forged in finance before and during the war had created somewhat chaotic conditions in the marketplace. The activities of the robber barons, a name deserved to varying degrees by many of the industrialists and financiers, are testimony to the climate at the time.

By the last quarter of the nineteenth century, a profound change began to occur in industry and on Wall Street. Consolidation was proving to be not only a trend; it was becoming a tidal wave that swamped American industry. The great cartels were beginning to form and within two decades would have a virtual stranglehold on entire sectors of the American economy. Wall Street helped finance that expansion and by the end of the century would represent one of the more powerful cartels in its own right. Only the fittest survived, but now they were colluding to ensure that they remained successful.

The Age of the Trusts (1880–1910)

Mary had a little lamb,
And when she saw it sicken
She shipped it off to Packingtown
And now its labeled chicken.

Nineteenth-century parody

In the twentieth century, television and the automobile would become the common denominators linking the United States. In the nineteenth century the links were the telegraph and the railroads. The explosion in railroad construction during the latter part of the century was the direct cause as well as the effect of much other industrial consolidation at the same time. After 1885 the face of the country began to change. Small, local industries were consolidated into larger ones that were able to sell their products worldwide as well as nationwide. The direct legacy of Carnegie, Rockefeller, Vanderbilt, and Gould was the trend they helped establish in concentrating economic power in the United States. In the latter phase of the consolidation, the great trusts were born. They would soon challenge the American ideals of individualism and self-reliance.

Once the trusts were in full operation, public reaction began to challenge some of the basic principles upon which they were built. Was it necessary to have so much economic power in the hands of so few? Why was it not possible to treat workers humanely rather than as mere cogs in the productive process? And could there not be more safeguards to watch over ordinary workers and citizens in the face of such overwhelming managerial power? As the great trusts were being established and becoming entrenched, voices from many quarters began to be raised in protest. Frank Norris and Upton Sinclair wrote about the abuses of whole industries in the name of profit, following the tradition of Émile Zola in France, whose novels about the coal mining industry and later anti-Semitism became extremely well known. The American protest, or muckraking, novel would soon challenge those contemporary favorites of Lew Wallace, Henry James, and the always popular Horatio Alger on the best-seller lists. In his book *How the Other Half Lives*, Jacob Riis deplored urban tenement life as the unacceptable side of capitalism. But the trusts and advancing industrialism still attracted their admirers. In 1888 Edward Bellamy reached the top of the best-seller list with his utopian *Looking Backward 2000–1887*, which sold over a million copies. Bellamy stated, "This tendency toward monopolies, which had been so desperately and vainly resisted, was recognized at last in its true significance, as a process which only needed to complete its logical evolution to open a golden future to humanity."[1] Henry Steele Commager, writing fifty years later in the *New York Times*, echoed this sentiment by admitting that "the trusts, like the poor, are always with us." The American fascination with wealth was deeply entrenched, and industrialists were still admired by many. Andrew Carnegie's *Gospel of Wealth* was one of the best-sellers of 1889. Yet Americans were ambivalent when dealing with great wealth; most envied it, but there was growing disenchantment with the way money was being made by the major industrialists. But many businessmen had a bit of the speculator in them. *The Economist* wryly noted that one in every three or four American merchants appeared to have some sort of speculative position in the stock market. Attitudes were beginning to change, but the gambling fever remained.

The term *trust* became standard American usage during the nineteenth century. Originally, it had been used as a synonym for *merger* when the term was more associated with monopoly than it is today. Monopoly was one of the great taboos of English common law, and the Americans inherited a dislike for it as well. The one exception was when the monopoly was granted by the state. All members of a pool of similar business interests would surrender their shares for certificates issued by a trust. Standard Oil employed this approach when the joint-stock company changed its status to a trust, which would entitle the owners to a portion of the earnings and a right to vote for the trustees who ran the trust. Standard Oil itself had nine. The company had reorganized as a trust in 1882 to circumvent state incorporation laws in Ohio. In 1879 the company had been investigated on several fronts, one of them the same New York investigation that had looked into the holdings of William Vanderbilt and the New York Central. Ohio began similar proceedings at the same time. Shortly thereafter, Standard Oil's directors were sued in Clarion County, Ohio, for restraint of trade. The company settled the suit, promising to engage in fewer monopolistic practices in the future. But the lesson had been learned well: the company's actions nationwide could be attacked from a single state. Standard Oil began to adapt in order to protect itself.

When a trust decided to take over another, smaller company, the shareholders in the smaller firm would simply be issued trust certificates in exchange for their holdings. The trust would grow in size and influence without having to issue new stock in the marketplace. Trust certificates replaced common stock in these enterprises and were traded on the stock exchanges. The early trusts were found in many of the agricultural industries, especially in the South, and required some investment banking services, usually on a small scale. As the trusts relied upon their own funds and those of the companies they absorbed, investment bankers were often left out in the cold. Rockefeller himself was wary of "finance capitalism" and preferred to find funds for expansion by issuing new certificates to his new takeover targets or by using cash on hand, avoiding Wall Street in the process.

The NYSE Gains Ground

Despite the momentous changes occurring in American industry, the stock exchange was still a battleground for bulls and bears intent on locking horns at every opportunity. Battles similar to those of Drew, Vanderbilt, and Gould were still being waged by other bear raiders intent upon seeking revenge upon bullish opponents. Now these raiders were often hired professionals, used by others to mount bear raids. But the belligerencies were becoming more difficult because the stock exchange had grown along with the economy; the battles would be proportionately larger as a result.

The number of shares bought and sold on the NYSE doubled between 1875 and 1885, as did their value. After the panic of 1873 had become a distant memory, stocks began to outnumber bonds on the exchange and dominated trading. Common stocks were traded much more avidly than railroad bonds, their nearest competitors. Among the common stocks, railroad companies still dominated, although industrials such as the Western Union Company and Edison General Electric were rising quickly. The railway stocks were still heavily watered, so bear raiders continued to favor them over others. The legacy of Gould, Fisk, and Vanderbilt lived on.

Railroad stocks became the battleground for two German-American speculators on the NYSE in a struggle that was truly in the tradition of Drew and Vanderbilt. Their particular field of battle was the Northern Pacific Railroad, once the darling (and ruin) of Jay Cooke. Before J. P. Morgan became involved, the railroad was controlled by Henry Villard, a Prussian by birth who became involved in railways when he obtained the receivership of the Kansas Pacific. Born Heinrich Hilgard, Villard came to the United States in 1853 at age nineteen and moved to Colorado. Shortly thereafter, he bought a steamship company using borrowed money and began consolidating his operations in the Northwest. By watering the stock and using planted favorable press reports, he forced its price to rise to almost two hundred dollars per share. As it rose, new share issues followed the old, paying immediate dividends and giving the impression that the company was a money machine, able to achieve exponential growth in the wild and woolly West. In fact, Villard's trick was not uncommon at the time. New stock was sold and the proceeds were used to pay immediate dividends on existing stock. The stock then began a phenomenal rise, presenting Villard and his colleagues with enormous gains. The stock-watering game, devised years before, was still very much in vogue in the wildly speculative market following 1873.

Villard then proceeded to "corner" the entire Pacific Northwest for himself by buying up all types of transportation in the region. But his plans appeared to go awry when he learned of the $40-million bond issue for the Northern Pacific led by J. P. Morgan and August Belmont and Company. The capital funds would help rebuild the railroad, posing a serious threat to his monopoly over regional trade. He decided to buy the railroad rather than compete with it. By forming pools, or syndicates, of investment money, Villard bought all the outstanding shares of the railroad and became its baron. When the final track was laid for the line to proceed to Portland, Oregon, Villard was the first to make the trip, breaking the old record for travel time to the Pacific coast. The magnate celebrated his apparent success by building a baronial mansion on Madison Avenue in New York that dwarfed many of the other robber baron's cathedrals.

But chicanery lay just around the corner for Villard. During his acquisition of the Northern Pacific, he had made a personal enemy of Charles F. Woerishoffer, another German immigrant described by Henry Clews as "the most brilliant bear operator ever known in Wall Street," a fair compliment considering some of the competition. Short sellers had become known as "plungers," and he was most often described as the master. Several years younger than Villard, Woerishoffer came to the United States when he was twenty-two and went to work for Henry Budge of Budge, Schwetze and Company, who bought him a seat on the NYSE. In 1876 he founded his own firm of Woerishoffer and Company and became well known as an adroit operator on both sides of the market. But Villard's acquisition of the Northern Pacific opened a rift between the two when Villard accused him of not being faithful to the deal and the pool that financed it. Woerishoffer sought revenge upon Villard by mounting a bear raid on his holdings, approaching the raid with the same sort of vengeance that Commodore Vanderbilt had displayed years before with the New York Central. Woerishoffer bet his firm and his personal fortune on the raid, which proved successful. The stock price of the Northern Pacific and other Villard-owned companies collapsed, ruining Villard in the process.

The raid was not as plausible as some of those in the past, and many have suggested that it was part of a conspiracy to drive Villard out of the Northern Pacific. Woerishoffer was merely the paid agent of others intent on running the railroad, among them Morgan interests. Smaller member firms of the NYSE made a good living acting as hired plungers for others throughout the post–Civil war period. Whatever the background, Villard was so penniless that he had to sign his Madison Avenue home over to the railroad. The directors responded by granting him a yearly allowance of $10,000 for past services rendered. Then the trustees of the Northern Pacific called in Morgan and August Belmont for financial advice. Villard temporarily faded from view but would return before long with an even more ambitious scheme, again aimed at creating a monopoly.

Competitors were not the only victims of financial skullduggery in the 1880s. Notable casualties included Ulysses S. Grant and his family, involved in a swindle that did little to enhance his reputation as a politician or financier. The Grant family naively fell victim to Ferdinand Ward, a New York native who emerged in the 1880s as a stock speculator in partnership with James Fish, then president of the Marine National Bank in New York and Ward's senior by twenty years. The two men showed a certain flair for the market, and by 1880 both had made sizable fortunes through many joint speculations. It was then that Ward set up his own shop on Wall Street with Grant's elder son, Ulysses Jr. The new house was appropriately named Grant and Ward.

The firm included the two Grants, Ward, and Fish. Ulysses Sr. and Fish were nonexecutive partners, while the younger Grant left the business mostly to Ward, who had the power to sign all checks by himself. The firm prospered, due to both the trading skills of Ward and the prestige of the Grant name. By 1884 the firm showed a profit of around $2.5 million, to the delight of the Grants and Fish. But Ward had devised a scheme, probably without the knowledge of his partners, to borrow money at high rates of interest and use the proceeds to buy stocks. Like Villard, he was able to pay the interest by using the new borrowings, a technique that in the twentieth century would become known as a *Ponzi scheme*.[2] But Ward's technique did not appear suspicious to his investors since the Grant family name was involved in the business. When more cash was needed than he had on hand, he simply took loans from Marine National, of which he became a director at the behest of Fish.

Unfortunately, the stock market fell in 1884 and Ward was not able to meet margin calls on his positions. He had borrowed substantial amounts of money from the bank, and when the firm failed, so, too, did the bank. By May 1884 the firm was bust, as was the bank, and Wall Street was abuzz with rumors. The Grant family lost a sizable amount of its wealth. Ward, once known on Wall Street as the "young Napoleon of finance," had met his Waterloo but not without tarnishing the Grant name in the process. His scheme was notable, however, since it would be practiced again many times, snaring gullible investors in the process.

Amid the skullduggery, Wall Street was still proud of its ability to determine the underlying causes of all sorts of phenomena. Social Darwinisim and crude utilitarianism were still as popular as ever and were often invoked when the role of finance in everyday life was questioned. The greatest good for the greatest number sometimes had a high price. But occasionally Wall Street took on topics best left to others. Henry Clews wrote that "a great number of Wall Street habitués are beginning to think seriously on the subject of earthquakes and are attempting to penetrate their causes." In 1884 a mild earthquake had been felt in New York City, preceded by a stronger one in Charleston, South Carolina. The southern quake had done some damage and interrupted commerce, and earthquakes quickly became the main topic of conversation in the financial district. The preoccupation with tremors was not totally unfounded, although the great San Francisco earthquake was still over twenty years away. But Clews's ideas concerning their causes provided a bit of light relief to serious science. "Among the population there is a large proportion of go-ahead, driving men who are constantly diving into the bowels of the earth to dig up the vast treasures which are there concealed," he wrote, referring to the mining companies springing up at the time.[3] These companies were upsetting the status quo in nature. He concluded that earthquakes were caused by such digging under the earth in places nature intended to be left untouched. Whether his remarks had anything to do with the performance of the very popular mining stocks was not mentioned.

The Octopus in New Jersey

By the 1890s the trusts had become the largest corporations in the country, challenging the railroads, which had held that distinction since their origins in the 1840s and 1850s. But what appeared to be a serious challenge to their influence was mounted when the Sherman Anti-Trust Act was passed in 1890. The first of two acts passed during the period bearing the name of the former secretary of the Treasury John Sherman, now Republican senator from Ohio, it proscribed trusts or business organizations that "restrained" trade or commerce. Any organization that did so and was found in violation could be sued for triple damages. While it was a useful source for defining monopoly, the Sherman Anti-Trust Act had few teeth. Nevertheless, it would soon claim one notable casualty.

The legislation was not overseen by any government agency, leaving potential challenges in the hands of aggrieved individuals or companies.

As a result, few prosecutions were successful during the early years. But at the time the act was understood as going hand in hand with attempts to control those industries that were protected by tariffs. Many of the agricultural trusts that had developed in the South were in enviable positions because they were protected against foreign competition by tariffs against imports. Having thus protected them, Congress later had a mild change of heart and passed the antitrust legislation to show that it had not inadvertently given undue power to the trusts. Ironically, Standard Oil was always the first trust that came to mind, but it owed nothing to tariffs. Its monopoly position was due purely to the abilities of Rockefeller and his colleagues to consolidate the chaotic oil refining and shipping business.

Many foreign investors (especially the British) clamored about the tariffs, but some found a clever way around them. The tariffs hurt British exports on one hand but made American investments very attractive on the other. While looking bad for those who advocated free trade, the tariffs did not deter foreign investment. In fact, they helped many British investors become extremely wealthy. That attraction also provided a magnet for immigration from Britain. Many skilled workers left Britain for the United States in search of wealth. In 1889 *The Economist* remarked that the immigrants "are the adventurous and the brave among their fellows and to pick them out of the less efficient must be a grave loss to any community, however industrious, as grave a loss as if the owner of a factory dismissed all his hands qualified to become overseers or foremen."[4] Stock traders also made windfall gains on many of the stocks and trust certificates issued by the monopolies during the period. Strong domestic sales for these large combines were almost assured when foreign competition was all but eliminated. But not all politicians were supporters of the law. Many felt, with some justification, that trusts were not subject to public scrutiny because they were not public companies. Detractors added that they did much interstate business, making them subject to federal law. The antitrust legislation was something of a compromise between the two.

The flurry of corporate activity created a need for increased financial reporting. In 1889 the quality of financial newspapers also took a positive turn when the *Wall Street Journal* was founded by Dow Jones. The original paper was an afternoon edition of four pages selling for two cents per copy. The editors immediately made their distribution area well known so that the paper would not be thought of as simply a downtown New York daily. The original circulation area stretched from Montreal to Washington, D.C. The front page was reserved for market news, and the paper promised to provide its readers with facts, not opinions, on the market.[5]

After New Jersey allowed holding companies to form in the 1890s, the door swung open for many of the trusts to reorganize themselves under that corporate umbrella. In business terms, the original trusts and the holding companies were horizontal organizations because they combined similar sorts of companies. As time passed, they extended outward and became vertical by absorbing other related companies. That was the intent of the first trust, the South Improvement Company, when it combined certain railroads with their best customers, the oil refiners of Cleveland. Standard Oil followed suit, expanding into all areas related to oil refining.

Since the formation of Standard Oil, Rockefeller had expanded his company both horizontally and vertically. He had bought pipeline companies, mining companies, and direct facilities for marketing his products. But monopoly power was under attack from many quarters. Many states were conducting inquiries into the leviathan corporations. Even before the Sherman Anti-Trust Act was passed, the handwriting was on the wall. Because of the vagaries of Ohio's attitude toward corporations, Standard Oil was reorganized as a trust to protect itself from what it considered a hostile state government. The "new" company's capital was represented by 700,000 hundred-dollar certificates worth $70 million. The nine trustees ran the entire operation. The subsidiary companies remained intact in the states in which they operated, and the individual parts were protected from litigation from outside their own states. One of the other Standards created at the same time was the Standard Oil Company of New Jersey. After the reorganization was complete, Standard Oil controlled about 80 percent of the country's refining capabilities and about 90 percent of its pipelines. In 1890 it earned over $19 million and paid dividends of slightly over $11 million. Throughout the 1880s it was the largest company in the world. But, unlike the railroads and some of the other monopolies that had developed, such as the American Tobacco Company, the company's stock certificates were never watered down. They were worth exactly what the certificates represented. There was no attempt to inflate their value or induce investors to buy watered stock.[6]

But the whole idea of a trust was about to die a quick death. Another suit filed in Ohio in 1890 again challenged Standard Oil, and the Ohio Supreme Court ruled against the company in favor of the state, finding that the trust had violated the common law by running a monopoly. As a result, Rockefeller and his other trustees rapidly began to shift the trust's operations to New Jersey, where conducive holding company laws helped Standard reorganize. In 1899 the shift was completed and the new Standard Oil issued shares in place of its trust certificates. Standard became a publicly traded company in the modern sense, with assets of over $200 million and an astonishing return on those assets of almost 30 percent. The management remained the same as when the trustees were in charge.

Standard Oil was not the only trust operating in the 1890s. About fifty operated nationwide, representing the major industries of the day. Many of the names are also recognizable today. Most of the industries that expanded nationwide did so through trusts and then holding companies. Many times their economic benefits outweighed their disadvantages, and they certainly attracted both admirers and detractors. They were usually associated with one individual, usually the founder of the company, regardless of how active that individual was in the actual workings of the company itself.

The well-known trusts of the period included the telephone monopoly named the American Telephone and Telegraph Company (AT&T) after 1889. The communications leviathan is normally associated with Alexander Graham Bell, the founder of the company, although it was run by Gardiner Greene Hubbard and later by Theodore Vail. Gustavus Swift's Swift Brothers became a major force in meatpacking and shipping by integrating its processing facilities with the transportation necessary to ship its products to market. Swift developed his own refrigerator cars to carry beef and other meats to market. The Edison Illuminating Company, founded by Thomas Edison but managed by several staff members including Samuel Insull, eventually became the General Electric Company. Tobacco came under a virtual monopoly when James Buchanan Duke integrated tobacco farming, processing, and distribution under the aegis of the American Tobacco Company.

The ingenuity displayed by these entrepreneurs lay in their abilities to understand the structure and potential markets of their businesses. In the process of consolidation, much of their competition was either absorbed or driven out of business. In this respect, American business had not changed markedly since the period prior to the Civil War, but the stakes had become larger as the American market grew. But one important factor distinguished some of these enterprises. Some were more capital-intensive than others and needed more investment funds to support expansion, and when they did they attracted Wall Street financiers. That attraction would be central to American development in the late nineteenth and early twentieth centuries.

Of all the emerging industries of the latter nineteenth century, there were no better examples than the General Electric Company and AT&T. Both Edison and Bell had quickly become American legends for their discoveries, but neither was particularly good at managing or expanding his business. From the very beginning, both relied heavily on professional managers and outside financing. Neither man would become as wealthy as those who assisted them, although their place in American folklore was certainly assured.

In 1876 Alexander Graham Bell received a patent for a "harmonic telegraph." Shortly afterward, he invented the telephone—the communications equivalent of all the American railroads and telegraphs rolled into one. It symbolized the high-tech equivalent of railroad, steel, and oil in one modern instrument. Like the steel industry, this revolution in industry also came from a Scot. But Bell, unlike Carnegie, came to the United States with an established profession and reputation.

Born in Edinburgh in 1847, Bell studied anatomy at University College, London, before traveling to Boston to teach at a school for the deaf established by the Boston school board. A year later he joined the faculty of Boston University to teach vocal physiology. During that time he developed the idea for a device capable of transmitting the voice, which he exhibited at the Centennial Exhibition in Philadelphia. For several years he was involved in a number of lawsuits defending his patent, and in in 1877 he formed the Bell Telephone Company to mass-produce telephones. But his first actual financial manager, Hubbard, was intent on selling franchises to local companies to produce the actual telephone networks, paying Bell a royalty in the process. Before any progress could be made, the company changed hands and a new group of investors took over; Vail became general manager. The new firm began to consolidate, buying the Western Electric Company, a manufacturer of communications equipment.

The franchising concept proceeded, and the local Bell companies were formed. Then American Bell, as the company was now called, formed a long-distance subsidiary, called AT&T, in an attempt to stave off further competition. But local manufacturing companies were providing stiff competition for the parent company's products, and American Bell required a further infusion of capital. Bell reorganized, with AT&T becoming the primary company in the group. It then entered an alliance with a syndicate of bankers headed by J. P. Morgan to provide fresh funds. Bell himself was by then out of the picture. By 1881 he was divorced from the Bell companies except for a small shareholding. He went on to other interests, among them founding the Volta Company, which served as an experimental firm that worked on a laserlike device for transmitting the voice by beams of light. He also served as president of the National Geographic Society until 1904.

Thomas Edison was a more active participant in his own company. Born in Ohio in 1847, he received a formal education for only three months. He spent his early years as a newsboy and a telegraph operator, recalling the early career of Carnegie. His early experience in telegraphy led him to experiment with electricity and its possibilities for communication. For a short time he was a partner in Pope, Edison Company, an electrical engineering firm that pursued patents and products such as the electric ticker tape, which helped revolutionize stock exchange reporting. When the firm was bought out in 1870, Edison used his share of the profits to open a laboratory in Menlo Park, New Jersey, so he could pursue his inventions. Edison's lab, the first industrial research laboratory in the country, produced many inventions, some of which were used by the Bell telephone company. The most notable was the phonograph, first put on display in 1877. Two years later Edison developed the incandescent light-bulb, for which he was best known. The bulb was only part of a larger plan for a series of power stations that would provide electrical power–generating facilities for entire cities. Edison was helped immeasurably in this endeavor by J. P. Morgan, who provided funds for an experimental power station located at Pearl Street, adjacent to the Wall Street district. Morgan's bank became the first user of electric lighting in New York City. Despite several mishaps at the station, Morgan continued to support Edison and would be instrumental in forging the General Electric Company out of Edison's original company.

During this period of entrepreneurship and invention, modern investment banking emerged as a major industry in its own right. There were so many projects requiring capital that investment bankers could pick and choose which ones they would support. But investment banking was still limited by the amounts of capital it could provide for new and established companies. Even the large banks such as Morgan, Kidder, Peabody, or Kuhn Loeb could not afford to provide all the capital their clients required, especially in new industries that were capital-intensive. As a result, the bankers began to use syndicates more and more. New issues of stocks and bonds were now regularly being sold to groups of banks, which would then sell them to the public. The banker who constructed the deal in the first instance was known as the lead underwriter and became the manager of the deal. Whichever bank assumed this position was able to dictate to the company needing funds, as well as to the rest of Wall Street. For the fifty-year period between 1880 and 1930, that position indisputably belonged to J. P. Morgan and Company, headed until 1913 by Pierpont Morgan.

Morgan's Influence Spreads

The last two decades of the nineteenth century also were Wall Street's first golden age. The number of listings on the stock exchange increased dramatically. The NYSE experienced its first million-share day in 1885. The investment banking syndicates became fixtures on Wall Street through which bankers would purchase large blocks of new securities from companies and sell them to investors. The power and influence of the investment bankers continued to grow. The influential houses such as Morgan, Kidder, Peabody, Lee Higginson, Kuhn Loeb, and Lehman Brothers gained in stature, and many became better known than their client companies. The well-known bankers became the thread holding together many of the various parts of American industry. But many were not content with being just intermediaries. They became active in trust creation and consolidating power in their own right.

The dependence upon foreign capital was still very evident in the latter nineteenth century. The United States was still a debtor nation, owing more to foreigners than it earned from them. By the beginning of the 1890s, this dependence became particularly clear when foreign investors began to panic over the gold-silver debates that had been waged in the United States since the Specie Resumption Act of 1879. In 1890 the second Sherman legislation was passed as the Sherman Silver Act of 1890, which required the Treasury to buy a specific amount of silver each month in order to maintain its price. This was Congress's bow to the western mining states. Silver was used mostly for coins and for backing silver certificates. However, many people saw little use for it, and much was returned to Treasury vaults shortly after being placed in circulation. Politically, maintaining a silver policy smacked to many of bimetallism, adhering to two metals backing currency rather than one. The clear preference was for gold, but politics intervened on behalf of silver.

Unsure of the Americans' devotion to gold as the single standard upon which to base the dollar, foreign investors began to sell American securities en masse. They had read of the fiery, eloquent speeches of William Jennings Bryan in favor of silver. Such populism only added to their anxieties, which in turn caused an outflow of gold from the country. Within a short time the panic of 1893 began, underscoring the Americans' continued reliance upon foreign investors. But the usually reliable British investors had become more wary of foreign investment. In 1890 the venerable Baring Brothers failed and had to be bailed out by other British banks. The bank's chairman had overextended the family-run firm by buying an excessive amount of Argentinian and Uruguayan securities; when both of these markets collapsed, Barings followed soon after. That panic bode well for American securities in the long run but made many British investors nervous about foreign investments in general.

The gold reserve of the United States had fallen to low levels because of revenue losses created by protective tariffs and increased bonuses paid to war veterans. When the reserves fell below $100 million, previously considered an acceptable level, investors became uneasy and began to sell securities. In February 1893 the NYSE witnessed its busiest day ever when 1.5 million shares were traded and over $6 million worth of bonds were sold. By April only about one-quarter of the money in circulation was backed by gold reserves. In May the NYSE index dropped to an all-time low behind massive selling of securities, wiping out many traders in the process. Railroad stocks were particularly hard hit. As a result, President Cleveland asked Congress to repeal the Sherman Silver Act of 1890 in an attempt to shore up reserves and restore order in the financial system.

A special session of Congress was called during the summer to determine the fate of the Sherman Silver Act, but it was not until October that the repeal finally cleared both houses. In the interim, the reserve situation had become more acute and a depression was setting in. Reserves dropped to around $80 million, the market was badly depressed, and numerous business failures followed. Over five hundred banks failed nationwide, over fifteen thousand businesses followed the same path, and unemployment soared. By the end of 1893, an estimated 30 percent of all U.S. railroads were in bankruptcy court. Such depressing economic conditions had not been felt since the panic of 1873.

Adding to the confusion, a group of five hundred men, dubbed "Coxey's army," marched on Washington to demand a reflation of the money supply. They were led by Jacob Coxey of Ohio, a professional activist, member of Congress, and social reformer who was involved in many social protests of the period. Somewhat prematurely, Coxey had proposed means of dealing with unemployment during the depression, including public works, a nationwide road system, and an eight-hour working day. His march presaged those of the 1930s, which became much better known in the Great Depression. The Washington march came at about the same time as a nationwide railroad strike. The latter was triggered when the American Railway Union, led by Eugene V. Debs, called a strike against the Pullman Palace Car Company. Sympathy strikes spread to many railroads, and President Cleveland finally called in troops to stop the strike in Chicago. The strike collapsed in July 1894, but not before it helped polarize tensions between management and workers. The great tug-of-war between labor and management had begun. In the same year, other strikes were occurring in the mining industry in Pennsylvania and the South and among clothing workers in New York.

Another blow to faith in American investments came in August 1894 when the federal deficit—the first recorded since the Civil War—reached $60 million. In response, the Cleveland administration proposed the first of two bond issues for $50 million each in order to shore up the Treasury's finances. Both were heavily subscribed by New York banks, which were asked to pay for their subscriptions in gold. That temporarily solved the Treasury's immediate problems. However, within a year the problem rose again since the Treasury was using the proceeds of the two sales to pay back other debt that was currently maturing. Reserves were again running low, and traditional bond sales would be of little use. The Treasury needed to regain some of the gold it had lost when foreign investors sold their securities. In a desperate attempt to stop the outflow, President Cleveland struck a deal that would allow gold to reenter the country through a sale of bonds to foreigners. His agents for the transaction were a syndicate headed by J. P. Morgan and August Belmont and Company.

In a deal that was highly criticized almost immediately, Morgan and his group sold $65 million worth of 3.75 percent bonds to the syndicate for a premium price. They were then sold to foreign investors for about 7 percent more. The bankers helped stabilize the exchange rate when bringing the gold into the country so that the dollar's foreign exchange rate would remain the same. Treasury reserves increased as a result, and the Treasury was spared the indignity of bankruptcy and a default by the United States on its obligations. But critics of the operation were numerous and very vocal. Silver advocates and populists were highly critical of the deal, as were those opposed to Wall Street's benefiting from public problems at Washington's expense (the syndicate netted about $6 million on the deal). This was not the first time such complaints had been raised, nor would it be the last.

Cries of anti-Morganism and anti-Semitism were heard from a number of quarters. The anti-Semitism was the most shrill. One populist rabble-rouser dubbed President Cleveland a tool of "Jewish bankers and British gold." The *New York World*, now in the hands of Joseph Pulitzer, was even more explicit, calling the syndicate a group of "bloodsucking Jews and aliens."[7] Henry Adams, one of the writers who wrongly labeled Jay Gould a Jew in one of the many attempts to disparage him, attempted to point out the dangers of having so much American debt in foreign hands when he claimed that the "Jews of Lombard Street" (referring to the Rothschilds in the City of London) "threaten to withdraw their capital if there was even a danger of free coinage of silver."[8] Besides controlling American finances, he implied that foreign investors also decided the silver question in favor of gold.

Not since the days of the Southern bond default in the 1840s had so much antiforeign feeling been expressed. But the story was not yet over. Within a year, gold reserves again declined and the Treasury again issued bonds to cover its shortfall. But the depression was ending and foreign investors were returning to Wall Street, bringing their gold with them. Silver had been defeated in favor of one metallic standard for the dollar. The problem eventually subsided but not without exacting a toll on the reputation of the U.S. Treasury. The country was sorely feeling the effects of not having a central bank. And the jingoists and xenophobes had established another link in their attempt to connect domestic ills to foreign and Jewish cabals.

America's dependence upon foreign investors came to the fore again after remaining in the background for decades. The ultimate bailout of the Treasury came from Europeans and their best-known agents in New York. Despite eighty years of progress, the situation appeared to have changed little since the War of 1812. This was annoying to many advocates of central banking because two private bankers managed to perform central banking operations for the United States, charging a fee in the process. Inadvertently, the mere presence of foreign bankers, some of whom were Jewish, was fueling the fires of jingoism that would be adopted by arch nationalist and hate groups for decades to come. Morgan himself referred to Jacob Schiff, his main rival among Jewish bankers, as a foreigner. But the gold operation was a personal coup for Pierpont Morgan, who had by then proved himself to be the most famous and influential banker in the country, rivaled by no one. But although the operation bolstered Morgan's reputation, it did not necessarily increase his popularity.

Morgan's position in finance was central to the heart of corporate America. Advising corporations had been good business for investment bankers since the early days of the railroads. But Morgan's influence extended beyond advice into the actual creation of many large trusts and holding companies. In this respect his bank had no peers, and his ability to be at the center of the financial universe earned him begrudging respect, but few friends, on Wall Street. Pierpont Morgan personified Wall Street during his tenure at the helm of his bank, but he was more feared than considered a colleague by other financiers. His personal yachts, all somewhat arrogantly dubbed the *Corsair*, suggested to some critics that investment banking and brigandage were one and the same activity. His haughtiness and authoritarian nature became legendary, but he did win the confidence of the U.S. Treasury, a relationship that was to endure for decades. But in terms of stock trading, he always kept on the banking side of the street rather than the speculative side. He preferred to use brokers when necessary and did not consider himself one of their number.

Morgan's influence on the creation of corporate America was as strong as that of many inventors and entrepreneurs on their own businesses. In the late nineteenth and early twentieth centuries, he had a dominant position in railroads, life insurance, steel, and electricity, in addition to banking. Of all of his activities, his role in the formation of the U.S. Steel Corporation and the General Electric Company were perhaps the largest feathers in his hat. In both cases, as in many others, all he brought to the table was financial advice. Thomas Edison and Andrew Carnegie had already laid the groundwork for these two companies.

Industry Expands Again

Edison's early enterprises had relied upon loans from Morgan since the time of the experimental power stations on Pearl Street. Morgan and his partners were also minority shareholders in Edison General Electric. The company remained relatively small until the 1880s, with sales remaining below a million dollars per year. The lightbulb was not to be the future of the electric industry. How it would be powered and where electrical power would originate were more important issues that would turn the industry into a battleground. Electricity production was about to become a central issue in American politics that would last for the next fity years.

In the early 1880s, one of Edison's avid supporters was Henry Villard, the erstwhile railroad baron. After the debacle in which he was forced into personal bankruptcy, he returned to his native Germany for two years before reemerging in New York in 1886. When he returned, he had the financial support of several large German banks and was intent upon forging a worldwide electrical cartel. One of his first targets was Edison's company. But in order to capture it, he would need the blessing of Morgan.

Edison himself was no longer interested in the business, preferring to return to tinkering and inventing. Villard and Morgan formed an alliance that effectively bought out Edison and the principals of Edison Electric for several million dollars. Edison himself got $1.75 million, while the others received $1 million between them. One of those receiving a small amount was Edison's chief lieutenant, Samuel Insull, a young Briton who had helped the inventor organize the company. Insull went on to become a vice president and member of the board of the new company along with Edison, while Villard became president. The money offered by Morgan and Villard was too much to resist, especially for the inventor. "Mr. Insull and I were afraid we might get into trouble for lack of money. . . . therefore we concluded it was better to be sure than to be sorry," Edison wrote, explaining his reasons for accepting the offer.[9]

But Villard's fortunes were not to remain on the rise for long. The new Edison General Electric Company prospered under Insull's management. By cutting costs, he was able to trim the operation while increasing profits from year to year. It became the most profitable of the three major electric companies, the others being the Westinghouse Company under George Westinghouse and the Thompson-Houston Electric Company. Westinghouse was the smaller of the two competitors, possessing an alternative product (alternating current rather than the direct current of Edison). In what proved to be a nasty battle between Edison and Westinghouse, each company set out to prove that its respective product was the safer form of electrical voltage. One of the products of that campaign was the introduction of the electric chair as a means of execution, adding a macabre twist to a corporate battle between two innovative companies. However, Westinghouse had better engineering skills than Edison Electric, and a merger would be out of the question. So Villard arranged a merger whereby Edison would take over the larger Thompson-Houston and approached Morgan for financing.

Morgan had ideas of his own, however. Arranging a counterdeal with the executives of Thompson-Houston, Morgan turned Villard's deal on its head by having the company take over Edison. He then asked Villard for his resignation. If the former conspiracy theories proved correct, it was the second time in his career that Villard had been defeated by Morgan. Insull and the other directors also lost their jobs, although they all gained financially. Edison made a few million more, which made him happy. In April 1892 Morgan formed the General Electric Company, which stood out as the leader in its industry, although it still had to contend with competition from Westinghouse. Morgan had effectively outmaneuvered the inventor and the principals of the company, emerging as the controlling force in electricity production in the United States. Villard and Insull moved on to other ventures. Insull's name would be found again in every national newspaper in the 1930s as America's most famous, self-exiled industrialist and financier of the Great Depression.

By the turn of the century, Andrew Carnegie's steelworks continued to prove extremely profitable, netting $40 million per year in profit. Carnegie himself was losing interest in the business, devoting himself increasingly to philanthropic enterprises as he grew older. "After my book, *The Gospel of Wealth* was published, it was inevitable that I should live up to its teachings by ceasing to struggle for more wealth," he wrote. "I resolved to stop accumulating and begin the infinitely more serious and difficult task of wise distribution."[10]

Carnegie's steelworks had been a prime target of J. P. Morgan for some time. However, Morgan did not think he would be able to control the company because of what he assumed would be its prohibitively high cost. But he did not count upon Carnegie's other interests providing him with the opportunity he needed. The steel man cum philanthropist indeed wanted to sell his enterprise. In 1900, at a dinner at the University Club in New York hosted by Charles Schwab, the president of the Carnegie Steel Company, the idea of selling the company was floated. After several furious weeks of negotiations, the asking price emerged. Carnegie would accept a bid slightly under $500 million for the company, an amount that would easily make him the richest man in the world. Morgan decided he must have the company and agreed to the price, of which Carnegie's own share would be $300 million. Payment was to be in bonds and preferred stock. Schwab also became extremely rich in the buyout and built a sixty-room mansion on Riverside Drive in New York. Carnegie himself was too wise to accept watered stock in payment. He had successfully negotiated with both Junius Morgan and now his son, although it was later agreed that his selling price to J. P. was a bargain. At the time, Carnegie gloated over the deal, summarizing his "victory" over Morgan in not uncharacteristic ethnic terms. "It takes a Yankee to beat a Jew and it takes a Scot to beat a Yankee," he said after the deal was complete.[11] Had he held out for $100 million more, he probably would have prevailed eventually.

While the price was considered a coup for Morgan, enhancing his reputation on Wall Street, Carnegie had a different explanation for his selling price. Testifying before a House of Representatives committee in 1912, Carnegie stated, "I have been told many times by insiders that I should have asked $100 million more and could have got it easily. Once for all, I want to put a stop to all this talk about Mr. Carnegie 'forcing high prices for anything.'"[12] Were former criticisms coming home to haunt the retiree? Whether the former steel man was playing a tune the House wanted to hear or was being serious is difficult to tell. But he wanted it made clear for posterity that a small part of the proceeds were spent upon his former workers when he established a benevolence fund for the Homestead Steel workers.

After acquiring the steelworks, Morgan proceeded to offer it to the public while retaining a large part of the offering for himself. The issue became the largest stock offering to date: $1.4 billion, representing the first corporation ever capitalized in excess of $1 billion. The syndicate was also the largest ever assembled, with over three hundred underwriters. In order to keep the price stable during the offering, Morgan appointed James R. Keene to manage affairs on the stock exchange floor. Keene, the most renowned stock operator of his day, admitted he had never actually met with Morgan despite being trusted with so large a deal. Morgan hired Talbot J. Taylor and Company to stage-manage the floor and officially dealt only with this firm, never with Keene. However, it was clear that Keene would be in charge since Talbot Taylor was Keene's son-in-law. The issue was an enormous success despite some dire warnings about issues of its size.[13]

Shortly after acquiring Carnegie's enterprises, Morgan scored another significant coup. Iron ore and other mineral supplies were crucial to steel manufacturing, and Morgan was constantly looking for resources to complement his business. Some of John D. Rockefeller's holdings attracted him, notably the Mesabi Range ore fields. But relations were not good between the two men, who simply did not like each other. Rockefeller had not lost his dislike of finance capitalism or financiers. Furthermore, he had previously chosen Stillman's National City Bank as his major New York banker rather than Morgan. However, Rockefeller was always amenable to a deal and in 1901 finally decided to sell the Mesabi fields to Morgan for $90 million. The deal was a personal victory for Rockefeller, although some early analysts considered it a personal victory for Morgan. More significantly, Morgan's desire to continue expanding the steel trust would cast some light on a deal to be done later, in the midst of the panic of 1907.

Some of the period's major industries were dominated by monopolies, while others were dominated by oligopolies. US Steel, AT&T, and American Tobacco were clear examples of monopolies, while meatpacking, agricultural production, and the investment banking business were oligopolies, to name but a few. Usually, those whose products affected the public directly became the targets of public indignation, muckraking novels, and congressional inquiries. While the bankers suffered the same fate, they usually escaped the harsher gaze of an unfriendly Congress or the press. But the cycle was still moving round. Another panic was on the horizon that would begin to change perceptions about bankers and their powers, raising the clamor for a central bank, much to the chagrin of many on Wall Street.

Judging Morgan

The trusts became a major topic of conversation in the late nineteenth and early twentieth centuries. So, too, did bankers, especially J. P. Morgan and his son Jack (J. P. Morgan Jr.). After the panic of 1893, it became clear that Morgan was able to exercise a power far in excess of his private position on Wall Street. But true to his nature, Pierpont exercised that power and then receded from public view. As far as the press and the reading public were concerned, the principles of Jeffersonian democracy were still safe in turn-of-the-century America. State influence in private affairs was still at a minimum despite the formation of some regulatory agencies such as the Interstate Commerce Commission. The America of Thoreau, where good government remains in the background, was still inviolate, or so it appeared. But behind this facade of private, trust capitalism was a relatively fragile financial structure. Too many panics occurred, and when they did they underlined the frailty of a system driven largely by private enterprise.

What was extraordinary about the first panic of the twentieth century was that it appeared to be a replay of those that had occurred so many times before on Wall Street. During the panics of 1857, 1869, 1873, and 1893, Wall Street had to come to its own rescue. Strong financial firms bailed out the weaker while allowing others to fail. Government was not much help. Traditionally, when a white knight appeared to help others by bailing them out or by helping the government with its financing, the rewards were minimal and the opprobrium could be great. The anti–Wall Street contingent was always quick to charge financiers with lining their own pockets at the expense of the public, as Pierpont Morgan had witnessed more than once. After Jay Cooke had beaten Drexel and Company into second place in investment banking in Philadelphia, his unraveling came quickly when the Northern Pacific bankrupted him. It was natural that anyone who stepped into the breach caused by the lack of strong central government power should make sure there was something in it for them.

The profits made by bailing out the Treasury in 1894 were criticized but well earned. But it became clear that an emerging economic power could not leave its lender-of-last-resort functions to Wall Street bankers. Even if the banking community looked after its own in reasonable fashion, the conspiracy theorists would always rant about the concentration of economic power at the corner of Broad and Wall. One of the more damning nicknames hung on Wall Street's lapel was destined to last for several decades. In the wake of the oil, steel, and tobacco trusts there was now the "money trust," the lofty Wall Street group that controlled the financial system, allocating credit at whim. This would prove a difficult characterization that would not be shaken off easily. During the panic of 1907, the notion would only pick up additional credence.

The stock market was approaching bubblelike proportions in 1906. Several previous bouts of volatility had left it open to criticism and manipulation. In 1901 the price of the Northern Pacific rose to over one thousand dollars per share as J. P. Morgan bid the price up in an attempt to stop Jacob Schiff and Harriman from gaining a majority control. The subsequent market collapse piqued the anger of the New York press and brought denunciations raining down on the heads of the trusts. In 1903 the market had also been hard hit by speculation. In that plunge the price of US Steel had dropped from the mid-fifties to less than ten dollars. But a bubble again began to expand and prices rose. The lack of a central bank became increasingly worrisome to almost all market operators. If the market fell, many banks would undoubtedly follow suit since they were integrally involved in the market as either underwriters or investors. This included the trust banks, a group of institutions separate from the commercial and investment banks. Trust banks were administrators of trust funds, money invested on behalf of estates, wills, and the like. They provided a tenuous link to the markets. Many of them made loans to market speculators, taking securities as collateral. If stocks fell, the trust banks would be severely hurt, as would their investors. Without a central bank, no one would loan them money if a depositor's run developed or they needed cash to prop up their positions under duress.

Wall Street began to recognize the problem, and the heads of many banks wanted to assemble a pool of money to be used as a standby if a crisis developed. They also had a substantial stake in the trust business. Four years earlier, many of the New York banks had pooled their money to found their own trust, the Bankers Trust Company, headed by Thomas Lamont, later to become a Morgan partner. Any vulnerability in this group was bound to have severe repercussions up and down the Street. Almost as anticipated, the reaction came on March 13, 1907, when the stock market began to fall. The press was full of stories about bankers and their deliberate attempts to make the market fall. Politicians, notably Teddy Roosevelt, also blamed the current economic climate on the economic concentration in the country. The next six months saw the market steadily erode. Then, on October 21, a run developed on the Knickerbocker Trust Company of New York. Depositors lined up in front of the bank's headquarters on the site of the future Empire State Building to demand their funds. Many of them were unsuccessful. The bank closed the next day after an auditor found that its funds were depleted beyond hope. The bank's president, Charles Barney, shot himself several weeks later, prompting some of the bank's outstanding depositors to commit suicide as well.[14]

After the Knickerbocker failure, the Wall Street community, led by J. P. Morgan, put together a rescue package designed to prop up the other trust institutions. Morgan, Jacob Schiff of Kuhn Loeb, George Baker of the First National Bank, and James Stillman of the National City Bank banded together to ensure that the banking system remained intact. Schiff especially had been an advocate of banking reform for some time and considered the way in which American banking was conducted to be nothing short of disgraceful. After the Knickerbocker failed, this group stepped in to prevent others from doing so. They met in New York with President Roosevelt's secretary of the Treasury, George Cortelyou, who provided them with Treasury funds of $25 million to keep the system from collapsing. The money was deposited in the national banks in New York with the intent of adding funds to a system sorely in need of more liquidity. It was the job of the large New York banks to apply the funds as they saw fit to prevent further panic and runs by depositors.

In many ways the act was an extraordinary gesture. Roosevelt's faith in Morgan and the more serious of the Wall Street contingent only underlined the vacuum in the financial system. The Treasury of the largest emerging economy in the world had to transfer funds to private bankers in order to prevent a financial collapse. More than one detractor claimed that those bankers had orchestrated most of the panics themselves in order to make speculative profits. The panic of 1907 was nothing short of a massive conspiracy designed to ingratiate Wall Street to Washington and make more than a few dollars in the process. Many pointed to the profits made by the Morgan syndicate in the previous panic. One of the strongest proponents of the conspiracy theory was Senator Robert La Follette of Wisconsin. Described as one of the few U.S. senators who was not a millionaire and one who had not bought his seat, La Follette represented the previous generation of Americans who favored competition rather than trusts.[15] There was little doubt that Morgan would enhance his own reputation if the financial sector could be saved, but the handwriting was on the wall. Those favoring a central bank would now win the day, but it would still take several years to work out the details.

Following hard on the heels of the Knickerbocker failure were problems at the Trust Company of America. Morgan organized a pool of $3 million designed to prevent the bank from failing. Funds were provided by First National and National City as well. The bank was saved and a measure of confidence was restored, although the crisis was far from over. The $25 million from the Treasury was judiciously used to support the banking system and keep the stock market from collapsing. But the stock exchange began to sag under the weight of all the margin selling the trusts and other banks were forced into to preserve themselves. On October 24 the NYSE president, Ransom Thomas, pleaded with Morgan to provide $25 million in funds to back the exchange, fearing it would not be able to remain open that day if help was not forthcoming. Morgan and the bank presidents responded quickly, pledging the funds, and the NYSE was able to remain open. When the support package was announced, pandemonium broke out on the exchange. Morgan heard a thunder of noise at his office across the street. When he asked about the cause, he was informed that the members of the NYSE had given him an ovation.[16]

After bailing out both the banking system and the NYSE, Morgan was deified in the press, being referred to as "our savior." He was portrayed as having saved the country from the excesses of speculation and watered stock. He was also portrayed as being above the common excesses of floor traders and minor-league capitalists, all of whom were hell-bent upon making a dollar regardless of the consequences. But Senator La Follette took a different tack. He suspected the Wall Street banking interests of manipulating the crisis to their advantage from the very beginning. Concerning the fiasco at the Knickerbocker Trust and the subsequent bailout of the Trust Company of America, La Follette presented a very different interpretation from that generally accepted. He blamed the run on the Knickerbocker and the Trust Company on enemies of Charles Barney who wanted to ruin him. Barney was also a director of the Trust Company, and that was why both banks were attacked at the same time. On the floor of the Senate La Follette stated:

> Morgan gave out, as reported in Wall Street, that the Knickerbocker would be supported if it met the demands of the depositors who had started a run on it. There was nothing in subsequent events to indicate that there was any sincerity in that promise. . . . Support was not given, it was withheld. . . . The raid [on the Trust Company of America] caused public suspicion to fall upon it. A strong run was started. This was not on the program but as the Vanderbilts, allies of the Standard Oil, were represented on the directorate of the Trust Company of America, Standard Oil was bound to offer some assistance. Though gold and bank notes were ostentatiously piled on the counters to impress depositors, and [a] young Vanderbilt offered as an exhibit of resources and placed at the teller's window, the excited depositors persisted in demanding their money.[17]

Only when the public relations tricks failed did the bank receive assistance from the three major banks.

Morgan's reputation was only enhanced by a rescue package put together for New York City in October of the same year. The unemployment and depression caused by ten months of market slide and bank failures had forced the city's back to the financial wall. The mayor appealed to Morgan, who agreed to underwrite a bond issue for New York for the required amount: $30 million. The 6 percent bond issue was successful, and finally, after several difficult months, the panic began to abate. Morgan was seen as the savior of the banking system, the stock exchange, and New York City all at the same time. But the lessons of the past had not been forgotten. If La Follette's views were any indication, the public would soon be clamoring for financial reform, despite the apparent largesse of the larger banks.

One of the stock market problems presented an opportunity for both profit and criticism by Morgan. Both quickly ensued. A NYSE member firm, Moore and Schley, had run onto the rocks and was over $20 million in debt. Its most valuable asset was a large stock position in the Tennessee Coal and Iron Company, a major competitor of US Steel, with vast mineral holdings. Another holder of large amounts of the stock was the Trust Company of America. The assets of the company were the sort that would blend perfectly with the operations of US Steel but would not be a viable target because of the Sherman Anti-Trust Act. Morgan agreed to rescue Moore and Schley if it would sell him its holdings in Tennessee Coal and Iron at $45 million, considerably less than the market price. He dispatched Henry Clay Frick, who had resigned from Carnegie Steel in 1900, to Washington to convince Theodore Roosevelt that the deal was in the nation's best interests. The president had been blamed by some for beginning the panic by expressing his strong antibusiness and antitrust sentiments in the press in 1906. Roosevelt, by all appearances a staunch antitrust man, quickly agreed after hearing the general arguments in favor of a shotgun merger. US Steel acquired the stock, Moore and Schley and the Trust Company of America were saved, and the steel trust became larger and more influential than ever. The deal was worth millions, but placing an exact figure on it was difficult. Detractors claimed that Tennessee's assets were worth as much as $700 million to US Steel and Morgan. Almost all were in agreement that the deal found remarkably little resistance given that Morgan made at least a $650 million profit.

Oil and Steel

The fall of Henry Villard, Charles Barney, and the Tennessee Coal and Iron Company demonstrated that large fish were still consuming small fish with relative ease on Wall Street. This was possible throughout the last two decades of the nineteenth century because of the large number of equity offerings in the marketplace. Stocks had replaced bonds as investor favorites, partly as a reaction to the stories of the fabulous wealth amassed by the industrialists and financiers. Only conservative investors were interested in bonds, as were those financiers who realized that bondholders could force a company into bankruptcy quite easily, thereby gaining control of it. Predatory investors knew well that the best investment in a company they wanted to take over was not stocks but bonds. Having forced their wills upon a company, these creditors could then accomplish the takeover for a fraction of the stock's previous price.

The presence of so much common stock, much of it watered, made the stock market a precarious place. Many of the investment banks, trust companies, and brokers bought and sold for their investors on a fiduciary basis, meaning they had total discretion over the funds and would invest them as they pleased. On the other side of the coin, the banks used their customers' deposits in the same way, making loans or investments as they saw fit. Few regulations stood in their way, and the annoying ones that did exist were easily circumvented. By the beginning of the twentieth century, it was clear that bankers had a virtual hold on the nation's money supply that would not be easily broken. But the stock market manipulations and raids causing panics endangered the banking system and wealth of bank customers who otherwise had little or nothing to do with the securities markets.

In 1896 the *Wall Street Journal* began publishing the Dow Jones Index on a daily basis. Begun a decade before by Charles Dow, the averages, as they were originally known, tracked the prices of the twelve best-known stocks for the paper, adding to the daily's reputation as well as the Dow's.[18] Now tracking the market's daily movements became possible for the first time, helping to alleviate some investors' fears. But the most significant financial change on Wall Street itself was the development of the syndicate. New deals were requiring more and more capital all the time, and the syndicate was a means of ensuring that deals would be underwritten. Normally, the syndicates were assembled to provide the money to buy an issue of securities from the issuer. At other times the term was used to describe pools of money used by investors to buy into a deal. Later, syndicates and pools would be separated and the term *pool* would be taken to mean that a group of investors had been assembled to buy a large portion of an investment. Syndicates were simply referred to as a group of underwriters.

Investment bankers always maintained that syndicates were informal groups assembled only to underwrite particular deals. Investment bankers invited into deals by Morgan often claimed they had no forewarning that they were being invited. Once invited, many were fearful of declining for fear of incurring Pierpont's wrath, which could be substantial. On the other side of the coin was the Rockefeller group, led by the Rockefellers themselves and Stillman of First National City Bank. Rivalry existed between the two major groups for obtaining new business, and many clients became captive to their investment bankers. Many smaller banking firms aligned themselves with the larger ones in the hope of being tossed enough crumbs to make a decent living, although their portion of a deal may have been small. Of the 350-odd investment banking firms that would form the industry's first professional trade organization in 1912, only about two dozen actually had an impact as underwriters.

Unless the investment banker wanted an entire deal for itself, the syndicates became larger as the deals themselves became larger. Most important, the deals were as good as the underwriters said because minimal securities or company analysis was being conducted at the time. Investors simply had to take the word of their banker that a deal was a good investment. With a system built upon so much blind faith it is easy to see why so much watered stock was making the rounds. Many of the stocks issued during the trust era resembled Daniel Drew's cattle. They were bloated, but not because they were fed nourishing food.

CHAPTER FIVE

The Money Trust
(1890–1920)

It's Morgan's, it's Morgan's
The great financial Gorgon's.

Nineteenth-century
beer hall tune

Before the outbreak of World War I, American business entered a consolidation phase. Great trusts like those of the latter part of the nineteenth century continued to be formed as financiers aided and contributed to the consolidation of many smaller, innovative companies by merging them into industrial giants. From the outside, it appeared that American industry was flexing its muscle in aggregate. Bankers were central to the process, but more controversy was building concerning their roles in capital raising and restructuring. As the war approached, bankers were considered by their critics to be plunderers, having done little, if anything, to help develop the economy in a meaningful way. Others considered them patriots, helping to finance the Allies and America's eventual entry into the conflict by raising billions of dollars. During the 1930s, however, interpretations became much more one-sided. Bankers would be referred to as "financial termites," tearing the financial system apart from the inside. Never particularly loved at any time during that twenty-year period, especially by Democrats, bankers became the most maligned professional group in the country during the Great Depression. But curiously, it was not their wealth that their detractors held against them. Instead, it was the combination of wealth and concentrated economic and political power that eventually made them such a vilified group. Wall Street was about to come under a cloud as Congress clamored for a new central bank. A natural question would quickly arise. In the absence of a central bank for over seventy years, how had the bankers managed to control the reins of credit in the country?

Although never popular in many parts of the country other than the East Coast, bankers underwent a transformation between the two world wars. The institutions they led became more powerful than ever, dominating American life as never before. They plunged into new areas of business with a fervor that helped revolutionize American society by steering it onto the course of consumerism that has dominated it ever since. The United States became a country where the economy was dominated by spending. Beginning in the 1920s, about two-thirds of the country's total gross national product was attributed to consumer spending, a percentage that has remained stable over the years. In order to finance that spending, bankers needed to supply credit, thereby making them central to the idea of American prosperity. Thorstein Veblen's idea of "conspicuous consumption," first outlined in his *Theory of the Leisure Class* (1899), was rapidly becoming reality. With a characteristic tongue-in-cheek description, Veblen likened modern man's desire to consume as conspicuously as possible to primitive man's desire to accumulate food or women by force. As American consumer society became more mature, consumption became a goal worth achieving for the middle class as well as the wealthy. The 1920s would witness its virtual explosion.

Events prior to World War I led to a burst of economic activity in the 1920s. It has been customary to think of the 1920s as a period unique unto itself. But the increased spending fueled by the banks (accomplished by granting of credit to companies and individuals alike), the mass production of automobiles and radios, as well as the continuing concentration of financial power all had their origins in the earlier part of the century when the modern foundations of corporate and industrial power were laid. Despite attempts to regulate the power of financial institutions, the 1920s were remarkably similar to the prewar years.

One of the unique aspects of American industrial and corporate development was the role of banking in the nineteenth and early twentieth centuries. The financial system operated without the benefits of a central bank, relying instead upon the large money center banks in New York and Chicago. The banks were shackled by a variety of federal and state laws dictating what lines of business they could engage in and where they could do so—sometimes limited to their own states. But despite their limitations, the banks were able to accumulate large amounts of deposits and influence, and, for the most part, they resisted any sort of change that disturbed the status quo. Having a central bank, once the focus of the states' rights arguments, now was resisted as being "too European," suggesting control of credit and money that bankers often painted as antithetical to the American ideal.

Immediately after the turn of the century, commercial banks were mainly wholesale institutions, deriving most of their revenues from businesses and wealthy individuals. During World War I, they strengthened their grip on corporate America by venturing into the investment banking business. There they provided competition for the older investment banks, which were still properly known as private banks. That expansion helped them penetrate another market that was just coming of age—retail banking. Emerging American industrial dominance was creating a new class of wealthy individuals, and the large banks had set their sights firmly on them.

The regulatory environment surrounding the banks in the early 1920s was extremely friendly. The only real constraint was geography. Banks were not able to cross state lines and, in many states such as New York, were not able to cross city and county lines. As a result, the most successful of them were concentrated in New York City and, to a lesser extent, Chicago. Their power derived from the connections they had forged over the years with businesses and corporations. The corporate bankers loaned money to businesses, while the private banks underwrote securities for them; in some cases select institutions performed both functions. Most of the extremely powerful dated from the middle of the nineteenth century.

Bankers' Influence

Within the seventy-odd years that the powerful had already existed at the outbreak of World War I, descriptions that would appear out of proportion to their relatively short histories quickly appeared. The adjective "great" was applied to the several top New York banks, and the families that sometimes headed them were referred to as "dynasties." These banks' domination over certain parts of the economy was so complete that only a wink or a nod by an investment banker was necessary to make or break a deal. Many of the private bankers still did not publish financial statements, so their customers did not actually know of their financial condition; they had complete faith in the banks based solely upon reputation and word of mouth. Because of this halo effect, many bankers likened themselves to the great banking families of Europe: the Medici in sixteenth-century Florence or the Rothschilds in nineteenth-century Britain.

The dynastic names were normally associated with the private banks and investment banking houses—J. P. Morgan, Kidder, Peabody, Kuhn Loeb, Lehman Brothers, Seligman, Brown Brothers, and Harriman Brothers. The larger commercial banks, notably the National City Bank and the First National, both located in New York City, were also headed by chief executives whose names dominated banking—in some cases more so than the private bankers who often preferred to remain relatively anonymous. George Baker of First National, James Stillman and (later in the 1920s) Charles Mitchell of the National City Bank were among the best known.

But these individuals were more than famous names in the banking business. They were also members of the *money trust*, a group that controlled the reins of credit in the country on an almost exclusive basis. The term was coined by Congressman Charles A. Lindbergh Sr. of Minnesota and became a household word in the years before World War I. They supplied credit to companies, raised bond and stock offerings for them, and had extensive holdings on corporate boards of directors that ensured a tight grip on American industrial policies. Without the bankers' access to money, industry would not have been able to expand as rapidly as it did in the late nineteenth and early twentieth centuries. But, as detractors would note, the money did little to develop business and new ideas. It simply helped the bankers accumulate concentrated economic power at the expense of those who founded and ran the businesses they financed. Memories of Jay Cooke had long since disappeared.

In the early part of this century, bankers were responsible for putting together deals that led to the rapid centralization of many businesses. Acting as both principal and agent in many deals, they helped rationalize industry into large holding companies, many with vast connections and power. The public utility industry, railroads, the rapidly developing telephone system, and the insurance industry were but a few examples. Using holding companies that acted as the parent company, many larger companies began to swallow up smaller ones with funds provided by their bankers. They also issued securities to finance those deals, and in many cases their bankers also invested in the deals as well as underwriting them. Often, many of the holding companies were related to each other although not officially on paper since they shared directors and bankers.

Holding companies appeared first in Ohio. Rockefeller founded Standard Oil there but moved to New Jersey when the state allowed corporations to hold each other's stock. Prior to that time, state laws had limited share ownership to individuals as a method of controlling monopolies. This principle began a revolution in American industrial and financial organization, which was widely used to avoid the Sherman Anti-Trust Act after it was passed in 1890. By hiding under the umbrella of a holding company, many companies were able to buy each other's stock, thereby disguising true ownership. Companies were able to acquire others in the same business without raising too many watchful eyebrows. Prosecutions under the Sherman Act would be difficult because it would be time-consuming to determine which company owned another.

The same form of organization was widely used in the securities business to avoid visible concentrations of financial power. Banks, forbidden to hold equity in other companies, organized themselves into holding companies to allow their newly founded securities subsidiaries to engage in the securities business. The best known of all securities subsidiaries prior to World War I was the National City Company, owned by the National City

Bank of New York. J. P. Morgan and Company's Drexel subsidiary was located outside New York in Philadelphia. Originally organized to venture into previously forbidden territory, after 1916 the subsidiaries were suspected of being used to avoid paying income tax. The same shroud of mystery that masked true corporate ownership could also be used to hide tax liabilities of individuals.

Few would argue with the positive economic effects of these mergers; they made American industry more efficient in many respects, and the country began to emerge as the dominant international economic power by World War I. But many objections began to be raised about the manner in which these deals were done and the soundness of the banking practices that financed them. Many of the most poignant criticisms came not from economists but from social activists who saw the great disparities the merger trend was creating in American society. In classic Marxist terms, the rich were getting substantially richer while the working class actually was losing earning power. This stood in stark contrast to the popular notion that the period from before the war to the end of 1920s was one of good times and prosperity for all.

Other criticisms over the extent of the amalgamation of industrial power could be heard from diverse quarters, from investors' groups to Woodrow Wilson. Investors were concerned that the concentration of power in holding companies was stifling new investment. As Wilson noted, "No country can afford to have its prosperity originated by a small controlling class. . . . Every country is renewed out of the ranks of the unknown, not out of the ranks of the already famous and powerful in control." Once having acquired power, the large companies were no longer interested in innovation or new products; they were simply happy to sit back and collect their existing revenues. Wilson concluded by noting, "I am not saying that all invention has been stopped by the growth of trusts but I think it is perfectly clear that invention in many fields has been discouraged."[1] American industry was going through one of its first consolidation phases, and the trend clearly had many worried. Critics claimed that growth had been stymied in favor of paper transactions designed to make bankers and financiers richer.

The industrial trusts, or holding companies, had vast holdings that could clearly be challenged as violations of the Sherman Anti-Trust Act. The United States Steel Corporation was an amalgam of 228 smaller companies scattered over more than a dozen states. The General Electric Company controlled directly or indirectly a wide range of water companies around the country. By controlling water, the company also effectively controlled much electrical power production and all the ancillary revenues that accompanied it. Before World War I, the U.S. Commissioner of Corporations feared that all water utilities in the country could actually fall into single ownership. The implications of such an event were even more shattering considering that these vast industrial holdings were either controlled directly by, or provided banking services by, the money trust, notably J. P. Morgan & Company.

The power of industrialists and bankers was the subject of heated discussion and scrutiny in the late nineteenth century, culminating in the passage of the Sherman Anti-Trust Act in 1890. Attempting to prohibit cartels and monopolies that constrained trade and competition, the Sherman Act still could not come to grips with some of the more subtle devices used to dominate certain industries. One was the central position that bankers had assumed on the American industrial scene. This was accomplished by sitting on the boards of many companies—some in the same sorts of industries—or on the boards of client companies. One of the bankers' main functions was to sit on as many boards as possible, ensuring an influence out of all proportion to the actual importance of the banks themselves.

It has long been assumed that American business and industry developed more quickly and exercised more power than the federal government, at least until the Great Depression. This is borne out by an examination of the banking industry in general. Subject to the regulation of their home states, most banks that carried the title "national" were not well regulated by the federal government. Until 1913 the country did not have a central bank, and the larger commercial banks in New York were accustomed to having things much their own way in the absence of a central banking authority responsible for money and credit creation. Their relationship to the industrial trusts extended indirectly to Wall Street itself. When many of these new, vast corporations had been formed, they certainly needed to sell stock in themselves to help finance new business and acquisitions. The banking houses stood ready to do business with them, having been steered the business by one of their own partners who sat on the board of the company. In such a manner, the banks dominated the money markets and the market for credit in general. When the proposal to establish the Federal Reserve gained momentum, the problem of bankers' power quickly emerged as a contentious issue. This concern led to a congressional hearing that became one of the most popular and revealing events in prewar America—the 1912 Pujo committee hearings.

Pierpont in Public

The committee hearings, called by Congressman Charles Lindbergh of Minnesota and named after Arsene Pujo, Democrat of Louisiana, were noteworthy because of the appearance of J. P. Morgan (Pierpont), among others, who was called to testify about the money trust. Although certainly

not known at the time, it would become one of two well-publicized testi-
monies given by a Morgan in the twentieth century, both equally famous
for revealing the amount of corporate power that bankers exercised. Morgan's chief inquisitor at the hearings was the chief counsel for the committee, Samuel Untermyer, a New York lawyer. Under close examination by
Untermyer, who had little use for bankers as a group, Morgan maintained
the traditional line about the extraordinary number of directorships he, his
partners, and other bankers such as George Baker managed to hold, especially in those industries vital to the national well-being. Hauling coal, in
which many utility companies had an interest as both user and producer,
on railroads owned by the same trust was but one of dozens of examples
brought out by the committee.

Morgan emphatically denied that he and other major bankers ever
controlled, or desired to control, sectors of the American economy. He
stated this matter-of-factly, although it was well documented that he personally controlled as much as fifty thousand miles of rail lines in the years
immediately preceding the hearings, as clearly revealed in a portion of the
badinage between Morgan and Untermyer.[2] Questioning Morgan about
his railroad holdings and the business the railroads conducted, especially
with the coal industry, Untermyer began:

MR. UNTERMYER: You and Mr. Baker control the anthracite coalroad sit-
    uation, do you not, together?
MR. MORGAN: No; we do not.
MR. UNTERMYER: Do you not?
MR. MORGAN: I do not think we do. At least, if we do, I do not know it.
MR. UNTERMYER: Your power in any direction is entirely unconscious to
    you, is it not?
MR. MORGAN: It is sir, if that is the case.[3]

Other witnesses called before the hearings professed to be equally puzzled
by what had become dubbed the money trust. George F. Baker, chairman
of the board of the First National Bank of New York, denied that such a
group had ever existed. When asked by Untermyer to describe what he
understood to be a money trust, Baker simply replied: "I give it up. I do
not know."[4] In fact, he and Morgan claimed that the banking system was
built upon honor and character more than money. Banking was a matter of
trust, and in such matters social background was an important factor. A
banker could expect honorable behavior from others of his own ilk or
those he subjectively trusted. Given this orientation, it was natural that
bankers should hold many directorships as well as owning a share of many
other banks.

In addition to his own bank, Morgan had extensive interests in many others, including the Banker's Trust Company, the Guaranty Trust Company of New York, and the National Bank of Commerce. He and his dozen partners held over 72 directorships in 47 major corporations of different types. Similarly, the First National Bank's officers held directorships in 89 other companies, 36 of which had at least one Morgan partner on the board as well. The Pujo committee found that in aggregate the officers of Morgan, National City, and First National between them held 118 directorships in 34 banks and trust companies with assets totaling $2.6 billion and deposits of $1.9 billion. In addition, they held directorships in 10 insurance companies with total assets of almost $3 billion. Outside the financial sector, they held 105 directorships in 32 transportation systems with total capitalization of some $11 billion. The sum of their activities was staggering for the time: in total they held 341 directorships in 112 corporations with resources of $22 billion.[5] When these connections were held up against their protests, the case for the money trust was well made. The bankers appeared to be claiming ignorance of something in which they had been actively engaging for years.

Despite the bankers' protestations, the Pujo committee went on to name the members of the money trust but admitted that it could not actually prove such a trust existed other than offer the overwhelming coincidence of interlocking directorships. The banking houses named were Morgan; First National Bank of New York; National City Bank of New York; Lee, Higginson and Company; Kidder, Peabody and Company; and Kuhn Loeb and Company. All were involved in deposit taking and securities underwriting to some extent, although Kidder, Peabody, Kuhn Loeb, and Lee Higginson were primarily securities underwriters. Almost as an afterthought to its report, the committee added that the money trust exercised two types of control over the credit process—controlling the supply of money and the way in which it was allocated.

In this latter respect, the testimony of George Reynolds, president of the Continental and Commercial National Bank of Chicago, was revealing. Untermyer confronted him with a copy of a speech given the previous year in which he categorically stated that six or nine banks controlled the processes by which loans were made throughout the country. Reynolds admitted having made the statement but went on to deny that such a thing as a money trust existed. He also stated that supplying funds and credit, especially in the absence of a central bank, was a natural function of the money center banks. In this respect his assertion was correct. The commercial banks between them had inordinate power over the supply of funds in the country because the federal government had given them that power de facto by never establishing a central bank. The lacunae in financial power had invested banks with authority they exercised as well as they could given the lack of governmental direction.

The hearings did not produce any tangible evidence of a money trust. Most of Wall Street and a large portion of the press thought they only helped shed a favorable light on financiers in general. The *New York Sun* commented, "The Pujo sub-committee is indebted to Mr. Samuel Untermyer for exhibiting to it, in the person of Mr. George F. Baker, that type of financial ability and integrity which is highly desirable that the legislative mind should study and comprehend."[6] Baker, one of J. P. Morgan's closest friends and confidants in the banking business, had shown remarkable restraint and ingenuousness when responding to Untermyer's questions, as had Morgan himself. While many began to believe that Lindbergh's characterization of the banks was nothing more than fantasy, the move toward a central bank had picked up momentum that could no longer be stopped.

Paul Warburg, a member of the German-American banking house and a member of one of New York's prominent Jewish banking families, was one of the architects of the principles creating the Federal Reserve System. He later recalled the opposition that some bankers raised to the central banking concept before it was passed and at various times afterward as well. Warburg was one of a small group of Wall Street bankers who met clandestinely on Jekyl Island, Georgia, in 1910 at the behest of Nelson Aldrich, Republican senator from Rhode Island. The meeting was intended as a forum for framing a Republican alternative to banking reforms making their way through Congress, which was then Democratically controlled for the first time in twenty years. The Aldrich Plan outlined what would become the blueprint for the newly created Federal Reserve three years later. Warburg was eventually offered the job as chairman of the Fed but turned it down in his characteristically self-effacing manner. He did, however, serve as a director until 1918. Although not passed by Congress in its original form, it was nevertheless the model upon which compromise would be centered.

As a partner of Kuhn Loeb and Company, Warburg was advised by its senior partner, Jacob Schiff, to keep his ideas concerning European-style central banking to himself in order to preserve his own reputation in the New York banking community. He always thought American banking was somewhat primitive compared with European models, many of which had support from both the local banks and their respective governments.[7] He also was fairly outspoken about the booming market in the middle and late 1920s. When confronted in his office one day by James Stillman, then chairman of the National City Bank of New York, he was asked why he wanted to propose such a radical change in American banking. "Warburg," Stillman asked, "don't you think the City Bank has done pretty well? . . . Why not leave things alone?" His answer came quickly, without much hesitation: "Your bank is so big and so powerful, Mr Stillman, that when the next panic comes, you will wish your responsibilities were smaller."[8] Such remarks did not sit well with the prophets whose major task was to keep a positive view of America's prospects. Bernard Baruch was later to remark, in typical New York fashion, "I cannot understand why people speak in such admiration of Paul Warburg. He's not so very rich."[9]

Although the Pujo committee had revealed a good deal about the close relationships in corporate America, its impact was less than might have been expected. For the most part, it was overtaken by events. The Pujo hearings were also the last public appearance for J. P. Morgan, who died a year later in 1913. Although his son and successor, J. P. Morgan Jr. (Jack), took over the reins of the bank, it would be some time before he established himself as a legendary figure in American banking in his own right. And perhaps most important, the Federal Reserve was established as the nation's central bank in 1913. One of its major functions was to oversee the supply of money in the banking system and see that it was allocated evenly among the nation's twelve Federal Reserve districts. Nevertheless, the Morgan partners recognized the potential threat to their dominance and withdrew from the directorships of almost thirty companies as a conciliatory gesture. They did admit that the seats on those boards were expendable. The combination of these factors helped push the money trust into the background, where it would remain active but mostly away from the public eye for the next twenty years. The bankers had had their day in the sun and now were retreating from the public view because most of the money trusters had a distaste for publicity and the accountability that accompanied it. But there were some dedicated to reform who did not believe the publicity generated by the hearings would be enough in itself to tame the bankers' control of American economic life.

Shortly after the money trust hearings, the U.S. Senate turned its attention to the New York Stock Exchange and its practices. The sentiment prevailing in Washington was still cynical. Now that the Fed had been established, the stock exchange bore closer scrutiny. The first witness called by the Senate was Samuel Untermyer. The former counsel of the House Banking Committee testified about the inside information that many corporate leaders had concerning their own companies but failed to make public. Usually, they used the information to trade in their own stock or the stock of companies in which they were outside directors. The committee was investigating the usefulness of stock exchange internal rules, which had prescribed more corporate reporting and uniformity in corporate accounts. The exchange had made some progress in uniform rules of reporting but was still woefully inadequate on others. Corporate leaders felt that uniform rules encroached upon their ability to run their companies and were essentially not the business of outsiders, even shareholders. Untermyer made something of a prophetic statement before the committee: "It will not be long before corporate officers will be prevented from withholding information and speculating on advance knowledge. . . . the time will come when those [members of the NYSE] who are bitterly assailing and slandering the champions of this legislation will find that it has marked the dawn of a new era of usefulness for them and the exchange."[10] Untermyer was perfectly correct, but the day was still twenty years away. The stock market crash and the Great Depression would occur before any serious legislation could be passed to prevent insider trading abuses and the lack of uniform reporting.

A "Constructive Adventure"

The Pujo hearings were one of the later factors behind the passage of the Federal Reserve Act of 1913. The creation of a central bank after a seventy-year hiatus was the most controversial topic to hit Wall Street since the Civil War. Probing bankers' power and influence was just one of the topics the hearings examined. In an instant, all of the previous controversies came to the fore—the Treasury bailout of 1894, the panic of 1907, and circumlocutions of the Sherman Anti-Trust Act. The Wall Street community was in an uproar that would not be quelled for years until the Federal Reserve had established itself.

Wall Street divided along traditional lines when the idea of a central bank was first proposed. The Jewish houses and those with strong European connections were mostly in favor of a central bank. Jacob Schiff was in the forefront of those in favor, who were accustomed to dealing with clients who themselves appreciated the benefits of a central authority overseeing credit and money. They realized that economic growth in the United States was always in danger of sharp downturns and depressions as long as the dollar was inelastic. Since the National Banking Act was passed during the Civil War, the supply of money had been backed by Treasury securities. Unfortunately, this made the supply of money unresponsive to the economy at times. There was no body that could adjust credit and money supply under different economic climates. The traditional Wall Street crowd did not favor a central bank because it would invariably get in the way of the Street's ability to create credit and possibly even interfere with market speculation.

Despite its lack of universal popularity, the creation of the Federal Reserve was inevitable. The two Morgan operations in the 1890s and in 1907 were still fresh in many minds, and it was now clear that what was quickly emerging as the world's largest economy was still being run by private bankers. Less obvious but still important was the strong role agriculture played in the economy. And the agrarian West did not like Wall Street. Ever since the days of the "western blizzard," those in the West had blamed eastern financiers for their problems, while Wall Street looked upon western agrarian interests as excessively populist and based upon loose money policies. Generally, it was felt that western social ideas were based on unsound financial premises. They represented opposite spectrums of American business practice. But in the case of the Fed, Wall Street did not have many allies in opposing the central banking concept.

The new Fed was vested with certain powers that were sure to make Wall Street uneasy. Those in political power also helped seal the fate of the opposition but not without a titanic battle. After Woodrow Wilson was elected in 1912, he held meetings at his home in Princeton on the bill that would shape the Federal Reserve before he was sworn into office. His soon-to-be-appointed secretary of the Treasury was William Jennings Bryan. Neither man had any particular fondness for Wall Street bankers. Wilson was one of those who firmly believed in the existence of a money trust, which he considered analogous to the great industrial trusts except that it did not operate on a day-to-day basis. In December 1912, before his inauguration, he began informal talks with Senator Carter Glass of Virginia, among others, on the composition of the new institution. Although Glass characterized him initially as a "schoolteacher" despite the fact that Wilson was governor of New Jersey and a former president of Princeton, it soon became evident that the president-elect would put his own stamp on the new central bank.

The powers to be vested in the new central bank were extremely contentious. The major bone of contention in the formative stages was the composition of the Fed itself. It would be governed by a board, resident in Washington, but its actual composition was not decided despite the Aldrich proposals made at Jekyll Island. The original Aldrich blueprint, submitted to Congress in January 1911, was not given much chance to survive a full congressional vote. It would have given the large New York banks a significant role in the new Federal Reserve Board. Many Wall Street bankers wanted to be represented on the board, but Wilson was firmly opposed from the very beginning. In his view, there was little point in allowing the fox into the henhouse before the roof was completed. In a meeting at the White House with key lawmakers framing the legislation, Wilson firmly rejected the notion of bankers sitting on the Fed's board. Countering their arguments, Wilson inquired, "Will one of you gentlemen tell me in what civilized country of the earth there are important government boards of control on which private interests are represented?" Senator Carter Glass, present at the meeting, recalled the silence that followed as the longest single moment he ever experienced before Wilson again inquired, "Which of you gentlemen thinks the railroads should select members of the Interstate Commerce Commission?"[11] Recalling the robber barons and the railroad bankruptcies apparently did the trick. From that moment, the issue died and bankers were excluded from the

Federal Reserve Board. They would find representation on the boards of the local Federal Reserve banks, however.

The new Federal Reserve became reality when the Federal Reserve Act was passed in 1913. The system was composed of twelve district banks spread throughout the country, each with a separate management board. Local bankers from the districts were allowed a limited number of seats. The actual capital of the local district banks was purchased by the commercial banks in their area, which became stockholders. The board in Washington, composed of five paid directors, made policy for the entire system. The new regulatory body was charged with maintaining watch over credit conditions in the country, requiring reserves of those banks over which it had authority, and was given powers to intervene in the market to influence conditions if necessary. But the most contentious issue of all was the Fed's ability to issue notes.

The elastic currency was the most prominent issue facing Congress when it passed the legislation. The dollar had to be freed from the Treasury securities that underpinned it if it was to become responsive to changing credit conditions. The new act allowed the Fed to issue Federal Reserve notes backed not directly by Treasury securities but by the full faith and credit of the U.S. government. If the economy slowed down and needed a stimulant, the new Fed could provide it without asking the Treasury to issue more bonds, which it would not need in times of a slump in business conditions. The commercial banks also needed the ability to convert bank deposits into cash if required. That would appease the public, which might be worried about their bank's ability to redeem funds. Both measures would go a long way in establishing more faith in the American banking system. Unfortunately, some would also think the measures would prevent future panics and runs on banks. Gold still was the standard for the dollar, but this matter would quickly become academic because war was about to break out in Europe. As a result, the Fed got off to a quiet start.

Despite the slow beginning, the role of the New York Federal Reserve Bank would be central to the entire system. Other cities had been chosen because of intense political lobbying. There was little sound reason for Federal Reserve banks to be located in Richmond and Cleveland except for reasons of political expediency. But New York reigned supreme among the twelve. Once the 1920s began, it became clear that the focus of financial power was still in New York rather than in Washington, where outside interests would have preferred it to reside.

Challenging the Trust

The creation of the Federal Reserve banks in 1913 did not necessarily mean that the money trust had been replaced by a higher authority. While the Fed developed its new powers, its relationship with Wall Street was still strong. Benjamin Strong, the first president of the Federal Reserve Bank of New York, had close connections to Morgan; as a result, Morgan's bank had the closest ties of any major New York bank to the new central bank. Some of the directors of the Federal Reserve Bank of New York mostly moonlighted in the position, keeping their lucrative private-sector jobs in the banking business as their main occupation. This arrangement, a product of the compromise that created the Federal Reserve System, was widely criticized by many, including Louis Brandeis, who immediately saw a conflict of interest. But as a result of the presence of the bankers, banks continued to do business as they had previously without much concern. In fact, their pursuit of profit, especially before the income tax amendment was introduced, kept the freewheeling spirit of the nineteenth century alive. This was so despite the fact that the Pujo committee hearings gave the impression that the bankers would be curbed because of the hearing's findings about the concentration of financial and industrial power. The unaccustomed spotlight caused the investment bankers to organize into the first trade group in their history. In 1912, meeting at the Waldorf Astoria in New York, they banded together to form the Investment Bankers Association, the body that would become their official sounding board. The new group had 350 original members, including Wall Street firms of all sizes.

In the year before the outbreak of World War I, the print media had fewer financial matters to report. American preoccupations turned toward things more mundane. Banking itself was not mundane because it did not have a human side. Other than the cult of personality that surrounded the Morgans and Baker, banking made for boring reading. The great muckraking novels and social commentaries of Frank Norris and Upton Sinclair concerned themselves with the human side of the trusts and industrial combines that ruled the corporate world, not the organizational or financial sides. Novels about banking were just not part of the popular literary world or the popular press. Ironically, that would change when the Great Depression began and Matthew Josephson's revealing historical book entitled *The Robber Barons* became extremely popular in 1934, created by a set of circumstances unforeseen at the dawn of the Prohibition era only fifteen years before.

When the banking community converged to make loans to France, China, and Germany during and after the war, the news was dutifully reported, but terms and conditions were hardly the stuff of which popular novels were made. The popular imagination was captured by the growing class tensions brought about by the clash of organized labor and management. Frank Cowperwood, the protagonist of Theodore Dreiser's 1914 novel *The Titan*, is portrayed as a man driven to achieve fabulous wealth simply by blind ambition. Ten years later, in *An American Tragedy*, Dreiser's characterization of the social-climbing Clyde Griffiths as one willing to kill in order to achieve some social distinction is a disturbing view of an unsuccessful attempt to arise above one's lot in life. The most popular author of the entire period, Horatio Alger, constantly emphasized the role of good fortune and hard work in his benign pulp novels about lost boys fighting their way up the economic ladder. In almost all cases, the emphasis was on the human side. Hidden from view were the machinations of the financial community and the trust makers who were striving to consolidate American corporate life even further.

Ironically, some of the more cogent comments about American social and economic life came from those most opposed to capitalism and consumption. The dominion of the money center banks was also recognized by V. I. Lenin, who understood their hold over what he called "financial capital." Citing Morgan and the Rockefellers in the United States and Deutsche Bank's control of the German economy, Lenin recognized that financial capital led to financial oligarchy and, ultimately, financial control. At the time, Lenin and his intellectual predecessor, Englishman J. A. Hobson, understood the close connection between money and power as a function of imperialism, not coincidentally the title of both of their respective books. But it was not this connection that would prove the most powerful in criticizing American economic life.

Only when Louis Brandeis began writing his articles about the trusts before the war was the mold broken. Finally, someone known as an interpreter and molder of public policy was speaking out against the unseen side of American life. During the first decade of the century, the money trust and Morgan in particular had developed an enemy in Brandeis. The son of Jewish immigrants, Brandeis graduated first in his class from the Harvard Law School in 1877. After practicing law in St. Louis, he returned to Boston, where he began to champion public causes. Because of his public advocacy, he quickly earned the nickname the "people's attorney," mostly for supporting workers' causes. His first official introduction to the concentration of financial power came in 1906 when he led an inquiry into the Equitable Life Assurance Society, a major New York insurance company controlled by Morgan. The study led to an idea that savings banks should offer low-cost life insurance for workingmen. The high premiums charged by commercial insurance companies were out of reach for many workers, who as a result had no insurance coverage. For the next ten years, Brandeis led investigations into other monopoly-dominated industries, among them the railroad industry. In 1907 he led a famous inquiry into the management of the New Haven Railroad, another company controlled by Morgan. He quickly became a nemesis to bankers and industrialists. His method of analyzing federal legislation from a socioeconomic

"Brandeis's Dream of Empire," *Truth*, 1913.

angle became known as the "Brandeis brief." One of his more famous briefs was to have far-reaching effects, extending into the future administration of Franklin Roosevelt.

Brandeis became interested in the activities of the Morgan-controlled New Haven Railroad in 1907. The company had been accumulating the stock of the Boston and Maine Railroad while producing some dubious financial reports in the process. It was illegal for a company to hold another company's stock in Massachusetts, where the Boston and Maine had its headquarters. The extension of Morgan's tentacles into New England caused the advocacy lawyer to begin questioning the finances and management of the New Haven. That, in turn, sparked a battle that was to last seven years, evoking unpleasant responses from Morgan and the railroad's management, aimed at Brandeis personally. After originally surfacing, the issue remained volatile but receded from public view. But Brandeis forged an alliance with Senator La Follette in 1910, who reopened the New Haven issue on the Senate floor. The battle continued, with salvos being fired by both sides for two more years when the *Boston Journal* ran an entire page on the skirmishes between the two factions, which neatly summarized Brandeis's positions with respect to the New Haven. It recounted him as saying, "A business may be too big to be efficient without being a monopoly; and it may be a monopoly and yet may well be within the limits of efficiency. Unfortunately, the so-called New Haven system suffers from both excessive bigness and from monopoly."[12]

This characterization and others like it evoked an equally blunt re-

sponse from Morgan and the New Haven's president. In a press release issued in December 1912, they stated that "every one of these attacks de-
faming New England and its railroad system, so far as I have learned,
traces back to Brandeis." Not leaving the matter there, a magazine called
Truth appeared, presumably financed by the railroads to attack Brandeis. It
sought to forge a link between Brandeis and Jacob Schiff of Kuhn Loeb in
a blatantly bigoted manner that invoked memories of anti-Semitic statements of the past. It stated that

> Mr. Schiff is the head of the great private banking house of Kuhn, Loeb and
> Company, which represents the Rothschild system on this side of the At-
> lantic. . . . Brandeis, because of his great ability as a lawyer and for other rea-
> sons. . . . was selected by Schiff as the instrument through which Schiff hoped
> to achieve his ambitions in New England. . . . the New England fight is sim-
> ply part of a world movement. It is the age-long struggle for supremacy be-
> tween Jew and Gentile. Schiff is known to his people as "a prince in Israel."[13]

The struggle lasted several more years before the New Haven finally cut
its dividend and some of its fraudulent expenses were made public. The divestiture from the Boston and Maine took place, and the New Haven went
into decline. But on the banking side, the troubles were attributed to
Brandeis's crusade, not to any malfeasance at the railroad itself.

In 1916 Woodrow Wilson acknowledged Brandeis's contribution to
social causes and the growing regulatory movement by naming him to the
Supreme Court, the first Jew ever so named. At the same time, Wilson was
paying off a debt because Brandeis was his unofficial economics tutor prior
to his election in 1912. The nomination was supported by many in the liberal community, although the hearings occupied many months before
confirmation. The young Walter Lippmann strongly supported Brandeis,
although his own writings until that time showed some signs of elitism. In
Drift and Mastery, published in 1914, Lippmann acknowledged that the
new managerial class had been extremely effective in keeping the vast economic power of the new corporations away from the hands of meddling,
unsophisticated shareholders. The managerial class had been successful in
matters that socialism could not cope with, namely, managing large economic locomotives of growth. But his support of Brandeis was unequivo-
cal, although he did admit in a 1917 letter to Oliver Wendell Holmes that
he did not personally understand French philosopher Henri Bergson or
Brandeis, two of his favorite authors, very well: "They don't seem able to
believe in one side without insisting that the cosmos justifies them."[14] It
was just this forceful combination of economics and law that made Brandeis a dreaded name in many quarters.

Writing in a series of magazine articles in *Harper's*, Brandeis became so widely read that the essays were turned into a book. Writing after the Pujo hearings, Brandeis claimed that only when the money trust had been broken would what he called the "New Freedom" in American society emerge. Citing the financial oligarchy as potentially dangerous to the future of American liberty, he stated that the development of financial oligarchy followed lines with which "the history of political despotism has familiarized us: usurpation, proceeding by gradual encroachment rather than violent acts; subtle and often long-concealed concentration of distinct functions, and dangerous only when combined in the same persons. It was the process by which Caesar Augustus became master of Rome."[15]

This was a fairly strong statement considering that the bankers and industrialists had been consistently denying that any form of collusion had ever existed in the marketplace. Brandeis had already proved to be a thorn in their collective side and would remain as such for most of his life. His first, and most famous, target was J. P. Morgan and his control of the New Haven Railroad. That particular concentration of economic power inspired the series of magazine articles and later the book *Other People's Money* (1914), which outlined his criticisms and remedies for the American economy.

Brandeis's criticism of bankers in general and Morgan in particular gave a functional definition to the term *money trust*. His criticism was not of investment bankers on one side or commercial bankers on the other; only when the two crossed did the threat to the public became clear. Bankers looked upon deposit taking as a source of easy money, which could be loaned to brokers so they in turn could make loans to stock market speculators or use the funds to finance the deals they were underwriting. Many of those deals involved the restructuring of American industry by corporate America and its investment bankers. Once the restructuring was complete, bankers often took a piece of the deal in the form of stock for themselves, thus inviting themselves into the corporate boardrooms of their clients. In such a manner, Morgan, Baker, and others had assumed a vast amount of power without actually having added value to any of the products or industries they controlled. This was what was meant by using other people's money. Using deposits as a power base from which to dominate American economic life was a form of tax that bankers were not competent to charge, especially since they were using them only to further their own wealth and influence.

Twenty years later, in the aftermath of the stock market crash, new legislation would be framed to separate investment and commercial banking. It has traditionally been assumed that the reason they were separated was to protect depositors from having their funds loaned to speculators who, if they failed to pay back the loans, would default to the banks, putting the entire financial system at risk. What was never assumed afterward was that the "wall of separation" dictated by the first major banking act of the century, which would be passed in 1933 (the Glass-Steagall Act), was also a method of curbing the power of the money trust, which was still very active. The 1933 separation of banking was one of the first, but certainly not the last, restatements of Brandeisian principles that would be made during and after the depression.

Brandeis showed how the money trust extended its tentacles into all aspects of banking. All of the large New York money center banks had securities affiliates through which they underwrote securities (mostly bonds) and operated in the secondary stock markets. National City and First National had subsidiary companies bearing almost identical names. Charles Mitchell, eventually the chief executive officer of National City Bank, began his rise through that bank's hierarchy by first successfully running the National City Company, the securities subsidiary. Morgan controlled the Philadelphia brokerage of Drexel and Company, while other major banks also had securities affiliates. But the web of interlocking directorships helped the money trust extend its grasp far beyond New York. The banks in and around Boston were connected by directorships so that about 80 percent were joined at the hip in some fashion. Many of them could then be traced back to the New York banks through the series of correspondent relationships whereby the larger banks would provide short-term loans to the smaller regional organizations.

Their influence was also felt in the stock market, where the money they loaned to investors had a great influence on the prices of securities. In the absence of a central bank, bankers could force up the price of stocks by creating additional liquidity in the marketplace by loaning money on easy terms. Conversely, the market could retreat when they made margin money less available. And the range in which they operated could be quite wide. At times, margin rates could be 50 percent or higher, while at others they could be very low. The bankers' total control of stock market liquidity was well known, but little could be done about it until the Federal Reserve System was established. They could aid their own underwritings greatly by supplying funds to the market when they had new securities to sell, giving the illusion of a hot market. Before the founding of the Federal Reserve, they had the market for stocks, bonds, and credit mostly to themselves through these interrelated activities.

Investment bankers' forays into related financial services could also be understood in this context. Prior to World War I, the insurance industry fell into the web of interlocking directorships, for good reason. As the Pujo committee had shown, three New York life insurance companies—New York Life, Mutual of New York, and the Equitable—had an annual cash flow of close to $70 million that had to be invested. A Morgan partner, George W. Perkins, was a vice president of New York Life and regularly sold the company investment securities. It was this connection that brought him to Morgan's attention in the first place. Equitable Life had Morgan himself as one of its major shareholders. The three major insurance companies had an aggregate investment of over $1 billion in bonds, the major underwriting emphasis of J. P. Morgan and Company and the other money center banks at the time.

Brandeis's comments are on the opposite side of the spectrum from the public statements of Morgan, Baker, and Reynolds. Despite the bankers' protests of innocence, Brandeis showed an intriguing web of relationships and back-scratching that seemed to describe many European corporatist states of the 1920s and 1930s, not the country supposedly built on hard work and individual freedom that was the cornerstone of American popular thought. One documented bit of pettiness provided more of a damning condemnation than any illustration of interlocking directorships at banks. About the time of the Pujo hearings, a New York City bond issue was sold but a listing was denied on the NYSE because the actual bonds were not engraved and printed by the American Bank Note Company. Listings were important because far-flung investors would buy such issues while sometimes eschewing nonlisted ones. American Bank Note bid $55,800 for the job, losing because of its high price. The contract instead had been given to the New York Bank Note Company, which bid $10,000 less. New York City had followed proper procedure in granting the contract to the best bid, but the American Bank Note Company had been granted an exclusive monopoly to do such work for the exchange. Upon further examination, it came to light that the more expensive bidder had some very well-known financial personalities as investors. The best known was its largest shareholder, J. P. Morgan.[16]

Before the war, Morgan's estimated annual income was reputed to be about $5 million, so his individual portion of a single contract was not really at issue. What the small deal typified was the extensive hold of the money trust over all manner of things financial, from arranging syndicates for corporate securities offerings to printing securities for the deals. This Morgan influence was not diminished by the Pujo revelations but actually grew stronger over the next twenty years. During World War I, Morgan would concentrate on many public financings for the U.S. Treasury as well as several foreign countries that would only solidify the decades-old tie the bank had forged with the U.S. government and others.

The Pujo revelations and Brandeis's popular crusade against concentrated economic power did not go unnoticed but helped contribute to the Clayton Act, passed in 1916. That legislation prohibited interlocking directorships but only when they could be shown to restrict trade. Brandeis's position on directorships was somewhat more pointed and went to what he considered the root of the problem. Going so far as to state that inter-locking directorships must be restrained, even if it could be shown that they provided economic benefits to their shareholders, he maintained, "Interlocking directorates must be prohibited, because it is impossible to break the Money Trust without putting an end to the practice in the larger corporations."[17] The origin of the American prohibition against these arrangements, however stated in later years, was the desire to put an end to the core power of the money trust. This Brandeisian origin of a point of American legislation would be seen several more times by the time the New Deal became a reality twenty years later.

Despite this fear, a fine line could be drawn between shared director-ships that helped restrain competition and those that actually helped make a company more competitive in its own right. In most cases, corporate America continued on the path that had been plotted earlier in the century without much fear of reproach because collusion and restraint of trade or competition, if practiced subtly, were difficult if not impossible to prove. Only egregious violations of the Sherman or Clayton Acts were apt to be pursued as the war ended. The money trust continued as it had in the past, reaping large profits on deals arranged and controlling the flow of credit funds to the markets. But at the same time it was also planting the seeds for the near collapse of the economy. Both Democrats and Republicans real-ized the nature of the problem, but the robust economy of the 1920s would make it politically hazardous to intervene. Will Rogers summed up the economic climate by saying that the country had grown "too damn big" to need anything. Such thinking was quickly to lead to economic and social convulsions.

Banking Fees Increase

One idea that appeared in Brandeis's writings won him no friends in the banking community: his opinion that banks performed a public service and, as such, should be considered as operating in the public trust, treated as public utilities. Electric power companies and water companies had a virtual monopoly and consequently were limited in their activities since they held that concentrated power as a matter of public trust. The same should be true of banks. Using other people's money was a matter of trust, not a license to print money at their expense.

While Brandeis expounded notions that sought to redefine banking, the banks themselves were on the road to internationalizing their activities in search of greater profits. Much of this occurred during the administra-tion of Woodrow Wilson, no admirer of banking practices by any means. Two loans made to foreign governments became the best examples of the new outward-looking reach and also helped exemplify the international outlook of Republicans, who were quickly becoming associated with banking and the new internationalism of the United States.

In 1911 an international banking syndicate attempted to put together a deal for the government of China. At that time, bonds were called loans, especially if they were made to foreign governments, emphasizing the generosity of the banking community. In contrast, when the American railways were financed in the late nineteenth century by foreign investors, mainly British, the loans were called by their more proper name, bonds. The banking community was developing a public relations program of its own that it used quite successfully in defending itself against detractors.

What would have caused critics to take notice were the terms and conditions of the loan itself. The amount, $50 million, was huge by contemporary standards, and the 9 percent interest rate was also very high, with a total fee structure amounting to 10 percent of the total issue. The underwriting fees were as high as those that had prevailed in the past, the Pujo committee revelations notwithstanding. When Woodrow Wilson was elected, he rejected the notion that the United States might be willing to send troops to China if the loan terms were abrogated by the new Chinese government after the Boxer rebellion. This attitude effectively quashed the loan, and the bankers eventually withdrew their support, writing off China as if it had been a bad deal from the start. The terms were detrimental to China and would only have led to greater international friction when the Chinese found themselves with their backs to the wall while attempting to make the ruinous interest payments. But it was Wilson's rejection of sending in the gunboats to make a recalcitrant China pay that effectively killed the deal.

Another example was a loan (bond) made to the governments of France and Britain during World War I in 1915, dubbed the Anglo-French loan. The purpose was to provide the Allies with credit so they could prop up their currencies and buy necessary war matériel from the United States. The $500-million loan, lead managed by Morgan, was the largest bond of its type ever floated until that time. The syndicate formed to underwrite and sell it was also the largest ever assembled, and the fees attached again were generous to the underwriters. The success of the loan would pave the way for a similar sort of bond floated for Germany after the war, intended to help it maintain its reparations payments to the Allies. Unknown at the time was the fact that the syndicate employed in assembling the loan would be cited over thirty years later as proof of a conspiracy to monopolize the investment banking business by the major New York underwriting houses.

The matter of the fees that bankers charged their customers was a contentious issue at the time of the Pujo hearings and remained as such until the early 1930s. As seen earlier, it was not unusual for bankers to charge as much as 10 percent of the amounts raised to underwrite a bond issue. Critics, including Brandeis, maintained that such fees were inordinately high for simply underwriting and selling a bond. In contemporary terms, they were more than twice the amount charged for a junk bond in the 1980s. But more important, they clearly showed why banks were so fond of the bond business, especially during the war. During the 1920s, many banks actively courted bond business from foreign governments and corporations with these sorts of fees in mind. In the absence of any meaningful regulatory authorities, the combination of high fees and foreign borrowers would prove to be a recipe for disaster after the crash.

The Anglo-French and Chinese loans provided good examples of why the banks were so quick to seize upon international lending opportunities. The same scrutiny that had been applied to the banks' domestic activities was not present on the international side, especially in a country that was not decidedly in support of American intervention in World War I. The legacy of Brandeis, by this time a Supreme Court justice (Wilson appointed him to the Court in 1916), had been passed down well, although he was not out of the public eye but certainly more restrained on non-Court issues than in times past. Although the idea of banks as public utilities did not take hold, it did live on in the memory of many and was raised again over the next seventy years, especially during times of banking crises and failures.

The private bankers recognized this attitude as a turning point in their dynastic histories. The Morgan bank especially took it as a personal attack from the past by Louis Brandeis, by 1933 a Supreme Court justice for almost seventeen years. Thomas Lamont, a Morgan partner, stated before the Senate committee investigating the stock exchange and investment banking in 1933 that Brandeis and *Other People's Money* were behind the specific provision in the act. He remarked to a Senate investigator, "I had a long talk with Justice Brandeis at the time he was bringing out that book. We spent an afternoon together on it and I entirely failed to convince him and he entirely failed to convince me."[18] Jack Morgan's personal dislike of Jews also had influenced some of his partners. But the antagonism was felt less on Wall Street itself, where several of the leading Jewish investment banking houses, notably Kuhn Loeb, the Seligmans, Lehman Brothers, and Goldman Sachs, had carved out lucrative businesses for themselves since their foundings around the Civil War. Morgan's sentiments never prevented business from being done between them.

The war caused severe shocks in the financial markets. The NYSE dived sharply when the Russian czar mobilized his army. Wall Street acted as if it had been caught napping, not anticipating conflict in Europe. Foreign investors also took the occasion to sell stocks en masse. The fall in stock prices gave testimony to the fact that the United States was still dependent to a great degree on foreign capital. In 1915, foreign investors liquidated almost a billion dollars in railroad securities, some at sizable discounts. Americans bought back almost $2 billion during the first three years of the war, and all of that liquidity put a serious dent in the stock market for several years to come. But the bond market prospered. Many European and Canadian governments and companies raised almost $2 billion during the war and met a favorable reception from American investors. The British inadvertently came to the aid of the markets despite all the selling. Large stocks of British gold were stored in American vaults, allowing American interest rates to remain low while war raged in Europe. This was to signal a major change in the country's international status after the war was over. The United States was finally on the verge of becoming a creditor rather than a debtor nation for the first time in its history.

The war provided Wall Street with a shock. Fearful that foreign investors, especially the British, would sell their holdings and repatriate them, the NYSE decided to close in July 1914 to "stabilize prices." Most of the world's other exchanges also closed. The obvious reason was that the United States did not want to suffer an outflow of funds at a crucial period. Henry Noble, president of the NYSE, was charged with the stabilization. The market remained closed until December when it finally reopened. The affair brought criticism from Samuel Untermyer, who stated that he was opposed to the NYSE acting alone in the matter. He complained about the ability of a ". . . handful of private citizens to seize and exercise such vast powers because there is no constituted authority to protect the public . . . or review their action."

Reparations or Extortion?

Despite the clear-cut distinctions between the reforming Democrats and the banking community, the two intertwined in everyday life. Several Morgan partners regularly advised Democratic as well as Republican administrations on financial and diplomatic affairs. Bankers and financiers were among the best emissaries of their day, possessing some of the finest diplomatic skills in the country. Bernard Baruch, Charles Dawes, Dwight Morrow, and Thomas Lamont were all affiliated with both finance and government service and were particularly adept administrators and diplomats, often to the dismay of their colleagues who preferred keeping a distance from the fray.

Bernard Baruch, a Democrat, was appointed by Wilson to the advisory commission of the Council of National Defense in 1916 and two years later served as chairman of the War Industries Board. His appointment surprised, even angered, many because he had spent most of his business life as a stock speculator. Immediately after the war he served as an adviser to Wilson at the Versailles peace conference and later went on to serve every president until his death in 1965. Dwight Morrow, a Morgan partner until appointed ambassador to Mexico by Calvin Coolidge, resigned his banking partnership to help smooth over relations between the United States and its southern neighbor, which were not particularly amicable in the 1920s. When his daughter later married the aviator Charles Lindbergh Jr. in 1929, it was considered further treason by the Morgan partners since it was his father, Charles Lindbergh Sr., who had called the Pujo committee in 1912 and coined the term *money trust* almost twenty years before.

Russell Leffingwell, another Morgan partner, originally served in the Treasury during World War I. Charles G. Dawes, a Chicago banker and probably the most influential banker outside of New York, perhaps had the most distinguished public career of any financier at the time. Originally serving under John Pershing as a member of the American Expeditionary Forces in Europe during World War I, he later served as director of the budget under Warren Harding, and vice president under Coolidge, and was the chief architect (under Morgan's guidance) of the massive loan made to Germany in 1924. His efforts helped persuade France and Belgium to withdraw from the Ruhr. That part of the Dawes plan earned him a share of the Nobel Peace Prize in 1925.[19] He later served as first director of the Reconstruction Finance Corporation (RFC) in 1932 under Herbert Hoover, a post that led him into further financial controversy involving charges of political favoritism and cronyism over the nature of the loans the RFC actually made in its early days.

But on aggregate it was the Morgan partners who reigned supreme over the political banking world. Morgan himself was too gruff and straightforward to be much of a diplomat, but his colleagues proved much more adept. Thomas Lamont, who became involved in international affairs during the last year of the war, became Wilson's most trusted adviser during the Versailles peace conference that began in 1919. The eventual reparations bill put to the Germans, $33 billion, was studiously analyzed by Lamont, among others. Wilson valued his counsel more than that of the other Morgan men who were plentiful at the conference. Bernard Baruch jealously remarked that there were so many Morgan men at the conference that it was apparent they were indeed running the show.[20] This was the beginning of a long relationship that Morgan partners would have with the government and later with the Federal Reserve as well.

Wilson's reliance upon bankers opened a new era in banking-government relations. Once openly critical of the money trust and the concentration of economic power it fostered, he came to rely, albeit somewhat late, upon its long list of connections with foreign heads of governments and foreign bankers. In many ways the war years were the heyday of the Democrats. Besides emerging victorious from the war itself, the Federal Reserve had been founded and the Clayton Act passed, both being the products of Democratic-inspired legislation. The Farm Credit Banks were organized and operating, giving great heart to the long-suffering agricultural sector. In the interim, the banking community had survived it all intact, with greater power than ever before. When Warren Harding became president, succeeding Wilson, the Republican decade would begin bringing with it a friendlier attitude toward banking, credit, market speculation, and all of the values that characterized Republicans of the period. It also brought with it one of the more simplified economic theories of the century, which would lead to ideological sides being drawn within the next ten years.

The size of the German war reparations was considered extreme by many, although the amount was certainly less than the French and the Belgians had requested. However, within two years Germany was unable to meet its payments and the French and Belgians occupied the Ruhr, threatening further action if payments were not forthcoming. This would put the bankers in a difficult position, for direct military action was certain to follow if an amicable agreement was not reached. The answer was the Dawes loan, negotiated and signed in 1924 at a great cost to Germany and a healthy profit for the banking consortium that floated it. The loan, or bond, again followed traditional Wall Street practice by charging the Germans 10 percent of its face value for underwriting costs.

Helping underwrite bonds for foreigners offset some traditional revenues lost during the war. Most bankers adhered to the Republican party line that international affairs, and international business, were intrinsically good for the country, aiding the balance of payments. This mentality was the direct result of the United States having been a net debtor nation for many years since the Civil War. During World War I, much international business was lost as the traditional northern European investors, mainly the British, divested themselves of their American investments, both portfolio and direct, to concentrate on the war effort. Lending them money for the same purpose was another way of recapturing some of that business at a time when commission business was becoming difficult to generate.

On the domestic side, bankers made inroads into new areas that would certainly help transform American life. As the general population grew and became better off economically, bankers recognized the possibilities of serving retail customers who had done well in the economy. About the same time as the Federal Reserve was founded, many of the large commercial banks began their forays into the securities markets, at the time confined almost exclusively to the bond market. The savings ratios of

World War I Liberty bond poster.

Americans had been increasing and a new middle class was emerging, especially on the East Coast, which bankers recognized as a potential source of profit. Many of the commercial banks began to acquire existing securities dealers if they had not done so already. The National City Company, the subsidiary of National City Bank, acquired broker N. W. Halsey and Company in 1916 in order to sell bonds to this rising middle class. This was a clever bit of marketing because until that time bonds had been the preeminent investment in the country among the wealthy. During and after the war, they would become even more popular when the government financed the war effort by selling, and then redeeming, war bonds.

The popularity of war bonds indirectly aided bankers' marketing efforts after the war, making it much easier to sell corporate bonds, among others. The Liberty loans, first authorized by Congress in 1917, were the largest bond issues of their time, with more than $21 billion sold to the public by 1919. At first, many investment bankers and the public alike were skeptical about the size of the issues despite the fact that they were tax-free. The bonds were denominated in small amounts—one hundred dollars each—and sold by investment bankers and securities dealers. They were sold without any selling commissions, and most Wall Street houses joined the effort despite the absence of any tangible profits. Inadvertently, the Treasury's marketing effort was bringing in millions of customers who were assumed not to have existed before.

Part of Wall Street's largesse could be attributed to the phenomenal response the bond issues evoked. In 1917 the bankers had estimated the bond market to consist of about 350,000 individuals. By 1919 over 11 million had subscribed to the war loans. These war bonds provided many Americans with their first experience in owning intangible property, and they soon learned that money could be made by the simple process of holding paper securities until they went up in value. The Treasury characterized the 1919 sale of Liberty bonds as the "greatest financial achievement in all history and a wonderful manifestation of the strength and purpose of the American people."[21] Inadvertently, the war effort had given the vast majority of small investors a taste for securities that would only grow stronger in the 1920s. Memories of Jay Cooke were evoked, but this time the public would channel funds from maturing Treasury bonds into the stock market.

While the public and the government alike were often cynical of bankers' motives prior to the war, the tension subsided and the bankers again began to tighten their grip on the credit system, despite the presence of the Federal Reserve. Prosperity in the 1920s brought with it a tolerance of bankers' actions that had not been witnessed before. In the 1920s, prosperity was evident (if not in all quarters), and the general sense of well-being and friendly Republican administrations helped cast a blind eye on finance in general, as long as it appeared to be producing profits for all. By the time the recession of 1920–22 ended (called *depressions* at the time), the money trust was a name that was more than ten years old and receding from the collective memory. Bankers and corporate America had learned to adopt a different tack. As journalist Matthew Josephson pointed out, "what the giant Trusts learned from the era of 'muck-raking' and the brandishings of the Big Stick was to move with a superior cunning and discretion about their tasks. . . . [They] sought nowadays to propitiate public opinion, hiring 'public relations counselors' who disseminated propaganda of great art, by which a mellower picture of themselves was presented."[22] But once the industrialists and the bankers had been under attack, they would try to keep their own internecine battles to themselves and put up more of a united front than would have been the case in the past. The money trust had receded from the public eye but, as the next ten years would prove, it was far from moribund. The 1920s were still to come.

CHAPTER SIX

The Booming Twenties (1920–29)

Everybody ought to be rich.

John J. Raskob

The 1920s quickly became the most paradoxical decade in American history. The prosperity that began in 1922, lasting until 1929, was not anticipated. During the war, dire predictions abounded concerning the state of the economy after the defeat of the Central Powers. Most conservative commentators saw inflation on the horizon, as one might expect after a prolonged European war. The introduction of the income tax amendment in 1913 originally helped diminish spending, as would also be expected. And most important, America could return to the self-sufficiency and isolation from European affairs that most of the population seemed to crave.

But events would overtake predictions and push the country into the forefront of world affairs. American productive capacity became the envy of the world and continued to attract immigrants. However, by the 1920s immigration was lower than in previous decades, and it would never again rise to the levels witnessed in the late nineteenth century. The growth in population continued. The postwar inflation rate remained low, sparking a massive rally in the stock and bond markets. At the beginning of the war, David Lloyd George boasted that London was conducting fully one-half of the world's financial transactions excluding domestic British business. But a shift soon took place. The New York capital markets wrested the international capital markets away from Britain and never again relinquished them. The income tax, roundly criticized, did not deter consumers from spending. Cars, radios, and telephones were being mass-produced on a scale not even imagined earlier.

Intolerance and xenophobia were on the rise. At the time the New York financial markets were reveling in their unexpected wealth, Oklahoma was placed under martial law to counteract the racial terrorism of the Ku Klux Klan. In 1925 John Scopes was arrested in Tennessee for teaching evolution in a public school. The same decade that witnessed the birth of the miniature golf craze was also the decade of Prohibition. And the money trust had no reason to hide itself from view in the 1920s because it was under constant pressure to provide loans to the stock market. While the markets were booming and investment bankers were reaping huge profits, however, the anti–income tax movement was gaining strength. Even the movement favoring repeal of the Volstead Act had come under surreptitious control of those favoring a rollback of the tax rates. A massive land boom occurred in Florida as investors frantically bought plots in the scrub pine barrens in the hope of making a quick profit. One of the better-known developers in the state was Charles Ponzi. Miniature golf courses were being built on the roofs of New York office buildings, but by 1929 they would not be safe places for brokers. By November 1929, Will Rogers noted that "the situation has been reached in New York hotels where the clerk asks incoming guests, 'You wanna room for sleeping or for jumping?'"

The decade was also the last gasp for the traditional American (and Wall Street) doctrine of self-reliance and the evilness of big government. As the disparities between rich and poor became greater and greater, even the philanthropy of the robber barons and industrialists could not mask society's have-nots. Big business and Wall Street were not providing a stimulus for those less well-off. The Scopes "Monkey" trial certainly did not deter the social Darwinists from believing that the survivors of Wall Street wars and raids were somehow stronger than anyone else, but it ironically presaged the 1930s. There was indeed a "higher" authority at work in human affairs other than business Darwinism. Government was at last catching up with the private sector and beginning to impose its own will on the commercial and financial sector. But the crash would have to occur first. In the 1920s the strong sense of individualism still prevailed. Herbert Hoover was perhaps its best exponent. His 1922 book, *American Individualism*, was a simple paean to the nineteenth-century values of hard work and self-reliance that were still ingrained in American social thought. Ironically, it would make him the last popular proponent of theories beloved by Wall Street when the crash occurred during his presidency.

Around the turn of the century, a now famous term first appeared, coined by Thorstein Veblen in his popular book *The Theory of the Leisure Class*. Writing about humankind's tendency to acquire goods and adorn itself with material possessions, Veblen likened the contemporary acquisition of wealth and all of its accoutrements to primitive man's acquisition of women by force. He simply took what he wanted by the hair and dragged it off to his den. This lusting after material goods was known as *conspicuous consumption*. Fifty years later, Vance Packard would dub this group intent upon acquisition for its own sake the "status seekers." Veblen's term has endured throughout the twentieth century, although his models undoubtedly got their start in the nineteenth. As a professor of economics at Columbia, he certainly did not have to look far for tangible proof of his theories. The lavish mansions of the industrialists dotted Riverside Drive, a stone's throw from the campus, and Morgan's *Corsair* was sometimes docked no more than a few miles away.

After a sharp recession in 1920, called a *depression* at the time, Americans demonstrated that Veblen's theory was not far from the mark. The country embarked on a manufacturing and consuming spree that permanently changed the face of American society. The number of American households owning a radio rose from a meager sixty thousand to over ten million, and the number of homes having a telephone rose by 20 percent. New AM radio stations opened weekly around the country, and more and more households bought automobiles. But the consumption had meager foundations in many cases. The average wage was forty-eight cents per hour for a forty-four-hour week. Buying consumer goods necessitated using credit more than ever before. The American economy began to take on modern characteristics. Over two-thirds of what the country produced was consumed by individuals. As soon as this trend was recognized, modern American consumer society emerged. Highways became dotted with billboards selling everything from cigarettes to shaving cream. Advertising was no longer just another way of reaching the consumer; it became a necessity.

On the surface, it appeared that the entire country was speculating in the market, buying all sorts of new consumer goods, and pretending to stay on the wagon in the process. But more striking ironies were beginning to surface that would eventually lead to economic disaster. The disparities in wealth were enormous, with the relatively few top earners in the population owning the vast majority of American assets. Karl Marx would have smiled, for he knew the formula. Five percent of the population controlled 90 percent of the wealth. Two hundred corporations controlled half of the corporate wealth in the country. Massive fortunes were being accumulated while the average annual wage was less than fifteen hundred dollars per year. In 1920 a terrorist's bomb exploded outside Morgan's headquarters at 23 Wall, killing thirty passersby. Not everyone was enamored with the wealth and consumption of the postwar period. Most ironically, it was the small investor and saver who was dragged into the maelstrom of the decade by the financial community, all too eager to use somebody else's money to continue its expansionist dreams for American industry. The bear raiders, ersatz bulls, and other assorted manipulators were still at work in their familiar locales. Those higher up the ladder in the financial profession had expansionist dreams of their own that would leave an indelible imprint upon the 1920s. As in the past, war had presented all of them with a golden opportunity to expand financial marketing to the newly emerging middle class.

During the 1920s, a trend began to develop some form of uniform credit in the country. The Federal Reserve was still in its early years, and its influence was felt mostly at commercial banks. Other sectors of the economy were still lagging behind and felt the pressures exerted by a patchwork of credit suppliers. Immediately after the war, Woodrow Wilson signed legislation creating the Farm Credit System, through which farmers could obtain credit at land banks, organized in a system analogous to the Fed. Now it was possible for farmers to find loans on easier terms and for longer periods of time. The credit made it possible for the United States to become even more efficient in agriculture. The Farm Credit System had the distinction of becoming the first federally sponsored agency devoted to aiding the private sector outside of commercial banking. While its success in the financial markets was at best limited, it was to become a model for many other better-known agencies created during the depression.

Despite the advances ushered in by the new farm legislation, conspiracy theories about Wall Street, the Federal Reserve, and farmers as a group began to emerge in the national press. The postwar recession of 1920–22 was accompanied by a sharp drop in prices as the last of the "depressions" before the catastrophe of 1929 occurred. Agricultural prices also dropped sharply, and the depression hit the farmers hard. But almost immediately, rumors began to circulate of a conspiracy by the Federal Reserve to depress farm prices by not making enough currency available for farm loans despite the new Farm Credit System. These reports raised the ire of Senator Carter Glass of Virginia, who had been instrumental in passing the Federal Reserve Act eight years before. Arguing that the rumors were unfounded, the work of anti-Fed forces, Glass contended that "no human being can form any credible conjecture as to why the Federal Reserve Board, except in aimless malice, could have desired to do anything of the kind suggested."[1] While the uproar soon subsided, it unfortunately continued the trend whereby American agriculture remained suspicious of East Coast finance. Wall Street became a convenient scapegoat for many agrarian interests and would be blamed for many of the farmers' economic problems for the rest of the decade.

On the other side of the coin, Wall Street had little ammunition with which to fight the conspiracy forces that were mustering against it in the middle and late 1920s. The populists of the agrarian Midwest began to organize against Wall Street. While the financial markets were booming, agriculture remained in the doldrums. A severe drought hit the farm belt midway through the decade. This angered many politicians from farming states, and they began to put pressure on the Federal Reserve Board to curtail the market rally that had enveloped Wall Street. The more prominent members of the movement were men not to be taken lightly. They all followed in the tradition of William Jennings Bryan, whose tirades in favor of silver were well remembered. They included Carter Glass of Virginia, Robert M. La Follette Jr. of Wisconsin, who carried on in his father's footsteps, J. Thomas Heflin of Alabama, and William E. Borah of Idaho. Together they would bring considerable pressure to bear in Washington, attempting to curtail credit to the stock market and paint Wall Street as responsible for all of the country's economic ills. But despite their political prominence, the group also had its detractors. Depicting them as less than saints, a commentator of the period described them as "gentlemen of high moral voltage and abysmal prejudice. One of them is reputed to be the leader of the Ku Klux Klan in his state. Another is afraid of Roman [Catholic] dominion, an apprehension he voices loudly—and continuously. Their utter lack of judicial temper and financial knowledge impeaches their competence to pass on matters concerning Wall Street."[2] The battle lines were quickly being drawn. The impending contest had a similar ring to that which had occurred during the first year of Woodrow Wilson's presidency surrounding the proposed Federal Reserve. Again Carter Glass appeared to be siding with the anti–Wall Street forces.

The End of the War

During Woodrow Wilson's second term, society was faced with several vexing problems. Income tax was being collected for the first time, Prohibition was passed, and the war itself was being fought. The war was not popular, and the peace negotiations and events that followed would be a disappointment to the president because Congress rejected American involvement in the League of Nations. At home, Americans' sense of patriotism was being pandered to by war financing. The result was overwhelming, but patriotism had its price in dollars.

When the Treasury issued war bonds to finance American involvement in World War I, memories were evoked of Jay Cooke and Civil War financing. Buying war bonds was a popular form of investment and patriotism, although actual American involvement in the war was much less popular. Advertising for the war loans was pitched at the small saver and evoked memories of many immigrants' personal flights to the safety of the United States. One of the most popular war advertising posters urged citizens to buy war bonds, recalling through a graphic illustration their own journeys to the new country through Ellis Island, in the shadow of the Statue of Liberty. Advertising was certainly needed. Between 1917 and

1919 the Treasury announced five Liberty loans totaling a staggering $21.5 billion—by far the largest financing in American history.

In order to keep investment bankers at bay and not allow them to make unnecessary profits on the deals as they had in the past, the Treasury would not pay the bankers and brokers a selling fee. The bonds were issued by the Treasury and sent to the Federal Reserve Bank of New York, which distributed them to banks and brokers for sale to customers. The Treasury itself supervised the sale, which was headed by Lewis Franklin of the Guaranty Trust Company of New York. Many of the techniques originally employed by Jay Cooke more than fifty years earlier were used again. Denominations were small, averaging around one hundred dollars. After a slow start, most of the issues were actually oversubscribed. The Treasury, which considered the financings a great success, hyperbolically described the financings as among the "greatest ever." Its use of the Federal Reserve as its agent in the marketplace gave the relatively new, independent federal agency a high profile in the market and established a trend that has lasted until the present day. Investment bankers were less than thrilled, but after achieving some doubtful notoriety in the Pujo hearings almost all joined in the selling effort. As it turned out, their efforts were not in vain.

All sorts of investors, large and small, bought the Liberty bond issues for one simple reason: they were free of income tax. Tax rates were high in the years immediately following the passage of the Sixteenth Amendment, and demand was unusually high. The fact was not lost on the investment community. Millions of individuals subscribed to the loans. Investment bankers estimated that only 350,000 individuals were invested in bonds before the war.[3] Suddenly, the number of investors dramatically increased, and their legions would make a lasting impression upon banks and brokers. Financial marketing would quickly begin to focus on the individual investor. While his individual holdings were of little consequence, on aggregate the potential market was enormous. As Charles Mitchell of the National City Company put it, "The development of a large, new army of investors in this country who have never heretofore known what it means to own a coupon bond and who may in the future be developed into savers and bond buyers" was the ultimate reward of the Liberty loan selling efforts.[4] And as during the Civil War, the program helped some firms on the Street gain a stronger foothold in the market. Salomon Brothers, until then a small money broker, took the opportunity to spread its name around by participating in the selling effort and eventually entered the government bond market on a full-time basis.

In the fifty years since the Civil War, bankers and brokers had directed most of their time and sales efforts at large investors, leaving the retail investors to small-time brokers and bucket shops. The latter were brokers who actually ran a form of betting shop with their customers' money. For small amounts of money, the bucket shop broker would allow a customer to buy into a stock position. If the stock rose, he gained; if it fell, he lost money. But at no time did he actually own the stock. The broker used his money to accumulate its own position in stocks on margin and paid off if it was honest. If it was not, it sometimes absconded with the money. One of Wall Street's better-known speculators of the era got his start in bucket shops. As he recalled, "One day one of the office boys came to me where I was eating my lunch and asked me on the quiet if I had any money. . . . 'I've got a dandy tip on Burlington. I'm going to play it if I can get somebody to go in with me.' So I gave him all I had, and with our pooled resources [of $5] he went to one of the near-by bucket shops and bought [bet on] some Burlington. Two days later we cashed in. I made a profit of $3.12."[5]

Not everyone speculated in the stock market. Herbert Hoover would attribute the 1929 crash to the activities of scores of small speculators, including even lowly "bellboys," who traded simply to make a quick profit. The bucket shops certainly catered to them. They had all heard the legends surrounding Jay Gould and Commodore Vanderbilt and had read the simplistic stories of Horatio Alger; understandably, they wanted to achieve their share of wealth. And many discovered that speculating in the market was a good method of avoiding taxes. The tax system was still fairly primitive, and it was not difficult to arrange purchases and sales of stocks to mask gains made in the market. Profits made by speculation were easier to hide than salaries. As a result, investors of all sorts and social classes tried their hands at the market. But many conservative investors, who were in the majority, preferred bonds or real property. But the great irony of the decade, like those preceding it, was that many savers who shied away from the stock market were still exposed to it indirectly. The commercial banks and the trust banks were heavily involved in market speculation and loaned large sums of money to brokers as well. When the brokers loaned the same funds to investors of all types, the financial system began to develop a pyramid of speculation built upon borrowed money.

After the war, the Liberty loans matured and much of that money became available for new investment, prompting one of the largest mass investments of the century. Many of the Liberty bond investors had purchased a financial asset for the first time, and when redemption came, so too did the assurance that investments were relatively safe. Wall Street and the banking community were well prepared to cater to the new investor class. In 1908 the First National Bank of New York City, headed by George Baker, spun off the First Security Company. The bank itself had been accumulating equities in its own portfolio, contrary to existing national banking laws, and it was criticized by the Comptroller of the Currency. The securities subsidiary was founded as a result to take those assets off the books of the bank. Shortly thereafter, in 1914, banks began to purchase brokerage firms with the intent of selling them securities. National City Bank of New York acquired Halsey and Company, a New York brokerage, in 1916 to gain a foothold in the corporate securities business as well as serve the emerging middle class. Prior to this time, banks were primarily commercial banks in the true sense of the word, serving mostly businesses. Individuals, if they banked at all, traditionally banked with savings institutions or with smaller community banks. The large banks now set their sights upon the retail investor, intending to use the securities business to identify the wealthier of them. In order to do so, they coined the first financial marketing term of the century, the *financial department store*.

The main thrust of the new idea was to sell corporate bonds to the public. While stocks were popular with many investors, bonds still dominated the markets after the war. Prior to 1927, a date that was to become crucial to the development of the stock market, bonds accounted for about 75 percent of all new securities coming to market. Sales on the NYSE were also heavily dominated by corporate and government bonds, outnumbering stocks in value ten to fifteen times over. While speculators abounded, the average American investor was conservative by nature, preferring a fixed return to the possibilities of a quick killing in the stock market. As a result, the largest part of the financial department store would be its bond department.

Since the turn of the century, bond underwriting had been a lucrative business. Fees ranged as high as 10 percent of the proceeds of a bond, and most of that fee was kept by underwriters. The underwriting group was also very difficult to enter and became increasingly so as time progressed. The nature of the investment banking side of Wall Street also provided a great opportunity for brokers. Bankers hired brokers to sell the securities they had underwritten for a commission. Brokers were keen for this business during the 1920s, especially when massive amounts of investment funds became available. While most of the major investment bankers in New York did not bother to sell directly, some of those outside New York did also endeavor to sell their own underwritings. But while the business was assumed to be lucrative, no investment bank ever published actual profit and loss figures for syndicates in which it was involved. So it was only natural that as business began to boom in the 1920s the number of brokers eager to get into deals initiated by the major underwriters would increase as well.

For the average investor, the array of bonds on offer in the 1920s was bewildering. In addition to Treasury bonds, those of municipalities, companies, and foreign governments and companies also existed. Railroad bonds were slowly giving way to those of industrial companies, and many municipalities were tapping the market to find money with which to provide for the increasing demand for municipal services. Many foreign governments and companies were also tapping the market for dollars, adding unfamiliar names to the growing list of borrowers. Borrowing countries came from Europe, both east and west, as well as from Latin America. Part of this rush to the market was created by a deal made between the British and the Americans during the 1920s that created a window of opportunity for American investment bankers.

One of the major issues in the postwar period was the gold standard. How currencies were valued in gold terms had much to do with where investors placed their funds, as the panic of 1893–94 had shown. When money departed from countries on the gold standard, gold would eventually follow because international transactions were settled in the precious metal. After the war, the British economy needed protection from international pressures, but the government still wanted to return to the gold standard, which had been suspended at the end of the war. As a result, the Bank of England and the Federal Reserve struck a deal that would protect Britain's postwar markets from capital outflows. The product was a particularly good deal for Wall Street.

The deal to stabilize the pound and open the New York markets to international deals came in the wake of the Dawes loan to Germany. After the French and Belgians occupied the Ruhr when Germany fell behind in war reparations, the United States and its Allies intervened to help stabilize the mark and prevent further hostilities. The Dawes loan was a two-part bond, with about $110 million each raised in the United States and Europe. Morgan was the manager for the issue. The Dawes loan was considered enormously successful and beneficial. Charles Dawes himself was awarded part of the 1925 Nobel Peace Prize for his efforts in securing the loan and averting another European war. Once the German currency was no longer under immediate pressure, attention turned toward the pound. It was also fluctuating widely, and there was a great desire to stabilize it as well since it was the world's major currency at the time. Most bankers wanted a return to the gold standard, hoping it would bring about price stability in Europe.

The proponents of a return won the day when sterling was stabilized in the spring of 1925. Opponents, such as John Maynard Keynes, were defeated after a lengthy public debate about the benefits and risks of returning to the gold standard. Montagu Norman, governor of the Bank of England, and Benjamin Strong, president of the Federal Reserve Bank of New York, struck up a close working relationship in the 1920s that helped forge strong Anglo-American financial relations for years to come. They agreed to keep the London stock and money markets closed to foreigners, forcing investors and companies to go to New York instead. American interest rates were kept lower than those in Britain so that companies and countries needing money would raise dollars rather than sterling. The deal worked remarkably well. The New York markets boomed while the London markets remained protected. America's first genuine boom without substantial help from British investors was under way. Most important, the United States had emerged from its century of debtor status to become a creditor nation.

There was substantial Morgan influence behind the agreement. Benjamin Strong, originally of Bankers Trust and the Federal Reserve Bank of New York, had been a Morgan ally for years and had audited the Knickerbocker Trust during the panic of 1907 at the behest of Pierpont Morgan. Now that J. P. Jr., or Jack, was at the helm of the bank, Strong's advice was often sought on international banking matters because he was the most international of the New York banking crowd, the Nicholas Biddle of his day. Somewhat reclusive, especially after his second divorce and a bout with tuberculosis, he became a close friend and ally of the governor of the Bank of England, Montagu Norman. Norman was equally reclusive and also extremely eccentric, giving the impression of being a twentieth-century version of a seventeenth-century Roundhead. He was originally associated with the British merchant bank Brown Shipley, the London arm of Brown Brothers Harriman. The men forged their alliance based upon their common belief that Britain should return to the gold standard. They began negotiations with the private bankers, notably Morgan, for assistance. In order to stabilize sterling, the British required the large loan, which was provided in 1925 by the Federal Reserve and Morgan.

The young Conservative Chancellor of the Exchequer Winston Churchill announced the support package in the House of Commons to the delight of the bankers. In their opinion, sound money had been given a vote of confidence. The idea of a paper money not backed by a metallic standard, propounded by Keynes, was defeated. Britain's role in world finance would be preserved and the integrity of sterling maintained. Needless to say, the profits on the loans were not bad either. The traditional view won the day, although British industrial capacity in the postwar period was not up to the task. The bankers felt justified in their faith in Britain and the pound. Keynes had other thoughts on the deal, however. He correctly anticipated that the pound was overvalued by at least 10 percent. Writing in a 1928 essay entitled "The Economic Consequences of Mr. Churchill," he attributed the chancellor's adherence to the gold standard as silly "because he has no instinctive judgement to prevent him from making mistakes; partly because, lacking his instinctive judgement, he was deafened by the clamorous voices of finance; and most of all, because he was gravely misled by his experts."[6] Keynes's anger derived, in part, from the immediate repercussions of returning to the gold standard. Morgan benefited by charging 1 percent of the $100 million it granted as a credit to the British as an annual fee.[7] The intention of returning Britain to financial stability and its former industrial glory did not pan out. The deal unfortunately bore the seeds of its own destruction. The pound was valued at $4.86 after the package was announced, a level that was widely condemned as being too high. The high pound sparked a general strike in Britain in 1926, which almost exploded into revolt. The government had to send heavy armaments and troops into London to prevent what it feared to be a revolution among the working class. The scars of the strike soured worker-government relations in Britain for a generation.

American interest rates were kept purposely low by Strong so that the British rates were seen as higher, supporting the pound in the process. Low American interest rates meant cheap consumer credit and equally cheap margin money, which was loaned to speculators in the stock market. The horse was out of the barn. The market bubble was beginning to expand, with the Federal Reserve dedicated to keeping interest rates below those in Britain. The only way to rein in the American market was to violate the basics of the deal struck between the two central bankers. Unfortunately, other bankers and speculators would also support the same position for very different reasons. The United States was on the verge of the greatest bull market in its history. No one bothered to think of any negative factors that could cause the economy to slow down in such a conducive climate. Those who were apprehensive about the boom conditions and the dangers that lurked behind the markets were simply written off as pessimists or, worse, as being unpatriotic. Wall Street was starting to fervently believe in its own sales pitches to the point where they were equated with the good of the country as a whole.

Prophets of Profit

Developing the financial department store was only one of the major Wall Street trends of the 1920s. The marketplace was still largely institutional and was dominated by the same investment banks that had controlled it since the late nineteenth century. But the commercial banks were mounting a charge into Wall Street despite the vague constraints imposed upon them by the National Banking Act passed during the Civil War. Like their industrial predecessors and the trusts, they organized themselves into holding companies and then purchased or expanded into brokerage and underwriting. The bankers saw this as a natural extension of their other activities. Detractors saw it as nothing more than an extension of Brandeis's basic maxim that they were still seeking other people's money to use in their expansionist plans.

Supporting the bankers' arguments was the peculiar nature of American banking. Most state banking laws prohibited commercial banks from crossing state lines to open a branch in another state. Many could not move into other parts of their own state either because of state laws prohibiting intrastate expansion. The country and the economy were growing but the banks were severely constrained. These restrictions limited their ability to make money and create credit. But commercial banks could open subsidiary companies across state lines and continued to do so. Morgan had its Drexel subsidiary in Philadelphia, and National City now owned Halsey. Other large commercial banks would acquire specialized subsidiaries in the scramble to find new customers despite the vagaries of many state and national laws regarding appropriate banking activities.

Equal strides were being made at the state levels to get a grasp on credit being created within their borders. Until the 1920s, much credit in the country was granted on a private basis. Individuals needing a loan usually found money available from small banks, credit companies, or individuals. This system sufficed until the boom following the war. Banks and companies found it more lucrative to loan money to companies and stock brokers in need of margin money. Interest rates for broker loans (made to brokers so that they could lend to speculators) were usually high, while other interest rates were still relatively low—in some cases only half the broker loan rates. Small lenders could not keep up with demand for consumer credit during the booming 1920s. High demand for money led to a rise in loan-sharking, especially on the East Coast and in major urban areas. Organized crime had gained a strong foothold during Prohibition by producing illegal alcohol, and loan-sharking became another of its lucrative activities. In response, many states passed usury laws limiting the amount of interest a lender could charge on a loan. These laws did not stop loan-sharking because few individuals were eager to come forward to complain about paying exorbitant rates of interest.

In the forefront of selling stocks to individuals were the securities subsidiaries of the major New York banks, most prominently the National City Bank, run by Charles Mitchell. Mitchell was a former electrical goods salesman for Western Electric with a distinct penchant for selling himself and the products he represented. Armed with its securities subsidiary, the National City Company, the National City Bank led the charge into investing for the average person. In its favor were its extensive ties with many parts of the newly emerging investors' community untouched by the traditional securities houses. The National City Company was able to forge a single financial department store that would become the model for future operations for the next seventy years. During the 1920s, it reigned supreme in parts of the investment banking business. It sold bullishness on America and investments in general and succeeded to an unprecedented degree.

National City was not alone. In 1925, advertising man Bruce Barton published a best-seller entitled *The Man Nobody Knows* in which he described Jesus Christ as the founder of modern business. A simple man with excellent foresight had handpicked twelve equally obscure men, and they had conquered the world. The prophets of profit came from a noble heritage. Toward the latter part of the decade they would bitterly resent any Joshuas come to blow the walls down.

National City used its numerous branches and subsidiaries to open outlets in over fifty cities nationwide. Most of these offices housed a combination of a bank branch (where permitted), a securities office, and a trust office as well. The intention was clear. It wanted to fully cater to its clients' needs, by selling them bonds, taking their deposits, and performing trust duties such as making wills and administering estates. Investing would be treated as any other mass-marketing operation. As Charles Mitchell told a bank training class, "Our branch offices throughout the United States are already working to make connections with the great new bond buying public . . . and are preparing to serve the public on a straightforward basis, just as it is served by the United Cigar Stores or Child's Restaurants."[8] To achieve this goal, the bank took out many advertisements in newspapers and magazines touting the bank's prowess in all things financial. National City tried to remain above the fray by not becoming a huckster of securities, and especially common stocks, like many of the smaller brokers. Instead it tried to educate its customers by producing pamphlets and other literature describing investment opportunities, especially in bonds. Unfortunately, it engaged in a fair amount of hucksterism as the late 1920s approached. The reason was simple. The National City Company was in the process of becoming one of the largest underwriters of bonds of all types. On average, the subsidiary company was able to issue between $1 and $2 billion in new securities per year for its various clients. Mitchell called this principal activity "manufacturing" securities, a term that would not endear him to investors or regulators. But it did seem that National City was indeed manufacturing by bringing so many issues to market. In order to do so, it was necessary to have the largest sales organization in the world.

Mitchell personally rode herd on his salesmen, exhorting them to sell more and more securities. He was known to take them to lunch in a New York skyscraper and show them the city from the heights, openly wondering how many citizens below had not yet bought securities from his bank. The message was clear, as were his intentions: sell securities or be fired. His tactics worked admirably. The National City Company became the financial department store writ large. What it was not able to accomplish directly it did by correspondent relationship. In addition to its almost two thousand employees, the subsidiary itself had sixty branches in over fifty cities, over eleven thousand miles of private communications wire between them, and formal relationships with hundreds of smaller securities dealers. The close relationships with other dealers would play an important role in the crash of October 1929.

One of the major bones of contention with the bank as it expanded re-volved around the types of securities it was selling to the public. Besides producing relatively simple literature for new investors, National City claimed that the bond issues it participated in were subject to the analysis of its own staff. They never knowingly sold bonds with dodgy reputations or weak balance sheets. Mitchell stated, "The time will never come, cer-tainly so long as I am connected with the National City Company, when, pressed with the need for securities for our own great selling organization, we will let down our exacting requirements. We have gained the confi-dence of the investor and we are building our institution upon that confi-dence."[9] And true to form, many bond issues remained at fairly high prices for most of the decade until the crash occurred. But the prices were more reflective of low interest rates than they were of quality. Unfortunately, many of the bonds issued during the boom times faded quickly from view when the 1930s began. The vast flow of investment funds from Liberty bonds into corporate and foreign bonds was to prove much riskier than many investors had anticipated. Politically, the Republicans would fashion a complicated response in order to fend off criticism of Wall Street in gen-eral and themselves in particular.

But there were still the stock speculators, who would not consider buy-ing a bond, with its low fixed return. They became the mainstay of the market, and brokers fell over themselves to cater to them. Later in the decade, many companies would join banks in lending money to the mar-ket to fuel speculators' desires to buy more and more stocks on margin. Speculation was still the centerpiece of the American Dream in the 1920s. Tales abounded of professional traders accumulating vast fortunes in short periods, and everyone wanted a piece of the action. The Vanderbilts and Goulds had been replaced by a more modern version of industrialist-spec-ulator whose trading profits made those of the legends seem tame.

The prosperity of the NYSE spilled over into the curb market. After spending a century out of doors, the New York Curb Exchange finally moved indoors to new quarters at 86 Trinity Place in 1921. Not officially called the American Stock Exchange for another thirty years, the curb market had made great strides in trading the shares of smaller, less capital-ized companies than those that traded on the Big Board. After the turn of the century, the curb market, under the longtime leadership of Emanuel "Pop" Mendels, began listing shares it traded, following NYSE practice. It also traded shares of larger companies such as Du Pont, Standard Oil, and Otis Elevator on occasion, providing competition to its larger counter-part. About the same time, the over-the-counter market began to emerge in New York, better known as the *unlisted market*. It provided competition for the curb market, which by necessity was forced to better organize itself to ward off the rivalry.

In all of the market lore of the precrash period there was no better-known industrialist-turned-trader than William Crapo Durant, better known as Billy. The grandson of a former Michigan governor, the short, dapper man was one of the founding fathers of General Motors. He had personally brought Oldsmobile, Cadillac, and Pontiac under GM auspices, but he later lost control of GM through a boardroom coup, selling out his interest to Morgan and the du Ponts. Durant immediately began to speculate in the market, having been freed from any responsibilities at GM, and his antics became something of a legend. Assembling a syndicate of wealthy friends and associates, he reputedly bought and sold over $4 billion of common stock. The syndicate was actually a pool of investors' funds that was becoming a common method of investing in the bull market. Durant was reputed to have made $50 million in three months by speculating in the months prior to the crash. Some newspaper accounts described him as the most successful market operator of all time. The dealings of the syndicate were well reported in the press, and the public quickly followed whatever stocks Durant favored. His group naturally sold when the public moved in. His reported winnings totaled over $100 million, which would have put him in the same league as Jay Gould, but he achieved his wealth in a much shorter time. His publicity also served as a model for many others with more modest means but the same sort of dreams. Bondholders may have been in the majority of American middle-class investors, but the speculator was still the most admired.

Manipulation of the press was still used widely by those seeking the public's help in raising stock prices. Many well-known journalists of the day were on the payroll of traders and market manipulators. Advertising was placed under more scrutiny than in the past. Placing ads promoting great riches or unusually high returns started to be frowned upon, at least by the more serious newspapers. The general public was highly gullible about investments, a fact that was widely known among professionals. Durant had used planted stories and published rumors to his own advantage when playing the market. As early as 1916, the *New York Times* began offering hundred-dollar rewards for information leading to the conviction of anyone placing false ads in the paper. Advertising revenues declined from certain advertisers, although many other newspapers followed suit in an attempt to protect the readership, and the papers' integrity, from bogus stock operators and land swindlers.

The Kreuger Empire

One of the most profitable lines of business for Wall Street in the 1920s was issuing bonds for foreign borrowers. Governments and foreign companies all took advantage of the Norman-Strong deal to float bonds in

New York, much to the delight of the investment bankers. The commissions and fees on these issues were usually quite healthy. Since the London market was effectively closed to foreigners, the American markets were now experiencing a new sensation: they were becoming sources of capital for foreigners rather than the target of foreign investments. Many pitfalls surrounded this new trend, but Wall Street's cheerful attitude was difficult to resist.

Most of these "Yankee" bonds were for foreign governments. Throughout the decade, borrowers came from a variety of places. The Dawes loan was included, as were bonds for Canada and Newfoundland (not yet a part of Canada). Later, Latin American countries would borrow, along with some from eastern Europe and more familiar places such as Great Britain. The terms of the bonds were very generous for the underwriters. The American portion of the Dawes loan cost the underwriters only about 87 percent of par, which meant a profit of over $13 million on the $110-million issue when they sold it at face value. As it turned out, the loan was never fully paid back. The Great Depression and German rearmament in the 1930s prevented investors from receiving all of their interest payments. But at the time, the Republicans were full of praise for the investment bankers who put together the deals. They were cited as having added to the U.S. balance of payments and to the general euphoria of the period. But not everyone was happy with the results. The sheer volume of foreign bonds suggested that not enough was known about the financial conditions of many foreigners. Isolationist America serving as provider of capital to the rest of the world was something of a strange phenomenon. The Seligmans served as underwriters for a Peruvian bond issue that was later to become infamous after the crash and the congressional hearings that followed.

The U.S. Department of Commerce began to raise some questions about the bonds. During the Coolidge presidency, Herbert Hoover was secretary of commerce. While the Republicans and Wall Street were extremely fond of Hoover, he did question the value of this spate of new issue activity. Slowly, the department began to recognize that the German loans in particular were going to provide competition for American companies by a major industrial power. As a result, it attempted to tie the bonds to agreements with the foreign borrowers concerning the actual use of the funds. But its efforts were futile. Wall Street continued to issue the bonds for foreign borrowers, ignoring the government in the process. Frustrated, a Commerce Department official remarked in 1927 that those on Wall Street had "utter disregard for all interests outside their own." Wall Street had come to tolerate the Fed but had little time for the executive branch. It had come to expect little interference from Republican administrations.

Among the corporate issues for foreign companies were some spectacular deals that did not bode well for the future. In 1923 Lee, Higginson
and Company became involved with Ivar Kreuger of Sweden, one of Europe's best-known financiers and industrial empire builders. Most of his
holdings centered around match and sulfur production and various chemical companies. His best-known holdings were the Swedish Match Company and Kreuger and Toll; the former was his core company, while the
latter was a financing arm that began borrowing money on the Yankee
bond market and then loaning it to foreign governments. One particular
bond's proceeds, floated in 1927, were loaned to the French government
to stabilize the franc. That particular deal earned Kreuger the everlasting
antagonism of Morgan and Wall Street, which liked to arrange sovereign
deals in their own good time. It was only one of many, helping to shore up
European finances in the postwar period, but it was indicative of the types
of deals Kreuger made. They invariably put him in good stead with many
European governments, which came to rely upon him as their intermedi-
ary in the American market.

In return for Kreuger's largesse, many governments granted him monopolies over match production in their countries. Swedish Match was
the jewel in his crown and helped bandy his name around the world. True
to the times, Kreuger did not publish financial statements, preferring to
rely upon his apparently spotless record with governments to speak for itself. In 1923 Lee Higginson helped him found the International Match
Corporation, which sold $150 million worth of shares in the American
markets. Two years later, the company and his Polish subsidiary transferred $25 million of the proceeds to his personal account, an amount
never to be accounted for again. Lee Higginson appeared to have never
fully understood the nature of Kreuger's business or was not perceptive
enough to realize that he was nothing more than a swindler. He had
adopted that well-known trick of the post–Civil war era of borrowing
large amounts of money at high rates of interest and then using the proceeds to pay dividends on the common stock of his companies. When the
stocks rose, he sold more, and so on. This form of leverage was quite
common up to the crash of 1929, and no one took much notice of it at the
time. No one suspected anything as long as the market continued to rise.
But when International Match and several other of Kreuger's companies
failed during the depression, Lee Higginson was placed in a very embarrassing position, professing to know little about the companies' financial
positions. The firm apparently had taken Kreuger's word about his financial condition rather than perform any credit analysis of its own. Another
deal involving Lee Higginson fell apart when it was learned that some of
the collateral Kreuger had pledged to a Yankee bond issue had been
switched after the issue and replaced with lower-quality collateral that

later became worthless. These shenanigans later forced Congress to pass legislation regulating collateral in order to protect bondholders. Kreuger himself committed suicide shortly after the bankruptcy in 1932 when many of his corrupt dealings were exposed.

Kreuger's deals and the rise of the Yankee market signaled a marked change on Wall Street. The United States found itself in an unusual position, in which foreigners were now tapping the New York markets for capital rather than supplying it. While this shift was healthy for investment banking fees, it invariably meant that Wall Street was finally going to be taken advantage of in much the same way that foreigners had been taken advantage of in prior decades. Wall Street was now in the position of being swindled rather than being the swindler. Bankers and brokers certainly were not happy about the results. Before long, it became apparent that many of the deals of the 1920s were indeed bogus or were so shaky that the underwriters should have known about the poor creditworthiness of many of their clients. When the reaction came, it was Wall Street that would bear the full brunt of the public's opprobrium.

Knowing a client company's financial condition is what is known in investment banking as *due diligence*. Before the Great Depression, it simply meant that an investment banker took all reasonable precautions to determine whether the company or government issuing securities to the public was in sound financial health. Before the explosion in new securities coming to market in the 1920s, the investment bankers' word was sometimes not good enough. During World War I, some western states had passed what were known as *blue-sky laws*, which required an investment banker to register the securities it wanted to sell in the state with the appropriate state securities authorities. Misrepresentation could lead to penalties. Prior to 1933, blue-sky laws were found only in a handful of states, not particularly known for their large investor populations, but they represented an important precedent nevertheless. Along with disclosure strides made in municipal bonds, they helped pave the way for reforms in 1933 and 1934.

Tax Issues

One topic that Wall Street was closely involved with in the 1920s was tax avoidance. An antitax movement developed quickly after 1922 when it became apparent that taxes were no longer a patriotic matter once the war was over. Many schemes abounded to avoid paying taxes, from the traditional wash sales used by Wall Street to investment schemes promising exponential returns to the investor, such as those of Charles Ponzi. But there was also a darker, more organized side to tax avoidance in the 1920s. In the tangled politics of the period, which seemed so simple on the surface, it was espoused by a group of corporate leaders who organized themselves into the opposition for the occasion. Their vehicle for opposing the income tax was not an antitax movement but the anti-Prohibition movement that was gaining ground at the same time. This curious mixture of alcohol and taxes became one of the most combustible issues of the decade.

On the surface, the movement pressing for the repeal of the Prohibition amendment was led by a former military man, Captain William Stayton. He headed an organization called the Association Against the Prohibition Amendment, or AAPA, founded shortly after the Eighteenth Amendment was passed in 1919. The organization was on record as a pressure group dedicated to rolling back the Volstead Act, prohibiting the manufacture of alcoholic beverages, as well as the amendment itself. It maintained that the ban on drinking and manufacturing alcohol was unconstitutional, and it sought to have both pieces of legislation removed. For most of the 1920s, it led the way against Prohibition and was victorious when Congress repealed the Eighteenth Amendment early in 1933.

But there was more to the anti-Prohibition movement. Over the latter part of the 1920s, it became a potent force with such sizable funds at its command that it was investigated by Congress in 1930 by the Senate Lobby Investigation. In 1925 the AAPA was nothing more than another "wet" group clamoring for the repeal, but a scant four years later it was the country's most powerful lobby. Between 1926 and 1930 it had found itself dozens of new contributors, all of whom espoused its principles. The counsel for the Senate committee investigating the AAPA was a young lawyer named Fletcher Dobyns. The committee amassed over five thousand pages of testimony, which, in retrospect, Dobyns categorized as "one of the most astonishing public documents in existence. . . . It reveals a group of men who are recognized as the industrial, financial and social leaders of America deliberately organizing, conducting and promoting a campaign to overthrow the Eighteenth Amendment."[10] Their avowed purpose was simple but convoluted. By repealing Prohibition, they wanted to abolish income taxes at the same time.

Stayton himself had experience working for another powerful lobby group before joining up with the AAPA. During the war he had been executive director of the Navy League, and many of the AAPA's employees were also on its payroll. The Navy League was a lobby group founded by J. P. Morgan, George Westinghouse, Charles Schwab, and John J. Astor dedicated to a propaganda barrage against the public and Congress to maintain a strong navy to ensure the protection of the United States. Not coincidentally, all of the founders had a vested interest in steel, steel production, and transportation. The Navy League was eventually denounced by Herbert Hoover as a selfish public interest group, and its star quickly began to wane.

Despite protests that the league was a narrow group dedicated only to its members' pocketbooks, other lobby groups used similar propaganda tactics. The Prohibition movement scored more successes during the war than at any other time because of the grain question. The "drys" had convinced a large portion of the American public that using grain for feeding the troops during the war was patriotic while using it for alcohol production was not. The war had been successfully used by all sorts of private interest groups.

Stayton had already changed jobs when Prohibition was passed and began running the AAPA. After 1926 he attracted some extremely wealthy patrons, notably the du Ponts and John Raskob, former president of General Motors and colleague of Billy Durant. The du Ponts were major shareholders in GM, as well as their own company. Raskob was the motivating force behind building the Empire State Building in New York, still under wraps in the late 1920s, and was chairman of the Democratic National Committee because he was a close ally of Al Smith.[11] He would also become the most vocal, and well publicized, bull of the decade. This curious group was avidly dedicated to repeal. Oddly, it was not the usual sort of group associated with Prohibition. The best known of the temperance groups had been women's organizations, church groups, and those affiliated with mid-America more so than with cities or big business. Business and finance had always been associated with New York and Wall Street, and Wall Street was traditionally known for its recreational drinkers. Fifth Avenue had more speakeasies during Prohibition than in many states combined.

Pierre and Irénée du Pont became active in the AAPA and were its major contributors after 1926. Their avowed interest was not in Prohibition but in the reduction of income taxes. In fact, until 1925 the du Ponts had been prohibitionists rather than wets. The economist Irving Fisher of Yale recalled that du Pont personnel practices at their Delaware companies were extremely intolerant of employees who showed up for work with even a hint of alcohol on their breath. That trait had been a du Pont hallmark since the company was founded almost a century before. Stayton himself admitted that Pierre du Pont was a "dry" prior to 1926. In testimony before the Senate committee in 1930, he was asked by Senator Arthur Robinson of Indiana whether fifteen of the twenty-eight directors of General Motors were members of the AAPA.

MR. STAYTON: Yes, sir; 15 of the 28.
MR. ROBINSON: American directors?
MR. STAYTON: Yes, sir.
MR. ROBINSON: Would you not think it would be a fair statement to say that the association is a du Pont subsidiary?

MR.STAYTON: I would not. Mr. du Pont for five years was on the other side. For five years after this organization was formed, Mr. du Pont was a dry.[12]

The motivating force behind the AAPA was the elimination of income taxes along with the Eighteenth Amendment. The British excise system levied against spirit production and consumption was the AAPA answer to the loss of revenue that the Internal Revenue Service would suffer if there were no income tax. An excise tax could be levied against alcoholic consumption. The idea was that the excise would replace income tax in a short period. When asked by an American reporter for his comments on Prohibition when he visited in 1929, Winston Churchill remarked, "We realize over £100 million a year from our liquor taxes, an amount I understand that you give to your bootleggers." Eliminating the income tax naturally would free many of the wealthy from high levels of personal and corporate tax.

The point was well taken. In the 1920s there was a fifty-fifty split between the personal and corporate sectors providing tax revenues for the government. For the wealthy who owned their own businesses, that meant a double tax burden. Corporate tax was paid first, and then their personal share of the income was taxed again. Despite the Republican administrations in power in the 1920s, the rates were considered excessive by the wealthy, who began to rebel, using the AAPA as their vehicle. Those who adopted a more traditional view were appalled by the entire anti-Prohibition movement and covert drinking in general. It was seen as a flagrant violation of the Constitution that was tearing at the social fabric of the country. Walter Lippmann, in a letter to Felix Frankfurter, wrote in 1926, "A very large minority of the American people is for all practical purposes in open rebellion against the Eighteenth Amendment, and the real lesson is not to enforce the Eighteenth Amendment, but not to pass amendments of this character."[13] Both the amendment itself and the Volstead Act were full of loopholes that made enforcement difficult, if not impossible. Both wets and drys recognized these loopholes and sought to exploit them for their own purposes.

The membership roll of the AAPA reflected some of the biggest names in American business. One that it did not include was Billy Durant, the erstwhile colleague of Raskob and the du Ponts. In fact, Durant took a different tack entirely. In 1928, while president of Durant Motors, he sponsored a nationwide essay contest to find ways to make the Eighteenth Amendment and the Volstead Act more effective. Contestants could not simply advocate repeal; those submitting essays were required to address themselves to the matter of enforcement of Prohibition. The prize was $25,000, an amount that drew over 23,000 entries, of which 102 were published. In his introduction to the book in which the essays were published, Durant wrote, "My collaborators are delegates from 37 states and Hawaii and Alaska. The list includes 34 public officials in the service of the United States, 23 state officials, 15 county officials, 30 town and city officials. . . . these contributors are not theorists but hard-headed officials up against the daily difficulties of enforcing this law."[14] Between them, they covered almost every conceivable method of tightening up the Volstead Act to make it more comprehensive and less of a laughingstock among the public.

Part of the great irony behind the anti-Prohibition movement was that little was made publicly of the fact that repeal would have seriously harmed organized crime. Gangsters had become the "beer barons" of their age by selling bootleg alcohol across the country. This created a curious set of circumstances where the fine line between producers and users became blurred. Nevertheless, the law was quite clear about the difference between producers of booze and beer and the users. Those purchasing contraband beverages were not guilty of breaking any law, but the producers were. This led Al Capone to his famous remark, putting forth a defense that has been used by many on the wrong side of the law ever since: "Everybody calls me a racketeer. I call myself a businessman. When I sell liquor, it's bootlegging. When my patrons serve it on a silver tray on Lake Shore Drive, it's hospitality."[15] Like many others of his era, he would have a difficult time explaining his reputed $100-million annual income as "legitimate."

The anti-Prohibition movement and the techniques used by the AAPA ushered in the modern era of American political advertising and propaganda. In its fight, the AAPA employed different groups that would lend credence to its cause. At various times it used a committee of authors and artists, composed of prominent members of the performing and literary arts, to rant against Prohibition. At others it used a committee composed of prominent members of the legal profession, also dedicated to repeal. Groups of wives and sons and daughters of members also formed groups designed to influence civic organizations. Some had names such as the "Crusaders." While condemned by many of the drys, these wet organizations proved extremely successful and eventually won the day when the Eighteenth Amendment was repealed. But the country had not heard the last of the AAPA, which within six months would reappear in a different guise to oppose the policies of Franklin Roosevelt under the new name American Liberty League.

The anti-Prohibition movement was not the only crusade waged against taxes in the 1920s. Once the war was over, the compulsion and patriotism surrounding payment of taxes began to recede quickly. Stock trading, along with land speculation, was one way to keep ahead of the tax man. In many cases, if the techniques were sophisticated enough, it was also a good way to beat him at his own game. One of the most common techniques involved what was traditionally known as a *wash sale*. An individual would sell a stock to another at an artificially low price, claiming the loss as a tax deduction. He would then buy another from the same party at a gain, having one side "wash out" the other. Careful manipulation always generated a loss while disguising gains.

But during the middle of the decade, the antitax movement became more serious. Individual tax rates were as high as 70 percent for those in the top tax brackets in the early 1920s, although they did dip later in the decade to about 25 percent.[16] A movement quickly developed to protest the high rates. Many corporate leaders devised methods of reducing the tax rates, including Charles Mitchell of National City Bank. While many of the proposals were debated in public, many Wall Street traders and business leaders had adopted their own personal method of avoiding income taxes. By arranging for wash sales, they would simply exchange shares at rigged prices to take losses and avoid gains. Pierre du Pont and John Raskob were involved in one such sale in 1929 just following the crash. Through a series of complicated transactions, they attempted to conceal $2 million in gains by claiming losses instead. Their transactions came under the IRS's scrutiny, and the tax courts eventually threw out their deductions, calling the wash sales flagrant abuses of the market.

One of the most flagrant abuses of the tax system was perpetrated by Albert Wiggin, chairman of the Chase National Bank in New York and was one of the small handful of senior New York bankers who composed the 1920s version of the money trust. Because of his position, he was Chase's largest shareholder, and he added to his holdings throughout the late 1920s. He actively traded the stock through a series of private Canadian investing companies established for the occasion. He continued to trade, using inside information even after the crash, making almost $11 million before he was finally exposed at congressional hearings in 1933. Those executives and traders without the wherewithal to establish offshore trading facilities devised other ingenious ways to trade without incurring taxes. More often, executives would arrange for wash sales with members of their own families, usually their wives. John Kenneth Galbraith, in his history of the crash, remarked that "tax avoidance had brought individuals of the highest respectability into extraordinary financial intercourse with their wives."[17] Before these methods were finally made public in 1933 and 1934, they were quite common and cost the Internal Revenue Service millions in uncollected revenues.

Throughout the 1920s, interest rates remained low, a single factor that alone helped the stock market maintain its steady climb. After the deal struck by Benjamin Strong and Monty Norman to keep U.S. rates below those in Britain, another international event occurred that caused the Fed to lower rates even further. In the spring of 1927, Norman traveled to New York accompanied by two other central bankers, Hjalmar Schact of the German Reichsbank and Charles Rist of the Bank of France. They came to argue for a deal similar to the one struck between Strong and Norman three years earlier, namely, a policy of easy money. If American interest rates were lowered, then pressure would be kept off the European markets and little gold would escape. Any gold that would cross borders would leave the United States, bound probably for Europe, and that would keep pressure off the European currencies. Strong agreed with the policy matter, and the Fed obliged by lowering interest rates by half a percent. The deal was seen as a victory by internationalists over those who argued that higher interest rates would help slow the growth in the stock market. But the stock market took heart from the lower rates and continued its historic climb. Within a year and a half, detractors of the policy would see the meeting between the central bankers as another reason the United States should steer clear of international affairs and pressures. Critics maintained that Strong had been persuaded by Norman and two sophisticated European wheeler-dealers into making a deal inimical to the interests of the United States.

The market continued to climb, rising over 200 percent between 1925 and 1928. Many saw the bubble building to unsustainable proportions, but their warnings and protests rang in vain. Secretary of Commerce Herbert Hoover spoke many times about the need to rein in speculation, but his calls, among others, went unheeded. Upon leaving office in 1928, when Hoover was elected to succeed him, President Coolidge proclaimed the market a "good buy," although prices were rising into unheard-of territory. The low interest rates were beginning to attract many banks and other companies that saw the clear opportunity for profit. While official interest rates at the Fed were 3.5 percent, money could be loaned to stock market speculators (margin money) for 12 percent or even higher. Rates at banks were low, but those found in the market were not. The rush was on to loan money to stock market speculators, who then used it to finance their purchase of common stocks.

Typically investors purchasing common stock put up between 10 and 20 percent of the purchase price, while brokers extended them credit for the balance. Brokers, in turn, found the money for lending at banks and companies that wished to lend them money. In some cases the banks were actually the parent banks that owned the brokers and thus were officially lending to a subsidiary. In any event, the process was extremely profitable for the lenders. Money could be found in the money market for slightly higher than 3 or 4 percent and loaned to a broker, who then passed it to its margin customer. This was a favorite trick of Standard Oil of New Jersey,

one of the larger corporate lenders to the call money market. The practice
became the subject of hot debate among bankers, brokers, and Fed officials in the late 1920s. The Fed well knew about the difference in rates but
saw little need to act upon it. Adolph Berle of the Federal Reserve Board
testified before a congressional committee in May 1928, "It may be that
there is such a considerable spread between the call rate in New York and
the Federal Reserve discount rate . . . as to put a temptation before the
member bank, if it has any money loaned on call in New York, to leave it
there and meet the demands of its local customers by rediscounting with
its reserve bank."[18] The banks were playing banker to the stock market,
along with many other companies that could not resist the interest rates
they could receive on what appeared to be minimal-risk loans.

But the question that has plagued the market for years after the crash
remained. Why did investors continue to buy stocks in the face of the rising chorus of critics who maintained that the market could continue to
fall? In some cases, prices exceeded five hundred dollars per share and
price-earnings ratios on genuinely speculative issues were 100 or higher.
At some time, prudence should have set in. Greed was certainly the answer
in the raging bull market, but it did have its structural dimensions nevertheless. For all of the critics who maintained that the Federal Reserve
Board was to blame, there were others who blamed the boom on the Federal Reserve banks, especially the New York bank. H. Parker Willis, the
first secretary of the board, banking adviser to several foreign central
banks, and professor at Columbia, put the blame squarely upon directors
of the twelve district banks: "They have sat tight and said nothing while
the 'small man' from Maine to California has gradually been led to invest
his savings in the stock market with the result that the constantly rising
tide of speculation at higher and higher prices has swept over the business
of the country."[19]

One of those directors mentioned by Willis also had an explanation.
The greatest stock salesman of his day, Charles Mitchell, provided another
answer, but no one was willing to listen. Prophets often are not taken seriously when the prophecies they help come true turn out to be more complicated than they seem on the surface. The designer of the financial
department store claimed that no one wanted to leave the aisles despite the
fact that someone began to smell smoke. The reason was the tax system,
which was proving too punitive for those who had already seen a profit.
While many pure speculators would buy and sell a stock quickly, others
sitting on large gains would not sell at a profit because they were unwilling
to pay the capital gains taxes. As a result, they often resorted to wash sales
and similar devices in an attempt to avoid tax.

When they could not take advantage of those techniques, they often
simply borrowed money against their stocks. The stocks were used as col-

lateral, enabling investors to hold onto them while borrowing substantial amounts of money against them. As long as stocks were considered good collateral, everyone benefited. Mitchell put his case succinctly: "The law has introduced scarcity values in stocks that have spelled high prices and it has created an enormous increase in the loan amount. . . . investors and speculators who have large profits in securities have been and are unwilling to liquidate and take profits, but go on holding these securities, leaning on the banks in order to do so."[20] The empire of paper assets was built by rising stocks, punitive tax rates, and the banks' willingness to extend loans based on stock for a few more percentage points than they could make by lending to an individual. Mitchell's solution for the problem was simple: eliminate the tax on capital gains. The argument was certainly more to the point than the convoluted arguments of the AAPA, but Mitchell's conclusion, reported in the *New York Times*, was not warmly received: "Let it be understood that this proposal is not advanced as a relief plan for the individual of large means. . . . Far outweighing all other consideration, however, is the fact that by this course it would be hoped that the key would be found with which to unlock the funds heretofore imprisoned in the stock market by a tax policy which discourages liquidation."[21]

One of the country's best-known and most highly paid bankers could not sway the public or Congress to his side. The idea that funds were locked up in the stock market was novel, to say the least, but would not win over the sympathies of congressmen from the South or Midwest. As disclosures later proved, most of Mitchell's market pronouncements were pure cant. Yet his argument does give some serious insight into the constant rise in the market. There was a substantial lack of selling pressure. Wealth accumulation appeared to be perpetual to many investors. But these conditions would not explain the frenzy of buying pressures that forced the markets to new highs almost daily, especially in 1928 and 1929.

Percolator Theory

One of the more simple economic theories of the twentieth century emerged in the 1920s. Called the *percolator theory*, it stated in no uncertain terms that the economic stimulus for society came from the top. Business stimulated society and government; rarely did the influence flow in the other direction. The latter usually kept well out of the way, and was expected to do so again despite the presence of the new Federal Reserve. Great inroads had been made by the federal government in controlling parts of business and industry, but in finance most of the major regulations were fairly recent. Government had made great strides in catching up with business since the nineteenth century, but events would prove that it was still one long step behind.

Alongside the percolator theory was the vision of the stock operator and manipulator making a fortune in the market using only his wile, or brilliance. Billy Durant, Jesse Livermore, Joseph P. Kennedy, Bernard Baruch, and scores of other well-known traders such as "Sell 'Em" Ben Smith and Michael Meehan were legends within the financial community and were envied by all who desired to become rich quickly. When they acted in the market, they inspired a following among others also desiring to become rich. But they, too, fit the percolator theory because it was generally assumed that they operated with "inside" knowledge of some sort or other. Such knowledge could come only from the top, from those who ran the companies whose stock they traded. As events would prove, this was only sometimes true.

Throughout the 1920s, most stock underwriting and trading was still in the province of the investment banks. The commercial banks remained committed to bonds of all sorts because they were clearly, if loosely, forbidden to engage in equities underwriting. But things began to change substantially in 1927 when the banks were given the green light to engage in equities underwriting. The Comptroller of the Currency, acting under the provisions of the McFadden Act, was given the power to allow banks to underwrite equities at his discretion.[22] After he did so, the new issues market for equities exploded, as did the stock market itself. New common stock issues increased eight times between 1926 and 1928, while new corporate bonds remained about the same. Stocks sold on the exchanges saw their turnover rate increase over two times. Loans made to brokers by companies other than banks trebled, while the index of common stocks also doubled. The comptroller's decision was certainly a boost for the stock market but did not have much effect upon the bond market. Charles Mitchell proclaimed that stocks had a place in every investor's portfolio because in some cases they were "as safe as bonds." What previously had been a bull market turned into a stampede. The bubble that was developing was the greatest ever seen in American finance.

Lost in the maze of what Ferdinand Pecora was later to call "New Era Frenzy" was a bit of regulation introduced by the Interstate Commerce Commission, in 1925, which required competitive bidding for new railroad equipment trust certificates. Any railroad wanting to put up its rolling stock as collateral for a bond had to ask investment bankers for competitive bids. It could not simply arrange the matter in private, as had been done previously. The bankers naturally howled in protest, but the ICC prevailed and now a small corner of the corporate bond market had the same sort of regulation as parts of the municipal bond market. Within nine years, the issue would rage again.

Hoover's victory over Al Smith in the 1928 presidential election was widely applauded as good for business and the market. The market rose in the weeks following the election, and a record number of shares changed hands time and again. Money continued to flow into the call money market from all parts of the globe, chasing the 12 percent lending rates that could be obtained for apparently doing nothing but helping to fuel the bull market. Previously critical of the market, Hoover remained silent in the months following his election, saying nothing that would dampen speculators' enthusiasm. His main adversaries, Al Smith and John Raskob, were left to consider their options for the future, although as two of the country's more vocal bulls, they had the market to console them against Smith's loss. Yet it was not long before the *Wall Street Journal* also joined the chorus of those expressing caution at the market's rise. It wrote, "It is time to call a halt in speculative activities because of their unsettling effect when they have extended out of Wall Street into every considerable town or city in the country. . . . It is not everybody who is built for successful speculation but it takes a check in a great bull market to disclose that important fact."[23]

A substantial portion of the economy was being supported by the wild rise in prices. Modern American consumer society, with its emphasis on excess, was born in the 1920s. Two automobiles were better than one, as were two radios and a host of other consumer goods. By 1929 Ford's production would surpass 3 million cars per year. Much of the marginal, or excess, spending was based upon the perception that economic life was getting better all the time. Most people looked to the stock market as proof of that. And few were willing to dissuade them.

The New York correspondent of *The Economist*, like many others, became wary of the bull market in the late winter of 1929. Responding to the Fed's inability to stem the rally, he wrote, "It is apparent that the Federal Reserve Board has once more failed to stem the flow of money into the stock market with half-way measures. Bullish sentiment has gained momentum . . . and the bull party is talking enthusiastically of its 'victory' over the banking authorities."[24] The "bull party" was not simply a figment of the writer's imagination. In 1928 various figures from business and finance had banded together to wage war on the Federal Reserve in order to keep it at bay. Intervention in the market to bring the stock rally to a halt was the last thing the bulls wanted. Numbered among the group were John Raskob, Billy Durant, and John Mitchell. Durant was especially hostile to the Fed, considering it an alien institution that had no place in American government. Because of his friendship with Hoover, he was encouraged by the others to make his views known to the president. He was rumored to have made a surprise visit to Herbert Hoover, bursting into the White House during an official dinner to denounce the board and suggest that it was leading the country down the wrong road. There is no record of Hoover's response to the intrusion.

But Mitchell in particular was the most notable dissenter. As a class A director of the Federal Reserve Bank of New York, he was the most prominent figure to denounce the Fed's attempts, however weak, to curb market speculation. In this case a member of a local Federal Reserve district bank of New York flagrantly thumbed his nose at the board in Washington. Pressure began to mount on the Federal Reserve Board to raise interest rates in order to cut down market speculation. The international deals cut between the Fed and European central banks in 1927 had caused an inflow of gold, and banks and companies from all over the world were loaning money to the call market. That was not the intent of the second central bankers' deal, but the strong market continued to attract investors from all over the world. By 1929 the bubble was rising to what seemed unsustainable levels. Shortly before his death in late 1928, Benjamin Strong had appointed Mitchell as a director of the Federal Reserve Bank of New York. In March 1929 the stock market began to fall, or "break," as the popular term for a sharp decline in prices at the time was called.[25] This exacerbated a situation already brewing between the Federal Reserve Board and the New York district bank. The board wanted the district banks to raise interest rates to their member commercial banks to cut down on the member banks lending to the call money market. The New York district bank had been in favor of a rise in the discount rate across the board to cut down on speculation. The New York bank's position appears to have been the wiser of the two. The board's position would have raised interest rates only for member banks, but a great deal of the call money being loaned to the market was from nonmember banks or large corporations that would not necessarily be affected by the board's proposal. The New York bank was beginning to look at the policies of the board with some disdain. And it did have some political support for its position. Congressman McFadden, sponsor of the banking legislation of 1927, stated in the House, "I do not think that the Federal Reserve System should concern itself about the condition of the stock market or of the security loan market."[26]

As the market began to fall in March 1929, the New York bank gave its approval for National City to add up to $25 million to the call money market to stabilize it and steady the stock market. Mitchell made the announcement of National City's intentions with characteristic aplomb, which would return to haunt him in the near future. He said that National City would add the funds regardless of the "attitude of the Federal Reserve Board." The results were dramatic. The call money market stabilized and the stock market stopped falling. A major crisis had been averted. Mitchell appeared to have assumed the role of the J. P. Morgan of years past in helping to calm a panic. He was becoming something of a Wall Street legend in his own right. One of the street's first fitness fanatics, he was known to walk the seven miles from his home in midtown to his office every day. But his detractors did not see his actions in a benevolent light. Carter Glass, indignant that Mitchell should openly fly in the face of the Federal Reserve Board, demanded his resignation. The *Financial Chronicle* sided with Mitchell, however. Acknowledging that Mitchell's public pronouncements were unfortunate, the paper still concluded, "Mr. Mitchell and his action has saved the day for the financial community. No one can say how great a calamity would have happened had he not stepped into the breach at the right moment."[27] The bull party won the day, but the agrarian interests and the anti–Wall Street crowd would remember Mitchell's action in 1933 when their turn came to express anger over the crash and the depression.

What was not apparent at the time of Mitchell's fateful announcement was that he was also helping a large stock position in which his bank had heavily invested. National City had invested in some three hundred thousand shares of Anaconda Copper Company with the intent of selling them to the public as soon as possible. But the market break intervened. Had it continued, the National City Company would have faced certain losses. The intervention prevented that from happening, although the Anaconda deal did not fare well for other reasons that developed later in the year.

Another significant position held by the National City Company also benefited from the announcement and may well have been the primary motive for Mitchell's feistiness in the face of the Federal Reserve Board. National City Company was actively trading the shares of the National City Bank, which stood at a lofty $785 in January 1928. Five months later they had increased to $940, boosted by the army of salesmen. A year later they stood at an incredible $2,000, three months after the call money crisis and National City's intervention in the market.[28] Mitchell and other senior officers of the bank were the major traders in the stock and profited from the rise. A good portion of their annual earnings took the form of performance-related bonuses in addition to salaries. Mitchell was routinely making over $1 million per year in bonuses alone. Such behind-the-scenes maneuverings made his pronouncements about interest rates seem rather slanted.

Over the years, the use of syndicates by investment bankers grew more sophisticated. As the underwritings grew larger, so too did the syndicates that bankrolled them. But special relationships existed within the syndicates. For years, Morgan, National City, and First National had an informal agreement that required whichever was leading an underwriting deal to allow the two others a 25 percent share of the business on the most generous terms. This helped ensure a steady source of revenue when times were good.[29] When a company or government decided to sell stock or borrow in bond form, the investment banker leading the deal would form a syndicate of other banks, buy the securities from the issuer, distribute to the syndicate, and then sell the new issue to the investing public. But a holdover still existed from the nineteenth century. The term *syndicate* was still used by professional traders to mean a group of investors who pooled their resources to trade in a particular stock; they were not underwriting, only speculating.[30]

The irrepressible Billy Durant also stepped into the argument by performing another civic-minded task designed to show the Fed the error of its ways. Speaking coast to coast on WABC radio, he told his listeners of a survey he had just conducted among five hundred top industrialists in which he asked them to declare themselves for or against the Fed's policy. Citing responses from 463 executives, he said that only 12 had supported the Federal Reserve Board's position. Claiming that the Fed's power was not accountable to anyone, he announced that a reform movement should be started. Assuming that the Fed had in effect caused the market panic, he also cited Mitchell's action as one of bravery rather than knavery: "For this patriotic offer he was threatened with excommunication. Senator Glass of Virginia, a member of the Senate committee on banking, demanded that Mr. Mitchell be removed as a director of the Federal Reserve Bank of New York. What an incident in American financial history!"[31]

The 1920s were the heyday of the investment pool. Traders and speculators would glance over the list of stocks they specialized in, looking for those whose prices could be manipulated in one way or another. Usually, the instigators of the pool operations were those traders who specialized in the stocks on the NYSE or one of the other exchanges. If an outsider organized a pool, he would need a trader who could be trusted, for the pool operations usually did not last very long. A pool was nothing more than organized stock rigging, and its intent, to be bullish or bearish, was known only to its members, and often not even to all of them. The blind faith that many pool members displayed only underlined the need for a trusted market operator. Usually, there was no shortage of them, for a price.

There was a fine distinction drawn between manipulation and outright rigging of prices. Although the practices were one and the same for all practical purposes, traders always drew the line for fear of criticism (or worse) from the exchange. The classic definition came from Edwin Lefevre, educated as an engineer, who later turned to the stock exchange and then to writing. "I do not know when or by whom the word 'manipulation' was first used in connection with what really are no more than common merchandising processes applied to the sale in bulk of securities on the Stock Exchange. Rigging the market to facilitate cheap purchases of a stock when it is desired to accumulate is also manipulation."[32] That was as true in the 1920s as in the days of Jay Gould, and the prevailing attitude was that the unsuspecting should be aware but were not really protected from price manipulation. In the percolator theory of applied economics, the traders were not at the top of the economic totem pole, but they certainly were higher than the general investing public.

Two of the best-known pools of the 1920s were organized for Anaconda Copper and for Radio Corporation of America, known simply as Radio. Anaconda was one of the first stocks to be underwritten by the National City Company after 1927 and had substantial Morgan backing. Several of the directors of National City were also officers of Anaconda, including Mitchell. The pool was managed by two floor traders on the NYSE, Tom Bragg and "Sell 'Em" Ben Smith. When the issue was first brought to market, there were already some doubts about the worldwide price of copper, Anaconda's major product. The price in Chile, where the company had much of its operation, was reputed to be falling, but that did not prevent National City from bringing it to market. Initially, the price rose because of the stock's backing, but shortly after the price began to fall. The general assumption was that the directors of National City already knew of the weak prices in Chile when they brought the issue to market. Even the pool managers were having trouble maintaining the issue's price.

Radio was run in the 1920s by David Sarnoff, who had made his reputation by being the first correspondent to report the sinking of the *Titanic* over the wireless. The specialist in RCA stock on the NYSE was Michael Meehan, a friend and acquaintance of the chairman, who thought the price of the stock was too cheap and decided to organize a pool to run it up. Such pools were not secret; they were usually accompanied by legal documents offering a piece of the pool to qualified investors. The stated objective could have been to buy or sell the stock short. Included in the Radio pool was John Raskob, subscribing for $1 million. Walter Chrysler of the auto company subscribed for $500,000. Also included were the wives of the other floor managers of the pool, Mrs. Thomas Bragg and Mrs. Ben Smith. Mrs. Meehan took a $1-million position and Billy Durant $400,000. Altogether the pool raised slightly more than $12 million.[33]

After a complimentary newspaper article or two, the stock began to rise and the price jumped from eighty-one to ninety-two dollars. It then rose again to over one hundred dollars when the syndicate began to pull out. The profits were enormous. The pool netted almost $5 million for its brief efforts, while those other investors who were short Radio at lower prices were badly hurt. In this case, wives' names were used to avoid any hint of impropriety by the floor traders. In most cases, pools were organized quickly and withdrew from their favorite stocks just as quickly. But when some pool members did not inform others of all their intentions, hard feelings developed that would contribute to the bear market after October 1929. Shades of Jay Gould and Daniel Drew could still be found on the exchange.

Best known as a pool operator, Meehan made another contribution to the bull market that was just the opposite of his specialty. He persuaded the Cunard Line to allow him to operate stock brokerage facilities from its ships for a yearly license fee. David Sarnoff of RCA provided the radio telegraphy needed to execute the orders. The NYSE quickly agreed to the proposal, eager to extend trading to all who cared to invest. Brokerage had graduated to the high seas. One of the first customers on board to execute an order was Irving Berlin who was en route to Europe.

Another popular investment of the day had a more appealing ring to it. This was called the *investment trust*. These pools of money were akin to what is known today as a *mutual fund*. Originally British inventions, trusts started to become popular in the great investment mania following the end of World War I. The managers of the trusts used investors' funds to purchase common stocks of chosen companies, opening a world of possibility for the small investor. For a relatively small amount, the investor was introduced to a wide array of common stocks, not just one. The management companies ranged from the highly prestigious to the highly suspect. Many of them failed quickly after having been snapped up by a hungry investing public. Others fared better for a longer period of time. J. P. Morgan and Company and Goldman Sachs organized some of the better-known trusts of the day.

One of the main appeals of the trusts was their ability to offer stocks to the public that were fast becoming unreachable by any other means. With the lofty prices asked for many stocks, small investors could not afford even one share of some stocks, but the trust idea allowed them to buy a piece of the action nevertheless. The 1920s in general were a period of consolidation rather than innovation in the markets. Many of the new stock issues that appeared in great quantities after 1927 were issues for holding companies that swallowed up smaller companies. Much of this consolidation occurred in the electric utility industry. The trusts then purchased shares in the holding companies. John Kenneth Galbraith has pointed out that there was a general shortage of stocks on offer during the latter 1920s because of the consolidation activities, and this also helped to push existing prices higher and higher.[34] Market conditions were ideal for new investment concepts, and many of the new trusts sold out immediately upon being issued.

Morgan created two of these large holding companies, which immediately dominated their industries: the United Corporation and the Alleghany Corporation. United was a holding company composed of public utilities on the eastern seaboard, while Alleghany was devoted to railroads. United encompassed a bevy of utility companies and was estimated to control one-third of all electrical power in the East. It was similar to the electric utility empire created in Chicago by Edison's onetime assistant

Samuel Insull. Alleghany was financed by Morgan and run by the eccentric Van Sweringen brothers of Cleveland. Like Jay Gould before them, they had purchased a bankrupt railroad and entered the business without putting up much cash. Originally property developers, Oris and Mantis Van Sweringen had developed Shaker Heights in Cleveland and became quite adept at leveraging their extensive holdings. They were introduced to Thomas Lamont at Morgan by Al Smith, who claimed, "I have had many experiences with these two boys. They are very capable. . . . I want you to cooperate with them in any way you legitimately can."[35] Within a few years, Lamont would come to regret his decision.

By developing holding companies and trusts, the organizers fared well despite the subsequent performance of the stocks. Management put the trusts together and devised an issue price that was invariably less than the offering price advertised to the public. With the appetite for new issues strong, the organizers made money simply by offering the shares, regardless of their performance afterward. Many also accepted common stock rather than cash as payment for the trust shares. They would devise a price for the trust shares to be paid in stock and accept shares from investors rather than money. What the investor did not realize was that he was swapping shares, which may have had some asset value for those simply built upon other shares, highly leveraged in many cases. This was another reason the stock market remained strong. Investors were liquidating for other investments without actually selling those shares showing a profit.

A good deal of the money used by those involved in pools was borrowed. Many senior bank officials borrowed money from the banks at which they worked and speculated on the company's stock through the pools. Technically these loans were not illegal, but many were discovered not to have been paid back. No interest was ever paid on many of them either. At one particular bank in New York City, the coyly named Bank of United States, the process was so flagrant that when the crash finally occurred, it appeared that the entire structure of the institution was set up simply to allow the directors to speculate with someone else's money.

Even at lofty levels, the stock market still had its supporters. Notable Republican politicians supported the market, while Herbert Hoover had less to say about market conditions in his first months as president than he did during his tenure as secretary of commerce. The ubiquitous Irving Fisher of Yale continued to believe in the strong market, based primarily on low interest rates. On the other side, Paul Warburg emerged as a leading doomsday forecaster along with Massachusetts-based financial forecaster Roger Babson, who was predicting a crash of significant proportions. As early as 1926, Louis Brandeis commented, "I wish to record my utter inability to understand why a lot of folks don't go broke. These consolidations and security flotations plus the building boom, beat my comprehension—unless there is a breakdown within a year."[36] All were derided for their "pessimistic" outlook on the market. Even A. P. Giannini of the Bank of America was having his doubts although the California banker had just recently purchased New York investment banker William Blair and Company and made it a subsidiary of his powerful Bank of America. His intention was to divorce himself from all dealings with Morgan and act independently of the very top tier of Wall Street banks. Some of the smart money took heed of the predictions and was starting to leave the market. Professional traders and investors saw the warning signs and heeded them more quickly than the general public.

In late summer 1929 the empire of British financier Clarence Hatry also began to fall apart. The flamboyant Hatry, who had originally made his name by transporting eastern European refugees to the United States and Canada, had built an empire of various enterprises, including retail stores, in Britain. In 1928 he made an attempt to gain control of United Steel, which accounted for about 10 percent of all steel production in Britain. The leverage he intended to use fell apart, however, and he made a last-ditch attempt to save his empire by visiting Montagu Norman at the Bank of England to ask for a loan. Norman flatly refused, sending the dejected Hatry back to the City of London to obtain the money he needed. The financing was never obtained, and Hatry's failure sent reverberations straight across to Wall Street in the autumn of 1929, just when the market was at its most vulnerable point.

An unheard-of refusal from the Massachusetts public utility authorities has also been cited as a primary cause of the crash. However, it had a strange ring of anti-Brandeis rhetoric of an earlier period. The Boston Edison Company was refused permission to split its stock. The authorities went even further by calling for an investigation into the utility company's pricing practices. Coming so close to the crash, the actions supposedly helped dampen enthusiasm for stock investments. In reality, the whole episode did little to contribute to the crash. It was the last gasp of companies that did everything possible to criticize outside interference in their affairs. Utilities' actions would be severely restricted within the next six years.

In August 1929 the Federal Reserve Bank of New York raised its discount rate by one point to 6 percent. The market reeled temporarily over a weekend before again assuming an upward course. This was one of the "breaks" in the action that many on Wall Street thought was only a temporary phenomenon, but it also created an odd situation not often seen in the financial world. People began to travel to New York to congregate around Wall Street as if they were attending a political rally or outdoor concert. The financial district had become the city's largest tourist attraction. Many traveled hundreds, even thousands, of miles to be where the action was. They cheered prominent Wall Street personalities as they arrived at work in the morning, applauding them for making so many investors rich and offering hope to many more average citizens that they too could be wealthy in a short time. Many had read about financiers and the stocks they touted in financial newsletters and from astrologers. One of the best-known soothsayers of the day was Evangeline Adams, who charged twenty dollars for her financial newsletter. She had no shortage of subscribers. Charles Mitchell, Baker, Lamont, and others became celebrities, considered by the assembled crowd to be financial geniuses. Wall Street began to resemble a pier where a large passenger ship was soon expected to dock. If it had not been apparent before, it was soon clear that the market was poised to drop precipitously. The small investor now considered Wall Street his mecca.

Market Cataclysm

There has been no shortage of interpretations of the causes of the stock market crash of October 1929. Some have been domestic, others international. Democrats of the period favored domestic explanations. The economy was already sliding into depression when the crash occurred, caused by stock market practices and shoddy banking. The Republicans favored international explanations, seeking links from the outside to show that the crash had foreign influences. Both interpretations are partially correct, but the crash owed its origins to one single factor. Wall Street itself was primarily responsible for the crash and the subsequent depression.

Throughout its history, the United States owed more to simple geography than to many other sophisticated factors. Even though there was never anything approaching a national banking system in the country, the link between the banks, first through the Banks of the United States and later through the large New York banks, was still uniting the country financially. The "western blizzard" of the nineteenth century was able to blow toward the East because of the links between the banks. British investors had been able to find investments, some in remote parts of the country, for the same reason. The rigid supply of money, jealously guarded by the eastern banks, had severe consequences for farmers during the panic of 1894. Jay Gould's audacious "gold corner" after the Civil War was felt throughout the country, not only in the gold market. The failure of Jay Cooke was a national disaster, not just for Wall Street alone.

As the stock market became larger and more sophisticated, especially after World War I, stocks began to take the place of bank savings for many. Even those who never played the stock market were still exposed to it because of the banks that loaned it money and accepted stocks as collateral. The banks, and later the market, unified the country as the railroads and

"The Goal" by Edwin Marcus, *Forbes*, January 1929.

the telegraph once had in the nineteenth century. Excessive speculation was creating inflated wealth and a sense of prosperity built upon borrowed money. It was also creating expensive money for manufacturers and farmers, who had to pay more for loans because of the high call money rates. Senator Smith Brookhart of Iowa pointed out in the Senate that "borrowed money will cost the farmer more in 1929 than it did in 1928, due to the high money rates enforced by the phenomenal industrial expansion and stock market turnover in the last five years."[37] Wall Street and the banking community were directly responsible for economic conditions as October 1929 approached. Any suggestion that they merely reflected the general state of the economy ignores their enormous effect upon the cost of money and human behavior in general.

The market boom meant that gold continued to flow into the United States from Europe as foreign investors continued to purchase American securities. Call money also continued to flow in from Europe and Latin America, including Cuba, in 1929 despite the lofty market averages. In bankers' terms, the country was borrowing short by taking deposits and lending long by allowing foreign companies and governments to borrow dollars and take them out of the country. This became a recipe for disaster because when foreign depositors pulled the plug, requesting their cash back from the banks and the call money market, the lenders had to scramble to find the necessary funds. When they could not do so, bankruptcy and closing down were the only alternatives.

And yet relatively few people had accounts at brokerage houses. When the tally was finally taken of exactly how many Americans had brokerage accounts in the early 1930s, the amount came to a meager 1.5 million out of a population of around 125 million. The stories about people from all walks of life betting on the market is true, but their numbers in relation to the overall population were relatively small. But the figure does not include institutional investors and banks, which accounted for the bulk of the trading. The market break, as it was known initially, was caused by the

"Airplane Warfare and Seesaw" by John McCutcheon, *Chicago Tribune*, 1929.

concentration of economic power at the top. It was the natural outcome of the percolator theory.

In 1928 Joseph P. Kennedy, the well-known speculator and founder of RKO Pictures, liquidated many of his positions, fearing that the market rally could not be sustained. Before doing so, Kennedy had walked into 23 Wall Street to meet Jack Morgan unannounced. He ostensibly wanted to discuss the condition of the market with the banker, assuming Morgan would see him because of his reputation. Seeing the senior banker without an appointment was a privilege not many Wall Streeters could exercise. Few were able to accomplish it, although Arthur Salomon, head of Salomon Brothers and Hutzler, was one of the few who could. Morgan refused to admit Kennedy, touching off a long-standing feud.

By early 1929, taking their cue from the March break, other speculators such as Bernard Baruch, John Raskob, and others were also beginning to liquidate their positions. Salomon ordered his firm to liquidate the margin accounts it had extended to customers. Bernard Baruch offered a piece of sagacious advice that helped explain why he remained relatively untouched by the market's fall: "Repeatedly in my market operations I have sold a stock while it still was rising—and that has been one reason why I have held on to my fortune."[38] He also urged bankers to form a pool to support the market in case it began to fall. He offered $6 million of his own money as a contribution but was turned down flat.

But those warning signs did not slow down the market. The New York Stock Exchange volume remained over 4 million shares per day for most of the winter and spring of 1929 until dropping back in the summer. All remained relatively stable until early October, when prices began to fall. Some stock prices were so high that the fall seemed all but inevitable. Measured by price-earnings ratios, the levels were extraordinary. Alleghany Corporation had a price-earnings ratio of 108, Goldman Sachs Trading Corporation, a large unit trust created by the investment bank, had one of 129, Columbia Gramophone's was 129, Cities Service's was 165, and National City Bank's was 120.[39] These were some of the stocks that would be hurt the most in October.

The market break occurring in March 1929, so adroitly averted by Charles Mitchell, turned out to be the first phase of the bear market to come. At the time, however, it appeared that the market was still healthy and poised to rise even higher. Mitchell proclaimed as late as October 16 that "market values have a sound basis in the general prosperity of our country." The dip in the market in early October was followed by a rebound before the selling panic began on Wednesday October 23. When trading closed that day, the Dow Jones Industrial Index stood at 305 on volume exceeding 6 million shares. The day before it stood at 325. The one-day drop of almost 7 percent left traders and investors extremely nervous. But the next day was to prove the most calamitous ever experienced by the NYSE. Thursday, October 24, was to become known as "Black Thursday."

Present in the visitor's gallery of the exchange on Black Thursday was a man whose policies four years earlier had contributed to the disaster that was unfolding by the moment. Winston Churchill watched the proceedings as the market completely lost its composure and was falling freely. Despite the enormous losses being incurred, Churchill observed in traditional understatement that the activity on the floor was taking place in an atmosphere of "calm and orderliness." By late afternoon the ticker tape was half a day behind and the back rooms of the brokerage firms and the exchange itself were having a difficult time keeping their heads above the avalanche of sell orders. Hours after the close, it was announced that the day's volume was over 12 million shares, a record.

By midmorning of Black Thursday, two groups met in an attempt to cope with the crisis. The Federal Reserve Board met in Washington, and a bankers' group met in New York at Morgan's headquarters at Broad and Wall. Of the two, the bankers' group was the more familiar with times of crisis. Included were Thomas Lamont of Morgan, Albert Wiggin of Chase National, Charles Mitchell, George F. Baker Jr. of First National, and the heads of Bankers' Trust and the Guaranty Trust Company of New York. As had been their custom in the past, they sought ways to bring the market out of its tailspin. Using a time-proven method, they committed a substantial amount of funds to the market in the hope that their buying power would be emulated by the investment community. But things did not work as well as they had in the past.

The bankers committed an estimated $130 million to stabilize the market. The press reported the amount to be substantially higher, recalling at the same time the rescue operation Morgan performed in 1907. The first buy order was performed on the floor of the exchange by Richard Whitney, president of the NYSE and brother of a Morgan partner. Whitney was known as Morgan's broker. The first stock he put in a buy order for was (naturally) US Steel, several points above the market price of $200 per share. Steel was the most actively purchased stock by the pool, accounting for some $27 million in stabilization alone. Other stocks supported were AT&T, Anaconda Copper, General Electric, and the New York Central, many with historically strong Morgan connections. The action, and others like it over the next several weeks, partially stabilized the market, which remained orderly for the next two days. Reassuring words flowed from all quarters, from the bankers to Herbert Hoover himself. Hoover made his famous pronouncement that the business of the nation was on a sound basis. But within another few days the slide began again. On Monday, October 28, the market fell heavily. Over 9 million shares were traded, and significant losses were seen in some major blue chips, including US Steel. Radio and Steel led the most-active list. Radio lost almost one-third of its value that day, while Steel lost about 15 percent. On the curb exchange, the leader in volume was Cities Service, losing almost 40 percent. The *New York Times* estimated that over $14 billion had been wiped off the markets' value.

The bankers changed tack slightly by stating that their actions were intended only to ensure an orderly market and that they had no other control over actual prices. However, some could not resist the temptation to cash in on the operation. Albert Wiggin of Chase began selling short during the intervention and continued to do so in the month after the crash. He sold over forty-five thousand shares short, buying at substantially lower prices when he covered. His total profit exceeded $4 million. Ironically, Wiggin even sold five thousand shares to the bankers' pool itself. Because he used his Canadian shell companies to hide the profits, he was also able to avoid paying tax on the profits.[40] His activities, even more than Mitchell's, gave banking and the stock market a bad name for at least two generations after the crash.

Tuesday, October 29, proved more disastrous for the market than the preceding days. Over 16 million shares changed hands, and the bankers' pool was already exhausted from its previous attempts to steady the market. The newspapers, which had been quick to point out five days earlier that the crash in prices was the result of inefficiencies in the back rooms of the brokerage firms, finally realized that a significant event had occurred. The *Minneapolis Star* reported that "the reaction came with the same abruptness as the one yesterday in which billions of dollars in value were lost." Thousands of margin accounts were wiped out, and when the account holders could not put up more cash they were liquidated, only adding to the drop in prices. *Variety* ran a headline that summed it up concisely: "Wall Street Lays an Egg." Within one week, significant losses were experienced from which some investors would never recover. The sidewalks were not perceived as safe anymore as the number of suicides increased and were well publicized.[41]

The Fed's actions during the crash were even less effective than those of the bankers. A rumor circulated on Black Thursday that the Fed had informed Thomas Lamont that it would lower the discount rate. But the action never came, and there were conflicting reports about its validity in the first place. The Federal Reserve Board lacked the leadership to impose its will, especially since the crash occurred in New York. Most of the financial district looked to the bankers for help, but even they did not have the financial wherewithal to prevent prices from dropping. One inescapable fact was rapidly emerging: no one individual or group was able to prevent the market from falling apart. There were too many stocks on the ex-

World

FINAL NEWS EDITION

W YORK, FRIDAY, OCTOBER 25, 1929.   IN TWO SECTIONS SECTION ONE   ★★★★★★ TWO CENTS In Greater New York | THREE CENTS Within 200 Miles | FOUR CENTS Elsewhere

TALIAN ASSASSIN MISSES HUMBERT IN BELGIAN CAPITAL

ttack at Tomb of Unknown Soldier on Day of Betrothal Stirs Two Nations

TALY DEMANDS ACTION AGAINST EXILED PLOTTERS

'rince Calm, His Fiancee Overcome by Emotion, Sobs in His Arms

Special Cable to The World

BRUSSELS, Oct. 24.—Crown Prince mbert, heir to the Italian throne, arrowly escaped death by a political ssasin's bullet here this morning, the ay on which he was one of the central figures in the public celebration of betrothal to Princess Marie Jose of elgium.

The shot which might have ended life of the Prince of Piedmont on anniversary his parents' marriage as fired at point-blank range of fif-en feet by Fernando di Rosa, one of own countrymen, an anti-Fascist oth of twenty-one, as the scion of house of Savoy was paying tribute Belgium's Unknown Soldier. It went ild because the quick hand of a motorcle policeman struck down the would-assassin's arm in the nick of time efore he could shoot again.

Brussels Outraged

russels was outraged by the attmpt on the Prince's life. It also rought immediate political repercus-ons in Italy, where demands were ade for extradition of Di Rosa and eassures against other plotters against Fascist regime. But the Prince remained calm, becoming the popular ero of two nations—Belgium and nly-by isolating upon going on with e ceremony which so nearly ended in eath.

"All's well that ends well," was his miling comment to the Count de ooperatife, Belgian Minister of War, hile the police were rushing off Di osa to prevent his lynching by an in-uriated public.

rincess Marie Jose was unable to ontain her relief over her fiance's scape from death. Sobbing with hankfulness she threw herself into the rince's arms as soon as she could ith his side after the attempt on his fe.

Their meeting took place on the steps he Italian Embassy here, which only ade the marks of recent anti-Fascist iding. Catcalls of the eyes of the eering crowds that had followed the rince there from the grave of the Un-nown Soldier who rushed up to him, ying hard to hold back her tears of ef.

Because of recent anti-Fascist monstrations in the Belgian capital recautions had been en by the authorities to forestall y such incident as occurred to-day.

Market in Panic as Stocks Are Dumped in 12,894,600 Share Day; Bankers Halt It

Federal Reserve Board Meets, With Secretary Mellon Sitting In, but Announces No Action—Rumors of Rate Cut

TREASURY, HOWEVER, FINDS BASIC CONDITIONS SOUND

Senators Renew Cries in Chorus for Sweeping Investigation of Wall Street Tactics

By Elliott Thurston
Special Despatch to The World

WASHINGTON, Oct. 24.—Reassurances from the Treasury that underlying business conditions are sound, an extended but unproductive meeting of the Federal Reserve Board attended by Secretary of the Treasury Mellon, and renewed cries from Capitol Hill for a sweeping investigation of Wall Street, came rapidly in the wake of the stock market debacle.

There were signs that when Secretary Mellon did the rather unusual thing of sitting in with the Federal Reserve Board at a meeting that began when the market closed and lasted for nearly two hours, some sort of statement was to be issued. Gov. Young emerged at the end of the meeting holding what seemed to be the statement, but it it was in had been vetoed. Nothing was said or intimated. The board kept its customary complete silence.

Rumors of Rate Cut

Rumors were going around that the rediscount rate might be cut back to 5 per cent. after the sudden full point advance that was intended but failed to halt the upward march of the market. Another rumor was that the board might announce credit would be available at tight points, if needed. This was meant to give a reassuring psychological effect like that produced in Florida by a similar announcement that halted the closing of banks there. The Treasury preserved an unshaken front of confidence, ascribed the latest cyclonic effects to technicalities, which appeared to indicate bear raiding, and heavily stressed the point that business is sound, and that even the worst spots, coal and textiles, have touched bottom and are on the upgrade.

Talk of Tax Cut

The tone of optimism was as strong that the high official who commented anonymously drifted into disturbing the hopes of ultimate tax reduction. He pointed out that such market upsets as the present one would have no effect on tax cut prospects, that the fluctuations of the market constitute a natural readjustment, that the mar—

Outside J. P. Morgan & Co.'s

By World Staff Photographer
Scene at Broad and Wall Streets During Stock Market Excitement. Insets Show THOMAS W. LAMONT, Morgan Partner (Left), and CHARLES E. MITCHELL, National City Chairman (Right), Who Turned the Tide of Selling

BUSINESS IS SAFE, FINANCIERS ASSERT

Leaders See No Economic Basis in Securities Panic

By Kenneth Campbell

"Considering the record-breaking earnings in many industries," said Lewis E. Pierson, Chairman of the Board of the Irving Trust Company last night, in commenting on the break in prices yesterday, "we may well remember that whenever fundamental values are lost sight of by the unthinking majority it is time for courage on the part of those investors who have a real sense of basic worth.

Mr. Pierson's opinion squared with

MEN ON EXCHANGE KEEP THEIR NERVE

In Face of Disaster, They Joke Amid Violent Scene

By Kenneth Campbell

The men of the Stock Exchange kept their nerve yesterday when the impending wave of financial disaster made the barricades of their money and running creak and totter about them.

They crowded the clamorous vaulted chamber 1,100 strong. It was as through the bear market had become a living, tangible thing. Elbow stood with feet wide apart and shoulders hunched forward as though to brace themselves

Richard Whitney's Cry of "205 for Steel" Halts Decline in Record Day's Disorder on Stock Exchange

EXPERTS TERM COLLAPSE SPECULATIVE PHENOMENON

Effect Is Felt on the Curb and Throughout Nation—Financial District Goes Wild

By Laurence Stern

The stock markets of the country tottered on the brink of organic yesterday as a prosperous people, gone suddenly hysterical with fear, attempted simultaneously to sell a record-breaking volume of securities for whatever they would bring.

The result was a financial nightmare, comparable to nothing ever before experienced in Wall Street. It rocked the financial district to its foundations, hopelessly overwhelmed its mechanical facilities, chilled its blood with terror.

In a society built largely on confidence, with real wealth expressed more or less inaccurately by pieces of paper, the entire fabric of economic stability threatened to come toppling down.

Into the frantic hands of a thousand brokers on the floor of the New York Stock Exchange poured the selling orders of the world. It was sell, sell, sell—hour after desperate hour until 1:30 P. M.

The Tide Is Turned

Then, in as dramatic a manoeuvre as financial history has ever known, the tide was magically turned by the organized power of the city's largest banking interests.

With prices at their worst and a buzz of rumors turning ordinarily sane men silly, a quiet group of financiers gathered in the austere offices of J. P. Morgan & Co., at Wall and Broad Streets. They included Thomas W. Lamont, Thomas Cochrane and other Morgan partners; Charles E. Mitchell, Chairman of the National City Bank; Albert H. Wiggin, Chairman of the Chase National Bank; W. C. Potter, President of the Guaranty Trust Company, and others.

No formal statement was issued. To writing newspaper men Mr. Lamont spoke words of reassurance—words dignified and restrained, expressing the calm views of men who refused to encourage panic by publicly recognizing it.

Behind the scenes a few simple orders were given, potent in the concentrated force of the money they represented.

"205 for Steel"

changes and the curb market (now the American Stock Exchange) and too much money in circulation for even $125 million to make much of a dent in prices.

One of the victims of the crash was Anaconda Copper. Prior to Black Thursday, National City was selling the stock to investors for as much as $150. When prices fell, the stock dropped precipitously, handing staggering losses to members of its pool, including Raskob, Durant, Al Smith, Bragg, and Ben Smith among others. Not all those participating in pools always made money, but price guarantees had been put in place for certain members by their bankers, unknown to the floor traders at the time. When this became known, some of the traders actively sought revenge upon the bankers by selling short in the marketplace until some of the stocks, including Anaconda, were trading at only a tiny fraction of their precrash prices. Short selling was used as a tool of revenge and would quickly become one of the best-known Wall Street trading techniques. Many would rail about it, from all quarters.

But the crash continued well beyond the original fateful days of late October. On the last day of October, the NYSE announced that it would close early for the weekend and work on Saturday to catch up with the paper backlog. During the crash, over a hundred thousand workers toiled around the clock to maintain some semblance of order in the record keeping. The commissions generated by all of the sell orders also helped many of the brokers keep afloat even as their customers floundered.

The market had gained a few points since October 29, and there was a feeling that the worst was over. The Fed then cut the discount rate, and the Bank of England did the same to prevent funds from escaping to Britain. Several companies also announced extraordinary dividends over the weekend in an attempt to attract investors back to their stocks. But the reassuring moves were short-lived. During the first week in November, prices were hit hard again, overcome by a wave of selling. The bankers' pool remained in operation but still could not cope with the selling. By mid-November the panic selling stopped. The market stabilized but at a much lower level than it had recorded only a month earlier. At the worst period of the crash, the Dow Jones Industrial Index had lost about 50 percent of its value, from 381 in September to 198 in mid-November, before rebounding back to 248. But the damage had been done. Several Wall Street myths had been dispelled, and the country was sliding into depression.

The financial supermarkets helped spread the news about falling prices and contributed to the spread of the crash. National City's vast network of private wires and sales offices meant that more customers were able to jump on the bandwagon than might otherwise have been the case. Size here was a negative factor. Good communications meant fast market reactions, and National City and the other large wire houses that once spread the gospel of getting rich quick now were inadvertently helping spread the word of imminent ruin.

Surprisingly, the brokerage community did not suffer as much as it had in the past. Previous panics actually took a greater toll on the investment community than did the crash itself. No major Wall Street firms were forced to liquidate, although many did suffer serious losses along with their customers. The losses were incurred on trading positions along with inventories of unsold new issues interrupted by the crash. But customers of the brokers fared much worse. The simple reason was that brokers liquidated their own inventories before they sold stocks for customers, getting in front of sell orders wherever possible (often known as *front running*). Many had anticipated a correction in prices and were poised to sell quickly. And many brokers were given extended grace periods by their banks, which did not call the call money loans extended to the brokers. The brokers, however, were not as kind to their individual customers, who were forced to pay or have their accounts liquidated.[42]

Late 1929 became a maelstrom for Wall Street. The effects of the crash, hardly finished, began to be felt rapidly as the economy began to slow down considerably. The last two months of 1929 witnessed some decisive government action. Herbert Hoover announced a 1 percent tax cut, designed to put more money into people's pockets. While that number sounds paltry in today's terms, it amounted to a 50 percent cut for some because the tax rates at the bottom of the scale were low to begin with. The Federal Reserve Board began easing interest rates in the hope that the economy would be stimulated. Hoover openly supported the policy and also tried his best to rally the country by appealing to all to work harder and avoid undue pessimism about the future. But society was swamped by events. American individualism and Wall Street folklore were soon to be relegated to the ranks of ineffective myths whose time had passed. But legends were not the only victims of the crash. The major casualty was the American financial system. Within a few years, as the depression deepened, Congress and the public would be looking for someone to blame for the country's problems.

CHAPTER SEVEN

Wall Street Meets the New Deal (1930–35)

These old Wall Street boys are putting up an awful fight to keep the government from putting a cop on their corner.

Will Rogers

The events of 1929 made an indelible imprint on the United States. Much of the faith that had been shown in markets, institutions, and politicians would quickly give way to skepticism and a longing for effective leadership. Bankers quickly moved from the pinnacle of public esteem to the bottom. Wall Street legends became symbols of avarice and greed, despised in all quarters. Those who once drew crowds of tourists on their way to work would soon lose those jobs after a public inquiry into their affairs revealed corruption and a total lack of interest in public accountability.

This did not mean that Wall Street was not going about its business. But business was dwindling. Tensions even developed between Wall Street traders and investment bankers as the floor operators realized that the top echelon of the banking business withheld trading secrets even from them. The old guard put a brave face on the declining economic conditions by invoking the myths of the nineteenth century. When times became tough, the larger fish naturally would swallow the smaller. But no one thought in late 1932 that soon a license would be required.

The crash produced some extraordinary gestures of generosity as well as some genuine tragedies. Samuel Insull, the Chicago utilities baron, provided personal funds to help cover his employees' losses in the market. Unfortunately, his empire was to collapse, leaving in its wake broken investors and calls for regulation of utilities. But for those experiencing prosperity before the crash, the events that unfolded in 1930 were a shock.

The stock market averages plummeted. New issues activity began to slow down conspicuously, and capital investment dwindled. Without capital investment, unemployment began to grow. Adding insult to injury, bank failures continued at an unprecedented rate. When banks failed, the savings of many depositors were lost in the process, never to be retrieved.

At first it appeared that the banking failures were simply a natural consequence of the crash. But on closer examination it became apparent that many were the results of massive looting by bank directors and officers who simply used their banks' money to speculate in the market or stole it outright. Fortunately, this phenomenon did not extend to the largest banks in New York or Chicago. Public mistrust of banks was not confined to ill feelings. Many voiced their displeasure by withdrawing money and hoarding it, causing severe strains in the banking system.

The idea of the rugged American individualist also was quickly waning. Herbert Hoover's well-known 1922 book, *American Individualism*, seemed somehow inappropriate only ten years later. Although the theme has managed to survive in the American psyche in folklore and advertising, it was doomed because it quickly became equated with runaway greed. Writing in *Harper's*, the historian Charles Beard best summed up the feeling of the times when he wrote that "the cold truth is that the individualist creed of everybody for himself . . . with investment racketeering at one end and labor racketeering at the other . . . is not applicable in an age of technology, science, and rationalized economy." His remedy was "stabilization, planning, orderly procedure, prudence and the adjustment of production." Senator Robert La Follette Jr. put it more bluntly in the *Nation*: "The bankruptcy of [Hoover's] leadership in the worst economic crisis in our history reveals the tragic failure of rugged individualism."

Within a short two-year period, the mighty indeed had fallen. The Republicans were in disarray, and bankers became the most maligned group in the country. Jack Morgan proclaimed in 1933 that private bankers were a national asset. On the contrary, many Democrats had begun to feel that they were a national liability and a danger to democracy. The sudden winds of change were prompted by a lack of direction from the White House and an equal lack of direction from the Wall Street community. Hoover believed that hard work and a strong individualistic ethic would set the economy aright. Investment bankers faithfully believed the market would rally, erasing the nightmare of 1929. Both proved to be misjudgments and carried a severe cost for the Republicans and the Street.

The market staged a brief rally in 1930. The Dow Jones indices began to rise from November 1929 lows and added almost a hundred points by April 1930. The bond market also rallied, and yields fell to lower levels. The number of issues listed on the NYSE actually rose before falling again the next year. On the surface, the markets appeared to be indicating an end to the economic slide, but the momentum could not be sustained. In the second half of the year the stock market again began to fall apart, much to the dismay of the Republicans.

The tensions between Washington and Wall Street that developed in late 1930 were the natural consequence of the crash. Politicians blamed Wall Street for the decline in the economy, while the Street simply shrugged its shoulders and wrote it off as just another depression (meaning what today is called a recession). Then the bandwagon began to roll a little faster. President Hoover denounced short selling as harmful to the economy. Many financiers wondered out loud if he knew what the term meant. Traders and investment bankers decried the lack of political leadership in Washington, while Washington caustically noted that bankers had no solutions for the economic malaise. Soon it appeared that Rome was burning and there was no one in sight to correct the catastrophe.

The social consequences were not long in coming. As the Great Depression set in, the rabble-rousing rhetoric of Huey Long and Father Charles Coughlin, the radio priest from Chicago, denounced elitism and advocated populist alternatives to social policies. J. P. Morgan became a favorite whipping boy of both. In a radio address in 1935 Long proclaimed, "Rockefeller, Morgan and their crowd stepped up and took enough for 120 million people and left only enough for 5 million for all the other 125 million to eat. And so many millions must go hungry and without these good things God gave us unless we call on them to put some back." Coughlin proclaimed via the airwaves that "today in America there is only one political party—the banker's party." Upton Sinclair would run for governor of California on a Socialist ticket. The presidential election of 1932 would reverse the Republican's ten-year hold on the presidency. In the congressional elections of 1930, the Republicans had already lost control of the House for the first time since 1916 and suffered a significant defeat in the Senate. Wall Street's response was predictably reactionary but muted. The one organized group to emerge from the postcrash period representing the top echelons of the financial community was the American Liberty League, the successor to the highly effective AAPA of the 1920s. The limited extent of the league's political success in the 1930s was an excellent barometer of the cynical public opinion concerning Wall Street, bankers, and industrialists in general.

Sophisticated economic ideas never troubled the Republicans in the 1920s. Simple ideas predominated and continued to do so even in the face of adversity, at least until 1933. What was good for business was good for the economy. The percolator theory did not die with the crash. The fact that much of business, and especially Wall Street, was heavily Republican made it even easier to make money. However, the top Republicans did not necessarily view Wall Street in the kindest of lights despite their similari-

ties. Many, including Herbert Hoover, viewed Wall Street investment
bankers in the same light as their Democratic opposition. They were considered the "anticompetitive" forces of the prior century. The Republicans
considered themselves representatives of a laissez-faire type of government where free competition prevailed. The percolator theory worked
well for those at the top. But those at the bottom got the grounds and depended on those at the top for the quality of the residue that trickled down
to them.

After a decade of being pushed into the limelight, no one wanted to
speak publicly for Wall Street after the crash. The simple pronouncements
of John Raskob and Charles Mitchell now were an embarrassment. The
age of hubris was over. People from all walks of life had overextended
themselves in a vain grab for riches. Quickly, the reaction was building.
Serious damage had been done to the American Dream by its greatest ex-
ponents. A new shyness from the public eye was being adopted by the
prophets of the 1920s. Nevertheless, the institutional bankers and securities men did not suffer much personal economic privation. They avoided
the limelight and continued their old ways. Jack Morgan donated one of
the *Corsair*s to the U.S. government. The 270-foot yacht was actually sold
for one dollar so the government could say it had been paid for rather than
donated. The annual upkeep of the boat would prove to be a problem for
Washington in the years ahead. On the other hand, Morgan had just com-
missioned a new boat, reportedly the world's largest and most expensive
private yacht. Its crew was larger than the staff of many small banks. Morgan's actions would soon cast him in the role of Nero, fiddling while the
system burned. Smaller investors who had aspired to wealth in the 1920s
boom were hurt by the crash, while the wealthy absorbed their losses and
carried on as they had in the past. One casualty of the crash, however, was
Michael Meehan's floating brokerage service on the Cunard Line, which
suspended operations in October 1930.

Wall Street did not produce much leadership during its darkest hour.
Partners of several Wall Street firms were quoted as lamenting the state of
affairs, but they did not offer any meaningful solutions. When asked by an
interviewer about solutions to the depression, Albert Wiggin of Chase
told *Time* that perhaps the Sherman Anti-Trust Act should be eased. Less
trust-busting would lead to greater financial stimulus, again from the top.
George Whitney of Morgan professed feeling inept when he was asked
why he had not done something constructive as the financial system began to crumble. Many followed a similar path, including Henry Harriman, who represented a utility company, an industrial group that would
be under the gun for much of the early and mid-1930s. Others simply decried the lack of what they considered "hard facts" surrounding the economic collapse, including Paul Mazur, a partner at Lehman Brothers and

an author, who went on record as saying he did not see what all the fuss was about.

Part of the skepticism concerning the extent of the depression was understandable. Many did not realize the seriousness of the economic problems the country faced. John Maynard Keynes wrote that many did not understand the enormity of the economic debacle that was unfolding or its historical significance. Nevertheless, those defensive responses, requiring "proof" of the depression by Wall Street's doubting Thomases, angered many in Congress who saw it firsthand in their constituencies and were more than happy to show Wall Street the economy's wounds. When the Senate hearings into stock exchange practices began in 1932, bankers would be in the public spotlight, but they never offered much advice on how to solve the country's economic problems. The depression was simply blamed on someone else. The lack of effective Wall Street leadership had been noted previously by Bernard Baruch: "When I first went down to the Street I was taught to respect certain great minds of those days. I found they were a pretty shallow set; in fact there were more overrated men in Wall Street than in any other street in the world."[1] The postcrash period did little to enhance their general reputation.

Ironically, American capitalism got a compliment from one of its most strident foes during the depths of the depression. Leon Trotsky, living in exile in Turkey, was interviewed by the *New York Times*. He stated unequivocally that he believed "the American hegemony's future inevitable growth will signify . . . the penetration of all our planet's contradictions and diseases into American capital foundations."[2] His comments basically repeated Lenin's analysis of capitalism before the Russian Revolution in which he begrudgingly admired the influence and power of the large American banks. The faith was not ill founded. For over a century, banks and the markets had provided the country with a framework that the federal government could not provide. The danger was that the framework was now showing serious signs of stress.

Sliding into Oblivion

One of the major casualties of the crash was the political career of Herbert Hoover. His 1928 victory over Al Smith was the culmination of a career dedicated to public service after an equally entrepreneurial business career. Originally a mining engineer, Hoover made his fortune abroad and by the time the war broke out was actively involved in public service. Having served as administrator for food relief in Europe under Woodrow Wilson, he became secretary of commerce under Coolidge. As early as 1920, he was urged by his friend Franklin Roosevelt to consider running for president. The first president to have his face beamed over the new, experimental device called television, he was at the height of his popularity in 1928. But by 1930 his star was quickly beginning to fade, and by 1931 his reputation and his party were poised for a massive defeat in the next round of elections. His political fall from grace would trigger changes in the very structure of Wall Street that no one would have thought possible in 1931 or 1932. One well-known anecdote concocted by the Democrats in the 1932 campaign had Hoover and a colleague walking down the street when Hoover stopped and asked if he could borrow a nickel. "What for?" inquired his companion. "To call a friend," responded Hoover. "Well then, here's a dime. Call both of them," came the reply.

The handwriting was on the wall fairly early. In December 1929 Billy Durant disclosed that he had warned Hoover about an imminent crash the previous April. Until that time, their impromptu White House meeting had not been made public. "I told the President how I felt about the situation and he listened with great interest. I believed that I was doing a service to the country and to the President himself in telling him what I believed was ahead."[3] Durant was still bashing the Fed, which he blamed for the crash. Someone else was to blame. Financiers were not taking the blame upon themselves. But Durant was putting Hoover squarely in the spotlight, making him look ineffective, especially since Durant had bothered to tell him what the source of the markets' problems were.

One of Hoover's colossal mistakes came in June 1930 when he signed the Hawley-Smoot Tariff Act into law. The tariff has been acknowledged as one of the major causes of the severe depression that followed. At first glance it appeared to be the very opposite of Republican principles. The GOP had always professed to be the party of laissez-faire economics, truly competitive in its principles. It also recognized the importance of international trade and capital movements. But when Hoover signed the tariff bill, he helped create a trade barrier that allowed the president to impose tariffs on imports so they would not have "unfair advantage" over American-made products. This was a clear attempt to protect American jobs from foreign competition as unemployment was rising. Over nine hundred items became eligible for the tariff. A month earlier, in May, a petition signed by a thousand economists had urged Hoover to veto the legislation, but he signed it nevertheless.

About the same time, Paul Mazur, a partner at Lehman Brothers and an advocate of international trade, published a book entitled *America Looks Ahead*. In it, he advocated increased international trade as preferable to tariffs, which would destroy American jobs and also hinder Europe's postwar economic development. But nothing could prevent the tariff from becoming law. It set off a wicked backlash. Within a year, over twenty countries enacted similar legislation aimed at foreign imports, and soon an international trade war was raging. What appeared to be an easy way to appeal to domestic voters turned into a major economic fiasco that helped make the depression even more severe.

The deteriorating state of the nation between 1929 and 1931 told a story of increasing woe. National income declined by over 30 percent, savings declined by 50 percent, unemployment rose fivefold to almost 16 percent of the labor force, and new housing starts came to an abrupt halt. Wall Street suffered, too, although it was offered few condolences. Stock market turnover fell by half, new issues of corporate securities fell by 75 percent, and broker's loans, once so popular, collapsed. Companies that once rushed to loan money to the stock market literally disappeared, leaving only the banks in their wake. A significant shift occurred in the voting population as a result. The Republicans lost their majority in Congress and the Democrats seized the presidency in the 1932 election.

December 1930 witnessed the largest banking fiasco in American history. The damage done by the failure of the Bank of United States (omitting *the*) to both depositors and the banking community was inestimable. Ironically, both in name and in scope, the bank was the epitome of what was wrong with the American financial system. Despite its grand, historical name, the Bank of United States was simply a local New York bank that had been preying upon immigrants in New York's garment district.

Nicholas Biddle would not have recognized his namesake institution, run by Bernard Marcus and Saul Singer, two former garment district entrepreneurs. The bank had over sixty branches and numerous affiliates. It was a member of the Federal Reserve but did not have access to any fed funds late in 1930 because it was already insolvent when its problems came to light. Most of its business was retail and it had a large number of recent immigrants, both Italian and Jewish, among its depositors. The uninitiated were easily beguiled by the operation, which displayed a large mural of the Justice Department in the foyer of its head office, festooned with flags. Marcus and Singer used many of the deposits to make purchases of their own stock, running up the price before selling at a profit. When the stock market would not always bid a high price, they sold their stock to their affiliate companies, cashing out at the bank's expense. Then came the crash, and the fall in prices wiped out their stock value, including the loans they had made to themselves in the process.

The New York banking authorities attempted a somewhat late rescue but were unsuccessful. Attempting to cobble together a rescue package of $30 million, the New York banking superintendent, Joseph Broderick, appealed to the New York banks for help but was refused. The Wall Street contingent appeared to have little interest in propping up a retail bank. After Governor Franklin Roosevelt ordered the bank closed, it was discovered that some four hundred thousand depositors had lost over $300 million. Some of the money eventually was recovered by depositors because the New York bank clearinghouse put up some funds to reimburse depositors. Federal deposit insurance had not yet been created by Congress.

Critics contended that Morgan and the Wall Street crowd could have saved the bank without much trouble. They pointed to the fact that the Wall Street firms had just banded together to bail out Kidder, Peabody, a firm that had been left short of funds after some precipitous withdrawals caused by nervous foreign depositors who withdrew funds because of the depression. The government of Italy and the Bank for International Settlements had both pulled out funds, leaving the old-line firm tottering on the edge. But bankers looked less favorably upon a retail bank, especially one run by outsiders that catered to immigrants. The failure of the Bank of United States was the largest in American history until that date. Significantly, it proved a harbinger of things to come. Marcus and Singer were sent to prison, and Superintendent Broderick was indicted for not acting quickly enough to close the bank. He was eventually cleared of misconduct charges. But the failure was to have an even greater impact that could not have been foreseen. The public, naturally distrusting banks, began to withdraw funds from banks around the country. The great "money hoard" had begun.

Other banking frauds had already come to light. The Union Industrial Bank in Durant's hometown of Flint, Michigan, had been systematically looted by its employees over the previous years. They used the funds to play the markets, and lost. But the largest banking failure was the straw that broke the camel's back for the country's banking system. As far as the public was concerned, the banks were no longer safe. And the saviors of the past were nowhere to be seen. There was no J. P. Morgan Sr. to step into the breach and hold things steady. In reality, the system was too large to be supported by private bankers. Individuals were not able to save the stock market. There was no reason to believe they could actually save the banking system either.

Herbert Hoover made a valiant effort to put things right. His plans to rescue the economy began in earnest in 1931. True to his style of consensus politics, he called to the White House twenty-five prominent bankers, including Thomas Lamont and George Whitney of J. P. Morgan, Albert Wiggin of Chase, and Charles Mitchell of National City. Hoover's plan was to forge an alliance between his administration and the banks in order to bail out the economy by creating a national credit pool, to be called the National Credit Corporation. The idea was to ask each bank to contribute $25 million for the rescue pool; the bankers, however, had different ideas. Despite the growing depression, they looked upon the credit pool as a bad idea, lacking collateral as well as a potential for profit. Some rejected Hoover outright, with little discussion. Others would pay lip service to the idea but put up no money, dooming the plan to failure. It would not prove to be the first time in the 1930s that banks would turn a cold shoulder to Washington.

Stung by the bankers' rejection, Hoover proposed that a government agency be established to provide the credit. Congress obliged by creating the Reconstruction Finance Corporation (RFC) in December 1931. Before the 1930s were finished, other agencies would be created to solve financial problems that Wall Street turned its back upon. The RFC's first chairman was Eugene Meyer, of the Federal Reserve, and its first president was Charles Dawes, recently retired from his diplomatic job as ambassador to Britain. Dawes was the ideal public servant, at least on paper, to sit on the RFC. His resume was perhaps the most impressive of any in government. He was also a banker with holdings in Illinois but had not been actively engaged in managing his bank.

Originally, the RFC was endowed with $500 million in capital and was meant to make loans to banks and other financial institutions, as well as to other industries in need of funds. While its aims were noteworthy, being a publicly funded institution did not always aid its objectives. One technical point concerning RFC loans was to lead to much further trouble for both Hoover and the banking system. The president originally persuaded John Nance Garner, the Democratic Speaker of the House, to keep the list of institutions that received loans from the RFC secret so that short sellers would not be attracted to them. Also, he was concerned that a public list of RFC loans would cause a run by depositors who might get wind of the loan and panic. Banks would receive discreet loans from the RFC without upsetting their depositors. This was particularly important because bank customers had been making large-scale withdrawals from those banks that were still solvent, hoarding currency instead of leaving it with institutions they did not trust. Stories about the Bank of United States, the Union Industrial Bank in Flint, and dozens of others had made depositors wary. Estimates of the hoarding exceeded $6 billion before Roosevelt restored stability to the banking system a year later. The lack of funds available to banks for lending caused a severe decline in the amount of money on hand, called "the Great Contraction" by Milton Friedman. Ironically, fear of banks made less money available, which only contributed to the lack of business activity. Secrecy seemed to be the best method to ensure some order. However, political connections came home to haunt Hoover almost immediately, destroying his plans.

Garner quickly reversed his position concerning RFC loans, and a few months later the agency was required to publicize its list of borrowers on a monthly basis. Bank runs and failures occurred at an alarming rate. Hoover claimed that Garner was acting irresponsibly, causing bank failures in the process. The financial climate was too fragile for depositors to trust banks. And the political climate was becoming more acrimonious than ever. It was clear that Hoover's proposals did not go far enough to satisfy his critics. He did not recognize the climate of public opinion that was building against his philosophy of government.

One of the early RFC loans was a $90-million facility extended to the Central Republic Bank of Chicago, headed by Charles Dawes. The loan represented almost 20 percent of the RFC's available capital at the time. Howls of protest arose in Congress, with cries of political favoritism heard everywhere. Lost in the melee was the fact that the directors of the RFC were chosen from both parties, so obviously Democrats had voted in favor of the loan along with the Republicans. One of them was Texan Jesse Jones, who would lead the RFC under Roosevelt. Jones later explained how the loan came about in the first place. The RFC advanced the funds to prevent the Dawes bank from failing, although it was solvent, fearing a run on other banks if it did not. In the end, the loan proved profitable to the RFC, which managed to earn $10 million in interest in the several years it was outstanding.[4]

Other RFC loans were made to both large and small banks, but the majority of its loans designated for financial institutions went to the major money center banks. The loans made to railroads also smacked of political favoritism. More than half of the original railroad loans were made to groups headed by Morgan and the Van Sweringen brothers, the two Cleveland railroad barons who had been closely involved with Morgan since World War I. They had put together the Alleghany Corporation, controlling several railroads, including the Missouri Pacific. Within two years, the corporation would be bankrupt. Ironically, the RFC loans made to it were used to pay back loans due to bankers, a ploy that distinctly violated RFC guidelines. Part of the money was owed to J. P. Morgan and Company. Harry Truman, then a senator from Missouri, later likened Morgan and the Van Sweringens to the railway bandits of the previous century. He claimed that twentieth-century bankers were more harmful to the railways than Jesse James had ever been. These relationships continued despite ICC rules attempting to limit the investment banker–railroad relationship that had been in place since the 1920s.

The railway problems and the power of the house of Morgan were again raised by Samuel Untermyer. The former counsel to the Pujo committee hearings of twenty years earlier was still a vocal advocate for controlling the money trust and protecting vital domestic industries from predatory bankers. As the depression deepened, many railroads were having serious financial difficulties, certainly not for the first time in their checkered histories. In a scathing speech delivered in Los Angeles in February 1933, Untermyer blamed Morgan for the railroads' current problems, citing the RFC loans to the Van Sweringens as proof. Assessing the bank's influence, he concluded that "in some respects J. P. Morgan & Co. has been a valuable asset to the country, but in others it has been a staggering liability." But his most radical proposals were to recognize the Russian government diplomatically while at the same time providing a mechanism whereby the railroads could come under some form of government control.

Untermyer's radicalism would soon be shared by many others. Among other things, he accused J. P. Morgan and Company of conspiring to involve the United States in World War I. The idea was not solely his.[5] Unfortunately, his ideas about possibly nationalizing the rails and recognizing the Russians would play into the hands of the ultraconservative right, which would quickly categorize anyone who even suggested such ideas as a communist. But it was his call to reinvestigate the money trust that rang most clearly. Although the term *money trust* was not as fashionable as it had been twenty years earlier, his plea did not go unheeded.

Hoover's Conspiracy Theory

During 1931 Hoover began his crusade against short selling. Believing that the practice was destroying the economy, he began to exhort the commodities futures exchanges and the stock exchanges to control the bears. Many corporate leaders from small companies also urged him to put a stop to the practice entirely. Their point was quickly adopted. Hoover urged the exchanges to make less stock available for lending so that short sellers would not be able to borrow shares to cover their short positions. Officials at the NYSE listened to his protests in the late winter of 1932 but did little in the way of meaningful reform despite the fact that Hoover threatened to regulate the exchanges if corrective measures were not forthcoming. Hoover remarked that "individuals who use the facilities of the Exchange for such purposes are not contributing to the recovery of the United States." He also urged the futures exchanges to discourage short selling in order to prop up prices of agricultural goods. Speculators had been earning strong trading profits by selling agricultural products short, correctly assuming that prices would fall.

The depression was creating havoc among farmers. Prices for their goods were falling so quickly that within a year it would no longer make sense for many crops to be harvested. Short sellers detected the trend and hoped to profit by the drop in prices across the board. Hoover blamed them for the phenomenon and saw a Democratic plot to discredit his administration in both markets. In his opinion, Democrats were conspiring to use the decline in values to paint his administration as inept. He was not entirely incorrect. "Sell 'Em" Ben Smith later confided that one of his motives for continuing to sell short after the crash was to cast the Hoover ad-

ministration in a bad light.[6] In that respect, the administration did not require much help. Unemployment was rising rapidly. Many of the poor and
homeless took to living in large shantytowns known as *Hoovervilles*. One of
the largest was located on the West Side of Manhattan along the Hudson
River. In better days, the same area was a vantage point for sightings of the
yachts of businessmen, including Jack Morgan. But Hoover, who steadfastly refused to believe that his policies were having a negative effect, continued to blame the country's economic woes on external factors ringing
with conspiracy.

The central part of Hoover's conspiracy theory came to light in 1932.
Secretary of the Treasury Ogden Mills and Eugene Meyer of the Federal
Reserve Board planned to use open market operations by the Fed to stimulate the banks and the markets, putting an end to the depression. They
planned to have the Fed buy government securities in the open market. By
doing so, the Fed would inject badly needed cash into the financial system.
The banks would then use that cash to make loans in an effort to give the
economy a much-needed boost. Hoover was in favor of the plan. Unfortunately, it did not work exactly as anticipated. The operation was not successful, partially because bankers knew it was coming and adjusted their
prices accordingly. And the added funds did not do much good in the
banking system because business activity was slowing down and demand
for loans was not strong to begin with. But the failure set off an even
greater problem for Wall Street. Hoover now believed that an international plot was afoot to discredit the American markets and his administration in the process. This had little to do with putting more cash in the
hands of banks but everything to do with the gold standard.

By putting more cash in the hands of banks, the Fed also lessened the
possibility that foreigners would demand cash quickly, eventually pulling
the United States off the gold standard. The British had abandoned the
standard only months before. As Hoover noted, "On February 7, 1932,
Secretary Mills informed me that the gold situation had become critical,
and that there was an immediate danger of not being able to meet foreign
withdrawals which were going on at the rate of $100 million a week."[7] In
response, Hoover called in key congressmen, including Carter Glass, and
pushed for a bill enlarging the powers of the Fed. The result was the first
Glass-Steagall Act of 1932 (not to be confused with a bill of the same name
passed a year later). Banks would now have additional funds, and the gold
standard would be secure.

But when the operations failed, Hoover saw conspiracy, and not without good reason. Writing anonymously at the time, Clinton Gilbert, a
highly regarded political correspondent for the *Philadelphia Public Ledger*,
recalled that Hoover "apparently believed a fantastic story. European capitalists had supplied much of the cash needed to engineer the greatest bear

raid in history. These proverbially open-handed and trusting gentlemen had accepted the leadership of New York's adroit Democratic financier: Mr. Bernard Baruch."[8] The old specter of foreigners controlling the American markets was raised again, with its convenient Jewish connection added. Hoover and Baruch had been rivals of sorts ever since their days as heads of relief agencies during World War I, so the idea was not totally absurd from the president's viewpoint. Baruch had suffered similar indignities before. In 1920 Henry Ford accused him of engineering a massive Jewish plot to control the world during the war. Ford, writing about the scope of "Jewish dictatorship" in the United States, claimed in his Michigan newspaper that Baruch was behind a conspiracy. Baruch himself later related that "similar attacks were picked up and mounted by the Ku Klux Klan, Father Charles E. Coughlin . . . to say nothing of Joseph Goebbels and Adolf Hitler."[9] He somewhat kindly attributed it to the anti-Semitism of the times. The latest conspiracy theory was passed to Hoover by Senator Frederick Walcott. The fear that it could discredit his administration prompted Hoover to action, attempting to control the bears.

Despite the attempts to stimulate the economy, the depression continued. Convinced that bear raiding was at least partially at the heart of it, Hoover asked Congress to investigate the stock exchange in late February of 1932. A week later the Senate Banking and Currency Committee complied when Senators Peter Norbeck and Walcott arranged for hearings to probe stock exchange practices. The great bear hunt had officially begun. Wall Street again was becoming the focus of unwanted attention, more so than at any time in its history. The outcome would change the way business on the Street would be done for generations.

Critics of the hearings contended that the economy was in such bad shape that a scapegoat was needed. As far as the economy was concerned, it was certainly in the worst shape in history. In 1932 the country's gross national product was at about 60 percent of its 1929 value, unemployment was almost 40 percent, and stock prices had plunged to about 10 percent of their precrash values. And the dire figures were beginning to take an even greater social toll. Social tension was simmering just below the surface. Although Hoover tried to stimulate the economy, he consistently vetoed any plans that attempted to put more cash in the hands of the population. The United States was running a fairly sizable budget deficit, and Republican thinking held that spending had to be held to a minimum. As far as the public was concerned, the president was simply standing in the way of an end to the depression.

Despite the open market purchases by the Fed and the loans made by the Reconstruction Finance Corporation to troubled banks, the general population was mired in the depression. In May 1932, one of the more embarrassing moments for Hoover's administration came when the Bonus March on Washington was organized. After World War I, a bonus to veterans had been promised, and payments had been actively sought by veteran's groups ever since. Requesting the bonus during Hoover's administration was premature since the veterans were not yet eligible for payments, scheduled for a few years later. But Hoover steadfastly refused to pay, citing the budget deficit and contending that the $2.5 billion in payments would have bankrupted the federal government.

As a result, veterans began to assemble nationwide and marched on Washington, reminiscent of Coxey's army of the 1890s. After the veterans stubbornly made their demands, the U.S. Army was dispatched to break up their encampment in the District of Columbia. The army, led by General Douglas MacArthur, George Patton, and Dwight Eisenhower, broke up the assemblage but not without incident. A detachment of marines sent to break up the crowd laid down their arms, refusing to march against unarmed fellow citizens. Unfortunately, an infant of one of the marchers was killed in the tear gas attack and cavalry charge. The newspapers had a field day with the news, which severely embarrassed the Hoover administration, now being portrayed as totally unsympathetic to the plight of the working man. The *New Republic* proclaimed that "the army in time of peace, at the national capital, has been used against unarmed citizens—and this, with all it threatens for the future, is a revolution in itself."

The Bear Hunt Begins

Wall Street was almost wholeheartedly against the Senate investigation. Its opposition came at a critical time for Hoover's presidency since 1932 was an election year. The president's popularity was continuing to slide. During the spring and summer of 1932, even Calvin Coolidge showed little inclination to support his former secretary of commerce, preferring to spend what were to be his last days on the sidelines. Bloodied but unbowed bonus marchers and renegade financiers dotted the newspapers and radio news, adding to the growing feeling that Hoover was out of touch with the country.

The conspiracy theories finally produced a reaction. The Senate hearings began on April 11, 1932. Senator Brookhart hurried them in order to forestall what many believed would be a great bear raid to begin about the same time. The conspiracy notions were not without foundation. On April 8, 1932, the French government seized a financial newsletter called *Forces*, written by Marthe Hanau. The publication was actively dedicated to eroding the financial standing of the United States by publishing information designed to instill panic in foreign investors, still a force to be reckoned with in the American markets. Hanau had a sketchy history in finance, having previously served prison time for running a bucket shop in Paris. The French charged her with being the agent of Russian and German elements committed to forcing down the Paris bourse and with it the NYSE. If the bourse declined, French investors would be inclined to sell their American holdings, eventually forcing the United States off the gold standard. The whole affair was reminiscent of communist guerilla theories about waging economic warfare against capitalist countries, written a generation before.

The plot thickened on April 7 when the Paris newspaper *L'Ordre* published an erroneous report that the National City Bank had suspended operations. It was the only newspaper in France to publish the story, and after quick pressure from the governments of France and the United States, it published a retraction the following day. Almost simultaneously, Senator Brookhart had assembled the full committee for the beginning of the Senate investigation. When asked by a reporter whether the recently published report from Paris about National City had anything to do with his haste, Brookhart replied that there were "a great many factors" behind calling the committee at that precise time. But reporters continued to press him further on the day of the hearings. One of many reporters covering the opening day of the hearings inquired, "What prompted the committee to meet so suddenly?" "Read the papers" was Brookhart's terse response. "Do you mean under a New York or a Paris date line?" the reporter continued. "Read both," came the reply.

Later Brookhart explained his motives in more detail: "There was no special information about foreign withdrawals but I have a confidential report that says they could put us off the gold standard in sixty days if they wanted to."[10] It was not clear whether the "conspiracy" as such was against the American stock exchanges or against the dollar. In recent weeks the greenback had been the object of intense currency speculation. The United States could have been forced off the gold standard by a run against the dollar more readily than a run on the stock markets. The economic fundamentals of 1932 made this highly probable without the help of any conspiracy theories. The economy was at its low point in the first quarter of the year, the RFC was coming to the aid of an increasing number of banks, and the stock market had hit rock bottom. Since the depression was hitting the United States harder than Europe, it was not surprising that foreigners would divest of some of their American investments.

Whatever the nature of the "conspiracy," it was certainly taken seriously by those in power. Brookhart and his Senate colleagues denied time and again that Hoover's desire to investigate the stock market had anything to do with their own investigation. They also stated that they were not keeping the White House informed of their progress, as was commonly assumed. But they all shared the common desire to see short selling investigated and wanted to see the list of those who were selling short and whom they represented.

In the nearly two years of on-and-off testimony, the investigators would hear from Wall Street's elite. Witnesses ranged from the heads of securities houses and banks such as Morgan, Wiggin, Mitchell, Clarence Dillon, and Otto Kahn to the prominent traders, including Meehan and Ben Smith. But continuity was lacking in the first year and the hearings had several chief counsels. The first was Claude Branch, who served for three months. The second was William Gray, followed briefly by John Marrinan. Only after Ferdinand Pecora took over the legal reins in late January 1933 did the meetings become more clearly focused. Although the hearings borrowed his name and became known as the Pecora hearings, the report that followed was named the Fletcher Report, after Senator Duncan Fletcher of the Senate Banking Committee.

The first witness to appear before the hearings was Richard Whitney, president of the NYSE and brother of George Whitney at Morgan. A former Morgan man and an East Coast Brahmin, he had attended Groton and Harvard and was a member of all the proper New York clubs. In his view, speculation was the cornerstone of American capitalism and the foundation of the NYSE. Without it, the exchange would be useless economically. He characterized Hoover's assertions about the deleterious effects of short selling as ridiculous. His position reflected that of most traders but certainly not all investment bankers. Short selling meant that sellers would ultimately have to buy back the stocks they sold, providing buying power for the exchange. This bit of circuitous logic rivaled Charles Mitchell's pronouncements in the 1920s about tax reform. Later on in the hearings, Otto Kahn of Kuhn Loeb took a much dimmer view of short selling. "The raiding of the stock market, the violent marking up and down of other people's possessions is in my opinion a social evil," he stated uncategorically to the committee.[11] His view was shared by most politicians and some other bankers as well.

Due to a hastily organized program, Whitney originally had his way with the committee. Carter Glass, a member, admitted that the proceedings were going nowhere within the first couple of days. In order to liven up the affair, Mayor Fiorello La Guardia of New York was called to testify. He had information vital to the committee, although his role was otherwise strictly on the fringes. La Guardia produced a suitcase full of proof that a publicist named Newton Plummer had paid almost $300,000 over a ten-year period to various journalists. Plummer was operating for the pools and had written articles about numerous companies that were not quite accurate but certainly flattering to them. The stories were then fed to the journalists, representing all of New York's major newspapers, who published them for a price. Despite the efforts made in the past to clean up "planted stories," the practice continued in the 1920s when the stakes were high. As a result, the hearings received a much-needed shot in the arm.

Later in the month the investigation turned its attention toward pools and investment trusts. Testimony followed about the RCA pool and the inflated prices and practices of the Goldman Sachs Trading Corporation. Goldman's investment trust company came under sharp criticism. Organized in 1928, it was originally capitalized at $100 million, with 90 percent of that amount being supplied by the public. Over the next four years it managed to lose over $60 million so that by early 1932 it was trading at only $1.75 per share.[12] The investment trusts managed by Dillon Read also came under severe criticism since control of them was wrested away from the public by the managers through a series of artful maneuvers after investors had put up the funds to float them in the first place. These revelations titillated the public. Although no conspiracy to drive the United States off the gold standard was ever uncovered, the stories about the pools and the financial losses of many popular celebrities (including Eddie Cantor, who had participated in the Goldman operation) caught the public's fancy. The bear hunt was not a passing phenomenon: it was proving to be good theater and was inspiring the public's wrath.

The hearings brought to light statistics about Wall Street that many brokers would have preferred not to have been made public. The most notable was the amount of commission revenues the brokerage business generated between 1928 and 1933, supposedly depression years. The members of the exchanges generated $1.6 billion in revenues, averaging about $300 million per year. The New York Stock Exchange member firms generated most of it, while the New York Curb Exchange and the twenty-seven other smaller, regional or local firms accounted for the rest. On top of that was another $325 million made by charging interest on margin accounts. Much of the margin interest was paid by short sellers since selling was far more popular than buying during that time. The total income of Wall Street commission business, before taxes, during that time amounted to $2.4 billion, including other forms of revenue such as underwriting.[13] The combination of brokerage fees and margin interest received was certainly high but would be exceeded in later decades.

The revenues would not help the image of brokers and investment bankers, who were seen to be profiting while the public suffered from poor investments sold to them. But Wall Street suffered with the public. By 1931, several notable firms had failed and the number of brokerage offices was starting to decline substantially. The crash brought down Kidder, Peabody and Company, which was only reorganized with the aid of a $10-million loan put up by Morgan and a number of other banks. Pynchon and Company, another firm founded in the late nineteenth century, failed as well, becoming the second-largest failure in Wall Street history after Kidder. The postcrash period witnessed the demise of sixteen member firms and over three hundred national sales offices. On balance, however, the damage was not as severe as in other postpanic periods, which only added credence to the idea that Wall Street was taking advantage of the fall in prices to make even more money while the investing public suffered the brunt of the depression.

The flood of statistics coming from the Senate hearings only added to that impression. The most damning practice uncovered was the activity of specialists (those who made markets on the floor of the exchanges). Because of their central location and functions, specialists were able to control the flow of orders in a stock and manipulate its price. The hearings showed that some stocks on the exchanges had over a third of their volume traded by their specialists for their own accounts. Thus the specialists were in a privileged position to see prices before executing for the public and would often act for themselves before filling an order from the public being executed through a floor broker.

But ironically, it was not the activities of brokers that would cause the greatest sensation during the hearings. The subsequent activities of investment bankers came to the surface when Ferdinand Pecora took over the reins of the committee. Crash stories and brokers' manipulations were essentially general news, but when individual bankers were connected with the dismal economic conditions, the stories took on a more personal note. Those revelations would make them the most hated professional group in the country.

Bond Defaults

Stocks were not the only major casualties of the crash. Many of the corporate and foreign bonds sold to an unwary public as safe investments turned out to be extremely risky. Another reason for the public's wrath against bankers was that 1932 was a banner year for bond defaults, which were destroying many savers' investments and weakening the banking system even further. In their great rush to "manufacture" securities, using Mitchell's unfortunate phrase, the bond underwriters often overlooked some very basic facts when bringing new issues to market. These oversights created as much trouble for them in the long run as the market crash itself.

Foreign bonds sold to American investors were some of the main casualties of the postcrash period. Most were bought not by large institutions but by small investors. Before his death Dwight Morrow, former Morgan partner, ambassador to Mexico, and senator from New Jersey, analyzed several foreign bond issues in an issue of *Foreign Affairs*. His conclusion was fairly startling at the time:

> When we talk about the person who is investing in foreign bonds we are not talking about a great institution in New York or Chicago or Boston. We are

talking about thousands of people living in the United States . . . about school teachers and Army officers and country doctors and stenographers and clerks. . . . he is a person who has saved something, who has done without something today in order that his children may have something tomorrow.[14]

The losses came about because of deceit or fraud. Kreuger and Toll bonds were virtually worthless because Ivar Kreuger had substituted the collateral that originally backed them. The bonds were originally backed by French government bonds, which Kreuger slipped out by substituting Yugoslav government bonds in their place. By the time the depression began, the Yugoslav bonds were virtually worthless, and the bondholders suffered the losses when Kreuger's enterprises began to fail. Donald Durant, a Lee, Higginson partner and the only American director of Kreuger and Toll, proclaimed no knowledge of the company's finances. He admitted to the Senate subcommittee that he had never attended any of the company's board meetings. Lack of responsibility was becoming the byword of financiers as the Senate revelations unfolded.

Because of Kreuger's sleight of hand, Congress eventually passed the Trust Indenture Act in 1939, a little-known but still valid piece of legislation that governs the behavior of bankers when collateral is involved in borrowings. Kreuger did much to help fashion the governance of trust relationships in this country ever since. Without the trust act, many later forms of Wall Street financings would never have developed.

Fraud was not limited to corporate bonds such as those sold by Ivar Kreuger's enterprises. Many Latin American government bonds also lost a substantial part of their value as every Latin American country except Argentina ran into serious financial difficulties. The notorious Peruvian bonds were the best-known casualties. Rumor had it that aggressive investment bankers at Seligman bribed the son of the president of Peru to have the bonds issued despite the country's poor financial condition. When the economic downturn began, the bonds naturally dropped in value, falling from par to only 5 percent of their value. The *New York Times* ran a story illustrating the price history of the bonds following their calamitous fall from grace. In the Senate subcommittee hearings, officials from the National City Company, one of the underwriters, admitted that the finances of Peru were perilously weak but maintained that this knowledge came to light only after the fact. The only person benefiting from the bonds was the president's son, who was reputedly paid $500,000 to have them issued in the first place.

One of Charles Mitchell's pet issues at the National City Company also caused a great stir after the crash. In 1928 the bank had arranged a $16-million bond issue for the Brazilian state of Minas Gerais. When the issue was arranged, Minas was already on the ropes, having a difficult time paying its existing bondholders, but that did not deter National City. The bond was probably the best example of National City "manufacturing" new securities. The state was portrayed in glowing terms in its sales literature and sold to a hungry investing public. About the same time, in a limp attempt to dissuade investors from putting too much cash into the stock market, Secretary of the Treasury Andrew Mellon stated in 1929 that investors probably should confine themselves to bonds rather than overpriced stocks, giving a boost to the bond market as a whole. National City was only happy to oblige by bringing as many new issues to market as possible.

Most of these bonds were sold to small investors through the National City Company. The Pecora hearings invited one, an Edgar Brown of Pennsylvania, to testify. In 1927 Brown had invested $100,000 with the National City Company, to be placed in bonds. Not being particularly sophisticated, Brown incorrectly assumed that his money would be invested in quality issues. He was mistaken. His broker bought mainly German, Peruvian, Chilean, Hungarian, and Irish bonds instead. Brown also was encouraged to buy on margin so that he accumulated $250,000 worth rather than only $100,000. When they began to drop in the market, Brown complained, but to no avail: his broker began to buy him stocks instead. When asked by Pecora whether the broker bought many stocks for Brown's account, Brown replied vociferously, "Might I answer that facetiously? *Did he buy stocks!*"[15]

But the worst was still to come as the number of bank failures increased dramatically. The American financial system was on the verge of collapse. The most surprising element was that the measures taken by the Hoover administration in 1930 to end the crisis were not proving particularly effective. Some commentators were quickly coming to believe that Hoover was as much a national liability as the investment bankers. During the election of 1932, shopkeepers were known to hang signs outside their stores, soliciting business with the threat that if consumers did not shop with them they would be forced to vote for Hoover again.

In the midst of the bond market's woes, J. P. Morgan and Company planned a support operation to prop it up. An operation called "Stars and Stripes Forever" was mounted by Morgan and thirty other banks, pledging $100 million to support the market. Their plan was to buy high-quality bonds in the market, leaving the poorer-quality ones to fare for themselves. Although it sounded very patriotic, the support group was rumored to have made more than a fair profit on the operation when it finished. Many of the bonds the banks purchased were those they had underwritten several years before when the bond business was booming. There were many opportunities for investment. During the latter 1920s and early 1930s, Kuhn Loeb alone had underwritten a staggering $1.6 billion of new bonds, twice Morgan's total. The support group certainly knew which bonds to buy. But politics were never far away. In response to the Senate hearings, Thomas Lamont touted the operation's patriotic nature and threatened to disband it if the Senate hearings were not cancelled, hoping to bring Hoover to heel. But Hoover remained firm, and the threat was never carried out as the hearings continued.[16] But Hoover made little political capital from the support operation because it was not clearly in the public eye. Again, it would have drawn the ire of critics only if Morgan and the banks again were seen making a profit while the economy floundered.

One of the depression's victims was Ivar Kreuger, the Swedish match king and swindler extraordinaire. Many of his affiliated companies were badly hurt by the crash and depression, especially since much of their cash and collateral had already been looted in better times. In March 1932 Kreuger committed suicide in Paris after learning that his companies were effectively bust. The Paris police provided a service by not reporting his death immediately, at least not until the NYSE was closed later that day. Although the full extent of Kreuger's dealings was not known for some time, his death badly affected the markets. Lee, Higginson and Company, his main American investment bankers, were in the dark concerning his financial dealings even at the end. The world mourned him as a financial genius lost forever. His death did little to calm jittery foreign investors because it occurred just before the Paris revelations that inspired the bear hunt in the first place.

The Political Tide Turns

The Senate hearings began to wind down as summer approached and the Democrats met at their convention to choose a candidate to oppose Hoover. No one candidate mustered enough votes in the early rounds to ensure a place on the November ballot, although Franklin Roosevelt was the leader in the voting. As the delegates began to bargain among themselves for the later rounds of voting, bankers entered the nomination contest. Their influence proved a negative factor. After the third round of voting by the delegates, Roosevelt still had not gathered enough votes to be declared his party's candidate. Sensing a deadlocked convention, many delegates began to turn to Newton Baker as their dark-horse candidate. Baker had been Woodrow Wilson's secretary of war and was one of the privileged on Morgan's preferred lists. If the convention stalled, he appeared to have the support necessary to garner enough votes to win. To support his candidacy, his partisans organized a telegram campaign aimed at undecided candidates. Unfortunately, most of the telegrams came from the financial community and from those employed by, or representing, public utilities—not two of the most popular industries in the country at the time. The delegates became so outraged that Baker's prospects dimmed from that moment.[17] In the next round of voting William McAdoo, another potential candidate and member of the Street's preferred lists, cast California's pivotal votes in favor of Roosevelt, putting him over the top for the nomination.

After Roosevelt secured the nomination, the ideological tone of the campaign began to take shape. Accepting his party's nomination, he proclaimed that "this is more than a political campaign; it is a call to arms." The New Deal began to form ideologically and practically as Roosevelt and his advisers fashioned a platform that promised to lift the country out of its economic quagmire and reject the ideas of Hoover and the Republicans. Roosevelt was advised by three Columbia University academics, Raymond Moley, Rexford Tugwell, and Adolf Berle. They were quickly dubbed the "brain trust" by the *New York Times*, and the sobriquet caught on. Their ideas were markedly different from those of the business community. There was a general sense of annoyance on Wall Street that academics with a penchant for government regulation had been chosen as Roosevelt's close advisers. In the place of the Republicans' stated Jeffersonian principles of states' prerogatives and local control of the political process, the original New Deal would propose policies designed to interject government into the process in a manner that had not been seen since the days of Woodrow Wilson. Wall Street was cast as a malevolent force rather than as the cornerstone of American capitalism.

Roosevelt adopted a domestic point of view rather than the Republicans' internationalist angle. The American market crash, the almost five thousand banking failures during the 1920s, the subsequent rise in unemployment, and the drop in industrial production to about 50 percent of capacity all had domestic origins that had to be remedied before any effective action could be taken. The depression was not caused by international factors, as many Republicans claimed, but by problems within the domestic economy and by rampant speculation. The internationalist explanation was seen as an excuse for the problems in the economy beyond the control of the incumbent administration. The brain trust attributed many of the problems to the basic inequities built into the economy. Although some within his own party urged Roosevelt to adopt the internationalist position, it quickly became apparent that he would not do so. The hand of government would now be felt in American society as never before. But in this case it would grip as well as guide. Two years earlier, in 1931, the historian Charles Beard had written, "For forty years or more there has not been a President, Republican or Democrat, who has not talked against government interference and then supported measures adding more interference to the huge collection already accumulated." Hoover certainly fell within this category. How this perception would be changed by the new Roosevelt administration would become more clear in the winter of 1933.

During the campaign, Roosevelt's image makers had a simple time portraying the Republicans as insensitive to massive unemployment, hunger, and starvation. Republicans steadfastly believed that Hoovervilles would disappear and fortunes would be restored if people would simply pull themselves up by their bootstraps. Despite the fact that the Republicans had presided over the near economic ruin of American society, their ideas concerning government were still markedly different from those that had prevailed in the nineteenth century. The Republicans represented an ideology that suggested that while intense concentrations of economic power were bad for society, government control of the marketplace was even worse. However, they did very little to supply any form of control even when it became apparent that the economy was facing disaster. Once the

"The March Lion" Talburt, *New York World Telegram*, 1933.

"The Rest of the Boys Might as Well Get Ready While There's Plenty of Hot Water," unknown artist, *New York Herald Tribune*, 1933.

new Democratic administration assumed office, it would seek to regulate the concentration of economic power using government intervention—something that was anathema to Republicans. This sort of regulatory environment had not been attempted before with any success.

A few days prior to the election of 1932, Hoover was on the campaign stump in New York. He described the impending contest between himself

"The Truants" by Elderman, *Washington Post*, 1933.

and Franklin Roosevelt in poignant terms that would reverberate in spirit, if not in style, for the next twenty years: "This campaign is more than a contest between two men. It is more than a contest between two parties. It is a contest between two philosophies of government." Hoover's assessment referred to the clash between those favoring a strong federal government and those content to let business and society take a more natural course. While the clash between the two sides was nothing new in American history, it would enlist some unusual recruits on the Jeffersonian side favoring a weak central government.

The election proved to be a runaway for Roosevelt, who garnered 22.8 million popular votes to Hoover's 15.7 million. The landslide was more pronounced in the electoral college, where Roosevelt gained 472 votes to Hoover's 59. Hoover's dire warnings about a Democratic victory, including a prediction that "grass will grow in the streets" if the Democrats gained office, was ignored by the public, which apparently felt the process had already begun. Unemployment was rising rapidly and commodity prices had collapsed. Wheat fetched only a tenth of its price from the 1920s, ruining farmers in the process. Many could not afford to harvest their crops. Able-bodied men went from door to door begging for food or work. Hoover continued to preach self-reliance and hard work, but the message did not sell.

Although the new Congress had a Democratic majority, it was unable to pass any meaningful legislation while waiting for Roosevelt to take of-

"Let the Seller Beware" by Kirby, *New York World Telegram*, 1933.

fice. During this time it picked up the nickname "debating body," which would be difficult to shed in the years ahead. The American Dream finally had begun to lose some of its luster. Recent immigrants began to emigrate again, in the opposite direction. Some settled in the Soviet Union, and their heirs were not heard from again for several decades. All of the social chaos produced a natural result, as some commentators began publicly questioning whether the United States could not use a bit of dictatorship to set it straight. *Barron's* remarked that a "lighthearted dictator might be a relief from the pompous futility of such a Congress as we have recently had."[18] Others suggested the same, in varying degrees, although the remarks show frustration with the political leadership more than a genuine desire for an American dictator. However, within a few years the idea would surface again with more negative connotations.

The Pecora Investigation

During the interregnum, the period between the election and Roosevelt's inauguration in March 1933, Ferdinand Pecora took over the reins of the Senate subcommittee hearings. A short, dark-complexioned Italian immigrant who had come to the United States as a small boy, he had worked as a law clerk and studied law at the New York Law School before entering the bar. As an assistant district attorney in New York in the 1920s, he successfully prosecuted many shoddy stock salesmen and corrupt politicians. But he never achieved financial success even at the time of the hearings; his compensation for his services on the subcommittee was a mere $250 per month.

One of Pecora's first orders of business was an investigation of Samuel Insull's utility empire located in Chicago. The depression had toppled hundreds of thousands of shareholders and bondholders in Insull's farflung operations. The former assistant to Thomas Edison had carved himself a monopoly out of Chicago's disparate utilities and at the peak of the bull market was sitting on a virtual empire that extended over two dozen states. His utilities group ranked as the third largest in the country before its fall, producing around 10 percent of the country's power. The group was controlled by five holding companies. The Insull family held sizable holdings in each.

At the height of its power, Cyrus Eaton began examining Insull's empire to see if any of it could be acquired. Insull mounted a corporate defense by creating two holding companies out of the previous five, financing the reorganization with borrowed money. The resulting two holding companies were heavily indebted, making them a less desirable target. When the crash occurred, stock prices fell and interest rates began to decline, leaving Insull with high debt payments and declining business.

But the financing was not free of manipulation. Insull sold shares in the holding companies at market prices but kept substantial amounts on option for himself. As the stock price began to rise, his profits mounted. Before the crash, in the summer of 1929, his estimated profit totaled some $170 million. The public, on the other hand, had subscribed t less favorable prices, although anyone who bought shares at the original offering prices did well if they sold before the crash.

Pecora discovered that Halsey, Stuart and Company had been employed by Insull to maintain the price of his shares while he was negotiating bank loans for the borrowed money for the financing. Halsey did not bother to mention that it too had sizable holdings in the Insull companies. Apparently, the financings and the subsequent fall of the businesses had been at the investors' expense, which ran somewhat counter to Insull's public image of personal generosity that derived from his lending money to overextended employees at the time of the crash. Fearful of being pilloried by the committee even before Pecora assumed the helm, Insull fled the country for Greece in the fall of 1932. President Hoover learned that Insull was in transit in Italy and asked the Italian authorities to detain him, but to no avail. Insull reached Greece and remained there for a year and a half. Several times during that period, the U.S. government attempted, without success, to have him extradited. Finally, the new Democratic administration exerted political pressure on a Greek-American organization in the United States to intervene on its behalf with the Greek government.[19] The Greeks responded by expelling Insull, who finally decided to return to the United States in 1934. He eventually was exonerated of state and federal charges and attempted a financial comeback somewhat late in life.

Jack Morgan was called before the subcommittee in May. His appearance was to be the highlight of the proceedings, and his testimony became one of the great celebrity events of the decade. No Morgan had appeared in public since his father testified before the Pujo committee twenty years earlier. Morgan was accompanied by his lawyer, John W. Davis, a onetime Democratic candidate for president and former ambassador to Britain. The discussions between Morgan and the members of the committee were cordial and professional, more than could be said for those that followed. But the stateliness of the proceedings was broken by Morgan enemies. A female midget, hired for the occasion by a Ringling Brothers Circus press agent, appeared at the hearings to pose with Morgan by sitting on his knee. Twenty years earlier, no one would have thought of embarrassing J. P. Morgan in such a fashion. Morgan maintained his dignity by actually talking with the woman, but the proceedings had clearly taken on a tone that the senior banker would not have expected.

Morgan testified about how his bank worked and gave his account of the role and functions of the private banker. He repeatedly told the committee that J. P. Morgan and Company did not solicit deposits or any other business from the public. If a man wanted to open a deposit he would have to be introduced to the bank before he would be considered. The committee was impressed with the fact that Morgan claimed that depositors came to him rather than the other way around. This was tempered by the fact that New York law prohibited private bankers from advertising or soliciting deposits, but Morgan's point was well made. His bank simply did not need business and extended it to new customers only as a favor.

Pecora personally led much of the examination of Jack Morgan. He discovered that the twenty partners of the bank did not publish accounts and that the Morgans had absolute control over the other partners, who served at the discretion of Morgan and could be dismissed at any time. Similarly, the partnership could be dissolved at the wishes of Morgan. Adding insult to injury was the fact that many of them had not paid income taxes in recent years and when they did, the amounts were minuscule in relation to their compensations. But as Pecora probed, it became clear that Morgan's absolute authority extended into other realms as well.

Well aware of the Pujo committee meetings, Pecora began to unravel the house of Morgan's interrelationships with other financial institutions. As it turned out, over sixty other prominent bankers had loans outstanding at Morgan, including Charles Mitchell and Charles Dawes. Morgan saw nothing wrong with the arrangements. When Pecora suggested that this might place these "customers" of his bank in a position to do favors for Morgan, he responded, "We do make these loans and we make them because we believe the people should have the money; that we should loan money if the gentlemen want it. They are friends of ours and we know that they are good, sound straight fellows."[20]

By carefully leading Morgan to describe his colleagues in the business as "sound fellows," his interrogators raised what would become one of the hottest issues surrounding the entire hearings—preferred lists. The house of Morgan used these lists, as did other private banking houses, to extend financial privileges to their best clients and others they wanted to influence. These revelations came at a time when the depression was hitting the working class particularly hard, and the news set off howls of protest in the press. It became apparent that the upper echelons of finance, politics, and business were not suffering at all while the average citizen was on the verge of desperation.

Preferred lists had begun when Morgan offered stock in its holding companies to a select group of individuals at cost. When the bank organized the United Corporation, the Alleghany Corporation, and Standard Brands in the late 1920s, stock in these companies began trading on a "when-issued" basis. The market put a price on the shares in anticipation of their coming to market. Morgan offered shares to the preferred group at the underwriting cost, substantially lower than the price that would be offered to the public. The opportunity for gain was obvious. Morgan was essentially handing anyone on the preferred lists an immediate profit.

John Raskob was one of those on the lists. He was offered two thousand shares of Alleghany at twenty dollars per share when the stock was selling at thirty-five dollars in the market. He wrote to George Whitney at Morgan, "I appreciate deeply the many courtesies shown me by you and your partners, and sincerely hope the future holds opportunities for me to reciprocate."[21] Even though his potential profit was only an immediate $30,000, the nature of the gift was obvious to the committee. When questioned about the lists, Whitney replied, "We did believe that we knew certain people who had the substantial wealth, the knowledge of their securities, and the willingness to take a risk with us in the underwriting of those common stocks." This did not ring true with the members of the committee since it was clear there were many people on the lists who were unacquainted with the intricacies of the market, including Calvin Coolidge and General John "Black Jack" Pershing.

The most ominous problem for Wall Street developed when some of the senators questioning witnesses turned their attention toward the past. Louis Brandeis's name arose several times during the course of the investigation. Because of the power of the house of Morgan, some critics, including Ferdinand Pecora himself, claimed that Morgan was really a government within a government. Because of the vast interlocking directorships the bank's partners still held and the different means it had of compensating friends, it effectively controlled the financial reins of the country. Outside the Morgan partnership, investment bankers generally had a monopoly hold over their industry. This situation was proving intolerable since they were perceived to be standing in the way of economic recovery.

Wall Street's monopoly was most clearly seen in the committee's investigation of the fees investment bankers charged their clients. The large fees attached to bond issues, sometimes amounting to 10 percent of the total amounts raised, were sometimes exceeded by the commissions charged on new stock offerings. Clearly, investment bankers could charge what they wished and clients would pay it because no one else could perform the function of raising new capital for companies. This was a difficult problem for the committee to tackle, but the size of fees was open to attack. While bankers, especially Otto Kahn, tried to explain their fees to the committee, the defense was very vulnerable to criticism. It seemed bankers were simply enriching themselves at the expense of the companies they served. The

"An Unfortunate Wait" by Clubb, Plainfield N.J. *News*.

clients to whom they sold new securities also paid high prices. It was difficult to explain how they could charge $10 million on a $100-million deal
when the country was mired in a depression.

The other side of the "monopoly" was found in the invasion of the
commercial banks into Wall Street in the 1920s. The fees were fat, and
National City and Chase National quickly moved into the securities-issu-
ing business. Pecora noted that they "had looked with hungry eyes upon
the savory meats that hitherto been the virtual monopoly of the private investment banker and they had decided to share more liberally in the feast."
At the heart of the investigation were Brandeis's admonitions of twenty
years earlier: "Compel bankers when issuing securities to make public the
commissions or profits they are receiving."[22] While bankers steadfastly

maintained that their securities affiliates were separate companies operating outside the direct sphere of the parent bank, Pecora knew otherwise.

Other senior bankers fared less well than Morgan under questioning. When he questioned Charles Mitchell, Pecora got to the heart of the matter very quickly, over Mitchell's protests. Despite the enormous growth of the banks during the 1920s, he quickly established a link between their personalities and those of their aggressive chief executives. Over Mitchell's protests, Pecora likened the banks and their executives to a body "with two heads, isn't it? . . . But instead of having one head it has two heads, and the two heads seem to be the one head in your personality." To which Mitchell tamely responded, "Yes."[23]

As a result of the investigation, Mitchell resigned from his bank job in February 1933. The press, members of the committee, and Franklin Roosevelt himself all called for his resignation. The *New York Times* remarked that "the resignation of Charles E. Mitchell was inevitable. No banking institution, not even the next to largest in the world, could afford even to appear to approve or condone the transactions of which he was a guiding spirit and one of the beneficiaries."[24] Far from being ostracized by the financial community, however, Mitchell became head of Blyth and Company after his resignation. Albert Wiggin of Chase also resigned from his post and was replaced by Winthrop Aldrich, brother-in-law of John D. Rockefeller Jr., who proved to be much more sensitive to the changing tide than his predecessor.

Reforms Begin

Although banking and securities legislation was the first item on the new administration's agenda, the preliminary proposals to regulate bankers and brokers were not well accepted by Wall Street. Tensions continued to mount. The upheaval caused by the crash and the depression was cast in a wholly different light, however, when witness after witness testified before the Pecora hearings. Pecora's tone was distinctly anti–Wall Street. He quickly became known as the grand inquisitor of the wealthy and powerful, earning the everlasting enmity of many investment bankers.

The banking crisis raised its head in the first days of the Roosevelt administration. Emergency banking legislation was rushed through Congress after FDR had announced a national bank holiday beginning March 6. Banks began to reopen on March 13. The emergency legislation took the United States off the gold standard. Everyone holding gold privately had to sell it to the U.S. Treasury at the prevailing price. Gold could no longer be exported. Like Britain almost two years before, the United States was now off the standard. Rumors of the great bear raid of 1932 were not completely forgotten.

Public distaste of investment bankers quickly found its way into securities legislation. Within weeks of FDR's taking office, the Securities Act of 1933 was passed by Congress. Drafting on the bill had actually begun during the interregnum. In the first weeks of the new administration, final drafting on the proposed legislation was furious. Respected figures from the legal community, such as Samuel Untermyer of Pujo committee fame, were consulted and contributed to the bill's theoretical framework. Untermyer's attacks on Morgan and the Van Sweringens had also extended to the stock exchange. Only a few months earlier, he had stated, "Some day when there is a real investigation of the history of the Stock Exchange we shall get a picture of the means by which billions of dollars have been literally filched from the public through the machinery of that institution that is still permitted to remain beyond official government regulation, supervision and control and above, and beyond the law."[25] For all of the Senate subcommittee's findings, Untermyer still believed it did not venture far enough.

Felix Frankfurter, of the Harvard Law School, and two assistants helped draft the final version. One of the assistants was James Landis, a colleague of Frankfurter and former law clerk to Louis Brandeis. Although there was nothing particularly new in the act, it was nevertheless the first piece of national securities legislation ever passed by Congress. The blue-sky laws already in existence in over twenty states, including New York, had been the first steps toward regulating new issues of securities. But the crash had proved they contained so many loopholes that unscrupulous brokers and investment bankers could easily circumvent. If a state's regulations were too strict for the seller of new securities, the broker would simply make his offering by mail rather than undergo a formal process of registering the stocks or bonds in the state. A federal law was needed to plug the gaps in the patchwork of state laws.

When Roosevelt submitted the securities bill to Congress in March 1933, it was clear that the proposed bill was part of an evolving trend. He stated:

> The Federal Government cannot and should not take any action which might be construed as approving or guaranteeing that newly issued securities are sound in the sense that their value will be maintained or that the properties which they represent will earn profit. . . . There is however an obligation upon us to insist that every issue to be sold in interstate commerce shall be accompanied by full publicity and information.[26]

Wall Street was given a chance to respond to the bill but fumbled the ball. Its defense was led by John Foster Dulles, an attorney at Sullivan and Cromwell, but the congressional committee taking testimony was not impressed with his defense of the old order. The Securities Act required new sellers of securities to register the offerings with the Federal Trade Commission. Issuers of municipal bonds and government agencies were exempt, but issuers of foreign bonds were not.[27] Congress had learned its lesson and would not allow investment bankers to indiscriminately issue bonds for foreign entities without subjecting them to the same process required of companies. The testimony of private investors who lost fortunes in foreign bonds was still fresh in the minds of Congress, as were the revelations about how bankers bribed those in power to gain mandates to issue securities.[28] So, too, was the banking system, still trembling under the weight of poor investments and fraud.

Wall Street did not appreciate the new law, but this was not the first time it had seen such requirements. The NYSE's listing requirements were actually more strict than the blue-sky laws and had been operating for a number of years. But even when combined with the state requirements, they were not able to prevent the crash and the hundreds of corporate bankruptcies that followed. Richard Whitney's vocal defense of short selling did little to reassure Congress that Wall Street would clean up its own backyard. Within a year, Whitney's characterization of the NYSE as a "perfect institution" would be seriously challenged.

The impact of the new securities regulations on Wall Street and the country could not be completely seen at the time. The new breed of regulators advising President Roosevelt were the second generation to recognize that the growth of American business had created a "bigness" that had to be regulated. The Pujo committee hearings had created the Federal Reserve but had done little to prevent the sorts of abuses that caused the crash and the banking crisis. This new breed, including Raymond Moley and Rexford Tugwell, as well as Felix Frankfurter and the omnipresent yet silent Louis Brandeis, realized that concentrated economic power would run rampant if not restrained. The new securities law was only the first shot in their war against unrestrained bigness in business and finance.

In his inaugural address Roosevelt proclaimed that "the money changers have fled from their high seats in the temple of our civilization. We may now restore that temple to the ancient truths." But the interregnum committee hearings only began the trend. The emergency banking legislation that followed FDR's inauguration was followed by the most revolutionary banking bill ever introduced in Congress. The Securities Act did not actually control the behavior of bankers; instead, it was meant to protect investors from fraudulent new securities offerings. But the new banking bill, which was aimed at private bankers, would leave an indelible imprint on American finance for the next several generations. By effectively destroying the ability to issue securities and take deposits, it would radically alter the face of banking. Most in Congress disagreed with Jack Morgan; the private banker was deemed a national liability.

The new bill introduced in the late spring was known as the Glass-Steagall Act of 1933, or simply the Banking Act. No one doubted its urgency. The *New York Times* conceded that it was necessary "if we are to remove from this country the reproach of having the worst banking system in the world." Point by point, the bill attempted to remedy the abuses in the market that had prevailed since the crash. The measures it introduced were fairly unique in banking. Most other countries had no comparable laws. On its back came nothing short of a financial and social revolution in the way finance was practiced.

Congress was bent upon reforming banking so that the poachers and the gamekeepers were kept separate in the new financial era. But Congress was taking no chances with generalizations. Any contradictions in banking were soon to be made very simple and clear. No longer would private bankers be allowed to control the financial system. The Banking Act created deposit insurance and separated investment and commercial banking. The combination of the two wiped out many of the traditional Wall Street power bases.

The Glass-Steagall Act passed Congress relatively quickly. The deposit insurance provisions posed the greatest ideological problems to some. Why should the government provide for insurance against malfeasance at the banks? At a rigidly anticommunist time, this seemed like socialism to some. But the concept was more practical. Without some assurances, hoarding would continue and economic recovery would be stymied.

But the separation between the two types of banking was the true revolution. Bankers had a year to decide which type they would practice, commercial banking or investment banking. A minority actually supported the separation, including Winthrop Aldrich, Wiggin's successor at Chase National, and James Perkins, Mitchell's successor at National City. But Jack Morgan remarked, "If we, for instance, should be deprived of the right to receive deposits . . . we should very probably have to disband a large part of our organization and thus should be less able to render in the future that important service in the supply of capital for the development of the country which we have rendered in the past."[29] Morgan's decision ran down to the eleventh hour. The *New York Times* reported that Morgan was leaning toward commercial banking rather than the securities business: "A majority of the private banking houses in Wall Street is expected to choose the securities business. J. P. Morgan & Co., however, will be an outstanding exception."[30]

Recognizing the handwriting on the wall, Morgan adopted the position that the new law would prove to be ephemeral. Accordingly, the company chose commercial banking, spinning off the securities activities into a separate company. It was joined by other banks from New York and around the country. Many of the new investment banks were partnerships that had no legal connection to the parent bank. The best known was Morgan Stanley and Company, which took with it Morgan's bond and stock business. Its first chairman was Harold Stanley, a partner at Morgan. Twenty members of J. P. Morgan and Company left their jobs with the bank to form the new firm. There was some suspicion that the functions would be shifted to Drexel, until then a Morgan subsidiary, but the partners chose to form a new firm instead. It did, however, keep its back-office operations in close proximity to those of the bank, apparently trying to remain close to home until the accursed Roosevelt-inspired reforms had run their course. Chase divested of the American Express Company and its securities affiliates. But the popularity of Roosevelt and the entire reform movement put paid to any reintegration of banking. Jack Morgan reportedly kept clerks busy simply cutting FDR's picture out of the newspapers so he would not have to look at the president's face when reading the morning newspapers.[31] Many bankers and other business leaders called FDR a traitor to his class for apparently biting the hand that had fed his own family for generations.

Even while regulatory legislation was being passed, traders on the NYSE were still up to their old tricks. In June 1933 a pool was operating in the stock of the American Commercial Alcohol Company. The pattern was not difficult to detect: in May the stock traded about twenty dollars per share; by July it had risen to almost ninety dollars. As it turned out, the run-up in prices was attributed to a new financing the company wanted to accomplish, and a price increase certainly helped. Company directors then wanted to sell the shares they had been able to obtain at cheap prices as high and as quickly as possible. The two floor traders employed in the manipulation were Thomas Bragg and Ben Smith, who managed to turn over more than ten times the company's outstanding stock in one month. After hitting its all-time high, the price collapsed back to thirty dollars.

Wall Street bankers knew the reforms were quickly changing the tide, but they characteristically ascribed it to personal vendettas. Russell Leffingwell, a Morgan partner, remarked to a colleague in 1934 that he thought Brandeis was behind the specific provision in the Banking Act that separated banking:

> I have little doubt that he inspired, or even drafted it. The Jews do not forget. They are relentless. . . . the reason why I make so much of this is that I think you underestimate the forces we are antagonizing. . . . I believe we are confronted with the profound political-economic philosophy, matured in the wood for twenty years, of the finest brain and the most powerful personality in the Democratic party, who happens to be a Justice of the Supreme Court.[32]

Leffingwell was not mistaken. Brandeis's influence, through both his past writings and his disciples in the Roosevelt administration, was apparent.

Much to the chagrin of Wall Street, the ideas of Louis Brandeis became even more entrenched among the trustbusters and those opposed to big business in general. The recent generation of his disciples—James Landis, William O. Douglas, and Felix Frankfurter—made sure that the master's ideas remained alive and well. The Supreme Court justice kept in regular touch with the New Dealers through an elaborate network of former students and disciples. Through them, his ideas reached FDR and his advisers, who referred to him as "Isaiah." Brandeis preferred to disseminate his views concerning the two securities acts of 1933 and 1934 through Frankfurter to avoid the appearance of impropriety or scandal.[33] That would account for the extraordinary impact his book *Other People's Money*, written over twenty years earlier, continued to have on the new breed of regulators.

Another abuse of the past was addressed in an addition to the Banking Act passed in another banking bill of 1935. Part of the new law was a direct result of Charles Mitchell's actions in 1929. The individual Federal Reserve banks could no longer conduct open-market operations by themselves. They now had to be done by all the banks under the auspices of the Federal Reserve Board. If funds were to be added to the banks when the Fed did a repurchase agreement (or repo), it could not be done by the Federal Reserve Bank of New York alone. That is what Mitchell had effectively done in 1929 by adding funds through National City as the system governors were trying to tighten money. Even a casual observer could see that specific parts of the new law were directed at past abuses of the financial system.

Other banks also divested themselves of their securities operations, and the modern investment banking industry was born. The First Boston Corporation was created when it was spun off from the First National Bank of Boston and moved to New York. Kuhn, Loeb reverted to the securities business, stepping away from taking deposits for wealthy clients. Goldman, Sachs and Lehman Brothers remained investment banks. Brown Brothers Harriman remained a private bank. Its investment banking side was spun off into Harriman Ripley and Company, taking with it a number of former National City employees. Despite this, it came under no criticism from the Pecora committee because of its otherwise unblemished record. The investment banking side of J. and W. Seligman was assumed by the Union Securities Corporation.

Although Congress had acted decisively to pass the new regulatory legislation, the bear hunt was not over. In fact, the most momentous part was yet to come. Wall Street and the New Deal would now become more opposed than ever. It was no longer the nineteenth century. Controlling new issues of stocks and bonds and those who underwrote them was not enough. The stock exchanges traded a vast number of issues. Richard Whitney's notion that speculation was part and parcel of their very existence would never quite die but was undergoing a radical transformation. The exchanges themselves finally were on the verge of federal regulation.

A Cop on the Corner

When Herbert Hoover originally threatened to regulate the stock exchanges if short selling was not stopped, he tried to use the threat as a political ploy as well. The NYSE was really in the realm of New York politics. Therefore it was the duty of the governor of New York, Franklin Roosevelt, to regulate the exchange. When it became apparent that FDR would not do so, Hoover tried to blame the exchange's problems on the lack of political leadership in New York. Yet, ironically, when FDR became president, regulation of all the stock exchanges became a priority.

When word began to circulate that the Roosevelt administration was seeking new laws to regulate the stock exchanges, the battle between Wall Street and the New Deal became more acrimonious. Richard Whitney organized the defense. An advocate of self-regulation, he wanted no part of federal regulation in any form. Joining the fight, he invited the heads of the major wire houses to New York to plan a counteroffensive. Shortly thereafter, he included corporate heads in his war group and found a receptive audience. Whitney claimed that if the new bill was not fought, activity on the stock exchange would go the way of new investment banking business. New issues of stocks and corporate bonds declined by 50 percent between 1933 and 1934. Sales on the NYSE followed suit. But these dismal numbers could hardly be attributed to the Securities Act passed in 1933. Economic activity was hardly exuberant. National income had dropped the previous year and was only slightly on the rise in 1934. Blaming the Securities Act was akin to blaming the messenger for bad news.

Almost a hundred businessmen answered Whitney's call to arms. They were joined by some former government officials, including Eugene Meyer, all of whom opposed regulating the stock exchange. The claims of the group reached out in different directions. Some insisted that small firms would now come under the umbrella of the federal government and that their ability to raise capital would be seriously impaired. Others were a bit more blunt. They saw the government encroachment as an attempt to introduce socialism. "The real object of this bill," said Republican Congressmen Fred Britten of Illinois, "is to Russianize everything worthwhile."[34]

The second of the securities acts, the Securities Exchange Act of 1934, was a direct challenge to the way Wall Street had maintained its independence since 1791. Stock exchanges now had to register with the Securities and Exchange Commission. Practices on the exchanges, including short selling, were subject to new rules. Margin requirements were now made uniform and were controlled by the Federal Reserve. The new law delved into each area that had been probed by the Committee on Stock Exchange Practices and plugged up many of the existing holes. The over-the-counter market and the commodities futures exchanges were not included because they did not trade stocks in an exchangelike atmosphere.

The new regulations did not restrain traders as Wall Street had feared when the bill was being drafted. Originally, reformers sought to separate the dual functions of the specialists and severely limit the activities of floor traders on the exchanges. But such severe measures were omitted in the final version, and specialists kept their dual functions. The compromise mollified the Street to some extent. The danger was that the new law would be too radical, severely restraining the ability of the stock exchanges to function. The restrictions placed on short selling and margin trading were thought to be ample to prevent abuses of the past from flaring up again.

The new SEC also assumed responsibility for the Securities Act of 1933 from the FTC. This gave the commission a dual power that annoyed Wall Street enormously. Investment bankers now found themselves accountable to a government agency for the first time. Any company that misrepresented itself on a filing statement with the SEC was liable, as were its investment bankers. In order to register, companies would have to supply financial information, such as annual reports, that many had never provided before. At the time, such disclosures were uncommon, and the rules did not please many bankers or their clients. As Jack Morgan and his partners testified, the house of Morgan had never published an annual report. Now it would have to do so if it ever sold a public security or represented a client doing so as an investment banker. This was one of the reasons the bank chose commercial rather than investment banking after the Banking Act was passed.

The SEC itself became the focal point of Wall Street's interest in the new law. Since it now had control over both sides of investment banking and brokerage, who ran it became extremely important. The five commissioners were the financial community's new czars, and there was no reason to believe they would be friendly. The great fear was that they would continue to support Brandeisian notions of "big is bad" and curtail the activities of the exchanges even more. No more than three of the five members could come from the same political party, but it was the chairmanship that carried the most weight. Given Wall Street's hostility to the whole idea, the choice of the first chairman would be crucial to the future development of the SEC. And Wall Street expected, and feared, that James Landis would be its first head. Brandeis had been politically reincarnated.

The new commissioners replaced the agrarian interests as Wall Street's main antagonists. Populists and progressives still were among the financial community's foes, and many of them openly supported the new SEC. The first commissioners named were Landis, Pecora, George Matthews of the FTC, Robert Healy, counsel to the FTC, and the surprise chairman, Joseph P. Kennedy. Kennedy was chosen over Landis for political reasons. He was a personal friend and financial supporter of Roosevelt's campaign. Landis was too strident a foe of Wall Street, but Kennedy was renowned as an astute businessman who would not ruffle too many Wall Street feathers. His nomination was supported by Raymond Moley and Bernard Baruch. Yet when Kennedy's appointment was announced, the outcry was loud and harsh. Roosevelt was accused of selling out to Wall Street, which had exercised considerable lobbying pressure against the new bill. As it turned out, the appointment was a master stroke, although Kennedy's reputation did not help matters.

Prior to his appointment, Kennedy was found to have participated in a bear pool organized around Libby Owens Ford stock in the summer of 1933. When this was discovered, even FDR supporters thought the president had made an ill-considered choice. But FDR remained adamant that Kennedy was the best man for the job. He was the only member of the SEC who actually had securities market experience. The others were all lawyers with varied backgrounds. Kennedy's background as a bear market operator meant he was the only member of the commission who actually had participated in many of the activities that were now proscribed by the new law. And he was no friend of Morgan since the banker snubbed him four years earlier. Many, however, found that a lame excuse for appointing a fox to guard the henhouse.

The critics were silenced within less than a year. Kennedy's administration of the new SEC proved to be highly successful. He carefully toed the line with Wall Street and the NYSE while actively setting up the mechanics of the commission so it could investigate and prosecute misdeeds by investment bankers and brokers. Shortly after the SEC officially began its work, Kennedy delivered a national radio address as one of his first official duties. Needless to say, the address was carefully followed on Wall Street, already apprehensive about the direction the commission would take. The Fletcher Report had already made it perfectly clear that "many of the abuses in investment banking have resulted from the incompetence, negligence, irresponsibility or cupidity of individuals in the profession. Such abuses can be eliminated only by the elimination of such persons from the field."[35] The new chairman made it clear that finance was not dead, as some had predicted when he stated, "We of the SEC do not re-

gard ourselves as coroners sitting on the corpse of financial enterprise. . . .
we do not start with the belief that every enterprise is crooked and that
those behind it are crooks."[36] More than a few brokers on the NYSE
rested easier that night than they had for several months.

Kennedy and his fellow commissioners made it clear that regulation
did not necessarily mean prosecution. Even Richard Whitney began to
make conciliatory gestures toward the SEC, recognizing that there was
less to fear than many on Wall Street originally had believed. But cleaning
up the acts of many brokers was a paramount objective. Many small bucket
shop operators were put out of business, and several minor stock exchanges closed. For his part, Whitney went on record against marginal
brokers, urging the public to deal only with reputable brokerage houses.

The original members of the SEC did not last long in their jobs. Ferdinand Pecora resigned after six months to take a job as a judge at $25,000
per year, ten times his salary as chief counsel of the Pecora committee. Joe
Kennedy could not afford to stay longer than a year and then left to return
to his own pursuits. His resignation was interrupted by the Supreme
Court's striking down of the National Industrial Relations Act—and with
it a central part of the New Deal's strategy for economic recovery—as unconstitutional. The SEC immediately came under a cloud because there
was some concern that the Securities Act and the Securities Exchange Act
could suffer the same fate. As a result, Kennedy postponed his resignation
until it became more clear that the SEC would survive.[37] He was succeeded by James Landis.

After the Securities Exchange Act was passed, the New Deal came under increasing criticism from the business community. Freewheeling
American enterprise was reined in. The resulting outcry was predictable
but futile. Richard Whitney's defense of the stock exchange had shown
that nineteenth-century ideas about speculation and competition no
longer won many adherents outside the financial community. The public
was tired of hearing about the deeds of bankers while they were having a
difficult time making ends meet. Some of the most enduring stories to survive the Senate investigation concerned personnel policies at the large
banks. While senior management helped themselves to their bonus pots,
ordinary employees were being asked to make sacrifices for the good of
their institutions. Many were laid off or asked to work extra hours with no
additional compensation. But many executives in Wall Street and at major
companies thought the country had taken a distinctly leftward turn because of what they perceived to be the New Deal's socialist tendencies.
Their reaction would not be long in coming.

Adding to the public relations woes of Wall Street and business was the
publication of a book on some of the great industrialists and bankers of the
nineteenth century, written by journalist Matthew Josephson and appro-

priately entitled *The Robber Barons*. It quickly became required reading, and the title remained firmly in the American lexicon for generations. Even after the book itself had been forgotten, the term was quickly associated with the likes of Jay Gould, Commodore Vanderbilt, and the Morgans. Josephson himself related how widespread the term had become when he heard of a potential Wall Street trainee who once told an interviewer why he wanted a job in the financial community; he had read the book and decided he wanted to become a robber baron himself. Wall Street had not completely lost its allure.

Wall Street Opposition?

Roosevelt's honeymoon with the business community ended with the Securities Exchange Act in the early summer of 1934. Even though many Wall Street personalities were impressed with Kennedy's handling of the SEC in his year as chairman, strong antipathy arose over this new form of federal interference with big business in general. Unfortunately, public sympathy for Wall Street and corporate America was nonexistent, so appeals to the average citizen would be useless. The business elite would rally to oppose Roosevelt and his brain trusters at every opportunity.

Opposition to the New Deal came from many quarters. Ideologically, much of it was more subdued than many New Deal programs. When it did become strident, it usually attacked on a personal level. Many writers and commentators professed to know what the Roosevelt administration was really up to as it tried to redirect the American economy. Those who did so subtly tried guilt by association to make their points. One such critic was Herbert Hoover, whose 1934 book, *The Challenge to Liberty*, attempted to show how America was drifting toward autocracy. He characterized the New Deal as a government by "regimentation," meaning that the federal government was probing into areas best left to private enterprise and the people. In his opinion, regimentation was in the same league as fascism, socialism, and communism. It eroded individual liberties when the executive branch usurped power from the other two branches of government.

The grassroots political movements produced a variety of demagogues and fringe movements. But at the very opposite end of the spectrum, it also produced an elitist, well-financed movement dedicated to opposing the New Deal on every possible front. Unlike Huey Long's "share the wealth" concept or Upton Sinclair's radical proposals for redistribution of wealth, it had all the funds it could ever use. Not showing any interest in the man in the street, this particular group struck a familiar theme in American society. The New Deal was impinging upon individual liberties and the principles of Jeffersonian democracy. By analogy, it was subverting the same principle that the Eighteenth Amendment to the Constitution had trampled during its short but memorable history several years earlier.

But the second time around, the reinvigorated group did not have a cause célèbre to wave in front of the public. It was simply an anti–New Deal organization. Organized by John Raskob, who believed the New Deal was too left-wing, it was headed by Jouett Shouse, a colleague of Raskob and his successor as chairman of the Democratic National Committee. The American Liberty League was formed in the summer of 1934 in Washington. Ostensibly, the league was to be above politics; its intention was to become a shadow force advocating constitutional freedoms. Shouse went to the White House to personally inform FDR of the league's formation and his own intentions. Roosevelt appeared to be perfectly happy to accept the organization since its aims appeared to be very general. But it soon became apparent that the organization was anything but apolitical, and its intentions were clearly hostile to New Deal reforms.

Members of the league included most of the du Pont family (especially Ireneé, Pierre, and Lammot du Pont), John W. Davis, former presidential candidate and lawyer to J. P. Morgan, Alfred Sloan of General Motors, Al Smith (at the time managing the Empire State Building), as well as a host of other well-known figures from industry and finance, including Jay Cooke II. The press gave wide coverage to the league's founding. The *New York Times* proclaimed that many Wall Street leaders would take an active part in the league, that most bankers and brokers "will join," and that employees and workers in the financial district will "follow along."[38] While Joe Kennedy's pronouncements only a month before may have assuaged some fears on the Street, joining the new organization would be a way of combating the new regulatory regime in Washington.

The Liberty League was nothing more than the AAPA under a different name. The same group that had Prohibition successfully rolled back reorganized itself into the business and banker group opposed to Roosevelt. Now that Prohibition was no longer an issue, having been repealed in the winter of 1933, the league was able to pursue its political agenda by opposing most New Deal legislation. But when it emerged, with it the antitax and anti-interventionist business clique that had operated behind the scenes for so long in the 1920s finally emerged with it.

Captain William Stayton was secretary of the new organization, running it on a day-to-day basis as he had done for the AAPA and the Navy League. At its height it claimed to have slightly under one hundred thousand members, but its membership was confined mostly to businessmen who simply wrote a check in order to join. The visceral popularity of many fringe and grassroots organizations was missing. Although the league had ample supplies of money and resources to fight the New Deal ideologically, its meetings were usually black-tie dinners dominated by very conservative Democrats and Republicans.

One potential member that the league could not convert was Herbert Hoover. Raskob asked him to join but was refused. The former president was not impressed with the league's membership or its aims. He wrote that he had "n̟ more confidence in the Wall Street model of human liberty which thi̟ group so well represents than I have in the Pennsylvania Avenue mod̟ l upon which the country now rides."[39] The only senior politician of na̟ional stature the league was able to attract was Al Smith, by 1934 no admirer of the New Deal or FDR.

Over the next five years, the Liberty League held dinners and testimonials to its members and organized active opposition to many of Roosevelt's policies. It also organized one of the largest pamphlet-writing campaigns in recent memory to counter, point by point, many New Deal proposals. In its short history, it produced over 175 individual pamphlets and brochures, on topics ranging from the veterans' bonus to the budget and the arousing of class prejudices. The league organized active opposition to Roosevelt in the 1936 presidential campaign by supporting Alf Landon, but it also had its darker side, which cast shadows over the nature of business and Wall Street in the early 1930s.

At the time of the Liberty League's founding, unsubstantiated rumors abounded of it having a paramilitary side. Claims were made that clandestine organizers were attempting to enlist the members of the American Legion and the Veterans of Foreign Wars to help overthrow Roosevelt and establish some form of fascist government in the United States. Names of senior corporate executives and bankers were immediately attached to the movement by those supposedly in the forefront of the military side. The claims were dismissed as bogus by all those associated with the Liberty League itself. Unfortunately for the league, many of the names were those of its original members. Whether the claim was true or not, the league picked up a sinister reputation almost from its inception. The fact that its members were very conservative did not help matters. They became associated with fascism in the same way that Roosevelt became associated with socialism. The Liberty League also became associated with the goals of other right-wing groups, whether deserved or not.

Other public relations campaigns proved more successful. The league organized a lawyers' association, similar to the one the AAPA had used to fight Prohibition, with many prominent Wall Street attorneys in its ranks. The group used the National Industrial Recovery Act as its rallying point. Firmly believing that the NIRA and its agency, the National Recovery Administration, were unconstitutional, the association actually advised corporate clients to ignore the law because it was invalid. Time proved them correct. The Supreme Court unanimously ruled the NIRA unconstitutional in May 1935, stating that the "Congress is not permitted to abdicate or to transfer to others the essential legislative functions with which it is vested."[40] Justice Brandeis voted with the majority, feeling that Roosevelt had replaced the bigness of business with that of government. The Liberty League felt vindicated. The NIRA gave the president too much power at the expense of Congress.

But circumstances did not vindicate the lawyers' group. A wave of protest was heard because of the way in which the association took it upon itself to pronounce a law unconstitutional even before it had reached the Supreme Court. The *Nation* ran an article entitled "A Conspiracy of Lawyers," which stated starkly, "If lawyers turn themselves into an organized body dedicated to inciting the public to disobey the law, that is conspiracy."[41] Numerous law journals also condemned the association for such a blatant violation of legal ethics. By the time the furor died down, the remarks probably cost the Liberty League more political capital than it had hoped to earn.

The league's financial muscle ensured it of an active role in the opposition until the presidential election of 1936. In its short history, it never put a candidate up for election. Its role was mostly polemical. In addition to the pamphlet campaign against the New Deal, it organized seminars and discussion groups to discuss the errant ways of FDR and his advisers. During the same period, in an interesting role reversal, FDR and the Democrats had been painting themselves as the successors of Andrew Jackson. But the league's major events were always treated as social events by the press. Its most infamous moment came at a black-tie dinner at the Mayflower Hotel in Washington, attended by almost two thousand people, prior to the presidential campaign of 1936. The featured speaker was Al Smith, and the list of dinner guests read like a who's who of American business and finance. Attending were Eugene Meyer, John W. Davis, Raskob, Shouse, Winthrop Aldrich, Jay Cooke II, Wall Street lawyer Frederic Coudert, and many members of the du Pont family.

Smith's speech became infamous when he equated the New Deal with communism. "There can be only one capital," he stormed, "Washington or Moscow. There can be only the clear, pure fresh air of free America, or the foul breath of communistic Russia."[42] Americans had a choice and clearly should reject FDR. He also threatened to walk away from the next presidential election and his party's candidate although he had been a Democratic candidate himself, bringing the crowd to its feet with his fiery rhetoric. Immediately after, he disappeared for a Florida vacation while the newspapers had a field day with his speech. Most characterized it as pure politics, given the black-tie, ermine, and emeralds ambience of the event, although some labeled it as cheap demagoguery since Smith occupied such a lofty position in the Democratic party. As it turned out, it was one of the last gasps of the Liberty League and its supporters. The apparently out-of-touch business elite and Smith probably did more to help reelect Roosevelt than they did to support Landon.

Politically, the Liberty League was something of a passing phenomenon in depression-era history. After the presidential election of 1936, when Roosevelt handily defeated Alf Landon by 11 million popular votes and an electoral majority of 523 to 8, it quietly began to disband and disappeared from the political stage by 1939. But even though it was relatively short-lived, its members' political preferences were well known. Despite the fact that the league was defunct, Wall Street was politically equated with its conservative ideas for years to come. Although the New Deal was highly successful in many of its objectives, Wall Street remained opposed to many of its principles—a fact that would again bring problems for the investment banking community both before and after World War II. Memories grew long among those who felt aggrieved by Wall Street's actions in the early 1930s.

Insull-ated

Despite the activities of the American Liberty League, by the end of 1934 the New Deal had delivered a severe blow to the independence and swagger of Wall Street. Within two short years, Congress had asserted more authority over banking and brokerage than it had over business in general since the end of the War of 1812. In the case of the banking and securities laws especially, the new regulations were aimed at individuals as much as they were intended to protect the public.

The Securities Act of 1933 was clearly aimed at National City Bank and the National City Company. The Banking Act was aimed at J. P. Morgan's extensive empire, while the Securities Exchange Act effectively brought Richard Whitney and his stock exchange under federal regulations. When the Trust Indenture Act was eventually passed in 1939, Ivar Kreuger was still on the minds of lawmakers. But one notorious industrialist in particular had not been forgotten. Even though he was cleared of the charges brought against him, Samuel Insull and his fallen utilities empire formed the background for a new law passed in 1935. Only then would the great bear hunt temporarily have run its course.

The collapse of Insull's empire led to the passage of the Public Utility Holding Company Act of 1935. Since the late 1920s, Congress and the FTC had been studying the utilities business and discovered the web of interlocking relationships that caused many companies to have a common ownership. Louis Brandeis also contributed to the bill's drafting, using his usual network of associates to bring his ideas before FDR. Brandeis wrote to an associate, Norman Hapgood, stating his support for the bill. Hapgood in turn wrote to Roosevelt that Brandeis had stated, "If FDR carries through the Holding Company bill we shall have achieved considerable toward controlling big business." Roosevelt responded, "I was glad to hear the comment our friend made on the Holding Company bill."[43] When passed, the new law required all holding companies owning public utilities to register with the SEC. The securities authority had the power to limit holding companies to a single system, meaning that it could break up the large empires such as Insull's. Before he retired from the SEC, Joe Kennedy protested this "death sentence" provision of the act, claiming that the SEC should not have the power to dictate the size of a utility. His protests went unheeded. Congress was in the mood to regulate those industries deemed vital to the public welfare, and the utilities industry had had too many strikes against it since the turn of the century. Additionally, the SEC would review bond and stock offerings of the companies to determine their suitability and would supervise their relationships with investment bankers. Most important, it included an "arm's-length" provision that required all utilities considering a new offering to divorce themselves from their traditional investment bankers. Six years later, this provision would be expanded to require competitive bids for the new issues—the first time the investment banker–company relationship had been tampered with in the history of Wall Street. And the investment bankers' role in utilities was never far from mind. While the Roosevelt administration was still working on the bill, a special committee reported, "Fundamentally, the holding company problem always has been, and still is, as much a problem of regulating investment bankers as a problem of regulating the power industry."[44]

The public utilities lobbied intensely against the act. Once it had been passed, they adopted a strategy similar to the one used by the lawyers' association of the Liberty League. They personally declared the law unconstitutional and refused to acknowledge it. They then searched about for a means to have the law struck down without actually involving the SEC. At the time, a case was pending in a federal court in Baltimore that provided a good fit. A utility had a reorganization plan pending in the court. The opposition to the law used a local dentist who happened to be a bondholder of the utility as a convenient way of attempting to have the act overturned. He would claim that the Public Utility Holding Company Act stood in the way of a reorganization and should be overturned.

But the Supreme Court did not agree. The Court ruled that the act was valid in this particular case and that there were no grounds for overturning it. The New Deal won a major battle after having lost a few in court, and the utilities barons were put in their respective places. The Liberty League's success was broken. Although crucial to the first two years of the New Deal, the league quickly became less relevant, although not without an ideological fight.

The aftermath of the crash and the depression became a lingering nightmare. The economy began to improve but only gradually. The new laws had done much to restrain the concentrated power of banking and industrial groups. Although not mentioned clearly by name, the threat of American fascism had been removed by breaking up the dominant power of bankers. But the conservatives responded by equating the New Deal with a creeping socialism. Neither side accused the other of being Jeffersonian or Federalist when foreign name tags were able to convey darker connotations. The battle between Wall Street and Washington was by no means over. The new breed of regulators would muster their forces for more attacks on the Wall Street establishment.

CHAPTER EIGHT

The Struggle Continues (1936–54)

We must maintain our vigilance. If we do not, Wall Street may yet prove to be not unlike that land, of which it has been said that no country is easier to overrun, or harder to subdue.

Ferdinand Pecora

Dark days were still ahead for the country and for Wall Street. The economic malaise affecting the country was deeper and much more serious than anyone anticipated. The golden age was gone, replaced by one of pessimism and gloom. Within ten short years, the fortunes of the Street and its major personalities had changed substantially. The 1930s proved to be a crucible for the securities business. Investment bankers entered a new phase in their history when their functions were deemed harmful to the public good rather than beneficial. Not only public attitudes and perceptions were involved. The SEC began to force changes upon the New York Stock Exchange in addition to those it already imposed upon investment bankers. The old guard rapidly lost ground to the commission brokers, who would slowly become Wall Street's new elite. The result was a changing of the guard that would affect the Street's development for decades to come.

Despite the legislation passed between 1933 and 1935, the New Deal did not give Wall Street much breathing space for the remainder of the decade. The bear hunt was not over and would not recede from memory for years to come. Despite all the publicity and circuslike atmosphere surrounding the Pecora hearings, they remained a major triumph for liberals over big business and Wall Street. But the revolutionary changes brought about by the new regulations did not allay fears that American business still had a monopoly hold over major sectors of the economy. Until those fears were put to rest, there would be no respite for financiers. The battle between Wall Street and Washington was not yet over. And many of the familiar players were still actively onstage when the latest part of the drama began to unfold.

Political criticisms of Wall Street continued. Harry Truman, senator from Missouri, ranted against bankers for their part in the railway financings and bankruptcies of the period. In a Senate speech in 1937, he cited the problems of the Missouri Pacific Railroad as an example, likening the role of bankers to that of Jesse James in the previous century. Bankers "used no guns but they ruined the railway and got away with $70 million or more. . . . Senators can see what 'pikers' Mr. James and his crowd were alongside some real artists."[1]

A distinct connection was made between the robber barons of the nineteenth century and the bankers and financiers of the twentieth. A year later, Truman went on to sound a familiar refrain about Wall Street leadership:

> It is a pity Wall Street with its ability to control the wealth of the nation . . . has not produced some real financial statesmen. No one ever considered Carnegie libraries steeped in the blood of the Homestead Steel workers, but they are. We do not remember that the Rockefeller Foundation is founded on the dead miners of the Colorado Fuel and Iron Company and a dozen similar performances.[2]

In the years following the Pecora hearings, Wall Street suffered from the same lack of leadership. No one from the Street was willing to take an active role in defending finance against its many critics. After Roosevelt's landslide victory over Alf Landon in the 1936 election, the major sources of political opposition to the New Deal crumbled. Wall Street continued to be silent. But that did not prevent political criticism of the Street from continuing. The silence only gave the antibusiness contingent more fuel for their criticisms.

Suspicions in 1932 and 1933 were that Wall Street and monopoly capitalists had helped cause the crash. In 1932 the depression was ample proof of this, according to anti–big business sentiment. The ideas of Louis Brandeis, echoed in the writings and speeches of William O. Douglas and some of the western populists in the Congress, proved as alluring to trustbusters in the 1930s as they had before the war. Although business activity began to rebound after 1932, the economy was hardly healthy and the depression continued, only adding to the negative sentiment. Then in 1937 tempers again flared and old accusations were raised when the stock market suffered another serious rout. Anyone reading the newspapers recognized the arguments on both sides. Wall Street claimed that the new regulations had stymied its ability to raise funds for industry; the market only reflected a strangling federal government. Conversely, the New Dealers claimed that the monopoly stranglehold on the American economy had not been broken.

The strong but invisible hand of Louis Brandeis was still felt within the New Deal. Through Harvard law professor Felix Frankfurter and his network of former students, the justice had supported the Public Utility Holding Company Act as well as the securities acts and provided suggestions for its framework, much to the chagrin of Wall Street. Perhaps it was not a coincidence that his code name "Isaiah," used by members of the New Deal, reflected the name of a prophet warding off other false prophets. Isaiah had his vision of Jerusalem, and the Supreme Court justice had his own version of the New Jerusalem in which big business served the society in which it had thrived for 150 years. In the past, messianic zeal had been the preserve of big business and Wall Street, but times most certainly had changed. The trustbusters discovered a continuity in their methods and ideology that spread over twenty years. Significantly, the New Deal was proving successful in its battle with business, which had been accustomed to uninterrupted success with little government interference until the crash.

In 1935 there were many who believed that Roosevelt would not win the 1936 presidential election despite the passage of the Social Security Act, the social welfare cornerstone of his first administration. Confusing opinion polls tended to bear them out. When those polled were asked if government expenditures were too great or too little, a majority of those polled thought they were too great. When asked whether voters would vote for FDR again in 1935, the president suffered a loss of support almost across the board. A majority said they would not vote for him again.[3] What was quite certain, however, was that no one from the Republican party was poised to defeat him.

Bankers and the NIRA

Some reforms had already been made in the organized stock exchanges in the first days of the SEC. Recognizing the drift of the New Deal, investment bankers and brokers immediately made an attempt to regulate themselves after the NIRA was passed. The act called upon industry groups to organize and regulate themselves in order to become more efficient, paving the way for an economic revival. This was done outside the confines of the Banking Act and the two securities acts. Once the NIRA was struck down as unconstitutional by the Supreme Court, there was fear that any reforms based upon it were doomed to failure. But the investment banking community continued to reorganize itself to show that it was keeping up with the times. Separately, in 1935 Richard Whitney was replaced as president of the NYSE by Charles Gay, another long-standing member of the exchange, after the SEC began to press for changes in the exchange's governance. The hold of the floor brokers over the exchange's governance had been broken, and now more commission brokers were represented on the stock exchange's council than ever before.[4] But the SEC was not finished with its drive for changes in governance.

The main industry group for the securities industry was the Investment Bankers Association, originally organized at the time of the Pujo hearings twenty years earlier. Representing most securities dealers in the country, the IBA prepared a code of conduct for its members in keeping with provisions of the NIRA. In early 1934 it represented about 440 securities firms with over a thousand offices nationwide.[5] But that did not account for the entire investment community. Nonmembers accounted for thousands more offices representing several hundred more firms, many of them small operations with limited capital resources.

While the new laws passed by Congress laid down stringent guidelines concerning new issues practices, the industry itself could still do a great deal to improve its public image while attempting to comply with the law. What was very revealing was how many securities dealers still existed in the country despite the crash and the depression. But despite their numbers, many were in a severely depleted state. Even one of the largest, Edward B. Smith and Company, needed a capital infusion and merged with Charles D. Barney to become Smith Barney and Company. Clearly, Wall Street was undergoing a major shake-up, although its numbers looked impressive on the surface.

The reform attempt by the investment bankers before the Securities Exchange Act was welcomed. The self-regulatory code they produced required financial disclosures by companies issuing securities, in compliance with the Securities Act of 1933, set standards of conduct for sales and syndicate procedures, and prohibited preferred lists. When the 1934 law was passed, these attempts at self-regulation were instrumental in getting the bill itself passed through Congress. But, more important, a precedent was established. The securities industry apparently was serious about complying with the new laws. Not everyone shared Morgan's hope that the new regulations would prove short-lived.

After the Securities Exchange Act was passed, there was still a glaring need for regulation within the investment banking business. The stock exchange regulations applied only to members; many within the investment banking industry were therefore excluded, and they traded in the bond market or the over-the-counter (unlisted) market where SEC rules did not immediately apply. In the two years following, there was still a pressing need to get some sort of self-regulation passed. After Joe Kennedy left the SEC, the climate became increasingly dark for securities dealers. The next two chairmen of the SEC were less than friendly to the Street. Attempts at self-regulation were practical as attempts at self-preservation as well.

Wall Street had good reason to worry. After James Landis resigned as chairman of the SEC to become dean at the Harvard Law School, William O. Douglas succeeded him. Landis was responsible for making sure that many of the SEC's early administrative procedures were firmly in place. Douglas was a foe of many Wall Street practices and was determined to carry the administrative inroads made by Kennedy and Landis to fruition. Upon obtaining the SEC chairmanship, he made it clear that "under Landis we were taught how to get things done. And we're now going to go ahead and get them done." Born in 1898, William was only six years old when his father, a missionary, died, leaving the family almost destitute. He worked his way through college and law school by taking a variety of odd jobs. He eventually took a job with a prestigious Wall Street firm before being invited to teach at the Yale Law School. He produced a prodigious number of casebooks on corporate finance and was probably the best-known academic expert on corporate law in the country. A fervent disciple of Brandeis, Douglas had wide experience with working-class people because of the many part-time jobs he had held to support himself while in college. He never forgot their attitudes toward money earned and saved. While a member of the SEC, he gave a speech at the University of Chicago in which he voiced his opinion of contemporary finance and financiers. His words hardly reassured the financial community, which had looked forward to his address, in which he stated:

> The financial and industrial world has been afflicted with termites as insidious and destructive as the insect termites. Instead of feeding on wood they feed and thrive on other people's money. . . . these financial termites are those who practice the art of predatory or high finance. They destroy the legitimate function of finance and become a common enemy of investors and business . . . one of the chief characteristics of such finance has been its inhumanity, its disregard of social and human values.[6]

Douglas's main concern was how Wall Street systematically helped loot companies, forcing many into bankruptcy. Prior to joining the SEC, he had worked on a major study examining the bankruptcy phenomenon following the crash. He brought a knowledge of corporate finance to the SEC, sorely needed in its post-Kennedy phase. As he saw it, Wall Street had turned on its original objectives and now was the enemy, not a useful ally.

During his tenure as SEC chairman, Douglas was unrelenting in pushing for financial reforms. The Brandeis theme surfaced time and again in his vision of a reformed society. "When a nation of shopkeepers is transformed into a nation of clerks, enormous spiritual sacrifices are made," he unequivocally stated when describing how large organizations become estranged from their own business roots. He constantly accused investment bankers of noncompetitive practices, bordering on collusion. In 1937 he gave his famous Bond Club speech in New York before becoming SEC chairman. The assembled crowd of bankers hoped to hear some conciliatory words from the soon-to-be head of the SEC, but his very first line dispelled any hope that he was friendly to their profession. He began: "In large segments of the business of investment banking a noncompetitive condition prevails." He went on to attack the fees charged by investment bankers on new issues and their use of options in underwriting to accumulate positions in companies' stocks, and he touted the virtues of competitive bidding, the bane of every investment banker's existence. He then confronted them with monopoly practices, a charge that would be heard time and again over the next fifteen years. *Time* magazine reported that when he concluded his remarks, "the spattering of handclapping was far from cordial."

The New Deal trustbusters saw themselves as the successors of the same crusaders who originally had passed the Interstate Commerce Act and the Sherman Anti-Trust Act almost fifty years before. Gradually, Washington had been forging its own tradition of antibusiness forces into an ideology designed to stave off Wall Street's incursions. The laws of 1933 and 1934 were not the last gasps of the trustbusters but only the beginning. To its credit, the Street recognized the trend and tried its best to respond by forming a self-regulatory body. Some of the senior members of prominent firms were opposed to any form of regulation, but the tide had changed. Commission brokers were now becoming a force to be dealt with in stock market governance. They had a better sense of the investing public's needs and criticisms. The floor traders' hold was slowly declining. Since commercial bankers were out of the picture, Wall Street was on the verge of an organizational revolution in the latter 1930s.

Through much of 1936, brokers and investment bankers thrashed out the blueprint for a new self-regulatory organization based upon work done in the immediate past. The group, known as the Investment Bankers Conference, originally enrolled about 20 percent of broker-dealers in the country. The group was separate from the Investment Bankers Association. It was also heartily supported by the SEC. William O. Douglas favored it but added cautiously that "government would keep the shotgun, so to speak, behind the door—loaded, well-oiled, cleaned, ready to use—but with the hope that it would never have to be used."[7]

Practicality and the implied threat of intervention won the day. The over-the-counter market was too large and amorphous for any single regulator. The SEC would have been at a distinct disadvantage trying to control it; the commission probably would have failed, which would have been bad for its image. So the new association proposed by the Bankers' Conference was a decent compromise. While the SEC was the cop on the corner as far as new issues and the exchanges were concerned, the self-regulatory body was more akin to a traffic cop. Many of the provisions of the organization were incorporated into new legislation passed by Congress in 1937 as the Maloney Act. Named after Senator Francis Maloney of Connecticut, the new law created the National Association of Securities Dealers, or NASD, which was responsible for overseeing the over-the-counter market.

Almost all broker-dealers joined the new organization. Complaints about trading practices and divergent prices were often heard in the unlisted securities market, so the new body was welcomed by almost everyone. The number of unlisted stocks (not listed on a stock exchange) traded on the over-the-counter market was significant, although the largest, best-known companies still were traded on the NYSE, the curb exchange, or one of the regional exchanges. About twenty-five hundred were listed as opposed to about three thousand unlisted. According to the new requirements, unlisted securities now would have at least a modicum of regulation because they too would be subject to disclosure and trading rules. But most of the regulations would prove extremely difficult to enforce. With more than six thousand members, enforcement of the over-the-counter market would be a serious problem. But the consensus view was that any regulation was better than none.

The new regulatory climate proved unfortunate for Michael Meehan. On August 2, 1937, the SEC expelled Meehan from his seats on several exchanges, including the NYSE, for rigging the price of a stock. Overlooking a lesser punishment of one year's suspension, the SEC imposed the maximum penalty at its disposal because of Meehan's manipulation of the stock of the Bellanca Aircraft Corporation. The stock had risen to heights totally unjustified by its financial position. In 1934 the RFC refused Bellanca a loan on the grounds that it had insufficient collateral. The Delaware corporation had earlier du Pont interests but by the mid-1930s was being manipulated solely by Meehan. The flamboyant trader became the first major NYSE figure expelled from the securities business by the SEC. Associates noted that Meehan had failed to recognize the drift of the New Deal and continued his old ways in the new financial environment despite clear signs that the SEC meant business. As the *New York Times* noted, "The transactions in Bellanca stock for which he was prosecuted by the SEC were the kind which made him the toast of trading circles in the Coolidge era."[8] In his case, the SEC kept the gun on the desk rather than behind the door. Ironically, the man who made his reputation running the price of Radio in the 1920s was brought down by manipulating a little-known and mostly worthless stock. Meehan's fall was a significant public relations triumph for the Landis SEC.

Repercussions on the Street

Some years in the 1930s were better for the markets than others. New issues of corporate securities began to rebound after a disastrous 1933 and 1934. New bonds increased fifteen times over from 1934 to 1936. Stocks followed, and private placements also increased. These were bonds not registered with the SEC and sold privately to just a few institutional buyers. Investment bankers opposed to the new disclosure requirements had been touting private placements to their corporate customers as a way to circumvent the Roosevelt administration, but by 1935 that ploy was falling by the wayside. The economy in general also showed some signs of recovery. Output increased after 1934 and reached its 1929 level again by 1937. In the same period unemployment declined from 25 percent to 14 percent of the labor force. But the bottom fell out again. Another slowdown hit the economy in 1937, and the markets responded by going into a tailspin. By 1937, sales on the NYSE had fallen by 25 percent and the new issues markets collapsed again.

The downturn in economic activity brought more criticism of the securities authorities, who, in turn, blamed the investment bankers for the problem. One of the investment bankers' complaints was about the overall decline in business in the several years immediately following the passage of the Securities Exchange Act. Underwriting commissions fell some 50 percent from the World War I period. Brokerage commissions also fell. In 1929 they amounted to $227 million; by 1938 they totaled only $43 million.[9] The largest wire house broker of the day, E. A. Pierce and Company, was forced to the wall and merged with another firm that eventually became Merrill, Lynch. Margins on underwriting fell, and the drop in stock exchange sales knocked down the commissions. These declining numbers also affected the capital of many established Wall Street firms.

One unmistakable sign of the shake-up was the reforms enacted at the NYSE. Feeling that the exchange was dragging its feet on further reform, Douglas pushed vigorously for sweeping exchange measures that would do away with the ingrained power of some of its older members. About the same time, the scandal that brought down Richard Whitney unfolded. Despite his patrician attitude and Brahmin background, Whitney was an inveterate gambler. He had taken positions in some dubious ventures that even a novice investor would have avoided, and he began running up debts as they went sour. His usual recourse for funds was his brother Charles at

J. P. Morgan. But as he became even more extended, he found another source of cash. He began embezzling money from a New York Stock Exchange fund designed to aid members in need, siphoning off almost $1 million. In an attempt to cover his tracks, he appealed again to his brother and some close friends for loans to bail himself out. By doing so, he admitted his guilt to them, hastening his downfall. When he was finally exposed, the house of Morgan was drawn into the fraud because Charles Whitney was a partner. Morgan itself emerged unscathed if slightly soiled, and Whitney became the first NYSE president ever to do time in Sing Sing for fraud. After his release, he never again entered finance but lived out his years in relative obscurity.

Whitney's actions were remarkably well publicized. In a poll taken at the time of the scandal, a majority of those responding acknowledged that they had heard of Whitney's case. An even greater majority answered that they would like to see further regulation of Wall Street.[10] The Whitney scandal also provided the opportunity for Douglas to press for more stock exchange reforms. In November 1937 the SEC formally demanded the NYSE reform itself. Charles Gay responded by appointing the Conway commission, which recommended widespread changes in the governance of the exchange, including appointing a paid president for the first time in its history. Douglas particularly wanted the NYSE to have a new president, salaried rather than a volunteer coming from the exchange community, so that the ultimate decision-making process would not affected by floor traders. His personal choice was the highly regarded William McChesney Martin, a member of the Conway commission. Martin was an exchange member who lived an austere life in New York City, renting a single room at the Yale Club and devoting much of his energy to his work. He was also a keen student of economics and an open advocate of exchange reform. It was the latter interest that brought him to Douglas's attention.

One of Douglas's other avowed interests in exchange reform was the matter of brokerage firms holding securities for customers in safekeeping. While the stocks were held, they could be used for lending to short sellers. Douglas recommended that a new trust company be established that would relieve the firms of holding the securities, in the name of greater efficiency. In reality, what he was suggesting was removing the source of short selling from the brokerage firms themselves, making it slightly more difficult to sell a stock short. According to Douglas, this new depository would "reduce the number of operations involved in the securities business and should effect substantial economies for the brokers."[11]

Douglas received at least one of his wishes when Martin was appointed president of the NYSE. The NYSE's governance was substantially broadened, and the old guard had effectively been displaced by younger, reform-minded members. The SEC had made its wishes known and caused the exchange to reform itself significantly for the first time in its history. In other areas, reforms would not be so easily effected. But the exchange clearly had been rid of those who had been identified with the crash and the depression. Following FDR's pledge four years earlier, many of the money changers finally had been driven out of the temple.

Rebuilding Institutions

In its attempt to influence more than one financial aspect of American life, the New Deal became enmeshed in the market for residential mortgages during the 1930s. Shoring up the banking system also meant finding ways of supporting mortgages so that the core of the American Dream would not disintegrate during the depression. As banks failed in droves, the mortgage market was in serious danger of splitting apart. Many good mortgages were still performing while the banks that made them failed. Besides creating some problems for the financial system, the disarray also threatened some previous measures to assist homeowners passed during the Hoover administration.

In 1934 the Roosevelt administration sponsored the Federal Housing Act through Congress. It was necessary because another law passed in the late 1920s mandated that Congress help upgrade federal housing standards. A major concern at the time was the menace of disease caused by substandard housing in many parts of the country. The act created the Federal Housing Agency in order to allow banks to make loans on homes. On the surface, the FHA looked like any other Keynesian-inspired agency designed to stimulate demand from homeowners. But its purpose was a bit more basic. Initially, it purchased only loans from banks that were meant for "home improvement," which in the 1930s meant only one thing—loans to install indoor plumbing.

These loans proved to be something of a watershed in banking. Previously, many consumer loans were made by finance companies, not banks. Now that the FHA was guaranteeing loans, a whole new world opened up for the banks, which began to recognize the value of consumer loans. FHA administrator George McDonald remarked, "I think the local banks which went into this business will never get out of it . . . and they will be enough to furnish competition to the finance companies."[12] He was correct. The era of commercial banks providing consumer credit had begun, thanks to a government agency. Business was beginning to learn a few tricks from its traditional rival, the federal government.

While attempting to improve residential health standards, the New Deal found itself on an interesting track. Another agency, the Home Owners' Loan Association, was also established. The HOLA bought mortgages from banks and helped change the terms to favor the homeowners, many of whom were delinquent in their payments. While it had only a short history, the HOLA nevertheless showed that government intervention in the market could aid consumers. It helped many thousands of homeowners from losing their homes during the depression. Because of its risky nature, it also ended up owning many properties it did not want or did not have the capacity to service. But its very existence showed a compassionate side to government that had been sorely lacking in the 1920s. The New Deal was quickly changing the face of banking. Banks were happy to be rid of the dodgy mortgages, and consumers were happy to keep their homes intact. But attempts to translate that success into broader action would be stymied by Wall Street, which found government activity in the mortgage market an unwarranted intrusion onto its own turf.

The New Deal hoped to expand the idea of mortgage assistance into a joint venture with Wall Street. Originally, it envisioned a private company with a government shareholding called the RFC Mortgage Corporation. The idea was to use the company to help prop up the mortgage markets, but there was little money available for private investment. The RFC founded a separate company devoted to buying and selling mortgages so that the mortgage assistance experiment would not die. But as Jesse Jones noted, "Times were so pessimistic that no one would put up money in common stock for such an enterprise." Wall Street had come to view the RFC not as a partner but as a government agency to be taken advantage of—an institution that would help failing banks and railroads at the taxpayers' expense.

This was not the first time the banking community turned a cold shoulder to requests for help from the administration. Jones noted that when he first joined the RFC, before he was named chairman, he approached J. P. Morgan about bailing out a small New York bank. The Harriman National Bank, located in New York City, was on the brink of failing in 1933 when Jones went to see Morgan about providing possible assistance to keep it afloat. His reasoning was sound enough. He assumed that since the smaller banks looked to the larger for guidance the big banks should help out when called upon. When the depression started, millions of dollars from around the country poured into the New York banks, where it was felt they were safer than if they remained outside the major money centers. Ironically, the large New York banks benefited from this, and Jones reasoned that the best known of all the banks would then come to the aid of a smaller, otherwise insignificant institution. But he was wrong. "Mr. Morgan told me that it was not his business to tell people what to do with their money. He said he had no responsibility to the depositors of the Harriman National Bank."[13] Morgan's refusal was not surprising since the Harrimans and Morgans had been adversaries in the past.

The sense of camaraderie that provided investment banking support for Kidder Peabody did not extend to small, retail banks.

A few private investors did venture forth and by all accounts appear to have done well with their investments. New York State Comptroller Morris Tremaine came forward and began buying bonds from the RFC that were supported by public works projects. He bought Jones Beach, New York, bonds as well as those supporting the George Washington Bridge over the Hudson River, both New Deal–inspired projects. But for the most part, investors remained on the sidelines. As a result, Congress created the Federal National Mortgage Association, or "Fannie Mae" in the good ole boy lexicon of depression politics, to help buy outstanding FHA loans. As Jesse Jones put it, "In setting up the Federal National Mortgage Association to work exclusively in the handling of FHA-insured mortgages, we again entered the field only after our offers to become partners with private capital had fallen on deaf ears."[14]

The RFC continued to seek investment partners with Wall Street and the private sector for several years after the HOLA had been founded but to no avail. In 1934 the private capital shortage could be blamed, although in reality it was nothing more than a small Wall Street strike against the new issue procedures of the SEC. Afterward, it was a strike against government interference in what financiers previously held to be their own preserve, the mortgage market. Wall Street's record with the RFC was one of borrower, not partner. Many of the railroads and banks assisted by the RFC were closely related to investment banking houses, which did not return the favor when the RFC asked for assistance in funding private mortgages and public works projects.

Wall Street's refusal to entertain the RFC necessitated the founding of Fannie Mae. It proved to be a turning point in American finance. The federal government stepped into the breach by creating additional agencies over the years that emulated and expanded upon Fannie Mae's basic blueprint. Prevailing Wall Street thought was that joint ventures with a dubious "socialist" administration were off-limits. After a century of business-led developments, a window of opportunity opened and the New Deal quickly rushed in. Wall Street's refusal to aid the New Deal left the Roosevelt administration no choice but to proceed without private assistance.

The TNEC

The resurgence in corporate financings after 1934 was misleading. Many of the new bond offerings were really refundings—old bonds coming due that could be refinanced at very low interest rates. They were underwritten by the same underwriters that had originally brought them to market.

In Morgan's case they were underwritten the second time by Morgan Stanley and Company. While this activity gave the appearance that economic activity was on the rise, it reflected the drop in interest rates during the depression more than a robust economy. But even the modest prosperity it brought to its underwriters would come to haunt them later.

Many companies refinancing bonds used the same underwriters they had used in the past. Those using Morgan Stanley simply followed the Morgan tradition to the new house. But wary regulators spotted the trend and began to cry foul. The underwritings were following a pattern. High-quality corporate bonds were underwritten by the top tier of investment banks while the lower-quality issues were handled by second-tier underwriters. Despite the Glass-Steagall Act, it appeared to some that the grip of the investment banker on the financial system had not been broken. Morgan Stanley's new prowess suggested that the house of Morgan was still very much in the investment banking business. If the power of the private cum investment banker was to be broken, they would have to be pursued with even more vigor in the future.

Ingrained in the continuing fear of investment bankers, even after the laws of 1933 and 1934 had been passed, was a general fear of syndicalism, although no one mentioned it by name. European syndicalism contributed to the rise of fascism in Italy and Germany, and the criticisms of the American variety flew in many directions. Hoover mentioned it in his diatribes against the New Deal, as did the American Liberty League. On the other side of the coin, the New Dealers thought they could detect it in banking organizations and utilities empires. Organized groups, formal or informal, affected capital formation, possibly led the country into the unpopular World War I, manifest themselves in groups like the Navy League, and controlled the access to credit by most banks outside New York. But most of all, they were very close to attaining significant political power. Charles Dawes had been vice president under Coolidge, John W. Davis and Newton Baker had been candidates for the presidency, and Dwight Morrow held a Senate seat. The delegates to the 1932 Democratic National Convention had snubbed financiers' requests to support Baker but only because of the economic climate. Under other circumstances, bankers and their lawyers might have been more successful. But in the nervous climate of the 1930s, close alliances between bankers and politicians were cause for alarm.

The two Morgans and some of the heads of other old-line houses had enabled Wall Street figures to transcend the tarnished image of Vanderbilt and Gould. The robber barons' counterparts during the depression were Michael Meehan and Ben Smith. But floor traders no longer possessed the wide influence they had had in the nineteenth century. Bernard

Baruch and Joseph P. Kennedy were probably the last traders to gain significant social status and influence, but even they fought for acceptance among the upper echelons of the banking elite. Kennedy still could not get a private meeting with Morgan, and Baruch was accused of every imaginable Jewish plot to undermine the WASP establishment. Wall Street's power was exercised at the very top, not in the middle ranks. The closed world of the private investment banker, with his access to political power and his unaccountability to the public, was beginning to have deleterious effects upon the profession, which had for so long enjoyed a remarkable amount of freedom.

Despite the strides made during the first Roosevelt administration, there was still a widespread suspicion that much of American industry remained under monopoly control in the late 1930s. Bankers had proved dexterous in maintaining their grip on the securities business in some cases, and the public utilities had proved resilient in the face of widespread criticisms. Before long, many who had testified at the Pecora hearings would be back in the witness chair at the instigation of the New Deal. This time the topic would be monopoly power.

The climate of the day was badly affected by the recession of 1937. After several years of slow but unspectacular recovery, the economy again sputtered, reversing the gains of the previous two years. While the economy slowed by about 8 percent, unemployment increased again to almost 20 percent of the workforce. Wall Street suffered as well. New corporate securities issues collapsed, and turnover on the NYSE diminished by half. The great fear was that, after its slow recovery, the country was plunging back into economic chaos. Roger Babson offered some advice for graduates of his Babson Institute in 1938, emphasizing an entrepreneurial spirit: "Your real goal should be to get a small business of your own. . . . My hunch is we're going to be in this economic struggle for a long time."

Cynics claimed that politicians were looking for a scapegoat by crying wolf in the name of monopoly. The New Deal countered by claiming that the country was still under the domination of monopolies that controlled vital industries, strangling recovery in the process. The inquiry into monopolies got its intellectual impetus from a 1933 book by brain truster Adolph Berle and Gardiner Means entitled *The Modern Corporation and Private Property*, which outlined the distribution of corporate power in the country. Their discoveries were startling since they resembled what would have been expected of the nineteenth century more than the twentieth. Half of all corporate wealth was under the control of the top two hundred corporations. AT&T controlled wealth greater than that found in twenty states combined. The book extended the findings found in the Pujo and Pecora hearings into a general indictment of American corporate structure. Apparently, America had changed little in the twenty-odd years since the Pujo investigation despite new regulatory legislation. These revelations would quickly make the book one of the most influential in the history of antitrust and the depression era.

As the recession took its toll on the workforce and industrial production, Roosevelt addressed Congress on the danger of monopoly power, stating that "there should be a thorough study of the concentration of power in American industry." Although the Sherman and Clayton acts had been on the books for decades, there was general agreement that their effect was very limited. Although J. P. Morgan and Company had been constrained by the banking and securities acts, there was a widespread feeling that it was still very much involved in investment banking. American Telephone, which had strong links to Morgan over the years, was the largest single corporate client of Morgan Stanley and Company after 1934, followed closely by US Steel and numerous utilities companies.

As a result, Congress and the president collaborated to produce a bill creating the Temporary National Economic Committee (TNEC) in June 1938, an eclectic group that became known simply as the Monopoly Committee. The committee was composed of members from the House and Senate, as well as from the executive branch. Among its members were Senator Borah of Idaho, a staunch defender of western interests who still bore a great deal of mistrust toward big business and Wall Street; also from the Senate was Joseph O'Mahoney of Wyoming, an early New Dealer who became the TNEC chairman; William O. Douglas was one representative of the executive branch. The committee launched a comprehensive investigation into the concentration of economic power that reached across many sectors of business life. Among the industries studied at length were life insurance; investment banking; steel, petroleum, and motion picture companies; transportation; public utilities; and manufacturing. From the beginning, the hearings were not meant to be adversarial. Bankers especially had been in the hot seat once before in 1933, and this time the inquisitors stated that they meant to study industries, not the behavior of individuals. Douglas made it clear that there would be no "witch burning" in the monopoly hearings.

Almost as soon as the investigation began, the opposition made itself heard. The U.S. Chamber of Commerce responded to the president's address by outlining a seven-part proposal designed to stimulate ecnomic activity without imposing further government controls on business by stating, "It should now be realized that expansion in employment and business cannot be produced by legislative fiat. The best and surest way to obtain such expansion is through the stimulation of private enterprise."[15] The New Dealers agreed, with one caveat. First, unfair practices should be attacked. Interlocking directorships and cozy relation-ships with investment bankers had made certain industries insulated from public account-ability. As a result, they were free to collude on unfair pricing. In the in-vestment banking business this meant the high underwriting fees charged to corporate clients with their obvious, if not wholehearted, consent.

The TNEC certainly found concentrated power in the investment banking business and did not have to go far to do so. SEC disclosure re-quirements, including publication of prospectuses and tombstone ads in the newspapers, made the job of tracking underwriting groups relatively simple. Six New York City firms dominated underwriting of corporate se-curities issues. Morgan Stanley, First Boston, Kuhn Loeb, Dillon Read, Smith Barney, and Blyth and Company shared 57 percent of new issues underwritten between 1934 and 1939. Another fourteen New York firms contributed 21 percent, while those outside the city contributed only 12 percent.[16] Those who believed a monopoly existed appeared to have am-ple evidence to press their case.

The way in which these issues were distributed added fuel to the fire. The top six firms underwrote the lion's share of high-quality issues, while the second tier in New York settled for the lower-rated issues. Firms out-side New York managed none of the highest-quality issues; their major in-fluence was in bringing the lowest-quality issues to market. Even more to the point was how well the second-tier New York group actually per-formed in the better-quality issues. Did they initiate deals or simply get in-vited into them by the top-tier firms? In many cases they were invited, making the argument against the top six underwriters all the stronger. They controlled more of the top corporations' access to the markets than many thought possible.

But even among the top six underwriters, the influence of Morgan was still dominant. Apparently, no one on Wall Street thought that Morgan Stanley was anything other than J. P. Morgan and Company in sheep's clothing. Charles Mitchell, in his reincarnation as a head of the investment banking firm Blyth and Company after leaving National City, told the TNEC that his partner Charles Blyth firmly believed the best way to get close to Morgan Stanley was to open an account at J. P. Morgan and Com-pany, to get "under the covers" with them as a means of gaining access to Morgan Stanley. From all outward appearances, he was not wrong. Most of Morgan Stanley's preferred stock was owned by officers of J. P. Morgan. This fact was not hidden from Wall Street by any means, although it per-petuated the notion that Glass-Steagall separability was more fiction than fact. In order to sever itself from the bank, Morgan Stanley finally bought back all of its preferred stock in December 1941, ending the formal link between the two firms once and for all.[17]

Critics of the TNEC were quick to point out that there was nothing unusual about the dominance of the New York investment banking firms since the depression had depleted many smaller firms' capital. Only those who had been around for years in a dominant position would be expected to survive the bad economic times. Besides, the Glass-Steagall Act helped create the contemporary investment banking industry in 1933, so it was actually a child of regulation. If not for that government interference, the industry would have been dominated by even larger firms with more capital at their disposal. But on the other side of the coin, their critics quickly pointed out that the investment bankers' influence was important because it was tied to the fortunes of large corporations to begin with. High-investment-grade companies used old-line firms, ensuring the survival of both during the depression. That alone was a sign of monopoly domination. The issue was far from settled.

Monopoly concentration was also found in the life insurance industry. Similar to investment banking, a few top firms controlled the bulk of the assets of the entire industry. The top five life insurers controlled over half the assets of all companies nationwide. The sixteen largest companies controlled over 85 percent of the industry's assets.[18] This was especially important because the life insurers were the largest clients of investment bankers. They bought a heavy proportion of new stock and bond issues, especially the private placements of bonds that dominated corporate financing in the late 1930s. The Metropolitan Life was the largest, followed by the Prudential. There were also strong historic connections between many of the insurers and some New York bankers, notably Morgan. The insurance business was the only other financial services industry besides investment banking to be investigated by the TNEC.

Even though the TNEC revealed much about American business, the New Dealers were moving on to other endeavors. William O. Douglas left the SEC in 1939 to accept an invitation to become dean of the Yale Law School. About the same time, Louis Brandeis announced his retirement from the Supreme Court and Douglas vigorously campaigned for the vacant seat. Douglas's departure from the TNEC after his Supreme Court appointment would remove one of Wall Street's most vocal critics from the public forum. Douglas was succeeded by Jerome Frank at the SEC. The hearings concluded on something of a whimper, and the TNEC was far from a qualified success. In fact, many thought it was an expensive, time-wasting failure. Senator O'Mahoney himself labeled the proceedings "boring." They lacked the emotionally charged atmosphere of the Pecora hearings. Although no charges or serious scandals emerged from the proceedings, the committee's voluminous findings did underline the structure of American industry and financial services. Investment banking played a relatively small role in the final reports, although its monopoly structure was clearly noted. But World War II intervened, putting any possible repercussions against Wall Street on hold until the conflict was over.

The Competitive Bidding Issue

The drop in the securities business in the late 1930s was also affected by the looming war clouds in Europe. There appeared little reason for optimism. Germany, fifteen years before a borrower on its knees, had repudiated its indebtedness and was openly militaristic. The Soviets showed signs of strength and were viewed as a potential threat as well. The recession within the depression had discouraged all but the most hearty investors, for it seemed that the New Deal had run out of tricks in coping with this latest economic crisis. When the government did propose new methods, they were usually signs of state intervention in the economy such as Fannie Mae. American capitalism was in deep trouble, partly because it was stymied by the federal government and partly because it lacked serious leadership.

If history had taught Wall Street anything it was that it often had been accused of profiteering while war was being waged. Ever since the War of 1812, the most prominent bankers to the government had been accused of profiting at the public's expense by charging too much for fees on government bonds although in many cases the opposite had been true. During the next war, massive bond borrowings would be sold with the help of investment bankers for no fee. Putting a positive face on an otherwise unprofitable situation, many of them simply concluded that history would repeat itself by helping to familiarize the general investing public with bond investment, following the experience of World War I. When the war finally was over, all of that cash again would become available for investment in more profitable financial products. The size of the financings required in the war effort against the Axis powers would dwarf any effort the private sector would be able to mount.

In the latter 1930s, many new securities issues were placed privately by investment bankers rather than being offered for sale to the public. The TNEC inquiries indicated that by 1939–40 almost half of new corporate offerings were placed directly with large institutional investors, avoiding SEC registration. Wall Street contended that this trend was a result of the onerous registration process. New Dealers maintained that American corporations were mature enough to sell securities to private investors on the basis of their good names and credit ratings, avoiding the costly fees charged by Wall Street. The fact was that private placements began to increase *after* the TNEC was formed, leading many to believe that investment bankers and their client companies were attempting to avoid the limelight and any appearances of impropriety. In 1939 the SEC launched an investigation into private financings. Through the TNEC, the SEC queried seventeen corporations that had sold private placements in the previous two years, asking them for specific details of the bonds. Foremost on its mind was the amount of compensation investment banks received for their limited service in packaging these deals.

By 1940 both the investment banking business and brokerage were suffering. New issues of corporate bonds picked up after the 1937 recession, but new stock offerings remained flat. The private placements helped investment banking, but the underwriting business was still mostly moribund. On the brokerage side, things looked even worse. Share volume on the NYSE fell to a quarter of its 1930 levels. The number of issues listed actually dropped slightly, and dividends increased only slightly. Membership dropped sharply and the number of nationwide sales offices declined. On balance, the situation in 1940 was as bad as at any time during the early years of the depression.

Brokers could not claim that the antimonopoly inquiry was hurting them. While the investment bankers were under a microscope, claiming that scrutiny and onerous SEC procedures were hurting their capacity to do business, brokers could not make the same claims. It was the new SEC rules and the NASD regulations that restrained their behavior. The effect fell on the specialists and floor brokers, who did the bulk of the trading. Now that their procedures were being monitored, floor traders were less likely to do the sort of deals they had in the past, especially after Michael Meehan was banned from the business. Without the churning created by floor traders, business was certain to drop. Since the public was in no mood to do any sizable trading, the net result was not encouraging for brokers. They would have to wait for an improvement in the economy before their businesses would show more promising results. While not everyone was severely hurt by the depression, "Hey Buddy Can You Spare a Dime?" was still a favorite tune among a large segment of the population.

The war helped put the economy back to work, but Wall Street was relegated to an ancillary role in war financing. The ranks of investment bankers and brokers were also reduced. Many brokers and bankers joined the armed services, depleting the Street of much expertise. The best-known conscript on Wall Street was William McChesney Martin, president of the NYSE. Dwindling business on the exchange and the constant pressure applied by the SEC disillusioned him, and he answered a draft call early in the war. The back rooms of many firms were also decimated by the loss of their clerks and began recruiting women to fill the vacancies. The war thus provided an opportunity for women to work in the financial district, but the jobs were mostly clerical and had to be given up when the permanent employees returned. The number of member firms on both the exchanges and the NASD also declined as poor business (mostly brokerage) conditions forced the smaller, marginal firms to shut down. Many of the larger firms were forced to continue merging as they had done during the 1930s.

The late 1930s and the early war years saw a continuation of the competitive bidding controversy that had raged for most of the latter 1920s and early 1930s. While Wall Street was overwhelmingly hostile to the practice, some regional investment bankers came out openly for it. Among them were Cyrus Eaton of Otis and Company of Cleveland, Harold Stuart of Halsey Stuart, two notable regional investment banking houses, and Robert P. Young of the Alleghany Corporation. They all favored competitive bidding for new issues and openly advocated it at every opportunity. But their motives were a bit transparent: all three favored it as a means of wresting business away from the larger banking houses in New York. Young advocated it as a means of getting out from under Morgan control at Alleghany. All had their "antiestablishment" motives. Federal Judge Harold Medina later concluded that "revenge for real or fancied wrongs played no small part" in their advocacy against the larger, established banking houses.[19]

Anticipating a formal SEC reaction to demands for competitive bidding, Harold Stanley stated his firm's opposition to the practice: "I believe that competitive bidding for new issues of corporate securities would be unfortunate for both the issuing companies and the investing public." He stated that he thought it represented coercion on the part of the government against private enterprise. He concluded by saying, "Investment banking is a useful business and its evolution must be toward, not away from, the professional standard and a greater sense of care and responsibility."[20] But Stanley's argument was cleverly refuted by an argument framed a year and a half later by Otis and Company of Cleveland. Coming out strongly in favor of competitive bidding, a pamphlet produced by the firm quoted Franklin D. Roosevelt, Louis Brandeis, and William O. Douglas, citing the dangers of a bankers' coterie. Referring back seven years to the NIRA, it denied that investment banking was a profession:

> The investment banker is primarily a merchant who buys securities at wholesale for resale at a profit. The fact that he is in a position to profit by the advice he gives invalidates any claim he may make to stand in the same position with reference to the issuer that a doctor or lawyer does to his client. . . . competitive bidding is the logical solution to the monopoly problem in the investment banking business.[21]

The argument proved much more persuasive than Stanley's.

The controversy came to a head in 1941 when the SEC formally required all public utility holding companies to obtain competitive bids from underwriters. The SEC passed Rule U-50, based on powers derived from the Public Utility Holding Company Act. The reason for enacting the rule sounded familiar. In its 1940 study, the SEC found that "During

the five and one half year period [January 1934 to June 1939] six leading
New York bankers managed 62 percent of all registered bond issues and
57 percent of all registered bond, preferred stock and common stock issues." It concluded that there existed "an unwritten code whereby once a
banker brings out an issue, the banker is deemed to have a recognized
right to all future issues of that company."[22] This was a not-so-oblique
reference to Morgan's domination of the public utilities business and the
problems presented by the fall of the Insull empire. The new rule required utilities executives to find the best price for their shareholders and
rate payers. Since the power companies already had monopolies in their
own areas, there was no reason to continue banker domination of them as
another monopoly within a monopoly.

Anticipating banker reaction, and perhaps even another "capital
strike," Jesse Jones stepped into the fray in May 1941. He proclaimed that
if investment bankers refused to provide competitive bids for utilities issues, the RFC would be prepared to do so itself, using its own considerable
resources. His reason was simple: "I think the competitive bidding rule is
right," he said as he announced his support of the idea after conferring
with the SEC. Technically, U-50 replaced the "arm's-length" rule used in
the Public Utility Holding Company Act. That particular clause usually
proved difficult but did score a notable success by preventing Morgan
Stanley from underwriting a new issue for the Dayton Power and Light
Company because the two were too closely affiliated.

As soon as U-50 was passed, several large corporations put out securities issues for competitive bids. AT&T, the Erie Railroad, and McKesson
and Robbins were three companies that sought the best prices for their issues. Competitive bidding brought about the demise of some long-standing banking relationships, at least temporarily. AT&T's move severed a
Morgan connection that had stood since the beginning of the century,
when it did not employ Morgan Stanley as its lead underwriter. The *New
York Times* concluded, "While the rule did not come without warning, its
operation in most of the cases so far has proved to be more confusing and
complicated to the industry as a whole than had been expected."[23]

The Fed in Control

The outbreak of war gave the Federal Reserve the opportunity to assert its
authority in the markets as never before. Douglas's departure from the
SEC took the spotlight off the agency and, when combined with the war,
gave the Fed increased visibility. In every war to date, government borrowing had crowded out corporations and municipalities, and World War
II was no exception. But the war also found the Fed actively operating in
the money and bond markets for the first time. Washington seized the op-

portunity from Wall Street, which had little choice but to play along. The size of the war effort and the general mobilization left Wall Street with little choice but to take its lead from Washington.

Also playing a major role in war financing was the RFC, headed during the war by Jesse Jones. Throughout the 1930s the RFC was the world's largest corporation because of the vast amount of money it distributed to industries in need. When war broke out, it became the natural organization to coordinate the war effort through industry. Most wartime production was coordinated through its subsidiary, the Defense Plant Corporation. Many vital smokestack industries contributed to the effort by accepting the RFC's estimates for expanded facilities and implementing them at cost. According to Jones's own estimate, profiteering was kept to a minimum, at least by the major corporations that joined or were co-opted into the effort. Over $9 billion was spent by the RFC and the Defense Plant Corporation to help American industry expand to meet the requirements for increased industrial production. But Jay Whipple, the president of the IBA, stated in 1943 that the first job of investment bankers was to help win the war while at the same time preserving private enterprise. "Without free capital markets," he proclaimed, "there can be no free enterprise system since industry would then be obliged to obtain its capital from the government."[24] The great inroads made by the RFC in helping finance the war effort were making investment bankers nervous. They were feeling the heat created by the RFC, which was only responding to their own lack of enthusiasm in the first place.

One of the interesting asides that came from the RFC's war effort concerned FDR's desire to purchase the Empire State Building. Viewing it as the perfect edifice to house federal offices, FDR asked Jones to look into purchasing it in 1942. The world's tallest building was not making a profit, with many of its offices vacant because of the depression. It was still owned by John Raskob, with minority stakes held by Pierre du Pont and Al Smith. A large mortgage also was held by the Metropolitan Life Insurance Company. The proposed offering price would have netted the shareholders a tidy profit of about $10 million. Jones assumed that FDR wanted to purchase it to repay old political debts to Raskob and Smith, who had supported him for the governorship of New York in 1928 when Smith ran for president against Hoover. Also, Raskob had once bailed FDR out of a debt he had incurred buying his Warm Springs property in Georgia. Despite their later flirtations with the Liberty League and the virulent anti–New Deal rhetoric that accompanied it, Jones saw the potential purchase as an opportunity in which the "President would be doing something for the two men who had done the most to make him President."[25] The transaction never went through, however, and the building remained in private hands.

The authority of the Federal Reserve was enhanced during the war when it intervened in the markets to stabilize interest rates. The intent was to keep interest rates as low and as stable as possible so that the borrowings in the bond market could be done cheaply. Between 1941 and 1945, the Treasury borrowed seven war bond issues in the market. The Federal Reserve bank in each Fed district coordinated the sales, allocating bonds to banks that joined the effort. Those in the selling group made no profit on sales and were not compensated for their expenses. Almost five hundred dealers and several thousand banks nationwide helped sell the bonds, with Kidder, Peabody selling the most on an individual basis. The gross debt of the United States rose from $48 billion in 1941 to almost $260 billion by 1945 as a result of these offerings, representing an increase of $1,500 per person in the overall population.[26] The increase in the public debt matched that recorded during World War I, but the sheer numbers were much larger. The commercial banks would be recruited into the effort to buy war bonds because they represented the largest pool of investment funds that could be channeled into Treasury bonds. But before they could be enlisted, consumers had to be deterred from spending too much cash.

The Fed was charged by the Roosevelt administration with reining in consumer credit, which it did after a speech by FDR in August 1941. The president asked consumers to sacrifice for the war effort even before the attack on Pearl Harbor. After credit expansion was put in check, the Fed turned its attention to interest rates, announcing that it would stand ready to buy or sell Treasury bills in the market at three-eighths of 1 percent. This ensured that money market rates would remain stable while bond rates also stabilized at around 2.5 percent. But bond investors were not tame investors and would sell if frightened by the prospects of rising interest rates, a real fear during wartime. But the peg proved successful and interest rates remained stable.

Unforeseen at the time was the psychological impact the peg would have on a future generation of investors. Interest rates became fairly stable until the end of the Korean War. Fifteen years later, during the latter 1960s, they again became volatile. An older generation of investors and savers, accustomed to relative stability, were caught unaware by the later volatility, and their slowness in reacting would cost some of them dearly as bonds became as volatile as stocks in the next generation. Volatile bond prices would become the major issue following the Vietnam War as inflation became the main enemy for investors.

In order to sell as many bonds as possible to the banks, the Fed devised a clever scheme that has been the envy of many ever since. In 1941 the Treasury changed its tax policy and began taxing the interest paid on its own obligations. It began by making sure that all new issues of Treasuries were taxable. Within fifteen years, it hoped that all the previously nontaxable issues would be redeemed from the market. It then offered banks an enticement to buy the bonds. When the banks bought the Treasury bonds, the Fed relaxed its reserve requirements for them, enabling them to keep more money in their vaults to buy even more bonds. The technique worked well throughout the early 1940s. Banks bought the bulk of the war bonds, with the public purchasing the rest. Loans to businesses and consumer credit suffered, but the massive war financing was very successful. Banks became the largest holders of Treasury obligations, an unaccustomed distinction for most, which ordinarily preferred business loans.

Preparations for war took their toll on Wall Street. New corporate securities issues declined by half between 1941 and 1943 before recovering and surging ahead in 1944 and 1945. New common stock offerings dropped to their lowest level since 1935. Brokers fared slightly better, with volume on the NYSE dropping between 1941 and 1942 before recovering in 1943 and surging ahead by 1945. Treasury offerings filled the vacuum. The Treasury issued $11 billion in new bonds in 1941, rising to $53 billion in 1944. After the attack on Pearl Harbor, a new issued was quickly snapped up by the public, netting the Treasury $2.5 billion. The Treasury asked investment bankers and companies not to offer any corporate bonds when it was in the market for fresh money so that corporate bonds would not collide with its own issues. When the market operations were combined with the industrial effort guided by the Defense Plant Corporation, the coordinated effort became the largest in history.

Investors began to change their familiar patterns once the war was under way. By 1942 the trading patterns on the NYSE began to change substantially. No longer did the major industrial companies dominate exchange trading. Traditionally called *wheelhorses*, stocks such as US Steel, Corn Products, Bethlehem Steel, Studebaker, and Anaconda Copper were losing their share of turnover volume on the NYSE. In 1942 over twelve hundred companies were listed on the exchange, twice the number listed during World War I. "Big Steel" had accounted for over 60 percent of annual NYSE volume prior to the 1920s, but by 1942 all twenty of the wheelhorse stocks accounted for only 18 percent of the total turnover. All the new listings and the smaller companies that had sprung up in the intervening years were attracting more and more of investors' attention. Although the new issues list for the war years covered no more than one column in the newspapers, investors were keen to find cheap stocks that had some growth potential.

During the course of the 1940s, the individual investor stayed clear of common stocks. The wire houses catered to them, but their overall effect was very limited. Little growth was found in the retail sector and when it was seen it was not particularly profitable. The favorite way of trading by the small investor actually increased, but brokers were not jumping for joy.

Odd-lot volume (less than one hundred shares) increased on the NYSE, but that would hardly translate into strong profits for brokers. As a result, the price of a seat on the NYSE hardly changed. The small investor, largely ignorant of or not interested in investments, turned his attention to housing immediately after the war. Mortgage debt and housing starts increased dramatically. Housing prices in 1945 were actually lower than in the 1920s and represented a better investment for most than stocks or bonds. Any bull market would have to wait until the great American housing boom developed.

After hostilities finally ceased in 1945, the markets slowly began to rise. Government issues of war bonds decreased dramatically, and new stock issues doubled. But corporate bonds did not increase much at all, and stock exchange turnover remained at its wartime levels. Municipal bonds increased dramatically, but the boom was not on the scale of that following World War I. Part of the reason was the Fed's determination to keep interest rates pegged. Corporate bonds still yielded only about 2.50 percent for the remainder of the 1940s, while Treasuries were about 2.25 percent. Treasury bills remained under 1 percent. As long as the peg remained in place, the Fed was in control of the markets. The margin requirements on stock market loans also rose in the late 1940s, driven up by the Fed. In 1945 the requirement rose from 50 to 75 percent and was raised to 100 percent in late 1946.[27] This meant that margin buyers and short sellers were virtually nonexistent; all deals had to be done for cash only. These were the highest requirements since the Fed had been entrusted with margin in 1934.

Inflation was a real bogey in the postwar period. Prices rose almost 15 percent between 1946 and 1947 when the Fed raised margin requirements, but because of the peg, bond yields remained steady in their narrow range. Harry Truman took a momentary lighthearted approach to the problem, writing in 1947: "I appointed a Secretary for Inflation. I have given him the worry of convincing the people that no matter how high prices go, no matter how low wages become, there just is not any danger to things. I am of the opinion that he will take a real load off my mind, if Congress does not." Continuing appointments to his imaginary cabinet, he also proposed a secretary of semantics, who would be vested with the most important task of all: separating East from West. Truman added, "He is to tell me the combination of words that will put me against inflation in San Francisco and for it in New York." While Wall Street liked to think of itself as representing varied interests, most outsiders recognized that it often marched to a different tune than the rest of the country.

The Fed was again asked to toe the line by extending its peg through the Korean War. Signs started to appear that the central bank was tiring of being the cofinancier of war efforts with the Treasury. But Truman stated emphatically that when it came to discussing finances for the war effort, "my approach to all these financial questions was . . . to keep the financial capital of the United States in Washington. This is where it belongs—but to keep it there is not always an easy task."[28] His own bias against Wall Street was still apparent. He was not alone. Many former New Dealers and trustbusters in his administration felt the same way. The suspicion still lingered that financiers had been conspiring to rig the underwriting business in their own favor for years. The last blast from Washington against the Street was still to come.

Antitrust Again

Just as the markets were returning to some normalcy in the late 1940s, the Justice Department showed its intent to pursue what it considered the continued investment banking monopoly. Trust-busting was proving to be a permanent fixture at the Justice Department under Attorney General Tom Clark, not the ephemeral pursuit it was earlier in the century. Morgan Stanley's links with J. P. Morgan and Company and the apparent National City/First National syndicate link with Morgan from pre-Glass-Steagall days provided evidence in the eyes of the antitrust division that investment bankers had never given up their old tricks and still maintained their long-standing relations with American industry. The Street was on the verge of the most important legal challenge in its history.

The Justice Department filed suit against Morgan Stanley and sixteen other investment banking firms in October 1947. The charges in the suit—officially known as the *United States v. Henry S. Morgan et al.*—were complex, and the case took several years to develop as a result.[29] In the complaint the Justice Department claimed that there existed an "integrated, over-all conspiracy and combination formed in or about 1915 and in continuous operation thereafter, by which the defendants as a group developed a system to eliminate competition and monopolize the cream of the business of investment banking."[30] The date referred to the time Morgan and other investment bankers put together the Anglo-French loan during World War I, the largest offering in history until that time. The suit sought redress on behalf of the United States as well as the hundreds of other investment bankers around the country whom the defendants had sought to exclude from the top ranks of the underwriting business.

Not as sensational as earlier inquiries into investment banking, the suit still proved to be a milestone in the history of Wall Street. Each investment banking practice was discussed and analyzed in great detail, and many were published for the first time. A brief history of each of the seventeen firms involved in the suit was published in the proceedings, providing some public relations for firms that otherwise were very private. The firms acquired bragging rights that became the envy of Wall Street: inclusion in the suit was considered acknowledgment of status and power within the profession. It was tantamount to achieving the lead position in a tombstone ad covering almost fifty years of Wall Street history.

One of the problems immediately encountered by Harold Medina, the presiding judge, was the precise nature of investment banking. While sounding silly, definition was still a problem to nonexperts. After years of front-page news and notoriety, investment banking was still not well understood. The only individuals who knew it well were those who practiced it, and no one was willing to take their word, especially when the top echelon of the business was busy defending itself against litigation. It therefore fell to the presiding judge to become well enough acquainted with the securities business to rule on the Justice Department's case, which relied upon a long line of apparent conspiracy for its credibility. Medina acknowledged the tenuous nature of the Justice Department's case. "And all this is said to have gone on for almost forty years, in the midst of a plethora of congressional investigations, through two wars of great magnitude, and under the very noses of the Securities and Exchange Commissions and the Interstate Commerce Commission," he wrote, describing the historical nature of the complaint. As far as he could determine, the government case depended "entirely upon circumstantial evidence."[31]

Fortunately for Wall Street, Medina himself was above reproach. He did not have the prosecutorial background of Pecora or the political leanings of Untermyer. Nor was he a politician. A graduate of Princeton and the Columbia Law School, he had already won some judicial fame presiding over a trial of prominent members of the American Communist party. He was in successful private practice when Harry Truman appointed him to the federal judgeship, and it was noted jurist Learned Hand who suggested that he be assigned the Morgan case. His major shortcoming was that he had no particular expertise in investment banking. He sought to make up for this deficiency by spending some time during the trial with an investment banker who showed him the intricacies of the business. He chose Harold Stuart, who had been called to testify in the case although Halsey Stuart and Company was not a defendant. Medina found him to be a "man of complete integrity upon whose testimony I could rely with confidence." An ardent exponent of competitive bidding, Stuart was something of an outsider to the large houses. Wall Street was not happy about his influence because, as one of the regional houses opposed to Wall Street domination of finance, Halsey Stuart and Stuart himself had gone on record in the competitive bidding controversy of 1941 as favoring sealed bids. However, he served his educational function well because Medina got a close look at the packaging of a couple of new issues, both negotiated and competitive bid. As a result, he was able to admit, "I felt possessed of the necessary background and could thereafter, with a modicum of assurance, interpret and assess the probative value of the documents which constituted the greater part of the plaintiff's proof."[32] Wall Street was relieved since the judge had no ideological ax to grind.

The crux of the Justice Department's position was that the seventeen firms had restrained trade under the Sherman Act by conspiring to keep the lion's share of the underwriting business to themselves. History played an important part in the charges. The government claimed that traditional investment banker–client relationships were built up over time. Once an investment banker did a deal for a client, it was expected to do similar ones in the future, at similar fees. This was not difficult to establish. The record of the seventeen firms showed that they were the major investment bankers to a large proportion of American industry and business. But proving this point with any continuity after 1934 was difficult because the traditional bankers had to divest themselves of their securities business after the Glass-Steagall Act was passed.

One of the intriguing questions that was asked concerned how the Justice Department settled upon the seventeen firms named in the case. At least twenty other firms had greater financial resources than some of the defendants, but they were not named.[33] On closer inspection, it appeared that the seventeen had close links with the money trust of pre–World War I days. When some of the names reappeared during the TNEC hearings ten years earlier, it was not surprising that they were named as defendants. Each firm had a history of continuity over the almost forty-year period since the Pujo committee hearings and the Anglo-French loan of 1915. On closer examination, the Justice Department could claim that Union Securities (a defendant) was really Seligman in disguise, Morgan Stanley was nothing more than J. P. Morgan, and Blyth was the successor to National City because of the Mitchell link. Dillon Read and Goldman, Sachs were prominent in the Pecora hearings, as was Kuhn Loeb. Kidder, Peabody had been in existence since the mid–nineteenth century and could be easily blamed for being closely allied with Morgan, while Drexel had its clear Morgan link. Continuity could easily be claimed, but whether it had a deleterious effect upon competition was another matter. Several firms were omitted from the suit simply because their chief executive officers claimed to be adherents of competitive bidding.

The continuity among the securities firms was counterbalanced by the financings they brought to market. Although Wall Street lamented the number of private placements done in the 1930s and 1940s, they may have helped bail the Street out of the suit even if they provided little income. Since private placements are distributed to only a few buyers, the fee structures for their investment bankers are very thin. In some cases investment bankers were not employed at all. Competitively bid issues naturally had thinner fees attached than negotiated deals. The Justice Department had a full record of public and private financings done between 1935 and 1939. Underwritten public bond issues, the mainstay of many houses' business before the depression, declined, while private placements and competitive bids increased. Thus, the traditional continuity the government went to such great pains to prove was not necessarily borne out by the facts. It would have to be proved by examining the underwriters of traditional negotiated deals. And while common stock financings also increased, many of the houses that specialized in them were not named in the suit because they were relative newcomers to the business. Merrill, Lynch was strengthening its position as a wire house that underwrote new issues of department store stocks, but it was not included in the suit because it did not fit the "continuity" mold.

In summary, the court held that "it is completely unrealistic, and a distortion of economic fact, to attempt to consider the 'securities business' even as defined in the complaint, only in terms of "underwritten issues."[34] Other forms of fee and commission business also contributed to most firms' bottom lines, but the Justice Department focused only on underwriting. Its strongest case lay there, although the other profit centers helped unravel the monopoly case in the end. The Street breathed a sigh of relief, because the longer the case dragged on, the more it became apparent that the government's case was weak.

After several years of testimony and arguments, Medina dismissed the case against the "Wall Street Seventeen" in October 1953. He stated that "each has followed its own course, formulated its own policies and competed for business in the manner deemed by it to be most effective." But the idea of conspiracy to violate the Sherman Act was unsubstantiated. Medina continued: "I have come to the settled conviction and accordingly find that no such combination, conspiracy and agreement as it is alleged in the complaint, nor any part thereof, was ever made, entered into, conceived, constructed, continued or participated in by these defendants, or any of them."[35] Wall Street finally was exonerated of collusion.

The *United States v. Henry S. Morgan et al.* became a watershed in the history of Wall Street. While not as well publicized as some past investigations, it finally freed the Street of its image as the home of monopoly capitalists. Despite the strong bias found in the White House and the Justice Department, investment bankers finally proved that they were vital to the economy. Their techniques and fees had been exposed and did not appear to be exorbitant, as many had believed. The image that had been built up in the 1920s and early 1930s was slowly starting to crumble. Wall Street dodged a large bullet when the Morgan case was dismissed. But after ten years of depression and five years of war, prosperity finally came knocking and would set the economy aright, putting criticism to rest. It was easy to identify with bull markets.

CHAPTER NINE

Bull Market
(1954–69)

A salesman has got to dream, boy. It comes with the territory.

Arthur Miller

When Harold Medina dismissed the case against the investment banking community, the modern era in finance began. Over the previous thirty-five years, Wall Street had suffered through the crash, the depression, and two world wars. For twenty of those years, it also had suffered at the hands of New Dealers intent upon wresting away the enormous power that bankers had accumulated over the years. The country had undergone vast and wrenching changes, and Wall Street had participated in all of them to the fullest measure.

A postwar boom developed in the early 1950s that was unparalleled in American history. Unlike the golden era of the 1920s, this boom was based upon strong economic fundamentals, technological advances, and a stock market that reflected solid optimism rather than rank speculation. Investment surged, the average American household became materially better off, and the country began to feel invincible once again. Consumerism retained its grip on the economy. The previous two decades of deprivation and war were replaced by optimism and a desire to acquire a wide range of goods. The nation's factories now were free to produce for the consumer rather than for the war effort.

One fundamental assumption spurred by consumerism did not materialize, however. There was a general belief that the vast array of consumer goods and the improved standard of living would somehow lead to a more egalitarian American society. Differences between people, based upon class, would disappear as everyone began to look alike in this new consumer world. No longer would it be easy to tell the boss from the worker, the bank teller from the bank president. The new prosperity and all of its trinkets would help workers blend in rather than stand out in a crowd. The media picked up the theme and discussed it frequently. America was becoming a "classless" society. Vance Packard, whose best-selling book *The Status Seekers* appeared in 1959, put it succinctly: "Whatever else we are, we certainly are the world's most self-proclaimed equalitarian people."

Wall Street certainly did its part to help perpetuate the idea. Having a stockbroker became as necessary as having a minister or a psychiatrist in the new American middle-class society. Investment recommendations from brokerage houses spelled the way to riches as investors tried to cash in on the boom in manufacturing and technology. Small shareholdings increased dramatically, and mutual funds began to grow as well. The average household income of investors was about seventy-five hundred dollars, six times what it had been in the 1920s. The new breed of investor provided the capital that the new breed of companies needed to expand. But he had to be careful. Hucksterism and get-rich-quick schemes were found around every corner. "Do you sincerely want to be rich?" became a familiar cry of stock promoters and bogus investment artists. The difference between consumer man of the 1950s and his predecessors was clear. As John Kenneth Galbraith noted, "People at the beginning of the nineteenth century did not need an adman to tell them what they needed."

Parallels between the 1950s and the 1920s started to emerge as the bull market continued. Swollen price-earnings ratios, aggressive stock promoters, corporate expansion, and a generally favorable regulatory attitude all contributed to the climate. The role of the stock salesman became all-important, as it had been in the golden era of the 1920s. The growing middle class became a source of funds for brokers on the one hand and targets on the other. Hucksterism now was becoming more than aggressive selling; it was becoming an art. Borrowing a page from the 1920s, hucksters made it clear that stock investment was vital to keep abreast with the neighbors. But the investor was still relatively unsophisticated.

The bull market that developed after General Eisenhower's victory in the 1952 presidential election continued for more than fifteen years. It represented one of the longest periods of general prosperity in history, although the market did experience a few bumps along the way. Economic growth was unprecedented. Industrial stocks raced ahead and were matched by those in high technology, namely, television and pharmaceuticals. American households bought television sets in the same way they had bought radios in the 1920s, and Zenith and Motorola became as entrenched in television as they were in radio. In 1954 Jonas Salk's polio vaccination was administered to over 2.5 million schoolchildren in an attempt to eradicate the crippling disease. Pharmaceutical stocks advanced as a result of that and other medical developments. The Supreme Court overturned separate but equal facilities in the public schools in *Brown v. the*

Board of Education, adding to the feeling that the country was becoming more egalitarian. Popular psychology had changed substantially since the war years. By the early 1950s, half the population sampled in a Gallup poll claimed they were able to get a good night's sleep, the highest figure in years. In the 1950s, everything seemed possible. Only ten years before it had appeared that the world was in the grips of the fascist menace.

Many of the new consumer discoveries of the period helped to produce record profits for the companies that developed them. The long-playing plastic disk was introduced at 33⅓ rpm and hailed as a technological breakthrough. The Columbia Record Company began producing the first long-playing albums. Automobile production boomed and seriously began competing with the rails as consumers discovered the joys of long-distance driving. Frozen foods, originally developed thirty years earlier by Birdseye, changed the shopping habits of millions as household freezers and other appliances became more plentiful. Aerosols became popular in packaging all sorts of products, and air-conditioning was in demand for homes as well as offices. The *Economist*, always looking to the United States for trends expected to develop in Britain ten years later, remarked that "the rump of a packaged air cooler protruding from a window sill of a block of middle class flats has become a social symbol as significant as a television aerial." But no one thought at the time that the power of television would become a key element in antitrust matters within ten years.

On a broader level, the 1950s proved to be the golden period of the American century in international affairs. The central role of the dollar in world trade helped pave the way. When the major allied industrialized countries signed the Bretton Woods Agreement in New Hampshire after the war, the dollar played the major role in determining foreign exchange rates. Remembering the chaos that the early years of the depression caused in the foreign exchange markets, it was agreed that currencies should have a stated value in dollars. The dollar was itself convertible into gold, although the precious metal was playing a smaller role in international finance than in the 1920s. The new order was designed in part by John Maynard Keynes and Harry Dexter White of the United States. For the next twenty-five years, the strong dollar that resulted helped the United States dominate international trade and investment.

American industry spent billions overseas in foreign investments as the United States exercised its strength as a creditor nation. While Western Europe and Japan were rebuilding their economies, the Americans moved several steps ahead by establishing a strong presence in foreign markets. Plants, factories, and distribution centers were established around the globe, although Europe received the bulk of American foreign investment. And since many countries were protecting their currencies with exchange controls, the dollar became the major international currency of choice.

The American multinational corporation grew so quickly in size and influence that cries of "Coca-Cola" imperialism were heard throughout Latin America and Europe. Pop culture was being exported through American marketing icons, and many foreigners objected to the advance. A best-seller in 1958 was Lederer and Burdick's novel *The Ugly American*, which depicted the American abroad as a powerful ignoramus, unaware of foreign cultures and social mores. Clearly, the Europeans considered Americans as nouveaux riches with potentially dangerous consequences for their economies if not resisted.

Rebuilding industry in Europe was more important than expanding abroad, and the American direct investment in Europe remained much higher than foreign investment in the United States.[1] The stock market benefited greatly. Canadians in particular shifted large amounts of funds to Wall Street, fueling the rally. The London stock market was open for trading, but severe restrictions existed for foreign investors so investors turned their attention to New York. Money was free to enter and leave the United States without restriction, making it one of the only major markets open to foreign investors. The last time that foreign investment was seen in such significant amounts was during the rumors of the great bear raid in 1932.

After the *United States v. Henry S. Morgan* trial ended in 1953, the regulations passed in the 1930s finally were accepted by Wall Street as a fait accompli. There was no more talk of capital strikes or government interference in private enterprise. Part of the reason could be attributed to investor confidence. A boom was coming, and it was clear that if the new investor of the 1950s was to be drawn to investments, he would have to feel comfortable in the markets. The NYSE extended its trading hours beginning in 1952 in order to service more orders during the week. Brokers now touted the safety and soundness of investments, but the get-rich-quick schemes were still abundant. The new trend on Wall Street called for increased investments by retail investors on a scale not seen since the mid-1920s. In the new environment, selling was becoming as great an art as putting together a deal. Many institutional houses began adding salesmen to their workforces.

The Market Recovers

The expected postwar boom was slow in developing. A stock market rally in 1949 was more of a speculators' rally than one of sound fundamentals, and the markets rose cautiously. But after Dwight Eisenhower defeated Adlai Stevenson by 442 electoral votes to 89 in the 1952 election, the markets became poised for a bout of positive feeling not witnessed since the 1920s. Harry Truman and his trust-busting administration were gone. Republicans had returned to office and had taken both houses of Congress as well (they would lose their majority again during Eisenhower's second term). After a twenty-year absence, the party of Coolidge and Hoover was back after five consecutive Democratic presidencies and would come to represent economic growth and booming markets.

The markets' fondess for Ike was rewarded when the Republicans began to slash the federal budget during his first term. Government expenditures remained steady rather than increase, and the amount of publicly issued Treasury bonds actually declined for a few years in the early 1950s. Then the opposite of what happened during the war occurred: Treasury issues began to account for a smaller portion of all bonds issued rather than more. This freed more funds for investment in corporate and municipal bonds, which were increasing month by month. Consumers and the markets reveled in the new positive atmosphere where belt-tightening was no longer necessary.

The housing boom that began after the war continued well into the 1950s. The recession of 1953 put a temporary damper on growth, however. Both the population and per capita income were growing as the postwar baby boom continued. Many of the new residential housing units were built in the suburbs rather than in cities. The exit to the suburbs began as suburban life became the goal for many city dwellers. Demand for municipal services also grew, putting enormous pressure on the municipal bond market to provide the necessary funds. The new prosperity was quickly felt on Wall Street, which expanded to meet the new challenges.

The Street reacted to the trend by increasing the number of salesmen in the brokerage branch offices around the country. The ranks of investment bankers also increased dramatically. Both doubled between 1950 and 1960. The price of a seat on the NYSE increased dramatically, and odd-lot volume also raced ahead. The public was becoming familiar with stocks, but the process was still slow, at least in the early years of the bull market. The NYSE itself began emphasizing the continuity of common stocks, listing those that had consistently paid a dividend over the previous hundred years.[2] Enormous publicity was given to stocks by some radio personalities. Walter Winchell, for instance, began suggesting stocks as good investments on his nationally broadcast radio show in 1954. While the recommendations were not those of an investment professional, his popularity indicated how far the public mood had changed since the depression. Twenty years before, Huey Long and Father Coughlin were busy excoriating financiers over the radio, hardly touting stocks.

The markets were not entirely free of government influence, however. The Treasury peg was lifted only at the end of the Korean War in 1953. The Fed made a decisive move to leave the markets to their own devices once the peg was lifted. Operations in the money market were scaled back as the central bank adjusted to the postwar environment. In the future, it would intervene in the money market only to influence short-term interest rates, allowing bond yields to go where they may. As a result, bond yields naturally began to rise in the 1950s as inflation pushed interest rates higher.

Margin requirements remained high until 1953. More margin money began to find its way into the stock market via the New York banks, and securities prices increased as margin sales rose. But most of the stock market activity came from institutional investors and professionals. The retail investor was still on the sidelines in the early 1950s. After twenty-five years of depressed prices and lack of interest, Wall Street still had to sell itself to small investors as a place where it was possible to make money without fraud or deceit. But investors were still slow in reacting. Housing and consumer durables occupied a large part of their personal finances.

Rapid expansion caused some problems. Scandals plagued the American Stock Exchange (Amex) in the 1950s, demonstrating that it was behind its counterpart at the NYSE in winning investor confidence. The New York Curb Exchange officially changed its name to the American Stock Exchange in 1953 in order to reflect a newer, more modern image, but some of its practices caught up with it in the bull market. A former SEC commissioner, Edward McCormick, had been hired in 1951 to improve the image of the exchange, which needed to have some of its internal practices overhauled. A popular choice for president, he was one of the few exchange employees who was academically qualified for the job. He was a CPA, held a doctorate degree, and was well regarded as a financial analyst at the SEC before becoming a commissioner. But his attention was directed at expanding the exchange to include more listed stocks. As a result, some companies of dubious value were listed. In addition, one of its leading floor members, Edward Elliot, became involved with illegal distributions of securities that were meant to be privately placed, violating SEC regulations. The problem mushroomed when it was discovered that other Amex members had also illegally distributed securities, using their positions and professional reputations as cover. Although the exchange eventually set the record right, its image as something of a backwater compared with the NYSE remained intact.

When Eisenhower was stricken with a heart attack in September 1955, the markets took it very badly. The president recalled, "I had thrust upon me the unpleasant fact that I was indeed a sick man." The markets experienced the same anxiety. The stock market loss exceeded $14 billion on paper, the largest drop in history, and almost 8 million shares were traded in one day, also a record. The drop occurred at the midpoint in the first Eisenhower bull market that lasted until 1957. The sell-off was a sign of how sensitive the markets were to news in the first bull stage. The overall cutbacks in government spending were to the markets' liking, and there was a great fear that the rally would fizzle out without Eisenhower in office. Within a year, the economy began to slump, although the administration kept to its course of cutting expenditures and fighting inflation. As the second recession of the decade approached, many economists in academia and Wall Street favored a reflation to stimulate the economy, but to no avail. Eisenhower steadfastly maintained that cutting government was his top priority. Then international events started to unfold that would have a profound impact upon the national psyche for the next generation. In October 1957 the Russians put the first *Sputnik* into orbit.

In the national furor that followed, the country began to doubt its own prowess in science, technology, and higher education. Walter Lippmann wrote to Russell Leffingwell, describing what became a characteristic American fear. Consumerism, so heavily relied upon to stimulate the economy, had come up short against an opponent with a totally different set of values. "[Our] adversary puts not only guns ahead of butter, he puts education and research and medical care ahead of butter. I do not feel that we can take the view that we must not cut into consumption, into our butter . . . in order to meet the challenge," he wrote.[3] The American emphasis on materialism appeared to have put the country in second place in high technology.

Immediately after the Russians made their announcement, Eisenhower addressed a concerned nation. He assured the public that the national defense was sound and that the country had nothing to fear. He also quickly increased the defense budget to allow for new research and development in weapons systems. The market rallied strongly after the president's address. The *New York Times* proclaimed that a "Boom Continues in Boron Shares: Talk of a 'New' Rocket Fuel Stirs Feverish Buying." Almost any company that made anything resembling rocket fuel or other aerospace-related products advanced in price, as did other defense contractors. The Russians provided the sort of external force that the market usually did not anticipate. The insularity of the postwar years showed in the reaction. The rush was on by makers of war matériel to sell to the government. Within two years the term *military-industrial complex* would become one of society's main buzzwords.

Certain that the country was far behind in education, Congress reacted quickly and created the National Defense Student Loan program. The federal government would grant loans to any college student who wanted to pursue science or language teaching after graduation. The student loan program blossomed in later decades, but not without great cost and embarrassment to the Department of Education, which was not equipped to be in the loan business. Students clamored for the loans and applied for several billion dollars' worth in just a few years. Ironically, within fifteen years Wall Street would be integrally involved with the program in much the same way it had become involved with Fannie Mae over the years. College students proved to be terrible credit risks.

After the country became uncomfortably aware of the Russian presence, the cold war began in earnest. It took the place of open hostilities, and the economy developed around it. Many of the industries that helped win the war against fascism now turned to high technology to develop weapons systems with liberal government support. On Wall Street this meant that many defense contractors and electronics companies would become the hot stocks for the remainder of the decade. Raytheon and Texas Instruments joined the traditional favorites such as IBM and AT&T as stocks to watch. A trend was emerging on the Street that was unsettling to some while being acknowledged as a sign of the times by others.

That established a link that made some observers clearly uncomfortable. The favorite stocks of 1957 and 1958 included many old standbys, including US Steel, Lorillard, American Motors, and Studebaker Packard. But many recently founded companies also grew quickly. Litton Industries, founded in 1953, saw its sales explode exponentially within only five years. Two new companies came to market in 1957 that were considered promising if somewhat novel. Polaroid made a camera that produced instant photos, and Syntex produced the new birth control pill. Hewlett-Packard came to market in 1959, initially trading without any earnings to speak of, and Loral Electronics was benefiting from the surge in defense contractors. Other hot stocks included the Equity Funding Corporation, a California-based insurance company cum mutual fund that sold an investment scheme not well known in the United States. Companies known for clever or new ideas became known as *concept stocks*.

The strong bull market attracted more new investors each year. In 1949 retail investors were few and far between, but by 1959 the number of retail investors buying securities doubled. The largest increase was among women. The NYSE began investor surveys in the early 1950s in a clear attempt to show that it was broadening its appeal beyond the traditional confines of institutional investors and floor traders. It also began an active campaign to show that its commission rates were not particularly high. But despite the increase in sheer numbers, individual investors accounted for about the same amount of turnover on the NYSE in 1959 as they did at the beginning of the decade. Retail investors accounted for about 55 percent, while institutions accounted for 25 percent. The remaining 20 percent was traded by floor members.[4] Broad geographic appeal was slower in developing, however. Half of all investors came from New York, and the other heavily populated states accounted for most of the balance. Wall Street was still lagging in promoting capitalism for the small investor.

The increased investment activity also had a profound effect upon

Wall Street firms. Partnerships began to decline and many member firms began to incorporate. Woodcock, Hess and Company became the first NYSE member to incorporate in 1953, starting a trend that would quickly accelerate. Changing to corporate status was prompted by the increasing need for capital and limited liability. The costs of doing business on the Street were increasing throughout the 1950s, and many firms found it necessary to incorporate. Within ten years, many more firms would go public, selling shares to investors.

The commission houses on the Street were also coming into their own after 1950. Many firms, led by Merrill, Lynch, began training their brokers to be clients' men and to serve the needs of small investors. Merrill was founded before World War I and by the end of the Korean War was the largest brokerage on the Street, followed by E. F. Hutton, Bache, Paine Webber, F. I. du Pont, and Dean Witter. The wire houses began producing investment research that they distributed to clients, based upon more sound economic research than in the past. The new retail investor was provided with more detailed information upon which to make investment decisions. The days of the shoddy, tendentious research produced in the 1920s were fading. Another sign of the times could be found in the social status of stockbrokers. Outcasts a generation before, they had crept into the highest-status group of professionals by the late 1950s. They now vied with corporate executives, federal judges, and medical specialists at the top of the status ladder.[5] In 1968 several investment bankers appeared in *Fortune*'s list of the richest people in the country, including Charles Allen of Allen and Company and Clarence Dillon of Dillon Read. They joined more familiar names such as du Pont, Rockefeller, Kennedy, Ford, and Mellon.

The Eisenhower administration was extremely friendly to the markets. The Justice Department did not stand in the way of many mergers that developed in the late 1950s, although some of these would be overturned after the fact. But at the end of his second term, the president reiterated a warning that was becoming a dominant theme of the latter 1950s. He acknowledged the increasingly vital link between the federal government and business that was providing such a boon for defense contractors and manufacturers. Warning against a concentration of power between business and the defense industry, he noted in his farewell speech: "We annually spend on military security more than the net income of all United States corporations. . . . In the councils of government we must guard against the acquisition of unwarranted influence, whether sought or unsought, by the military-industrial complex. The potential for the disastrous rise of misplaced power exists and will persist."[6]

In just a short generation, the "enemy" of American society had changed. No longer was it the monstrous trust or monopoly extending its tentacles by destroying competition. Now it was a combination of industrial and military power whose influence appeared to be growing at a rate never attained by the monopolies of a generation before. Critics argued that the old monopolies had never been broken; they had simply taken on a new complexion. This new concentration of power served its own best interests by whipping up public distrust of the Soviets in order to win more government contracts. The Navy League had been born again, only on a massive scale. Others claimed that the close relationship was the price of defense. The United States had never had a permanent armaments industry before because it had never had a "permanent" enemy before. Whatever the interpretation, Wall Street boomed along with the defense contractors. Yet some of the contractors recognized their dependence upon government business and took steps to ensure their survival if the link was ever broken. Critics contended that they were simply using their glorified positions in the market to begin dominating other businesses.

Under the Democrats in the 1960s, the stock market generally prospered, although there were some nasty hiccups along the way. In 1962 a major sell-off occurred because of the administration's spending policies and some policy fiascoes such as the Bay of Pigs invasion. In May 1962 the stock market was seriously routed by fears over Kennedy's economic policies. On one day, May 28, the Dow dropped almost 6 percent on 9 million shares, one of the largest drops in history on one of the busiest days. In the past, this clearly would have been called a panic, but the very next day, the exact opposite occurred. The market staged one of its sharpest one-day rallies in history, regaining all of the loss and adding a couple of percentage points. After the smoke cleared, it became apparent that a new phenomenon had struck the Street that was a harbinger of the future. Stock price fluctuations were possible without the implications of a panic or a crash. The age of volatility had begun.

Kennedy's unbalanced budget was not well received. This led the Street to take a less than favorable attitude toward the president, but the reaction was short-lived. The day Kennedy was assassinated, the market dropped sharply. The market indices fell by 3 percent before making it up when it became apparent that Lyndon Johnson was in full command at the White House. Before the NYSE closed at 2:00 P.M. on November 22, many investors experienced serious losses and blamed the specialists for their problems. Many specialists on the exchanges were swamped with orders, and prices on many well-traded stocks were not even quoted as the day wore on. Critics contended that the specialist system was outdated and not able to withstand crisis conditions. The criticisms faded eventually but would be repeated when the market experienced serious difficulties in the future.

The market indices rose during Johnson's presidency and touched historic highs on several occasions. The Dow Jones Industrials flirted with 1,000 in 1965 before retreating. But at the same time, interest rates were rising. Money market yields rose, and short-term rates equaled long-term rates. Inflation also doubled but still remained relatively low, touching almost 3 percent. The major stimulus was the rise in federal spending, which increased at a greater rate than the growth in the economy in the mid-1960s. But a new pattern was being seen for the first time in years. The market, although extremely volatile, was actually gaining along with inflation. One thousand on the Dow again seemed possible in both 1966 and 1968 before retreating a year later. Inflation rose and became entrenched at around 5 percent for the remainder of the decade. The number would seem like a trifle in the latter 1970s.

Picking Up Momentum

The bull market created the greatest merger trend on Wall Street since the days of the nineteenth-century trusts. Companies discovered that the strong market had left many older firms with dimmer prospects behind. While investors shunned them, their low price-earnings ratios and mediocre prospects presented opportunities for takeovers. These companies were a bargain since their book values were cheap. They could be bought for less than it would cost to start up a new company, so they became takeover targets for more successful companies, sparking a trend in mergers and acquisitions that reflected the mood of the times.

Because of the high prices found in the market during the latter 1950s, many of the new, aggressive companies found themselves in a position to capitalize on their lofty positions. Some had multiples of forty to fifty times earnings, enabling them to raise new stock quite easily. Bargain hunting became the trend of the decade as they went in search of other companies. Litton Industries aggressively began accumulating others both within and outside the electronics industry, becoming one of the first "conglomerates." Diversification became the new buzzword on Wall Street, and companies actively sought bargains outside their own industries in order to hedge their operations against downturns in the economy.

Conglomerates were the products of merger activity. The trend began in the mid-1950s and lasted well into the 1960s. The theory behind a conglomerate was simple. An acquiring company brought under its umbrella other companies, sometimes in totally different lines of business, to enhance the parent company's profits. If business was bad in the core business, the others would help balance losses. The company was protected against business cycles, and its investment bankers made healthy fees by advising on the takeovers. In the patois of the 1960s, some investment banks advised the "bride" while others advised the "bridegroom."

Some of the "marriages" were friendly, while others were hostile. They were arranged by investment bankers, who usually received a fee based upon the size of the deal. But conglomerates spelled serious problems for regulators. Traditionally, mergers had occurred between similar companies or between two companies in the same food chain; if competition was restrained, the Justice Department could take action under the antitrust laws. But conglomerate mergers were a new breed. Since dissimilar companies were uniting under one umbrella, they usually did not fall within the ambit of antitrust legislation. A concentration of economic power was occurring again without any federal regulations to prohibit it. The SEC chairman Manuel Cohen called conglomerates "one of the very serious problems that is facing the American industrial capital structure . . . requiring the type of SEC remedies employed after the analogous 1920s' merger wave had developed the public utility holding companies."[7]

Before long, Wall Street analysts figured out how to sell the stocks of the conglomerates to investors. They touted them in much the same way, using the diversification idea: they were hedges against the parent company losing money. Theory suggested that they should be stable and grow along with the company's acquisitions. That was safer than investing in a company that was not so well diversified. If the conglomerate was well established overseas, so much the better. Far-flung industrial empires provided the best hedge against downturns in the domestic business of a company. Investment analysis now was a more complicated discipline than in the past when the word of investment bankers was all a client needed to know about a company. The diversification principle was well known, however, having been widely used since the late nineteenth century.

Those who built the conglomerates became the notable Wall Street and corporate personalities of the era. Harold Geneen of International Telephone and Telegraph (ITT), Charles Bludhorn of Gulf and Western Industries, Charles "Tex" Thornton of Litton Industries, and James Ling of Ling-Temco-Vaught (later LTV Corporation) were the best known. Employing very different personal styles, they constructed conglomerates that dominated their respective core industries and, in ITT's case, had substantial influence overseas. They took electronics companies benefiting from the new emphasis on defense and technology and molded them into multi-billion-dollar businesses. They were the contemporary heirs of Billy Durant and J. P. Morgan Sr. in that they created vast industrial empires by absorbing other companies. But Durant had mastered acquiring similar companies, while Morgan focused on acquisition for its own sake. The new breed was following in Morgan's footsteps more so than in Durant's.

Ling founded the Ling Electric Company in the late 1940s and became acquisition-minded in the mid-1950s. A native Oklahoman with a youthful, 1950s demeanor, he reputedly raised capital for expansion by selling subscriptions for a new stock issue door-to-door. Within ten years his empire grossed nearly $50 million and was listed on the NYSE. He then moved seriously into the defense business by acquiring an electronics and missile manufacturer named Temco. Shortly thereafter, he acquired an aircraft manufacturer and changed the name of his company to Ling-Temco-Vaught. The LTV Corporation soon followed and became one of Wall Street's darlings. The company continued to acquire others, and within twenty years was involved in aerospace, meatpacking, and steel production. The acquisition of the Jones and Laughlin Steel Company proved disastrous, however. It eventually helped sink the company into bankruptcy in the 1980s, becoming the longest-standing bankruptcy in American history until the company was totally reorganized in 1993. LTV remained a major steel producer but otherwise divested itself of many of its former holdings.[8]

ITT's expansion under expatriate Briton Harold Geneen was no less spectacular but more mainline since Geneen, formerly an executive with Raytheon, signed on with ITT in 1959 when it was already a mature company. Historically its main business was manufacturing telephones and telephone equipment. Because of the ATT-Bell monopoly in the United States, most of ITT's business was overseas. Having previously worked as an accountant, Geneen also was determined to expand domestically and embarked on a series of acquisitions that left Wall Street breathless and begging for more. His best-known buy was Avis Rent-a-Car. At its height, ITT had a presence in seventy countries, as well as two hundred thousand shareholders and four hundred thousand employees. Yet Anthony Sampson characterized the company as having a dual personality. In addition to having its corporate tentacles extended everywhere, it still "was accountable to no nation, anywhere, and was held together and inspired by one man, against whom no one cared to argue. A man, moreover, who in spite of his famous accounting skills and discipline yet had the unmistakable style of a buccaneer."[9] Geneen was one of the first postwar industrialists whose style would have been recognized by the robber barons.

The conglomerates often gave the United States a bad name abroad. Many meddled in the domestic politics of their host countries. ITT was no exception. The company, under its founder, Sosthenes Behn, acquired the international operations of the Western Electric Company in the 1920s and set out to challenge Bell's domination of telephone manufacturing and systems operation. In its early years the company had close links with many governments, including the Third Reich and Franco's Spain, and became accustomed to dealing with political regimes of all stripes. By the time Geneen took the helm, the company was tottering. Avis was the first large-scale acquisition for Geneen, and it proved profitable for ITT and its advisers. ITT's main investment bankers were Kuhn Loeb and Lazard Freres. Lazard became the more important of the two because it was more aggressive in seeking acquisitions that suited Geneen's style. The firm was headed by expatriate Frenchman Andre Mayer, by the early 1960s a legend on Wall Street, and his lieutenant, Felix Rohatyn. Between them, they helped ITT with a series of acquisitions that produced fat merger and acquisition fees and made the conglomerate a modern legend.

Growth remained strong with the acquisition of many disparate companies. By the end of the 1960s, ITT was the tenth-largest conglomerate in the world, with sales of about $7 billion, putting it on a par with Unilever and Texaco. Other notable acquisitions included the Hartford Insurance Company and the Sheraton hotel chain. But growth in the 1960s was not always smooth. In addition to a failed bid for the American Broadcasting Company, Geneen had to endure a Justice Department antitrust division under President Nixon that was far more zealous than its predecessors of either political party. For the first time since the TNEC hearings thirty years earlier, the term *concentration of economic power* was again being used, this time referring to conglomerates. The Justice Department forced ITT to divest itself of some of its recent acquisitions, although it allowed the Hartford merger to proceed.

Despite its many organizational achievements, ITT made headlines in the early 1970s when it planned to overthrow the proclaimed Marxist government of Salvador Allende, recently elected in Chile. The Allende regime had angered many multinationals by nationalizing the Chilean copper industry. One of the victims was the Anaconda Copper Company, still thriving since its first public offering on Wall Street in the 1920s. ITT's opposition, and the eventual assassination of Allende, cast a dark shadow over the power of multinationals in general. Tampering in the domestic affairs of foreign countries proved J. J. Servan-Schreiber's warnings in his book *The American Challenge*, first published in Paris in 1967, ahead of their time. He wrote that the creeping influence of American business must be met by political forces strong enough to oppose it while preserving local cultures and politics. Clouds began to gather over conglomerates, and ITT in particular, for being quasi states without any rules governing their behavior.

Conglomerates proved to be less than successful for their shareholders over the long run. They employed accounting methods that tended to overstate earnings for the parent company almost as soon as a consolidated earnings statement could be put together after a merger. Most of them used *pool accounting*, a technique that allowed them to account for the acquired companies' assets at cost. The alternative, *purchase accounting*, required them to record the difference between the merger's cost and book value as goodwill. Geneen was especially gifted in this respect, and ITT's earnings appeared to grow constantly. A congressional study found that if ITT had used purchase accounting, its earnings between 1964 and 1968 would have been 40 percent lower than reported.[10] But Wall Street believed the growth rates. When the market started to soften and fall dramatically in 1970, however, the stocks of most conglomerates began to drop. By the early 1970s, the gilt had come off many of the conglomerates' share prices, and they gave up many of their gains.

The growth of conglomerates set off an unexpected reaction in Washington reminiscent of the case against Morgan Stanley et al., but it came during a Republican administration, not a Democratic one. John Mitchell, Richard Nixon's attorney general, assembled a strong antitrust division within the Justice Department, headed by Assistant Attorney General Richard McLaren. Using two general arguments against conglomerates, it set out to block several key mergers, among them ITT's proposed takeover of the Canteen Corporation, LTV's bid for Jones and Laughlin, Litton Industries' proposed takeover of a German typewriter company, and Northwest Industries proposed takeover of B. F. Goodrich. Once again, the government went to war to fight the spread of concentrated economic power.

Some powerful trust-busting had already been occurring in government. In April 1967 the Supreme Court upheld the FTC's ruling that a merger that occurred ten years before between Proctor and Gamble and the Clorox Chemical Company was illegal. To the dismay of Proctor and Gamble, the court held that the merger allowed Clorox to gain an unfair edge in television advertising because of the marriage. Despite the fact the Clorox was already the nation's largest producer of bleach, the unfair elements came to the surface because it was already controlling nearly 50 percent of the national market. *Consumer Reports* remarked, "If effective national competition with Clorox was difficult before the merger, it became well-nigh impossible afterward. The power to pre-empt commercial time on network television presents a virtually impregnable barrier to other companies."[11]

Mitchell proposed in 1969 that potential mergers between two companies that were among the two hundred largest manufacturing corporations should be automatically reviewed by the Justice Department. The acquiring companies would have to account for the mergers and show that they did not restrain competition. This was the first time that an automatic explanation would be required of companies thinking of going to the altar. Mitchell stated that "a superconcentration exists in the manufacturing sector of the American economy today, as a result of mergers that have brought 58 percent of all manufacturing assets into the hands of the 200 largest industrial corporations and 75 percent into the hands of the top 500."[12] The major mergers challenged by the Justice Department all fell into this category. *Fortune* ranked ITT as the 11th-largest manufacturer on the list; LTV was 25th, Litton Industries was 40th, and Northwest Industries was 142nd. B. F. Goodrich, the apple of Northwest's eye, was 82nd.

Adding fuel to the government's fire was the release of an antimonopoly report submitted to Lyndon Johnson in 1968. It was written by a task force that studied antitrust laws and made recommendations that Johnson, for unexplained reasons, never made public. The Nixon administration did release it since it fit the tenor of its own battle against the conglomerates. The task force, headed by Phil Neal of the University of Chicago Law School, recommended radical changes in the antitrust laws that would permit the government to break up large companies dominating an industry. A "leading" company was one that was in the top four in its industry with sales of at least $500 million or having assets of $250 million or more. If it could be shown that the proposed takeover would result in unfair domination of the industry, the government could require the company to divest itself of some holdings.

Although the report was only a recommendation, it came like a lightning bolt. The *New York Times* was quick to point out that the major mergers being investigated by the Justice Department would probably be allowed to stand under these guidelines. This may have accounted for Mitchell's use of the top-two-hundred companies formula. But its release was also fortuitous on another account. The same day that the release was made, Jim Ling and his main antagonist, Richard McLaren, debated the two sides of antitrust policy at the Hotel Pierre in New York. Each took his expected stance on the issue. McLaren claimed that the Justice Department was not opposed to conglomerate companies or conglomerate mergers as such but did oppose mergers with "discernable anti-competitive effects." He added that while his views differed from those of previous heads of the antitrust division, there had been "no radical departure from established law."

When Ling rose to address the audience, McLaren did not wait to hear his position but departed early. The LTV chief defended his acquisition program, noting that the acquisition of Jones and Laughlin gave LTV only a "toehold, not a foothold," in the steel industry, in which over a hundred companies shared the market. "As I see it," he concluded, "LTV is not accused of having done anything to monopolize any business or to lessen competition in any industry, but the Government's case is based upon what LTV *might* do in the future in the way of reciprocity."[13] Ling also called for full disclosure of the Johnson task force report, already rumored but not yet released at that time of day, knowing that its contents generally would be favorable to LTV's merger plans.

Ling's arguments were supported to an extent by some antitrust experts. Joel Segall, a specialist in antitrust at the University of Chicago, claimed that McLaren's arguments against the LTV merger were ingenious but highly debatable. Arguing that LTV would not affect competition by acquiring one of many steel firms in the industry, he claimed not to see what all the fuss was about. "Even so, potential competitors in the steel industry must number in the hundreds and the loss of one does not seem devastating," he stated in a speech given shortly before Ling's in New York.[14] More to the point, his analysis suggested that large companies were less efficient than smaller ones and that shareholders would eventually feel the bite of bigness. The weak stock market just around the corner would certainly prove that prognosis correct.

Manufacturing was not the only industry coming under public scrutiny. Banking was again under the microscope. Emanuel Celler, long-time Democratic congressman from Brooklyn and the chairman of the House Judiciary Committee, attacked banks' expansionist tendencies during the 1960s. He claimed that they "threaten the basic structure of the American industrial system." The banks had been reverting to what were called *one-bank holding companies*. They then were expanding into other businesses that the Federal Reserve forbade. But the fact that their holding companies owned only one bank exempted them from most Fed regulations. Celler sought to plug up this loophole. He stated that "this country has had its full share of bitter experience with abuses that flow from bankers to pursue business ventures that are not closely related to banking. . . . purely [nonbank] business operations must be excluded."[15] As one of the few old guard trustbusters left in Congress, Celler strenuously tried to prevent banks from reverting to tactics employed during the 1920s.

Criticism of the conglomerates, while shrill at times, never took on the messianic fervor that had pursued financiers during the Pecora hearings. It became a more prolonged chapter in the fifty-year history of antitrust. The failure of the Justice Department's case against Morgan Stanley proved that the tide had indeed swung away from pursuing financiers, although the new breed of corporate kingpin was carefully monitored by consumer advocates' groups as well as the Justice Department. Ralph Nader became accustomed to following the movements of ITT under Geneen. But within a few years, the Watergate affair would dominate politics, and active policy against conglomerates would be seriously curtailed. At the heart of the matter, the conglomerates led the charge of American business on a global scale. The twenty-odd years since the end of the war had produced great prosperity, and the conglomerates were responsible for much of it. Criticizing them was tantamount to biting the hand that fed society at the time, something few critics were willing to do. But at the end of the day, size proved to be the conglomerates' largest headache since the market eventually turned against companies whose disparate businesses were considered too unwieldy.

As a result of conglomerate activity and the spate of other consolidations, mergers and acquisitions became a highly profitable area for many Wall Street houses. It was especially popular because it was not capital-intensive, requiring only advisory services and not much up-front capital. Lazard, Morgan Stanley, and Goldman Sachs rose to the forefront of the business and continued to dominate it for years afterwards. Many smaller "boutique" firms also opened, providing glamorous but limited service in mergers and acquisitions. Many also specialized in bringing new, small companies to market. Those who did require large amounts of capital were arbitragers, traders who speculated on the probabilities of mergers actually being consummated. Houses that specialized in arbitrage were Bache, L. F. Rothschild and Company, Salomon Brothers, and Goldman Sachs, as well as smaller, purely arbitrage firms. Their activity was extremely risky because it had political as well as economic risks. Often the business of mergers was more risky and less glamorous than was generally thought. As one noted arbitrager of the time stated, "A deal, more often than not, is worth neither what the newspapers, nor what the merger parties say it is worth. It is generally worth less." In the 1960s the major risk to a proposed deal was the Justice Department. By blocking proposed mergers, it helped erode many arbitragers' capital. They would take positions in the stock of the bride and the bridegroom almost immediately after a proposed marriage was announced. If the deal did not go through, the arbitrager's position stood the chance of being unsuccessful.

Hucksterism Appears

One of the largest growth sectors of the securities business in the 1950s and 1960s was mutual funds. Not since the 1920s had they been so popular. In the 1950s their growth exploded as more and more investors decided to take a plunge in the stock market. In the 1950s alone, their growth increased ten times over. They were unlike any investment ever before sold by Wall Street. Salesmen often actually paid house visits, similar to insurance salesmen, to sell to anyone who could put up the necessary cash. And their timing was impeccable. The market kept rising, and so did the value of the funds. Investing in them became a no-brainer.

Although investors were increasing in numbers, they were not particularly sophisticated. Mutual funds became the ideal vehicle for the small investor to participate in Wall Street's tremendous growth. And there was no shortage of companies willing to satiate their demand. The number of funds and fund managers also proliferated with the trend; by the time the 1960s began, their numbers were in the hundreds. Although there were many mutual fund whiz kids who managed to produce healthy returns through excellent stock selection, none could match the flair of Bernard "Bernie" Cornfeld, who took his fund to new heights.

The premise behind the funds was simple. Investors bought shares in mutual funds, while the funds bought shares of common stocks. For relatively small amounts of money, investors could participate in the growth decades without having to expose themselves to the risks of only one or two stocks. For their part, the funds had stated purposes, and they constructed their own portfolios to satisfy them. Many were growth funds, but others emphasized income or growth by investing in new issues. As the funds proliferated, investors found themselves facing a cornucopia from which to choose.

Despite diversification, fund investment was far from safe. Some funds charged very high fees by loading their commissions into the purchase price; others behaved less than prudently in their choice of securities. Complaints started to mount at the regulators, mostly over the matter of the fees charged. The SEC was ultimately charged with reviewing the complaints because funds (technically investment companies) had to be registered with the commission. But there were other funds over which the SEC had no authority, and these were the ones that gave the industry a black eye by the late 1960s.

Bernie Cornfeld was synonymous with the mutual fund industry during the bull market. He was not a Wall Street insider by any means, only someone who was admired because of his apparent organizational and sales abilities. And neither did he possess a traditional background for his adopted profession. Born in Turkey, the son of an expatriate American, the former social worker drifted into selling mutual funds in the 1950s, finding it more rewarding than casework. His genius was in spotting aberrations in the marketplace. He quickly noticed that demand for funds was phenomenal but nevertheless regulated by the SEC. But the same was not true overseas, where a large amount of dollars resided. As a result, he began marketing the funds of his Investors Overseas Services (IOS) to expatriate Americans and to foreigners clamoring for a piece of the action in the bull market. He found no shortage of customers.

Cornfeld feverishly began selling the various funds to all and sundry. He claimed to be an advocate of "people's capitalism," the movement that would make everyone better off no matter how small their investment. Not since the 1920s had such hucksterism been seen in the securities business. IOS salesmen were renowned for pounding on doors all over Europe, selling a piece of the action. Their targets were expatriates, as well as servicemen and foreign nationals. Over half of their clients were Germans. But while Wall Street was not acquainted with Cornfeld's sales techniques, it was impressed by the sales totals. Corporate treasurers approached him about buying large blocks of their shares because he represented such enormous buying power. Within ten years he had over $2 billion under management, representing a million shareholders, and was always searching for more. Sales managers at IOS seriously believed that they would have over $100 billion under management within ten years.

Growth in value was not the only attraction of Cornfeld's funds. On the front page of one of his funds was the following statement: "The names and addresses of all investors are held in strictest confidences at all times." Clearly, this was an appeal to domestic investors to recognize that investment in an offshore vehicle would allow them to avoid tax (Cornfeld's companies were registered in Canada).[16] Taxes were not the only problem the IOS presented. One of Cornfeld's superfunds, the Fund of Funds, was actually a holding company that owned other funds, many of which were owned by the IOS. Its charges were quite high, often more than 5 percent, but his investors did not usually complain because of the anonymity factor.

By the late 1960s, Cornfeld's mutual fund empire was in tatters. An apparent white knight appeared on the horizon, bidding for the IOS. His name was Robert Vesco. Born in Detroit into a working-class household, Vesco dropped out of high school to take several jobs as an toolmaker. He later moved east with his family to Connecticut, where he claimed to have endured prejudice because of his background. He became known as the "Bootstrap Kid," a name that showed he had come up the hard way. He openly bandied about his humble origins as he moved up the ladder, fulfilling his boyhood dream of becoming a CEO of his own company. But other parts of his background would haunt him, such as his early run-ins with the law in Detroit when he was a teenager.

Participating in the conglomerate trend of the decade, Vesco had turned his small New Jersey–based International Controls Corporation into a hydralike manufacturing conglomerate owning more than twenty-four companies. Sales rose from an original $1 million to over $100 million in just a few years. Vesco mastered the art of leverage early. During the bull market, he prospered. But when the stock market began to turn down, he, like Cornfeld, began to feel the pinch. The IOS represented a vast sea of wealth for him because his own companies had become strapped for cash by the end of the 1960s.

The IOS ran into trouble in the same market. Only several months before, in 1969, it had made a huge offering of new shares to investors, and many executives within the company had bought shares; Cornfeld himself owned about 15 percent. When the market turned down, many were wiped out because they had financed their purchases with borrowed money. When the IOS became vulnerable, Vesco spied his chance to bail it out. Cornfeld himself was not sure. When told of Vesco's interest, he responded by screaming, "That hoodlum Vesco isn't going to touch this company!" But the handwriting was on the wall. The IOS needed funds, and Vesco appeared to be its savior. The deal was sealed.

Other mutual funds also made a large splash in the market. The Equity Funding Corporation, based at Century City in Los Angeles, was one of the high-flying stocks of the decade. The company sold an investment product more familiar in Britain than in the United States: a combination of life insurance and mutual funds. Salesmen sold the package to investors as life insurance whose premiums would be paid by the dividends on a mutual fund. As the market moved up, the increased dividends would pay off the insurance and soon it would be paid off in its entirety, ahead of schedule. The idea had been used in Britain but had never been tried in the United States.

At first the Equity Funding Corporation made some admirable gains, and its sales soared. Many of the policies it wrote were sold to reinsurance companies so that the company could ostensibly raise cash to write even more policies and spread out its risk. Investors were impressed, especially by the number of customers who were enamored of the new concept. One of its directors was even a regional member of the NASD board. The stock rose from six dollars to over ninety dollars a share in five years and became a favorite. Investment advisers put all sorts of investors into it, from the usual widows and orphans to large university endowment funds. But the declining stock market and under-the-table practices had the company on the financial ropes as the 1970s began.

Ironically, all three companies began to become unwound at about the same time. The effect on the stock market was devastating. Three of the favorite companies of the 1960s were doomed to failure because of what Wall Street feared most: fraud. Their highly visible CEOs, especially Cornfeld and Vesco, became synonymous with chicanery. Wall Street quickly began to ask itself how so many sleights of hand could have gone undetected.

After Cornfeld lost control to Vesco, it became clear that the self-styled financier was not interested in mutual funds. His sole intent had been to loot the IOS of its cash, leaving its investors in the lurch. Vesco was estimated to have siphoned off $500 million from the funds before becoming an international fugitive with no fixed address. The story of his dealings continued into the 1970s when two members of Nixon's administration, Attorney General John Mitchell and Secretary of Commerce Maurice Stans, were charged with obstructing justice and perjury in their dealings with Vesco and contributions he made to Nixon's reelection fund (ironically dubbed CREEPs for short). Although both were acquitted in 1974, the Nixon administration and members of the president's family had been tainted by dealings with Vesco. It was perhaps the closest a confidence man had come to dealings with the First Family since the days of Ferdinand Ward and the Grant family after the Civil War.

Cornfeld migrated to Beverly Hills after the IOS began slipping from his control. Maintaining an opulent lifestyle, he went into the movie production business. He was arrested after he returned to his former haunt in Geneva and held by Swiss authorities for almost a year before making bail. The Swiss court that held him took a dim view of the amount of money he personally made on the last sale of IOS stock, reputedly almost $7 million, especially when his salary was only about $125,000 per year. Professing ignorance of Vesco's actions to the end, Cornfeld died in 1994.

The Equity Funding Corporation came unraveled when a disgruntled employee revealed to financial analyst Ray Dirks that the company was perpetrating a massive fraud by creating false insurance policies and then selling them to reinsurers, pocketing the cash. The company was effectively looted and apparently had been operating fraudulently for some time. The investigation that followed showed that it had been successful in fooling its auditors, investment bankers, and bankers, in addition to insurance regulators and investors. The loss to investors exceeded $300 million, with the list of unhappy investors including many celebrities who had been attracted by the company's glittering Los Angeles headquarters. On the day the fraud was announced in 1973, the stock market dropped a full 3 percent in value. The entire affair had a serendipitous quality to it because the disgruntled employee came forward only after receiving what he considered to be an insultingly small Christmas bonus.

When he went public with the information that brought down the company, Dirks found himself rewarded several times over. The NYSE threatened to bar him from working for any member firms for disclosing confidential information—in short, for violating its own internal rules. Shareholders of Equity Funding sued him for $100 million, and he faced a loss of his living forever. Yet he persevered. He wrote that the entire affair raised several questions involving SEC regulations, accountability, and public morals. One question certainly involved the internal procedures of the NYSE. He noted that, "There is the question of the New York Stock Exchange, a venerated American institution which advertises the safety and security of investing in its listed companies, but which, in fact is an antique, costly and dangerous system perpetuated for the convenience of its members."[17]

The two major scandals cost investors over $800 million. Equity Funding became the country's largest scandal to date because the IOS was considered "offshore" for all practical purposes. Both scandals and their wide-ranging implications were strangely reminiscent of days past, when schemes bilking investors were more common. During the latter stages of the bull market, however, they were reported very much as separate incidents. Their negative effects hurt investors, but now there were many more of them than in the past. The spirit of the age was affecting investor losses. The more investors there were, the less any one small group lost, ensuring that the financial system did not topple. The principle of diversification was alive and well, if not operating in the manner intended.

Consumer Credit Gains

The bull market in both stocks and bonds led to other institutional changes that greatly affected Wall Street. The Street helped to develop the source of credit cards, a radical departure for most houses unaccustomed to providing credit for consumers. In 1959 the Ford Motor Company announced that it would open its own finance subsidiary to make car loans. Ford detected a profitable business in borrowing money and then loaning it to its dealers and their retail customers. Until that time consumer finance had been provided by credit companies such as CIT Financial, as well as by the banks. When Ford announced its intention, the stocks of many other financial company shares dropped in response. The other major manufacturers were forced to look at the possibilities of opening their own subsidiaries as well. Within fifteen years, the big three automakers' finance subsidiaries would account for billions of dollars of lending to car buyers and other consumers. The funds came from the money market for commercial paper, and the demand provided the market with its most momentous changes since the Jewish banking houses of the mid–nineteenth century helped develop it in the first place.

The widespread use of credit cards also began in the 1960s. Western Union had offered cards to customers since the 1920s. The actual term had been around for years. Edward Bellamy used it in his *Looking Backward, 2000–1887* to describe how citizens would spend their money in the advanced society of the late twentieth century. Diners Club and American Express had offered simple buy-and-pay cards since the 1950s, but they were used mostly by business travelers. But as the finance companies were established to fund consumer purchases of cars and home appliances, it became clear that the market had even more potential. The next step was to establish credit cards providing revolving credit. The Bank of America picked up the idea and established VISA cards in 1963; Mastercard was introduced in 1965. Both allowed customers credit on time. Clearly, a revolution in consumer finance was born.

Wall Street benefited from the surge in credit cards by providing the funds for the credit companies. Most of the finance companies and bank holding companies borrowed money in the commercial paper market and then used the funds to make purchases from merchants using their cards. Wall Street houses acting as agents for companies then had to provide issuing facilities for very small underwriting margins—so small, in fact, that many decided against participating in the market. One investment bank that continued its past tradition was Goldman Sachs, which consistently remained the Street's premier commercial paper agent. Because of the peculiar nature of the Glass-Steagall Act, investment banks had the market entirely to themselves for years. Commercial banks were wary of entering it for fear of being shown to act as underwriters for corporate securities.

Wall Street Woes

The stock market's weakness in the late 1960s marked the end of the great bull market that had begun in 1953. Although there were many hiccups along the way, the market indices all had quadrupled in value, the price of a seat on the NYSE had increased four times over, and the number of individual investors was estimated at slightly over 20 million. Dividends on common stocks listed on the NYSE increased five times in value, and share volume increased almost six times. But as the 1970s began, the market was set for a serious price correction. The only uncertainty was the direction from which the bad news would come.

The "go-go" decade took a heavy toll on the securities business. Failures of member firms became common as fraud and inefficiency pulled the financial rug out from under more than one. Two well-respected member firms ran into serious financial difficulties in 1962 because of their involvement in the affairs of Tino De Angelis. De Angelis ran the Allied Crude Vegetable Oil Refining Corporation, which had just filed for bankruptcy. He traded oil futures with Ira Haupt and Company, and his bankruptcy severely affected the company because he was unable to provide it with any cash for his outstanding positions. Another member firm, Williston and Beane, was also involved with him in other ventures. The NYSE eventually had to salvage the two firms, and its own reputation for self-regulation, by cobbling together a rescue package to preserve the firms' client accounts.

In the 1960s, over 150 firms failed, a record. In the previous twenty-five years, only one NYSE member had closed its doors because of insolvency. Many of the problems were caused by backroom inefficiency. Volume increased to the point where many firms found themselves seriously behind in squaring their books, alienating customers and causing liquidity problems for themselves. Others had been busy churning customers' accounts, and squaring the books was not in their own best interests. At the end of the decade, the failures continued. Orvis Brothers, Blair and Company, McDonnell and Company, and Pickard and Company all failed and required winding down by the NYSE. F. I. du Pont merged with Glore Forgan and Company to become du Pont Glore Forgan, and Hayden Stone, a large wire house, was reorganized. When the market started to fall in the late 1960s, many customers failed to meet margin calls and the firms at which they kept accounts fell short of cash. Some firms absorbed others, relieving the need for other assistance from the exchange. Merrill, Lynch assumed the operations of Goodbody and Company, the country's fifth-largest broker, which had been buried under the backroom crunch. The NYSE had established a special reserve earlier in the decade to meet such emergencies, but it was in danger itself as more and more firms folded their tents. Unless something was done, it was conceivable that Wall Street would begin losing customers in droves or, worse, face massive liquidations by customers of existing accounts.

One of the major worries about securities investments was the fact that while offering higher interest and the possibility for capital gains, market investments were not insured. For all of their shortcomings, banks and thrifts were insured and deposits secure as a result. It would be very difficult to entice future generations of savers to become investors if brokers could not be trusted. While the shakeout on the Street may have been natural, convincing investors who had lost money or had their accounts frozen because of brokers' irregularities was difficult. As a result, Congress responded in 1971 by creating the Securities Investor Protection Corporation, better known as SIPC. This was the equivalent of FDIC insurance for the securities industry. Accounts at brokers were now insured against fraud or mishandling. It guaranteed that they were residing in a safe place regardless of what happened to the broker.

Equally problematic for the NYSE was the manner in which it charged commissions. The exchange adhered to a fixed commission basis, which it had vigorously defended in the past as fair and efficient. Many customers begged to differ. They claimed that the brokers' fixed rates were too high and that rates should be negotiable instead. Many investors received research reports from brokers as part of their services. The cost of producing the reports was included in the fixed commissions, so lowering the rates meant that the research costs would have to be absorbed by brokers. The SEC, under Manuel Cohen's chairmanship, became involved to determine for itself the merits of the arguments. The major worry among brokers was that institutional investors would begin buying seats on the exchange so they could lower their costs of trading. Retail investors had no such options available, but many longed for negotiated rates because they would allow brokers to discount their services to good customers. If a customer wanted only bare-bones brokerage services, he should not be forced to pay a full commission rate, went the argument.

Aside from the consolidation of many firms, the bull market had other marked effects upon the investment banking community. The old-line underwriting houses were being challenged for new business. Salomon

Brothers and Merrill, Lynch made inroads underwriting by successfully competing for and winning business from companies such as AT&T and TWA. In 1962 the two firms combined with Blyth and Company and Lehman Brothers to form an association—nicknamed the "fearsome four-some"—that would challenge the old-line firms for underwriting business. They met with success and their underwriting revenues increased several times over. Many of their deals were in the utilities business, where they successfully bid for competitive issues.

Underwriting was not the only part of the business that was changing rapidly. Sales and trading, especially to institutions, were on the rise. Even the old-line firms began adding their own institutional sales departments to sell directly to clients rather than simply employ other brokers as sell-ing agents. Morgan Stanley was one of the last holdouts but by the early 1970s added an institutional sales force. Block trading also became more popular as many firms, led by Salomon, realized that the best way to an in-stitutional client's heart was through his wallet. By buying and selling large blocks of shares off the exchanges, they were able to obtain better prices for clients than specialists on the exchange floors were able to offer. This was especially important as institutions began challenging the NYSE over its commission structure. Block trading became known as *fourth-market* trading.[18]

By the late 1960s, it appeared that another bubble was about to burst on the Street. But the crash never came and despite the myriad problems caused by the bull market, relative calm prevailed. The expanding econ-omy and money inflation helped create an economy that was becoming al-most too large for wide-scale panic. In the 1960s it was certainly too large for even the NYSE or the SEC to save by themselves, using either regula-tions or reserve funds. Part of the reason a panic never occurred was the safety net legislation provided by the early New Deal legislation. Bank customers now felt safe because of deposit insurance. The link between banks and brokers had been severed, so deposits were free from the va-garies and risks of the stock market.[19] The stock market could now de-cline, even precipitously, without fear of the entire financial system collapsing. SIPC insurance would help reassure securities investors. Wall Street fears about the Glass-Steagall and Securities Exchange Acts had long since receded. These laws were now recognized as bringing more sta-bility to the markets than they ever experienced before. This was some consolation for the securities business in the late 1960s, which was under-going wrenching change. But despite remedial measures, there was more bad news yet to come. The decade of gloom was just over the horizon.

CHAPTER TEN

Bear Market
(1970–81)

*I am determined that the American dollar must never again
be a hostage in the hands of international speculators.*

Richard Nixon

Momentous changes and a strong bull market helped restore Wall Street's image in the 1960s. But the Street's overall power continued to decline against its old nemesis, the federal government. The antitrust movement of the Johnson and Nixon administrations demonstrated that finance and industry did not have free rein. Concentrations of economic power and anticompetitive practices were still under the microscope. But if industry did not push the issue to the limit, there was plenty of serious money to be made as Wall Street helped finance the reshaping of American industry. Wall Street and business were again leading the dance, but the federal government reserved the right to cut in when it desired.

The last days of the 1960s brought a wave of change to Wall Street. The 1950s and 1960s were decades of optimism, but as the bull market began to wane, shades of pessimism were cast over the horizon. The frauds and scandals were perhaps the best-remembered institutional developments of the bull market, but they were certainly not the most important. The Street had changed its complexion since the end of the Truman era. New competition abounded for underwriting business, sales and trading had come of age, and a legion of new investors had been introduced to investments. Most important, however, was the increase in market volatility. The stock market was becoming increasingly susceptible to outside influences as it accommodated itself to technological change.

Within the next ten years, the markets would receive more distressing news than ever anticipated. The world was becoming smaller as a result of vastly improved communications, and much of the news was international.

Developments from outside the domestic markets always had an unsettling effect upon the Street because of the insular nature of the American markets. Since the war, the only international event that had had much impact on the markets was the launching of *Sputnik*. Economic events in other countries were largely ignored. Foreign factors played a small role in financial affairs except for the cold war. Wall Street adopted the slogan of New York City after the war and never changed its tune: "If you're good enough to make it here you can make it anywhere."

But international factors were about to encroach on American prosperity. Wall Street always assumed that foreigners liked to invest in the United States because of the safety factor. American politics were sensible, the Treasury had never defaulted on its debt, and the dollar had been mostly free to move from money center to money center without any restrictions. Except for wartime controls on investments from hostile countries, the United States had an impeccable record for treating foreign investors well. The few scandals that enveloped foreigners stained the record but did not permanently tarnish it.

Few of those on the Street in the early 1970s would recognize it ten years later. The volatility that had raised its head in the past would only reach its peak by the time Ronald Reagan took office in 1981. Inflation, rising gradually since the late 1960s, would explode, helping interest rates climb to their highest levels in American history. Social unrest and uncertainty followed such as had not been seen since the depression years. Accompanying all this was a feeling of American impotence in world affairs. The decline of the dollar, a series of foreign policy mistakes, and the rise of the obscure oil-producing nations to a central place on the world stage all contributed to a general feeling of helplessness. But that did not necessarily mean inaction in the financial world.

Dozens of new financial products made their appearance, many of which were unfamiliar even to seasoned Wall Street veterans. The name "Wall Street" began to include parts of the financial business not traditionally associated with it. Large parts of this new business were not even located in New York but in Chicago. Far-flung parts of the financial world developed products designed to hedge stock and bond investments. The Chicago commodity futures markets began experimenting in financial instruments that were designed to hedge traditional products. Sacrosanct Wall Street notions about stocks and bonds were replaced by the more realistic idea that they were nothing more than different types of commodities.

The volatility experienced in the financial world had its counterpart outside. The affluent society began to turn introspective. No longer was society willing to blindly follow its leaders as it had during the Eisenhower and "go-go" years. Dissent prevailed during the Vietnam War, and pa-

Oliphant@Universal Press Syndicate. Reprinted with permission.

tience with the status quo was wearing thin. The same impatience was evident in the financial world. Investment bankers and others began designing instruments that would help investors adjust to the new environment rather than simply sit back and wait for better days. Part of the motive was restiveness; the rest was practicality. Without new instruments to hedge investments, it was possible that investors would abandon the markets in droves.

While Wall Street was learning to cope with a weak stock market and rising interest rates, international economic affairs began to raise problems. Until the mid-1960s, the dollar's value was mostly a forgotten issue at home. Then monetary strains began to appear in the Bretton Woods system as the deutsche mark and the yen rose. The British pound began to weaken considerably and was devalued more than once to lower its value. The dollar remained as the anchor in the foreign exchange system, but balance-of-payments problems put it under pressure as well. After twenty-five years of dollar supremacy, rising interest rates and budget deficits were having a negative effect. Soon many commentators believed that the United States was attempting the same goal the British had achieved for years by devaluing its currency without addressing more fundamental problems at home.

The reaction on the Street was muted. The United States dominated international trade, so there appeared to be little reason to worry. With so many overwhelming issues to be faced on the domestic front, the international side appeared nothing more than a minor annoyance. The NYSE was facing the continuing pressures of realigning its commission rates, the SIPC had just passed Congress, the shakeout in the number of firms on the Street continued, and the NASD market was growing in size and influence. Added to these were a slowdown in the new issues market and increased government borrowing in the Treasury market. Looking outside was only looking for trouble. But by the summer of 1971, trouble officially arrived. Probably the most singularly important financial event in the postwar period occurred. Naturally, it was draped in a shroud of international mystery.

Bretton Woods Collapses

This international event came dressed in familiar clothing. It was part of an anti-inflation package put together by the Nixon administration after months of equivocating about the best way to combat rising prices caused by the Vietnam War. Investment bankers and brokers preoccupied with abolishing fixed commissions and raising more capital for themselves could be forgiven for not noticing events unfolding on the international stage. But soon they would be painfully reminded that they avoided international affairs only at their own risk.

Inflation was the major economic concern in the early 1970s. Since foreign exchange rates were fixed against the dollar, investors realized that their holdings were losing purchasing power. The same had happened to the British pound several years earlier. Prime Minister Harold Wilson blamed the pound's problems on international speculators, whom he claimed attacked it so often that he was left with no choice but to devalue. This vast oversimplification had great publicity value. During the 1960s, a British official coined a term that has been become a well-known financial cliché. When discussing foreign exchange traders, he referred to them (and their mysterious ways) as the "gnomes of Zurich." Gremlins had subverted the pound, and now they were turning their attention to the dollar. Foreign speculators had not been blamed for poor markets since the early days of the depression.

Nixon inherited an inflationary spiral when he took office. Treasury bond yields were near 8 percent, and the Dow sank to around 700. Nixon proved something of a prophet by proclaiming that it was a good time to buy stocks, echoing Calvin Coolidge's similar proclamation of forty years earlier. But in 1971 circumstances were different. Unions were pushing for larger and larger wage increases and were winning. Autoworkers at General Motors had just recently negotiated a multiyear package worth 20 percent. Manufacturers passed the increase along to consumers, and prices were rising. Certain that consumers wanted change, Nixon and his advisers huddled at Camp David for a weekend in August before making a scheduled television address designed to combat the spiral of inflation.

Treasury Secretary John Connelly, one of Nixon's closest economic advisers, had recently rejected Fed Chairman Arthur Burns's suggestion that wage and price controls be implemented. Burns had succeeded William McChesney Martin as Fed chairman. Under more normal international conditions, Connelly may have proved a good secretary, but the extraordinary events unfolding required someone with a greater grasp of international monetary affairs. As the point man on Nixon's team of advisers, Connelly did not appear to have a full grasp of the ramifications of devaluation and possibly abandoning all surviving links to the gold standard. A consummate politician, he was nevertheless described by Robert Solomon, chief economist at the Federal Reserve Board and participant at the major international economic conferences, as a secretary with "no broad vision of how to improve the economic welfare of his own country or the world."[1] The former Texas governor adhered to the traditional line of a free economy setting itself aright without government interference.

No one in the administration had publicly discussed a devaluation of the dollar, but it had been rumored in international circles for months. After a weekend of intense discussions, Nixon adopted wage and price controls, which would freeze wages and prices for ninety days, presenting his plan to the public on August 15. Toward the end of his televised address, after discussing the domestic sanctions, he delivered the bombshell that foreign exchange traders feared most. He devalued the dollar by cutting its convertibility into gold. The idea was to make imports more expensive while lowering the price of exports. As he somberly addressed the public, the gnomes made an appearance. "Now who gains from these crises?" the president asked. "Not the working man, not the investor, not the real producers of wealth. The gainers are the international money speculators: because they thrive on crisis, they help to create them."[2]

At the time, tinkering with the dollar seemed less momentous than wage and price controls. It was a devaluation, but it seemed pale when compared with the other parts of the anti-inflation package. Wall Street rallied the next trading day. The NYSE registered a record trading day of 31 million shares, and the Dow added 32 points to close at 889. But foreign investors saw it another way. Recognizing trouble, they began selling dollars. The foreign exchange markets disintegrated into chaos. They would remain unsettled for a year and a half before the major currencies were allowed to float freely against each other. The main worry was that the gold standard had been abandoned. Although gold backing for the dollar was more theory than reality, fears arose that the dollar had become debased. Many traditionalists still held that without gold backing, it was nothing more than funny money. In that respect, the worriers were correct. No one thought that the dollar would be allowed to float freely for long. But once rates began to float there was no turning back. The die had been cast for the international monetary system for the remainder of the century. Traditionalists were still lamenting floating exchange rates on the twentieth anniversary of the currency float. In 1991 *Fortune* characterized it as "a baleful anniversary of a misbegotten decision that is still costing us, and the world, dearly." But the domestic markets were not bothered in the late summer of 1971. After twenty-five years of strength, the dollar was not a major area of concern to Wall Street. Negotiated commissions and higher interest rates still occupied center stage.

Over the next ten years, the dollar's travails set off the most fierce round of inflation since World War II. By late 1972, the world's money markets became very unsettled as the dollar declined and other currencies appreciated. A major crisis occurred in the British banking system as the pound also declined. Then the bombshell exploded. The Organization of Petroleum Exporting Countries (OPEC) announced a sharp rise in the price of oil in early 1973. The shock waves were immediate. A barrel of oil doubled in price. The days of cheap energy were over. Industrial democracies, accustomed to uninterrupted sources of cheap, imported oil, were soon to learn that the price was going to be substantially higher in the future. Once-obscure Arab sheikhs now appeared with industrialists and bankers at all of the major banking and industrial conferences.

The oil crisis added insult to injury. Oil was denominated in dollars, so most OPEC producers saw their income drop as a result of the devaluation. Then the Arab members of OPEC began an embargo of oil sent to the United States in retaliation for American support of Israel in the October 1973 Yom Kippur War. The result was long lines at American gasoline stations, where drivers, usually accustomed to paying around 30¢ per gallon, now faced prices of over $1.20. The consumer had been rudely slapped in the face. Critical dependence upon fossil fuels was now very apparent. Adding to the intrigue, rumors abounded of a contrived crisis by the major oil importers. New York harbor was really full of tankers loaded with oil, in no hurry to dock, according to the conspiracy theorists. The producers made certain that the delivery was as slow as possible to ensure constantly rising prices. The stories were reminiscent of those surrounding John D. Rockefeller in the nineteenth century. The United States again appeared at the mercy of a cartel. But this one was not of its own making.

Shock waves reverberated throughout the country. The price of a barrel of imported oil ratcheted upward, to over $11.00 per barrel from only $2.50 a barrel a year and a half before. Interest rates started to rise as well, marking the beginning of a chaotic bond market that would last for over a decade. Since the new issues market was quiet and the stock markets depressed, more companies were borrowing bonds than ever before, adding to the debt explosion. As interest rates rose, the debt explosion met head-on with the inflationary spiral. The combination proved disastrous for Wall Street, already facing vast structural changes in the way it did business.

Although the OPEC price rise became the major news of the new decade, the dollar devaluation was the trigger that set off most of the other inflationary events. Within a few short years, the financial community would be wooing the newly enriched OPEC nations. Their wealth caused a serious redistribution of investments in the markets and helped bolster the emerging euromarket as a major financial market in its own right. Currency crises began to make an impression on Wall Street. No longer was talk of currencies a peripheral issue.

The market felt the impact of expensive oil immediately. The stock indices dove sharply in late 1973 and 1974. Bond yields rose, as did short-term interest rates. Later in the year, a severe recession set in as the cost of imported oil forced an economic slowdown. Soon, the talk of Wall Street centered around those stocks that would perform well under the circumstances. Oil producers naturally led the list. The prices of producers rose substantially in the market. The *Wall Street Journal* reported that Exxon Corporation and the other producers reported constantly higher earnings in 1973. Exxon's income rose 50 percent by midyear and almost 90 percent for the entire year. All the oil companies increased prices that year, and their shareholders were rewarded across the board. Exxon increased its dividend from 95¢ to $1.10 per share. Oil and anything related to it were touted as some of the only hedges against inflation.

Negotiated Commissions

The wide-ranging debate about NYSE commissions begun in the 1960s continued into the 1970s. Advocates of more competitive rates favored freely negotiated commissions on trades, while most NYSE members (naturally) favored their established fixed rates. But outside pressures were being brought to bear on the Big Board. The second and third markets were encroaching, accounting for a higher percentage of trading. Then a champion emerged for negotiated rates that no one expected. Robert W. Haack, president of the NYSE and previously a broker and the governor of the NASD, addressed the Economic Club on New York in November 1970. He made his own position perfectly clear, to the chagrin of many colleagues and floor brokers:

> The New York Stock Exchange, to put it crassly, no longer has the only game in town. . . . I personally hope it might well consider fully negotiated com-

missions as the ultimate objective. . . . While I question whether or not the industry is presently sufficiently strong financially to completely disregard fixed minimum rates, I personally think it might well consider fully negotiated commissions as an ultimate objective.[3]

Haack's suggestions did not sit well with many NYSE members, who ultimately voted for any change in direction at the exchange. He acknowledged that the comments could eventually cost him his job. But the point was well taken. Less than a year later, the NASD, or over-the-counter market, opened its automated quotations system, dubbed the NASDAQ. The computerized system allowed market makers in over-the-counter stocks to post their prices on a computer screen that could be accessed by brokers nationwide. It was the beginning of a nationally quoted market for unlisted securities and would make trading in many of the smaller stocks easier. NASDAQ commissions were not fixed but flexible. Slowly, it appeared that the NYSE would have to bend if it wanted to maintain its hegemony as the country's premier stock exchange.

In 1971 the SEC required the NYSE to proceed with negotiated commissions on trades involving more than $500,000. A schedule was adopted giving the Big Board four more years to adapt to a fully negotiated basis for all trades. The exchange moved ahead with the directive, realizing that it would be bucking the trend to do otherwise. Commissions on block trades naturally were affected, and those houses that entered the fourth-market trading in the 1960s were obliged to cut their commissions. On May 1, 1975, negotiated commissions replaced fixed commissions on what became known as 'May Day.' The once-clubby atmosphere of the exchange, whether it was under Richard Whitney and the old guard or under the more recent dominance of broker-dealers, had been replaced with a more open atmosphere of competition with the other markets.

The first member firm of the NYSE itself to trade on the Big Board was Merrill, Lynch, whose shares became listed in July 1971. Donaldson, Lufkin and Jenrette, a relatively new member firm, announced that it was selling shares to the public in 1969. The increasing need for capital as the markets grew larger made this a historic move and one that was to be followed by many other investment banks in the years ahead. Without additional capital on their balance sheets, underwriters found it difficult to participate in underwriting deals that were getting larger and larger. Bache and Company and Reynolds and Company soon followed by going public as well. Traditional partnerships were in a bind because much of their capital was supplied by partners themselves. Potential liabilities also followed the partners, especially in the wake of scandals. Expansion became the priority for most Wall Street firms.

Expanding into the commodity futures markets was not a top priority, however. Futures contracts were traded by many brokers and investment bankers, but the largest houses were usually specialty houses that understood the intricacies of the markets. The largest futures exchange was the Chicago Board of Trade (CBOT), which traded a wide array of contracts on agricultural products and metals. Smaller exchanges were also found in Chicago and other Midwest locales, and several were located in New York. Then, in 1973, the CBOT took a bold step by opening an exchange dedicated to trading options on common stocks. Since the days of Daniel Drew and Russell Sage, options to buy and sell stocks were sold by brokers to customers on an over-the-counter basis. The popularity of the new exchange, called the Chicago Board Options Exchange, or CBOE, became painfully evident to those who believed any sort of stock-related trading should naturally take place in New York. The number of options outstanding exploded in a short time. What was thought to be only a new game in town became entrenched very quickly. The American Stock Exchange took up the gauntlet almost immediately and opened its own options trading facilities on a separate floor of its facilities in New York. The NYSE did not respond. The CBOE—particularly adept at adding stocks quickly—already had introduced traded options on most of its well-known stocks. When oil prices rose substantially in 1973, it introduced options on Exxon within a matter of months.[4]

Immediately after the breakdown of the Bretton Woods system, derivatives trading in foreign currencies was introduced in Chicago as well. As early as 1971, the International Monetary Market (IMM) began trading currency futures in what became one of the best examples of timing ever seen. This opened up an entirely new world by introducing the markets to financial futures. Customers could buy and sell contracts on currencies as easily as they could on soybeans or live hogs. For the first four years of the exchange's life, financial futures meant foreign exchange. But in 1975 the IMM introduced futures on Treasury bills. Contracts on bonds followed, and a new creature was born in the markets: the interest rate futures contract.

Brokers sold these new contracts to investors as hedging vehicles. The floor traders who stepped up to trade them saw a potential for profit. Over the years, futures traders had earned their livings buying and selling contracts on volatile agricultural commodities. Now volatility had become the norm for financial instruments, and the opportunity for gain was just as great. Gyrating markets made futures contracts on financial instruments and options necessary. Volatility had become entrenched and showed no signs of receding.

The Chicago markets seized another opportunity from New York by introducing financial futures. Options and futures quickly became known as *derivatives*, a category that grew rapidly over the next twenty-five years.

As more and more bonds and stocks appeared in the new issues market, ways of hedging them became more sophisticated. Institutional investors and Wall Street houses themselves were drawn to the new markets, recognizing their potential for hedging and speculation. Broad and Wall remained the center of the capital markets, but derivatives found their home base in Chicago.

The NYSE responded to the Chicago challenge by opening its own futures exchange in 1980. The New York Futures Exchange, or NYFE, began trading contracts in financial futures and its own NYSE index. But technical problems relegated it to a distant third place behind the Chicago exchanges. The Amex's experiment with options, however, continued to flourish, and the Amex became the country's second-largest options exchange behind the CBOE. Other regional stock exchanges also opened their own options trading facilities, and many listed options on the same stocks as the CBOE. Many traditionalists complained that the new markets were nothing more than gambling dens, taking business away from the stock exchanges. Brokers, on the other hand, welcomed the new products because they represented new ways to generate business in an otherwise awful stock market. Commissions on options were proportionately higher than those on stocks, even after negotiated commissions, and they could be bought and sold for relatively small amounts of money. Futures were riskier, appealing to more sophisticated investors who understood the extensive risks involved.

In June 1975 all of the stock markets, including the NASDAQ, made a giant leap forward when the consolidated tape was introduced. All trades, regardless of market, were reported on the ticker shortly after they were executed. The move was made possible by new technology. The markets became more integrated than ever before and helped bring the smaller exchanges into the mainstream. Now trades in Boston or Philadelphia were announced alongside those on the Big Board. The regional exchanges would benefit because trades could now be placed on them by brokers without being accused of trading on a backwater market. Arbitragers, however, appreciated the consolidated tape less because one of their favorite ways of making money quickly disappeared. Buying in New York and simultaneously selling in another market became very difficult because those discrepancies were now in full view for everyone to see. "Sell 'em on the coast" became an outdated war cry of the arbitrager.

New Financial Products

The 1970s turned out to be an excellent time for marketing new financial products. Unlike the 1960s, however, money was certainly not pouring into the stock market. Inflation became the enemy that investors wanted to defeat. The Penn State football team went to the 1975 Cotton Bowl with "WIN" inscribed on their helmets—short for "Whip Inflation Now." Rising prices clearly had become a matter of public concern, but the stock market was not considered the place to do battle. Consumers behaved much as they had in earlier periods of inflation and recession. During the recession of 1974–75, their savings increased. When inflation surged in 1971 and 1976, they spent more money and their savings fell. Unlike previous business cycles, however, this time they had a vehicle that allowed them much greater flexibility in the way they saved and spent.

Although the investment world was becoming accustomed to minirevolutions in the 1970s, nothing caused as much commotion as a new mutual fund. Introduced in the early part of the decade, this new type of fund did not offer growth or speculative features. In fact, it offered only a market rate of return, nothing more. Even its name lacked the glamour associated with some of the trendier funds of the day. Yet within a few years of being launched, it had attracted billions in new investment and even threatened the stability of the banking system. This did not appear to be the sort of vehicle associated with revolutionary concepts or products.

These new instruments were money market mutual funds (MMMFs). Their managers sold shares in them to the public, just like any other mutual fund, but these funds invested only in money market instruments such as Treasury bills or commercial paper. The rates on them were higher than bank interest at the time and continued to rise throughout the 1970s. Since the Fed limited the amount of interest banks could pay depositors, their rates of return became increasingly unattractive.[5] The new funds did not have to do much advertising. They simply advertised the recent returns and watched cash pour in. At a time when new stock investors were few, the MMMFs attracted astonishing amounts of new investment.

Most brokerage houses and investment companies were offering their own versions of MMMFs by the middle to late 1970s. Merrill Lynch, in the vanguard among the securities houses, offered its Ready Assets Trust beginning in 1975 for a minimum investment of five thousand dollars. Two years later it followed with its cash management account, or CMA. This took the concept one step farther by allowing investors to write checks against their funds and make VISA charges against them as well. Merrill was clearly stepping across the line into banking by offering these additional services. Banks complained but to no avail. The tide had turned against them as an old concept made a comeback. The new term was *department store banking*, now offered by brokers. The term had not been used since the financial department store had faded from use after the crash in 1929 when banks were breaking into the brokerage and underwriting business. And the apparent motive for offering MMMFs had not changed much either over the years. Eventually, some of that cash (estimated at almost $200 billion by 1979) would find its way to the stock market when conditions were more favorable. Although more profitable, the MMMFs were on par with Liberty bonds and the war bonds of the 1940s because they represented sizable buying power. If only a portion could eventually be directed toward the stock markets, brokers would be happy for years to come.

Eurobond Market Challenges

During the 1960s, when Wall Street was wallowing in insularity, an offshore market development occurred that would profoundly shake up the investment banking community. Many foreign investors had accumulated substantial dollar bank accounts in the postwar years, and those dollars needed a home. Normally, they would have been deposited in American banks or invested in the U.S. markets, but tax regulations were cumbersome. A tax was withheld against foreigners, meaning that a penalty was imposed on those holding dollars in the United States. A potential market existed for anyone with the foresight not to tax foreigners' interest income.

The British were the first to exploit the situation. The London markets had been losing ground to the United States since World War I. The British still had regulations protecting the pound, and while foreign investment in the United Kingdom was encouraged, there was a maze of regulations to wade through. But British bankers saw an opportunity. British banks could offer deposit facilities for dollars free of withholding tax. The only stipulation was that the dollars always remain external to the British banking system. What was envisaged was an offshore market in dollars located in the United Kingdom. Journalists and bankers began to call them *eurodollars*.

Eurodollars were originally created when the Soviet government was looking for a place to deposit its dollar holdings in the late 1950s. Naturally, the mainland United States would not have been the ideal place for the Soviets to bank. A French bank obliged by accepting the deposit, unofficially beginning what was to become one of the world's largest markets for short-term (and later long-term) investments. In the beginning it remained highly secretive. Paul Einzig, a London-based journalist who began writing about the market almost from its inception, noted that many bankers did not even want to discuss it at first. He wrote: "When I embarked upon an inquiry about it in London banking circles several bankers emphatically asked me not to write about the new practice, except perhaps in articles in learned journals or in books which were too technical for the uninitiated."[6] But the market could not maintain its anonymity for long.

The Bank of England quickly recognized the advantages this potential market could have for the City of London, the British equivalent of Wall Street. Lord Cromer, its governor, stated as early as 1962, "The time has come when the City once again might provide an international capital market where the foreigner cannot only borrow long-term capital . . . but will once again wish to place his long-term placement capital." He was certainly correct. As banks located in London began to offer deposit facilities, hundreds of millions of dollars poured in from all over the world. In a sense, the old deal between Montagu Norman and Benjamin Strong ironically had been turned around almost forty years later. Now the "offshore" market picked up a distinct competitive advantage over the United States.

The eurobond market competed directly with the older Yankee bond market. Since its resurrection after World War II, the Yankee bond market had raised billions for foreign companies and some countries as well, just as it had in the 1920s. Investors favored Yankee bonds because of their high yields and their relative safety factor. No more Ivar Kreuger bonds were found in the market; it was dominated by high-quality foreign companies and countries needing dollars. The eurobond market coveted that business and successfully lured much of it away from New York. London was now the ideal place to raise capital.

Most of the dollars flowing into London were deposited in banks. But many investors preferred long-term investments. Then, in 1963, S. G. Warburg and Company, a British merchant bank, launched the first eurobond for a foreign entity in dollars. The syndication took place entirely in London for Autostrade, the Italian highway authority, which was in the throes of building a nationwide highway system in Italy. The issue was dubbed "the Italian version of the New Jersey Turnpike without road signs" by some market cynics, but it sold well. It was doubtful that it would have found much of a reception in the Yankee market, where it was virtually unknown. But Autostrade was a success, and the bonds were sold to international investors happy to supply dollars for a long-term investment.[7]

As the eurobond market grew larger every year, many companies needing cash recognized its major attraction. Unlike Yankee bonds, new eurobonds did not have to be registered with the SEC. In addition to avoiding the SEC registration fees, the more important issue was one of accounting. When registering, companies had to adhere to American accounting standards. Many foreign companies were opposed to this and never borrowed dollars as a result. But now the door was open to dollars without that inconvenience. The Yankee bond market suffered as a result of the eurobond market, and the SEC lost some of its authority over foreign companies borrowing dollars. The SEC finally reacted fifteen years later, bowing to market conditions rather than the indirect challenge.

The euromarkets received a major boost from the collapse of the Bretton Woods system in 1971–72. When the OPEC members began to build up substantial dollar balances, the money naturally was deposited in banks in London and other euromarket centers that had sprung up since the 1960s. Placing dollars in the United States was not attractive because there was talk from time to time, especially during the Nixon and Ford administrations, of seizing foreign assets and even the oil fields themselves. Such rumors were bad for the domestic U.S. markets but excellent public relations for the euromarket. OPEC money continually was deposited in London banks throughout the 1970s and early 1980s. Saudi Arabia alone had over $50 billion deposited in the European banks. By 1979 the total amount of eurodollars was estimated to be at least as large as the narrow measure of the U.S. money supply (M1). Eurobonds also were becoming significant, although new issues activity certainly lagged behind those in the U.S. domestic market.

Investment banks quickly realized that they needed a presence in this new bond market. Their American and foreign corporate finance clients were using the market, and if they could not underwrite from London, a foreign bank would happily do it in their places. As a result, the investment banks began to open London offices in the 1970s. Morgan Stanley and Lehman Brothers were among the first on the scene and actually led the league table of underwriters in the latter 1960s. Salomon Brothers and Goldman Sachs arrived a few years later, followed by Merrill Lynch and some of the smaller houses. But they were not completely at home in the new environment. While the eurobond market was very similar to the domestic market, striking differences did exist, especially in syndication methods. Underwriting agreements did not allow the lead managers control of the syndicates as they did in the United States. But underwriting fees were higher than they were at home. That incentive, plus the desire to gain new business, made the eurobond market a vital new area for established underwriters willing to venture abroad.

The investment banks that succeeded in the eurobond market competed with some highly successful foreign banks, most of which were huge commercial banks that practiced investment banking legally. Their home countries did not separate the two sides of banking as the Glass-Steagall Act mandated. While Morgan Stanley and Goldman, Sachs were lead managers for some of their domestic client companies floating eurobonds, on other deals they were competing directly with huge universal banks such as Deutsche Bank and Credit Suisse. These banks had capital far in excess of that at the investment banks and also had access to international clients unknown to the Americans. Their combination of financial muscle and capital became the envy of American bankers, who wanted to emulate their organizations if the Glass-Steagall Act was ever repealed. They were known as *universal banks,* and all large American money center banks wanted to adopt their techniques.

Other than raising large amounts of capital in a variety of currencies, the eurobond market served as a mechanism for importing new ideas into the United States. Wall Street's insularity had helped develop huge markets, but the features on the menu could be somewhat small. Almost all bonds sold in the bond market were traditional fixed-interest-rate bonds with semiannual interest payments. Eurobonds were more varied. One popular type was the floating rate note, a bond that changed its interest payments periodically, using eurodollar rates as the base reference. These bonds were favored by investors because their interest payments rose along with short-term interest rates. Although alien to the American way of borrowing, floating or adjustable rates would be imported into the United States in the early 1980s as part of the internationalization of the marketplace.

New York City Woes

The turbulent times came close to home for Wall Street in 1975 when New York City tottered on the verge of bankruptcy. The city was one of the largest borrowers in the municipal bond market, and a default would have had catastrophic consequences for the tax-free market. The city found itself in desperate straits with very few friends, especially with Republican Gerald Ford in the White House. It appealed for help from both New York State and Washington. The federal government was in no hurry to help, so the state picked up the gauntlet. The Municipal Assistance Corporation (MAC) was established with state support to put the city back on its feet financially.

New York's plight was no different than that of many other cities in the 1970s. As people moved to the suburbs, many cities lost their property tax bases. Many companies were also beginning to move away, lured by lower rents and better environments elsewhere. In fact, the trend, which began in the 1960s, had severely hurt many large New York banks at the time. As many of their customers migrated, the banks were helpless to follow them because of restrictive banking laws. Many turned instead to making loans and doing international business from foreign branches—types of business that did not fall under the banking laws. Banks found that loans made to foreign governments were more profitable than those made to domestic companies. So the combination of suburban migration and constricting laws forced many banks overseas. Walter Wriston, the president of Citibank, claimed that loans made to foreign governments were among the most profitable on his books. Besides, he stated that "no sovereign government has ever defaulted." Such remarks came back to haunt him after 1982.

New York City's budgetary problems started coming to a head in 1975 as the prices of its outstanding bonds and notes began to fall. Mayor Abraham Beame, besieged by militant unions and escalating costs, could not keep abreast of the problem. New York's major banks banded together to find a solution. Doing so was in their own best interests, for they held large amounts of New York City paper on their own books. The investment banks were market makers in municipal paper, while the commercial banks were large investors. They also helped underwrite city issues since municipal paper was exempt from Glass-Steagall Act restraints.

Bankers approached President Ford about federal help for the city but were met with a polite no. They then approached New York State, hardly in a position to be so cavalier. Governor Hugh Carey and members of the banking group hammered together a special agency designed to put the city back on its financial feet. The MAC was formed to issue bonds backed by the state, with proceeds going to the city. A syndicate was formed to lead the city out of its financial morass. Morgan Guaranty Trust and Salomon Brothers were prominent in heading the syndicate of commercial and investment banks.

The first "Big MAC" bonds hardly fared well in the market initially. On the first day of trading, they dropped 10 percent in value, causing a near panic among investors who bought them. The city's continuing problems with its unions and continuing pessimistic forecasts for its financial future forced many investors and market makers to sell the new issues as soon as they reached the market. Problems were compounded later in the year when New York State declared a moratorium on its own debt. Now the federal government was compelled to act, and President Ford put together a rescue package of credits in Washington to tide the state over. Matters took a turn for the better when the governor appointed Felix Rohatyn of Lazard Freres to succeed William Ellinghaus as MAC chairman. A supporter of Democratic causes, Rohatyn had made his mark at Lazard during the conglomerate trend of the 1960s. Well known for his keen financial mind, he applied strict measures to ensure that the MAC itself did not fail. The *New York Times*, likening him to Hugh Casey, a legendary Brooklyn Dodgers relief pitcher, dubbed him New York's "fiscal relief pitcher." It reported that he "is linked with the so-called hawks on the MAC—the group insisting that New York City take the strongest possible measures to preserve its fiscal integrity. I'm not a hawk. . . . But I'm not a chicken or an ostrich either," he responded after hearing the remark.[8]

After a long and arduous road, the city and the state were restored to respectability in the bond market. Many banks continued to hold New York City and New York State paper. Individual investors also continued to be attracted because New York paper was double or triple tax-exempt since the state had one of the highest income taxes in the country. That was vital to the city's well-being because without the support, buyers of its obligations would have been far fewer. The city reflected the urban crisis that was hurting cities from coast to coast. Fortunately, stability was restored, but memories of the crisis would linger.

The Street Expands

The Dow Thirty broke the 1,000 barrier in 1975. That proved to be a brief respite in an otherwise depressing market. The recession of 1974–75 was painful, and the economy continued to react negatively to rising oil prices. The weak market could be seen in the numbers of shareholders participating in the market. The number rose from twenty million in 1960 to thirty million in 1970. Then the bottom fell out as they abandoned the market in droves. By 1975, five million of them defected. Those who remained had a higher household income than did stockholders of only five years earlier. The number of women equaled that of men, but their numbers as a percentage of the population fell. Society was growing, but the number of shareholders was declining.

The market's weak performance was not the only reason investors voted with their feet. Money market mutual funds were competing for funds as interest rates rose. Companies themselves shared some of the blame. After 1970 many companies began to scale back dividend payments made to their shareholders. By 1975 the payouts were declining dramatically. A fair amount of profit was being reinvested by companies, using the cash rather than raising funds in the markets. The Internal Revenue Service also changed its tax rules for capital gains in 1977 and 1978—the first time since preferential rates were established in 1942 that they were tampered with. Investors now had to hold securities longer to obtain the preferential tax rates. Clearly some did not agree with the change.

Brokers did not follow the same pattern. Most of the wire houses continued to add personnel to their ranks in the 1970s. The large reduction in personnel had come at the beginning of the decade in the immediate aftermath of the Bretton Woods collapse and the oil price increases. Then almost 30 percent of the brokerage force was cut. But new products encouraged brokers to expand beginning in 1975, and in some cases their bottom lines were encouraging because of the wide range of products offered to investors. After the recession, 1975 was a banner year for Wall Street. Merrill Lynch's profit touched $100 million, a 30 percent rise over the last good year, 1971. The number of member organizations of the NYSE continued to slowly decline, however, as the quests for capital and incorporation continued to take their toll. Partnerships were still on the wane. In 1929 over 650 member firms were partnerships; by 1979 barely 200 were left.

Even institutional investors were becoming wary of stocks and were opting for bonds instead. Daily volume on the NYSE reached its height in the late 1970s at about 65 million shares, a fairly paltry number given the two thousand–plus shares listed on the exchange and the number of institutional investors that dominated the market. In 1974 Congress created Employees Retirement Income Security Act, or ERISA, in part dedicated to protecting employees from pension fund managers who imprudently invested their funds. The law came as a response to many bogus investments made by pension funds, including the Teamsters, reputed to be under the control of organized crime. Now fund managers were legally responsible for choosing appropriate investments. And many of the recent academic methods of evaluating stocks became more popular. For the first time, academic research was beginning to have an impact upon ordinary Wall Street practices. Those fund managers on the "buy side" needed more sophisticated tools to assess the risk of stock investment. Those who sold them the stocks also needed to understand the same jargon in order to keep their business.

Despite higher interest rates, the bond markets were doing a booming business. There were plenty of entrées on the menu. The debt explosion could clearly be seen in the number of mortgage-backed securities in the market. In 1970 when Ginnie first started selling bonds, about $475 million were issued. By 1979 there were over $90 billion in existence. Similar numbers also could be found for Fannie Mae and for Freddie Mac, the newest entrant into the mortgage market.[9] The country was rapidly expanding residential housing, and the agencies helped with the financing, but prior to 1979 they were not accustomed to taking serious losses on bond positions. The bond markets, while enormous, were still relatively quiet compared with the stock markets. Dark days were yet to come for the fixed-income markets.

Outside the orbit of the established markets, a new market slowly was beginning to develop on the Street. After finishing his studies at the Wharton School, a young Californian named Michael Milken made his way east to start working at Drexel Harriman Ripley. The firm boasted an old name but was only a shell of the former Drexel that J. P. Morgan once operated. The firm gave the young Milken an opportunity to pursue his vision: high-yield bonds. He was named a director of research and allowed to pursue his ideas, based upon his Wharton thesis, that junk bonds—the name given to bonds that had fallen from grace—could be decent investments for the investor desiring high yield and understanding the associated risks. Milken embarked on a career dedicated to the proposition that there was a market for companies with low credit ratings to borrow new junk bonds. Equally, on the other side, he sought to find the investors to buy them, proving him correct.

Milken embarked on his mission in the 1970s with a messianic zeal, but he would always be viewed as a Wall Street outsider, someone not from the East Coast establishment. He later moved his entire high-yield department to Los Angeles, to be as far from New York as possible. The goal of Drexel at the time was best summed up not by Milken but by Leon Black, a colleague at Drexel: to identify those robber barons who would become owners of the major companies of the future, but not to such a degree that Drexel would actually share the stigma of such clients.[10] Even though the markets were far from robust, those with insight could see ahead to days when they would again be booming.

The Fed Changes Direction

When William Miller retired from the Fed chairmanship to become secretary of the treasury in 1979, the central bank desperately needed a fresh look and new leadership. Both Miller and his predecessor, Arthur Burns, had been less than successful in combating inflation. Wall Street lost confidence in Miller, who came to the Fed from industry rather than from banking or government. To satisfy the Street and keep confidence from waning further, Jimmy Carter appointed veteran central banker Paul Volcker to head the Fed, a move that was loudly applauded on Wall Street and in the banking community. Carter desperately needed the support of the Street. The day he was elected in 1976, the bond market had dropped precipitously in response to the "bad" news. Having a popular man at the helm would not do his flagging presidency any harm.

When questioned by the Senate Banking Committee before being confirmed, Volcker steadfastly maintained that his Fed would be completely independent of the Carter administration. He won lavish praise for his stance, especially from Senator William Proxmire, the committee chairman. The six-foot, seven-inch, cigar-smoking Volcker, president of the New York Fed, was an imposing figure who had played a major role in many international financial conferences and deals. International affairs had come to occupy center stage, and Volcker's appointment was a recognition of this shift. Volcker had an extensive background at the Fed and at the Treasury; he had been active in the negotiations following the breakdown of the Bretton Woods system and was probably the most popular and visible candidate for the job. "Seldom has President Carter used his appointive power so well," said Gabriel Hauge, retired chairman of Manufacturers Hanover Trust. David Rockefeller of the Chase Manhattan described Volcker as "eminently qualified" and "tough and determined." When the markets received news of his appointment, the dollar staged a rally on the foreign exchange markets in support. His actions after assuming the job, however, did not receive such universal plaudits.

   The problems facing the Volcker Fed were enormous by any measure. Prices had doubled in the 1970s, the money supply was expanding quickly, and interest rates continued to rise. The stock market and the bond markets were extremely wary of higher inflation and zigzagged at the slightest bit of negative news. Wall Street needed reassurance from Carter that something was going to be done to stamp out inflation. While Volcker's appointment did not address this issue, nevertheless he was the one person the Street wanted to see appointed. As one of Carter's closest advisers said of the appointment, "Volcker was selected because he was the candidate of Wall Street. This was their price, in effect. What was known about him? That he was able and bright and it was also known that he was conservative. What wasn't known was that he was going to impose some very dramatic changes."[11] He was about to force the very issues that the Street desperately wanted to avoid.

   In order to attack inflation, Volcker shifted Fed tactics. He adopted a policy designed to attack the monetary base, the amount of cash and reserves at banks. By controlling the base, the idea was to control the amount of credit the banks could create. Once bank lending was curtailed, the pressure on interest rates would subside and things would return to normal. The way to accomplish this was to attack the rate banks paid for reserves in the market, the federal funds rate. If it was forced to rise, banks would eventually get the message and cut back on loans made to industry and individuals. The immediate response from the press was that the Fed was becoming monetarist. In reality, Volcker recognized the limitations of strict applications of monetary theory. Three years earlier he had stated before the American Economic Association in Atlantic City that "we need to realize the larger question is not tactical but substantive—how much weight to put on the monetary aggregates as opposed to other considerations."[12] The pressures he would bring to bear would not please all monetarists.

   The announcement of the direction for Fed policy was made on Saturday, October 6, 1979. The discount rate was raised, and other special measures were taken to rein in the supply of money. The fiftieth anniversary of the 1929 crash was only two weeks away, and the markets celebrated early by all going down in tandem the following Monday. The new dose of monetary policy was not what they had anticipated. But the infamous day in Wall Street history did not end there. On the previous day, the first ever bond issue for the IBM Corporation was in syndication, being lead managed not by its traditional investment banker Morgan Stanley but by Salomon Brothers and Merrill Lynch. The issue was the largest in history for an American company: $1 billion of 9.5 percent notes.

   Morgan Stanley refused to participate in the managing group of underwriters since it was not named sole lead manager. The firm then accepted a substantial underwriting commitment but did not want to be seen at the top of the tombstone ad along with Merrill and Salomon. The strategy was openly criticized by many on the street. At the time, Morgan Stanley stood third behind the other two firms in total underwritings for the year. It had not retained the top underwriting spot for a number of years, but it still had the largest number of corporate clients for which it had traditionally served as sole lead manager in securities offerings. An informal survey at the time indicated that Morgan had 53 major corporate clients, 41 of which used it as sole lead manager for new issues. Goldman Sachs had 68 clients but only 23 sole manager positions. First Boston had 26 of 42, respectively.[13] Merrill and Salomon competed individually for new issues and did not count many firms as "sole" clients.

Theories varied on why Morgan Stanley adopted the hard-line position. Some saw it as sour grapes for not remaining sole lead manager. Others attributed it to a superb sense of market timing: knowing that the bond market was in bad shape, Morgan did not want to be seen leading a deal that was bound to dive in value. Others saw it as a sign of the times. One competitor commented, "Having one investment banker is an outgrowth of the period when Wall Street dominated American business. We have seen a great change in the 1970s as more and more companies decide not to have sole managers on their issues." What was neglected was any mention of the size of the issue. The billion-dollar size would have created a financial strain for Morgan, for it had the smallest capital of the three top underwriters. But the deal clearly marked the beginning of a new era.[14] Old relationships, once so valued in the antitrust trial more than twenty years earlier, were now being replaced by competition for underwritings by the newer entrants into the field.

Other Morgan Stanley clients also admitted to actively rewarding other firms for services performed, even at the risk of offending their traditional Morgan Stanley relationship. American Brands, a long-standing client, awarded underwriting mandates to Goldman Sachs after dealing solely with Morgan for years because it wanted to reward Goldman for performing valuable mergers and acquisitions work during the "go-go" years. Many client companies were becoming more transaction-oriented. They needed investment banking firms that could serve their trading and merger needs as well as their underwriting needs. Morgan Stanley was not well suited as a trading house and until recently it had not possessed a sales force. Business began to go elsewhere as a result.

Volcker's policy announcement came over the weekend following. When the bond market began to tumble on Monday, it was assumed that the entire issue was in trouble. Over 225 investment banks were involved in underwriting the issue. But Salomon announced that its major share of the underwriting was already sold and that it did not suffer any losses as the market fell. Merrill, Lynch and the other underwriters, on the other

hand, were not as lucky. They still had a large amount of unsold inventory
on their hands. The estimated size of the loss after the weekend was put at
around 10 percent of unsold bonds. Rumors on the Street put the loss
somewhere between $35 and $50 million for the syndicate as a whole.
John Gutfreund, managing partner of Salomon, put the Street's losses at
under $10 million, attributing the problem to the change in direction at
the Fed. Salomon continually claimed that it had no advance knowledge of
Volcker's announcement and that it had simply been efficient by selling
the bonds early. But almost no one believed the story. Salomon's sharp
reputation was only enhanced by the deal.

The change in Fed policy marked the beginning of the slide into the
deepest stage of the bear market. Yearning for effective political leadership
was also showing in the market. Discontent had not been as intense since
the last days of Hoover's presidency. None of the major political figures
since the Watergate affair had inspired the markets, and the Fed was drifting behind the times until late 1979. The dollar continued a weak performance on the foreign exchange markets, and the United States continued
to run a budget deficit. Congress authorized the Treasury to begin issuing
thirty-year bonds in 1977, indicating longer repayment periods for its
long-term debt. The debt revolution was shifting into high gear. Americans had developed a taste for imported goods, which were rapidly taking
more and more market share. Most disconcerting of all was the surge in
foreign investments. Foreign companies were buying American assets
with their strong currencies, creating the general impression that the
country was for sale at bargain prices.

The Fed's battle was hardly over. The 1979 announcement was only
the beginning of a prolonged attack that would last another three years.
The dose of medicine it applied to the markets was homeopathic as like
was used to combat like. In order to bring inflation and interest rates
down, the Fed ignored interest rates and let them go wherever they might,
which meant straight up for the next several years, to the highest levels
ever seen. But at the same time, inflation was also on the rampage, causing
yields to become distorted. The unthinkable was happening on a large
scale as a result. Short-term interest rates were higher than long-term
rates. Money market mutual fund investors loved it, but industry was in a
bind. Where was the supply of long-term debt capital to come from if investors were busy snapping up high-yielding short-term investments?
Comments in the press from economists did not help. Many likened the
inflation rate, at a high of about 15 percent, to "Latin American," or highly
double digit, inflation. Fed governor Henry Wallich recalled his days as a
boy in Weimar Germany, when inflation rose so high it could not be
counted. While the current inflation did take its toll on the quality of life,
most of the analogies were vastly overstated, as events were soon to prove.

Spiraling

As the new Fed policy began to be felt, interest rates began an inexorable rise. The new IBM issue plus other corporates and Treasury bonds all came under additional pressure as their prices fell and yields rose. Bad days had arrived for the bond business. The *New York Times* ran headlines reading "At Bond Desks, Trying Times" as journalists and economists alike began to give the bond markets more attention than they had done in the past. Commentators furiously began brushing up on arcane Fed terms. Older terminology was not adequate now that the Fed was committed to fighting inflation by centering on bank reserves, not necessarily on interest rates in the first instance.

The Fed began performing in the money market with its dealers. It sold Treasury bills to the dealers and then bought them back within a short time. On Tuesdays or Thursdays it would call its member primary dealers, mostly investment banks and some large commercial banks, to arrange the deals. At 11:45 A.M. the dealers knew that the Fed was actively in the market. The operations became a source of dread for many observers because the fed funds rate continued to rise throughout 1980. Wall Street felt it was starting to come apart. Volcker's Fed was screwing interest rates tighter and tighter while attacking the monetary base. At some point rates should stop rising and the monetary base should begin falling. But where was that point?

The October 1979 announcement and the Fed's actions afterward were not always coherent. Open market operations began but were not always consistent and often confused the market. Then, in the spring of 1980, the Carter administration entered the scene with a plan designed to bring down interest rates and curtail credit. Ordinarily, that part of policy making was left to the Fed, but 1980 was an election year and the administration was not faring well in the polls. The plan was a problem for Volcker because he had vigorously proclaimed his independence from Carter at his confirmation hearings less than a year before. Now politics was making a blatant entry onto the scene. The Fed's reaction would be vital to the success or failure of any administration's attempt to defeat inflation.

Carter planned to introduce what became known as *special credit controls*. Normally, credit restraints lay within the Fed's authority, but in this case the central bank could do little but go along with the administration and help implement the controls. To refuse would have precipitated a crisis between itself and the administration by publicly undermining Carter, something Volcker wanted to avoid. On the surface, the controls seemed spectacularly effective, but within several months they proved to be the administration's undoing. Special, higher reserve requirements were placed on banks and credit card companies as well. The latter roused such public ire that the Fed banks actually began receiving cut-up credit cards in the mail from members of a disgusted public. But the controls appeared to work temporarily. Interest rates dropped during the summer and stayed down until the administration lifted the controls, which would look bad during an election campaign. But interest rates began to rise again as quickly as they had dropped as the Fed tightened up and the markets were back where they started. Carter lost the November election to Ronald Reagan. One of Reagan's planks in the election was tax cuts—the sooner the better. The credit controls were roundly considered to be a political bandage that accomplished almost nothing in the end.

The zigzagging interest rates of 1980 and the wide swings in the money supply were openly criticized by Milton Friedman, the best-known monetarist in the country. Volcker testified before Congress in 1981 that the fluctuations in the money supply and the volatile interest rates of 1980 were the results of a sharp second-quarter recession followed by a stronger than anticipated recovery, all in a relatively short period of time. The culprit, of course, was the special credit controls. Friedman begged to differ. "This explanation reminds me of the man on trial for murdering his parents who asked for mercy on the ground that he was an orphan," he wrote in an open memorandum to the Fed in the *Wall Street Journal*. In his opinion, Volcker had not been tough enough or consistent enough in the battle. He continued: "I have said nothing about the precise monetary growth targets the Fed should specify because that is not where the problem is. The Fed has known what monetary growth it should aim for. But it has been reluctant to adopt procedures that would enable it to achieve those goals."[15] The Fed was not being consistent enough in applying its policy. Friedman actually advocated an even tougher policy than Volcker had pursued.

As soon as the election was over, Volcker began to tighten interest rates even more. In the short interim before Inauguration Day, the Fed had some breathing space before having to deal with Reagan, an unknown quantity when it came to economic policy. The various strains that ran through his public speeches of years past made it difficult to say what economic policies he would follow. Reagan had always proclaimed to be in favor of gold backing for the dollar. Volcker, on the other hand, was present at all the post–Bretton Woods meetings that finally spelled the death knell for fixed parities based on gold. The only place they appeared to have any common ground was on monetary policy. Both favored some form of monetarism, although Reagan was probably closer to Milton Friedman. Volcker had received the brunt of Friedman's criticism, and some in the administration were opposed to the chairman and were willing to use it against him.

The first two years of Reagan's presidency were the greatest challenge for the anti-inflation fight. Within weeks of his inauguration, the president stated that the United States was in "the worst economic mess since the Great Depression. We are threatened with an economic calamity of tremendous proportions." He then went about searching for policies to ward off what many thought would indeed be a depression unless the economy could be stimulated. Reagan espoused several philosophies that gave the market heart. The problem was that they were all espoused at the same time, confusing the markets and economists alike. On one side, monetarism was held to be an excellent means of reducing inflation. Reagan shared this view with Margaret Thatcher, elected the Conservative prime minister of Britain the year before. Several years earlier, Keith Joseph, one of her chief advisers, had written a monograph entitled *Monetarism Is Not Enough*, closely reflecting some of Volcker's ideas on the subject. Reagan seemed to take the idea literally. He also supported tax cuts in order to stimulate the economy. This was part of a bow to supply-side economics, a growth-oriented philosophy that had many supporters on the Street. Lowering tax rates would make more money available for investment. Naturally, a large part of that investment would come from those in higher income brackets, who were best able to invest large sums of money. But the two sides did not necessarily complement each other. It would be difficult to strangle inflation on one hand while encouraging spending on the other. There was no guarantee that the lower tax rates would encourage only investment. Spending could follow as well, helping to undo monetary policy. And the cold war once again raised its head. Defense spending quickly was to become the largest item in the federal budget.

The other major economic plank Reagan supported was the one that would haunt both his administrations. A balanced budget was widely discussed as a way out of the country's economic slowdown. Wall Street heartily welcomed this doctrine, but it proved to be mainly lip service, as budget deficits began to swell shortly thereafter. Reagan's choice for secretary of the treasury was Donald Regan, the chief executive of Merrill Lynch. Regan followed in the tradition of Wall Streeters migrating to Washington; William Simon of Salomon Brothers had served as treasury secretary under Richard Nixon. The Street was happy to have one of its own at such a high level in the administration. The *Wall Street Journal* described Regan as a tenacious competitor with a fine eye for detail, but being second in command was not a quality that many thought would suit him. Clashes with Volcker were bound to arise. This was especially true because Regan had to run the Treasury without much help from the White House. He later revealed that in his entire time at the Treasury he never discussed economic policy with the president on a one-on-one basis but rather ran the department by the seat of his pants. In March 1981 he wrote, "To this day I have never had so much as one minute alone with

Ronald Reagan! . . . How can one do a job if the job is not defined? I have been struggling to do what I consider the job to be. This . . . is dangerous."[16] Regan clearly was accustomed to better. He had favored abolishing fixed commission rates at the NYSE as early as 1970, and he espoused the traditional Wall Street line by advocating less bias in the tax system toward spending and consumption while advocating tax breaks for savings and investment. He certainly was in the Reagan camp when discussing taxes. "The only argument against reducing the top marginal tax rate is that it would remove a penalty for being successful," he added, echoing generations of Republicans favoring lower taxes.[17] But he was not conservative enough for some conservative Reagan backers. "He's going to be the mouthpiece for Wall Street who says we've got to balance the budget before we cut taxes," quipped one.

Balancing the budget received lip service from all presidents, but it was a particularly old Republican chestnut. When combined with supply-side arguments, it began to sound like Republican economic platforms of old. Herbert Hoover claimed he could not pay the veterans' bonus in 1932 for fear of bankrupting the federal government, but he granted tax cuts to stimulate the economy, especially after the crash. Much of Reagan's program sounded suspiciously like the old percolator theory, but it still had great psychological value. The three very different philosophies all appealed to the public at one time or another.

By the time the decade began, most securities houses with established research facilities had their own "Fed watchers." Analyzing the Fed's actions in the market and interpreting the minutes of the Fed Open Market Committee became standard Wall Street routine.[18] Correctly anticipating the Fed's moves in the market could prove profitable for many houses that served as primary dealers with the central bank. The dealers were required to make a price for the Fed when it called. Having Treasury bill and bond positions that were the same as the Fed's could save them a fair amount of money. Money and bond market analysts superseded stock analysts as the most quoted Wall Street gurus as long as inflation and interest rates remained high. Henry Kaufman of Salomon Brothers, in particular, was given widespread attention because of his pessimistic economic forecasts in the early 1980s. Albert Wojnilower of First Boston echoed many of Kaufman's bearish sentiments, and before long the two were referred to as Dr. Doom and Dr. Gloom. In May 1981, at the height of the Fed's tightening of credit, Kaufman characteristically stated that the prospects for the bond markets were poor: "This week's market developments provided further evidence that the Federal Reserve is attempting to conform to a monetarist approach. . . . the effort appears to have been intensified recently . . . and contributes to the instability of the credit market."[19] Such pronouncements marked the first time Wall Street had adopted a pes-

simistic prognosis for the economy in place of the prevailing growth theories that had characterized so much of the past thirty years. Not everyone
agreed, but the gloomy news certainly captured many of the headlines.

The gloom was well placed. Inflation continued to rise, hitting 15 percent. Short-term interest rates exceeded long-term rates. The bond market remained in a state of turmoil as a result, and the Dow Jones Index
refused to break 1,000. New equity issues remained low, and many companies turned instead to short-term commercial paper financings. The result was a drastic change in the way companies financed themselves. By
using debt, they leveraged themselves, only adding more interest payments to their expenses. The costs of doing business were increasing.
When they did, they would eventually be passed on to the consumer.

The net effect was dramatic. Investment by companies declined, and
much research and development was put on hold, waiting for better days.
Manufacturing and smokestack industries began to decline, and their
stocks plummeted. Both required large doses of capital at relatively low
rates in order to make investments for expansion. But since buyers of equity were on the sidelines and new bonds cost too much to issue, many
canceled their plans. As a result, industry began to fall behind and imports
grew. Foreign manufactured goods developed a reputation for quality,
while domestic goods were considered shabby. American-produced
consumer electronic goods, automobiles, and steel quickly began to lose
market share. Imports took their place. The decline in American competitiveness became the buzzword of the early 1980s.

Inflation combined with low economic growth produced "stagflation,"
the economic description for the last two years of Jimmy Carter's presidency. In 1981 it appeared that it would characterize Reagan's as well.
Then an unanticipated phenomenon occurred that proved a political
windfall for the Reagan administration. The Fed had been combating inflation at home by tightening up reserves and the fed funds rate to unheard-of levels. Fed funds touched 20 percent, and the prime rose to 21.5
percent at its height. High numbers usually spelled chaos for the markets,
but in one case a financial market actually picked up a great deal of steam
from high interest rates. The dollar began a major rally on the foreign exchange markets. Foreign investors became convinced that Volcker's fight
against inflation was being won and that the dollar was a good buy. The
dollar began a meteoric rise as investors sought to buy American bonds
and money market investments that yielded more than any other investments in the major industrialized countries.

While Americans feared the high interest rates, foreign investors recognized them as a healthy return. Within the next four years, the dollar
rose 40 percent against the other major currencies. After almost a decade
of slow decline, the dollar was on the rise again, a fact that was well publi-

cized by the administration. Investors were attracted by high bond and money market yields that persisted despite the fact that the inflation rate at the end of 1981 was only a touch below 9 percent. The opportunity was too good to miss in another respect. The strong dollar allowed consumers to buy those high-quality foreign goods at reasonable prices. When the recession of 1981–82 ended, that produced a surge of consumer spending unseen for years. Wall Street was able to smile as well, for many of the foreign investors began turning their attention to American securities. A rally was in the making. But some felt that the hard money policies of the Fed contributed to an unnecessarily harsh recession. Donald Regan wrote that Volcker's constant tinkering with interest rates and bureaucratic maneuvers "did indeed cauterize inflation, but the burn cost that patient the use of his right arm for nearly two years."[20]

In the summer of 1982, the stock market would begin a prolonged rally that would eventually see it rise by over two thousand points on the Dow. In 1981 Congress gave it substantial help by passing the Economic Recovery Tax Act, containing several Reagan principles that the market immediately took to its liking. The tax rate was lowered substantially on all long-term capital gains; this was the most substantial reduction ever seen and showed the administration's supply-side bent. It also changed depreciation rules for companies so that write-off periods were shortened, helping add to the annual depreciation expense. After suffering through a Democratic administration portrayed as highly ineffective, the markets found something to become excited about. This administration was willing to put legislation in place of empty promises.

When the recession ended, the market was poised for a rally. Falling interest rates gave it a substantial boost. Then, in the summer of 1982, the Mexican debt crisis unfolded. Within a short time, it would become the third world debt crisis as well. The Mexican minister of finance, Jesus Silva-Herzog, informed Volcker that his government had run out of money and was unable to meet its external debt payments to international banks. Mexico's external indebtedness stood at about $77 billion. Much of that debt was denominated in dollars and had been made by the banks over the previous ten years. Technically, most of it was in eurodollars, having been made from London branches or subsidiaries. American banks were in the forefront of the lending. Both Bank of America and Manufacturers Hanover Trust had loaned Mexico in excess of $4 billion each over the years. An outright default would threaten the existence of these two banks, not to mention the score of other sizable banks with significant Mexican exposure. The Fed clearly had to do something. In August it began to relax its hold and let interest rates subside. Nancy Teeters, the first woman governor to sit on the Federal Reserve Board, recalled that she first heard of the problem while making spaghetti sauce at home on a summer day.

Paul Volcker called her with the news. Interest rates would have to be lowered to stave off the crisis. No one actually anticipated the severity of the Mexican problem. High interest rates had taken their toll on the markets and domestic industry. Now they were set to put enormous pressure on international borrowers as well.

The immediate threat to the American banking system was not yet clear, but the market was thrilled by the falling inflation rate, slow growth in the money supply after several years of high growth, and the upbeat manner of the new president. The pessimistic days of the 1970s, stagflation, the Iranian hostage crisis, and a general feeling of American impotence were in the past. The new environment emphasized increased defense spending, tax cuts, defeat of unionism (Reagan fired the air traffic controllers rather than accede to their wage demands), and increasing capital investment. The 1950s appeared to be returning. But the intervening thirty years had brought problems that would not recede. Budget deficits were increasing, and the trade deficit was growing by leaps and bounds because of the strong dollar. Wall Street was growing as well, but the shift in power was still increasing. Government remained dominant while the once substantial power of financiers continued to slide.

But the tide had turned on the Street, and there was no looking back. The older investment banks saw their dominance challenged by newer upstarts offering clients services they themselves were slow in recognizing. Transaction-oriented services became the trend. In addition to the traditional underwriting, that meant block trading, mergers advice, foreign exchange trading, and derivatives hedging. Many of these practices were not recognizable at the time of the Justice Department's suit in the 1940s, but the times had changed. Partnerships were on the decline and in ten years would be almost extinct. The demand for capital by corporations meant that investment banks themselves had to have more capital to keep abreast. And the new internationalism found in the eurobond market meant that the top-tier firms also had to expand internationally to follow their clients. The 1970s introduced Wall Street to international competition, and the 1980s would add even more of a "cutthroat" element to the equation. The bull market that was developing also gave increased prominence to the Federal Reserve as a tough inflation fighter. But by 1989 the Fed assumed a role previously exercised only by the SEC or Congress. It would bring about a profound change on Wall Street by reinterpreting the Glass-Steagall Act all by itself. A turning point had been reached on the Street. Change followed change in rapid-fire fashion. The more placid days of the past were gone forever.

CHAPTER ELEVEN

Mergermania (1982–97)

*We have entered the era of the two-tier, front-end loaded,
bootstrap, bust-up, junk bond takeover.*

Wall Street Journal, 1985

The financial chaos left by the 1970s finally led to a giddy bull market in the 1980s. The cycle of Wall Street had proved again that the bad days were followed by the good. The boom and bust cycle was still very much in evidence. The wild market ride that would develop in 1982 and 1983 owed much to renewed investor psychology. After more than a decade of inflation, shaky stock markets, and ineffective political leadership, investors were ready to seize upon any good news. The election of Ronald Reagan and the chairmanship of Paul Volcker at the Fed gave the markets heart, and the new administration soon rewarded them. As in all other booms, there were strange and wonderful products on the menu to excite the investor.

The 1980s are usually remembered as the decade of junk bond takeovers, insider trading scandals, enormous merger deals, and general financial excess. But the decade was also one of momentous financial change, more so than at any time since the 1930s. Many of these changes came through the back door with little fanfare, the exact opposite of how the changes of the Great Depression were introduced. Once the SEC had been in the vanguard of the reform movement on Wall Street. In the 1980s the Fed was clearly in charge. The second major stock market collapse of the post–World War I era made it apparent that many links still allied the investment banking community with the commercial banks. The 1987 market collapse demonstrated that change was necessary to keep the financial system intact, but Congress was not interested in pursuing repeal of the Glass-Steagall Act. As a result, the Fed would begin interpreting some old laws more liberally in order to effect change on the Street.

Since 1979 the Fed had acquired a strong reputation in the market because of its monetarist policies used in fighting inflation. Within ten years it would use that reputation to create changes on the Street, sweeping aside regulations put in place after the 1929 crash. Congress remained unwilling to repeal the Glass-Steagall Act, and commercial banks were kept separate from investment banks. The banking system still was as balkanized as it had been in previous decades; full-service banking was just a dream. But the Fed would allow a marriage of the two without the law being changed. When it did so, a familiar player from sixty years earlier again emerged at the forefront of the decision—J. P. Morgan and Company.

The 1960s produced dozens of "growth" stocks, and the 1970s had their share of energy-related stocks. In 1982, high-tech stocks emerged as the market leaders. Apple Computer and other affordable personal computers challenged IBM for a dominant market share. The desktop computer was beginning to challenge the mainframe and forever alter the work habits of millions. Biotechnology companies boasted advances in genetic engineering that left most laymen puzzled, to say the least. New gene-splicing techniques promised advances in medicine and agriculture that made the scientific advances of previous decades look snail-paced by comparison. Computer software made advances almost daily in a rush to make the new, more powerful PCs more accessible. Software entrepreneurs were establishing their businesses in converted garages with almost no capital and were soon becoming millionaires, at least on paper. Smokestack industries were on the decline, however, with imported steel and other staples capturing a larger and larger portion of the market. The shift to a service-industry society was under way. The economy was by no means vibrant enough to ward off talk of the United States' having become a second-rate industrial power. The popular image was of an aging industrial society expanding by opening hamburger stands rather than creating value and jobs through new industry and capital investment.

Obituaries for American industry proved premature, but they certainly captured their share of the news. The American worker also came under fire. He was too lazy, overweight, and inefficient compared with his Japanese counterpart, who was trim, did jumping jacks before work, and thought in team terms. But cultural differences alone could not explain the apparent American decline. Wall Street knew the problem, however. Raising capital was an expensive process in the United States in the early 1980s. Real interest rates were still high, and the stock market, while moving up, still had some distance to cover before producing relatively cheap new equity. Foreign interest rates, especially in Japan, were lower; as a result, companies were able to continue borrowing for development. Ten years earlier, talk of a capital shortage (equity capital) had made the rounds on the Street. Now those gloomy projections seemed to be reaching fruition. Real American interest rates were still high, and bonds still captured the majority of corporate financings.

Wall Street clearly changed during the bear market. The derivatives markets were doing a booming business and, while technically at a distance from the Street, would prove to be much closer than anyone might have thought. The dollar remained extremely strong, creating a consumer boom and a looming trade deficit at the same time. Interest rates fell from the highs of the early 1980s but still had deleterious effects, especially among farmers. And the Street was ready for the challenges. The securities industry grew enormously during the middle part of the decade, making up for the time lost during the bear market. Brokers, investment bankers, and analysts were added to the ranks to keep abreast of the market and provide financial innovations at the same time.

Yet the decade had something in common with the 1960s. The conglomerate trend that began in the late 1950s never really ended but entered another phase. After the consolidation period in which conglomerates bought all sorts of companies of varying sizes, the downsizing began shortly thereafter. Many investment firms recognized that large companies had bits and pieces that were more valuable to someone else. The famous Wall Street trick with mathematics was again going to play a major role in American life. When the parts were worth more than the sum, it was time to begin a new merger trend. In this case, it was the leveraged buyout and merger phenomenon that spawned the bull market.

Enter Rule 415

Many of the major events on Wall Street over the past thirty years have centered around changes in the shape of the industry. For the most part, underwriting took a back seat in Wall Street headlines. It was a time-proven technique to which all securities firms aspired. Many firms were considered major players on the Street without having a substantial presence in the underwriting league tables. The change in underwriters' status in the 1970s was a notable exception. The emergence of Merrill Lynch, Salomon Brothers, and some of the other wire houses to prominent underwriting positions continued. Advances in the actual underwriting process were small, however. But in 1982 a major change came about in underwriting regulations that heralded the first substantial change since the 1930s. The major force behind the change was foreign, not domestic. The international financial markets were making another intrusion on Wall Street. This one almost slipped through the back door unannounced.

Despite the rise of Merrill Lynch and Salomon Brothers to the top tier of underwriters, the actual underwriting syndicates had not changed materially in decades. Then, in the 1970s, a trend began in the euromarket that would radically shake the ranks. The eurobond market in London was crowded with all sorts of underwriting houses—large and small, from all the industrialized countries. The bond underwriting fees generated were almost half of what Wall Street produced on an annual basis for corporate bonds. All of these underwriters competed for underwriting mandates from the same international companies. Often they sought lead managements when they were really happy to receive a major bracket underwriting. The underwriting syndicates became quite crowded as a result. Large underwritings typically had more than a hundred securities firms in the tombstone ads, and the large ads themselves became a major source of revenue for many financial newspapers.

By the late 1970s it was apparent that there were too many players on the field. Competition was fierce. Some of the smaller houses underwrote bonds, took them on their books, and then dumped them in the market to the first buyer at a discount. These practices gave the market a bad name, and the larger houses openly complained about the behavior among themselves. Some of them began to muscle out the smaller ones by introducing the *bought deal*, in which one or two lead managers bought the entire deal from the bond issuer, often not syndicating it but selling it themselves. This demonstrated the financial muscle of some larger houses while underlining the relative weakness of the smaller. The average $100-million deal required a fair amount of financial commitment from the lead managers. The smaller houses could not compete with the larger; they simply did not have enough capital to do bought deals.

Back home, the American underwriters were still playing the underwriting game according to the rules of the Securities Act of 1933. An underwriter obtained a commitment to manage an issue from a borrower and then went about assembling an underwriting syndicate while the issue was in SEC registration, normally for twenty days. When it was approved, the syndicate stepped up and purchased the issue in order to then sell it to the public. The SEC procedure made the whole process quite methodical. The underwriters were given ample time to organize the syndicate. The time period became risky when the market became more volatile. The stock market changed considerably within three weeks, and after 1979 the same was true of the bond market.

The process also was causing the market to be inefficient and risky. The twenty-day cooling-off period meant that the market could change drastically, making an issue difficult to sell. Companies that wanted their money quickly turned to the euromarket (usually for bonds only), where money could be raised faster. Wall Street needed to change its procedures to win business back from the eurobond market. Besides, the SEC realized that it was also losing its authority to London, where its registration procedures were meaningless. In March 1982 it decided to fly a trial balloon by introducing a new procedure.

The result was Rule 415. The SEC allowed companies to preregister their financing needs. When they wanted their money, they could quickly get their investment bankers to organize the actual new issue. The process was called *shelf registration*, and its merits became obvious very quickly. An issue could remain shelved for two years. Anytime within that period, the financials could be freshened up and a new issue launched. While Rule 415 sounded simple, it wreacked havoc with traditional syndicates. There was no time now to assemble a syndicate in gentlemen's fashion. Underwriters wanting the mandates from companies had to step up and agree to buy the whole issue and then organize a syndicate *after* making the commitment. The bought deal came to Wall Street through the back door. But once it arrived, it quickly revolutionized business. Corporate clients favored it because it allowed them quick access to the markets. Rivals of Morgan Stanley saw its advantages almost immediately. Still the most traditional of the old-line firms, Morgan had been one of the originators of the modern syndicate. Many Wall Street executives noted that a trend was beginning to take even more business away from the old-line houses. A window of opportunity was open for new, aggressive firms that banked on their expertise rather than tradition. The last bastion of traditional investment banking was under pressure from more contemporary forces.

The trend that originated in the 1970s was picking up steam. More and more corporate clients were becoming transaction-oriented, abandoning old investment banking relationships in the process. By the mid-1980s, even General Motors, a long-standing Morgan Stanley client, was using other investment bankers to underwrite its new issues. Morgan still accounted for more single-manager deals, but it was losing its grip. Corporate clients were now actively shopping around for investment bankers. But it was the capital issue among the underwriting houses themselves that spelled success or failure for securities firms for the remainder of the 1980s.

Rule 415 also attracted the Japanese to Wall Street. Over the years, the Street had been almost exclusively American; foreign securities dealers were not a factor. But the new environment attracted foreigners. Always eager to participate in Wall Street's wealth, British firms, along with some Swiss and Japanese, began to make appearances in New York. The best-known among the British was Morgan Grenfell, an old firm that had had ties to J. P. Morgan in the 1930s. The Swiss were led by the large banks that had securities subsidiaries, such as Swiss Bank Corporation. Credit Suisse made its presence felt by buying into First Boston, which changed its name to CS First Boston (CSFB in London). The other Europeans were inconspicuous for the most part, although Deutsche Bank was slowly increasing its presence on the Street. British and Swiss firms had always done some business on the Street and were also among the largest foreign investors in Treasury bonds. But the Japanese were a different matter. Since the early 1980s they had carved out a substantial presence in the eurobond market. Now they were planning incursions into Wall Street.

Japanese success in London was striking. Within a few years of its arrival, Nomura Securities, the world's largest securities house in terms of capital, had quickly challenged Deutsche Bank and CSFB as lead manager in the eurobond market. With enormous amounts of capital at its disposal, Nomura raised the bought deal to a new level by simply offering to buy new issues and then resell them at stable prices. But when Nomura approached the Street, the reception was cool, and its success rate proved much less enviable than what it enjoyed in the eurobond market. Nomura found that simply buying its way into lead managements was not as easy as it was in London. Relationships between companies and clients in the United States were stronger than imagined. Although multiple investment bankers were used by companies, old relationships were not necessarily abandoned altogether. Nomura and the other large Japanese houses found themselves invited into some underwritings but gained few precious lead management positions. The *Wall Street Journal* reported that many Japanese houses went looking for business in some strange places as a result. Some even ventured onto Indian reservations in search of business. They made more significant gains in the Treasury bond market, where the enormous Japanese appetite for Treasury bonds was well recognized.

The Fed helped the matter substantially by allowing several foreign houses to become recognized primary dealers. The relatively small group of select dealers received a blow in 1982 when Drysdale Securities, a New York dealer, was forced to close its doors because of fraudulent money market deals with Chase Manhattan. A backroom scheme was discovered in which employees of the two firms was recording fictitious trades; the incident cost Chase over $100 million. Since the British, Japanese, Germans, and Swiss had been such large purchasers of Treasuries, many houses had actively sought to become members of the dealing network. They would not have to pay transactions costs for themselves or their clients but could buy and sell directly in the market. The quid pro quo was simple. The Fed wanted those countries to open their doors to American firms. The internationalization of the marketplace was moving into high gear. Success in the Treasury market was no guarantee of success anywhere else on the Street. But failure would be taken very seriously, for foreigners as well as Americans.

Banks were beginning to make themselves heard on the Street again in 1982. The Fed gave a J. P. Morgan subsidiary the right to trade financial futures during the summer, a move that clearly distressed brokers. The Bank of America moved to acquire Charles Schwab and Company, a large discount broker, in a clear attempt to intrude into the brokerage business. The Securities Industry Association responded by announcing that it would sue the Comptroller of the Currency in an attempt to block the banks from acquiring brokers, but to no avail. Schwab was acquired and other banks actively sought brokerage houses, but only those without underwriting capabilities. Robert Linton, the head of the SIA and also the CEO of Drexel Burnham Lambert, read the trend correctly, suggesting that if banks acquired brokers they should do so only through securities subsidiaries. The trend toward financial supermarkets again was picking up some momentum. When asked whether there was a future for independent brokers, Linton responded (as expected), "I think so. We don't necessarily believe in one stop shopping."[1] But the idea picked up further momentum. Sears Roebuck acquired Dean Witter Reynolds, and the Prudential Insurance Company bought Bache and Company with just that in mind. General Electric also acquired Kidder Peabody in the best-known transaction involving one of the Street's oldest firms. But no one realistically saw customers at Sears taking a break from shopping to do a trade or two at the Dean Witter desk in the stores. Within a decade, the acquisition trend began to reverse itself.

The Glass-Steagall wall was still inviolate, and no one wanted to be seen challenging it. But the debate was heating up in Congress. The SEC's chairman, John Shad, came under fire for being too friendly with the Street, especially in dealing with Morgan Stanley, adding to purported regulatory laxity. Critics and friends of the Street were lining up on both sides of the debate. Republican Senator Jake Garn, architect of the Garn–St. Germain Act of 1982 and a chairman of the Senate Banking Committee, was in favor of revising the Glass-Steagall Act without actually repealing it. "Bright lawyers are using creative methods to blur the line between commercial banking and investment banking," he wrote. "If the legal and business talent that has been debating whether to amend the act (and in finding ways around it) were to be harnessed toward creating alternative, workable and fair means of dealing with such issues, the entire financial system would be better off."[2] But his views were certainly not shared by all. Democrat Congressman Charles Shumer of New York was among those in favor of maintaining the act, mostly to preserve the protections it offered. "Eliminating Glass-Steagall is likely to create risk-averse behemoths that squelch entrepreneurial initiatives," he stated, adding that "a banker with nothing to sell will be a better custodian than one with a direct interest in the outcome."[3] The trend for the future was becoming clear. Glass-Steagall was likely to remain, so new attempts would need to be made to circumvent it with a few well-timed end runs.

Merger Trend Begins

Shelf registrations turned out to be only one of several Wall Street revolutions in the 1980s. The Street was witnessing more changes within a short period than it had in decades. Usually, the radical changes were precipitated from outside. The enormous growth of the options and financial futures markets took place in Chicago. The conglomerate trend of the 1960s was another example, originating within companies themselves. The Street got rich by helping in the merger trend, but it did not originate it. But in the case of junk bonds, the revolution began on the Street at a house with a familiar name.

Over the years, the term *junk bond* had meant a "fallen angel." Wall Street was fond of theological metaphors. Once a highly rated investment-grade bond, the issuing company had fallen upon hard times and its bond price fell. The yield rose to the point where its speculative nature was clear. Would it be able to climb back to grace? If it did, the price would rise again and the bondholder who bought it cheap would be amply rewarded. Some favorite junk included bonds of countries in default. The best known was a Cuban bond, issued before the Castro revolution. Although it technically matured in 1977, traders continued to make a market in it although it had paid no interest in twenty years. Even with no prospects of being redeemed, speculators still bet that some day the bond would be redeemed after Castro eventually fell from power. The wait proved to be lengthy. All securities houses had junk bond specialists who traded the market looking for turnaround situations, but no one ever *created* a turnaround situation.

Enter Michael Milken at the rejuvenated old firm of Drexel. After a couple of mergers and infusions of cash, its name became Drexel Burnham Lambert, with the last part added after a capital investment from Banque Bruxelles Lambert of Belgium. Drexel was only a minor player on the larger stage, and its corporate finance presence was meager. But Milken's idea for a new market, first formulated in the early 1970s, had come a long way in ten years. New issue high-yield bonds, a more polite name than junk, were being issued in larger numbers every year. Although some had been brought to market by more established houses like Lehman Brothers, Drexel had most of the market to itself. The idea required as much selling and distribution ability as corporate finance expertise. That is where Drexel had a leg up on some of its larger competition.

Milken developed a new issues market for companies in purgatory. Companies that could not access the corporate bond market because of their low credit ratings now could borrow in the junk bond market. There was a price, however. The yield to the investor had to be substantially higher than for higher-quality bonds to compensate for the risk, so the new bonds were usually issued at a discount from their face value. The result was a higher yield for investors and cash for companies that otherwise may not have been able to find any money at all. Market timing was important for junk bonds. Rule 415 helped immensely by allowing the underwriters to get the bonds to market as quickly as possible once approved.

Drexel had the market mostly to itself until competition started to develop from other established investment banks in the mid-1980s. Junk bonds were enormously profitable for underwriters but also bore substantial risks. The underwriting fees for junk bonds were double those for ordinary, investment-grade bonds. Milken reputedly negotiated a deal with Drexel that personally gave his junk bond unit one-third of the fees as a commission. On a bond with a 6 percent fee structure, that meant two points. If the issue amount was $100 million that was $2 million for Milken's team—larger than the entire underwriting fee on a quality bond. He had discovered a product that yielded fees like those produced by bonds had in the heyday of the money trust during World War I. Both Milken and Drexel quickly accumulated large amounts of money and influence. The *Wall Street Journal* dubbed Milken the "king of junk bonds."

But selling junk bonds was another problem. Not all investors could be persuaded to buy them because of their lowly credit ratings, BB or lower in the alphabet soup of credit rating agencies. If the new market was to develop properly, Milken had to find an ample supply of investors. As with any good investment idea, if it did not sell it had no practical value. Politics entered the picture. The timing was superb because the market was still in its infancy. In 1982 President Reagan, with Secretary of the Treasury Regan at his side, announced a proposal to liberalize the existing banking laws. The Depository Institutions Act, better known as the Garn–St. Germain Act, proposed that banks and savings and loans be allowed to buy corporate bonds. It actually expanded upon some of the provisions of an earlier law passed in 1980. This was the first change in the Glass-Steagall Act affecting banks and corporate securities since the original law was passed. Calling the proposal the greatest financial development in years, Reagan cheerfully predicted that it would help banks out of the problems created by high interest rates.

More than good timing was involved. Drexel spent lavish sums to ensure that junk bond financing had legitimate support. Every year it held an annual Predators' Ball at which dozens of academics and politicians spoke of the market's virtues. Show business celebrities were invited to give the proceedings a lighthearted ambience. Potential buyers of junk bonds were regaled with sumptuous dinners and a bevy of professional models for companionship. The annual fete, held at Ivan Boesky's Beverly Hills Hotel in Los Angeles, sometimes attracted as many as fifteen hundred revelers. But the purpose was dead serious. The invited politicians were those with financial connections that could potentially help Drexel. The financial people were those with the greatest buying power to purchase the steady stream of new issues. Among the political stars making appearances at one time or another were Senators Bill Bradley, Ted Kennedy, and Howard Metzenbaum. Drexel contributed to the campaigns of Senator Al Damato and Alan Cranston, among others. Cranston was later implicated with Charles Keating in the massive California savings and loan scandal that bilked hundreds of millions from Keating-controlled institutions and left the Senate in disgrace.

Suddenly, a new potential market opened for junk bonds. Savings and loans were especially hurt in the early 1980s and desperately needed investments yielding more than their traditional mortgages. Junk bonds filled the bill from the yield side but not necessarily from the quality side. But the new law only allowed banks and others to place a certain proportion of their assets into bonds. The damage that junk bonds could potentially cause seemed minimal. So the thrift institutions became a prime marketing focus for junk bond merchants. The market for junk was mostly institutional; buyers included savings and loans, bond funds, and some insurance companies. The growth of the market was explosive. Halfway through the decade, it seemed that the junk bond would become as popular as other bond novelties had been in the past. But investors, at least the clever ones, recognized that a junk bond was really a substitute for a stock, which behaved in much the same manner and certainly was as risky. In the first several years of their lives, however, junk bonds appeared to do no wrong. They paid more than other bonds and found many willing investors. Although demand was not universal, and many investment banks refused to become involved in a meaningful way, Drexel nevertheless reaped the rewards. The firm increased its presence in the top underwriting tables, and its profitability rose commensurately. Milken's bonuses alone made him the highest-paid Wall Street employee ever. He was reputed to have accumulated over $3 billion in personal wealth from the junk bond craze before Drexel closed its doors in 1991. His bonus in the last year of Drexel's existence, some $550 million, made him the country's highest-paid executive in history.

Drexel established an elaborate scheme for selling junk. The nature of the distribution network obviated the visionary element behind Milken's original ideas for the market. In many cases, buyers were well compensated for buying Drexel-originated issues. One such example was the Finsbury Fund, managed by David Solomon. This was the high-yield fund of Solomon Assets. The fund inflated the price of the junk bonds it bought and sold to investors and then kicked the cash back to Drexel and Milken. Milken, in return, kicked back benefits to Solomon's personal trading account at Drexel.[4] Deals of this nature proved to be Milken's undoing.

Rather than be satisfied with the ample commissions that junk generated, greed entered, providing fuel for prosecutors when it was discovered.

The economics of the 1980s certainly helped Drexel and Wall Street. After the economy recovered from the recession of 1981–82, growth remained strong for the rest of the decade, with no recession developing until 1990. Those eight intervening years were one of the longest periods in post-World War II history without a downturn in the economy. Many of the junk bond companies continued to do well, although a recession certainly would have hurt many of their prospects and slowed down the market. The market collapse of 1987 did put a serious damper on the growth in the market and eventually led to a major shakeout. After October 1987, investors began to assess junk bonds' performance and discovered that they did in fact behave much like stocks. They discovered that declining earnings affected junk bond companies badly because most did not have strong enough financials to weather a poor quarter or two before finding themselves on the verge of default. The junk market began a serious decline after the stock market collapse of October 1987.

Takeover Candidates

Although the Fed had been relaxing monetary policy in 1982, the result was more dramatic than might have been expected. Money supply growth jumped over 13 percent by early 1983, and the budget deficit widened. Some commentators dubbed Volcker's policy a shift from tough to permissive monetarism. Then interest rates took another serious spike upward in 1984. The thirty-year Treasury bond yield hit 14 percent before subsiding later that year. Yields finally began to fall, then continued to do so for the next three years. The bond market began its largest rally in the twentieth century. Everyone wanted to take credit for it. The Fed remained characteristically quiet, but not so the administration. The bond market rally accompanied the stock rally, and waves of optimism swept over Wall Street.

Foreign investors helped considerably. British and Japanese investors in particular began buying American stocks. The SIA reported that they favored the blue chips, especially IBM, Eastman Kodak, and Johnson and Johnson. But inflation had taken its toll on corporate America, and many industries were still in the doldrums. Stock prices were below book values in many cases. New technologies made many companies' prospects bleak. All those cheap assets became the prey of a new breed of mergers and acquisitions specialists. Companies that wanted to expand found themselves in a difficult position. Building new businesses from scratch was expensive because new assets reflected the rise in inflation over the previous eight years. Existing assets could be bought more cheaply. Regardless of a company's corporate strategy, there were enough cheap assets to trigger an acquisition boom that made the 1960s seem tame by comparison.

Wall Street rejoiced at the boom. Goldman Sachs estimated that a major portion of the stock market's climb in 1984 came from the anticipation of mergers.[5] Investors bought companies that they thought had a reasonable chance of being taken over. The traditional firms that advised on mergers and acquisitions were doing a thriving business. The boom started at the same time as the stock market rally. Within the next five years, the number of mergers and their average purchase price tripled in value. By 1987 the annual value of merger activity almost reached $300 billion, a record. The investment banks dominating the business were the top-tier firms: Goldman Sachs, Morgan Stanley, First Boston, Merrill Lynch, Lehman Brothers, and Salomon Brothers. Some of the smaller firms, such as Lazard and Dillon Read, also figured prominently in the trend. Many small boutique firms also opened to take advantage of the boom. In many cases mergers and acquisitions was their only activity. The larger firms averaged 110 to 200 deals per year during the boom. Compensation was usually based upon a percentage value of the deal, which could produce sizable fees for the advisers. Even if investment banks negotiated fees of only 1 to 2 percent of a deal's value, the prices being paid at the time allowed some of them to reap rewards of $50 to $100 million per year.

Some practices during the boom gave Wall Street a less than savory reputation. One strategy that particularly irked many corporate boards was *greenmail*. Not illegal, it was frowned upon for producing little value except for the greenmailer himself. In this approach, potential buyers accumulated enough stock in a company to become a nuisance. The price for getting them to go away required the company to buy the stock back at a premium. The strategy worked successfully many times, although most raiders emphatically denied that they had greenmail in mind when approaching the brides. Most of the approaches were hostile, often because the management of the bride did not trust the bridegroom's intentions. The takeover specialists, whose names became household words during the 1980s, often were feared at target companies because of their labor or management intentions. Carl Icahn, the soft-spoken yet predatory greenmailer, made almost $100 million from his approaches to companies such as Hammermill Paper, Tappan, Marshall Field, and Phillips Petroleum. Thomas "Boone" Pickens, an outspoken Oklahoman, used his own Mesa Petroleum Company to begin acquiring stock in other oil companies. He realized about $100 million by acquiring stock in Cities Service and General American Oil Company before selling both holdings back to the respective companies. Following in Reagan's path in dealing with the striking air traffic controllers, some mergers were finalized only at a great cost to the unions at the companies being purchased. Several were effectively busted as a result, beginning a trend away from unionization. Carl Icahn's takeover of TWA in 1985 was but one example.

One way to deter hostile takeovers was to make the cost so prohibitive that they were simply too risky. Companies began to employ "poison pill" defenses to ward off unwanted buyers. Companies could spot unwanted suitors when they were required to file with the SEC after having accumulated 5 percent of their targets' stock. Using investment bankers to design the strategy, companies would begin issuing preferred stocks or bonds at the first sign of a hostile takeover. All of the increased leverage in the form of dividends and interest was added to deter hostile takeovers. The buyer would be forced to pay all the extra costs in order to acquire the company. Rule 415 made this much easier by allowing companies to shelf register the pills. But the problem was only magnified if the poison pill worked. The company might be free of the takeover bid but could emerge from the battle very weak as a result of the extra dividends and interest it accumulated in the process. Investment bankers came under fire for advising on the deals. Helping underwrite new preferred stock and bonds added to their underwriting fees but left many companies in the lurch after the smoke cleared.

The deals made some of the 1960s takeovers look small by comparison. Rather than costing hundreds of millions of dollars, the new deals ran into the billions. The stakes involved suggested that many were no longer friendly takeovers. One of the first, and most successful, deals of the post-1982 recession was former Secretary of the Treasury William Simon's leveraged buyout of Gibson Greeting Cards, netting about $70 million. After that, the rush was on. The takeover of Beatrice Foods, a major food company, was accomplished by Kohlberg, Kravis, Roberts, a specialized buyout firm that frequently used high degrees of leverage. The three principals in the firm, Jerome Kohlberg, Henry Kravis, and George Roberts, all cousins, were among the first firms organized to take part in the conglomerate trend of the 1960s. They were correctly positioned to take part in the emerging trend in the 1980s and became its biggest players. They used Drexel as their investment banker in the takeover, which quickly became hostile. Beatrice was a large, diversified company that had extensive interests in areas other than food. It also possessed a stodgy management that KKR sought to replace. The company would have more potential value broken up than it did in its present form while still retaining the core business. KKR bid fifty dollars per share for Beatrice in 1985 but reconsidered when Drexel informed it that the price was too high and that investors in junk bonds would balk. The price was eventually lowered to forty dollars. When the deal went through, the cost to KKR was $5.6 billion. KKR acquired the company, and Drexel made a small fortune on the underwriting fees and warrants created for the deal. In addition to an estimated $50 million in fees, Milken made another $250 million by acquiring warrants created by KKR for him at a nominal sum and then later selling for one hundred times their value.

The buyout firm went on a spending spree and acquired many companies with well-known names. By the time it made its bid for RJR Nabisco, it had already acquired Beatrice, Safeway Stores, Motel 6, and Duracell, among others. It also began acquiring a fairly sizable magazine publishing empire bit by bit. But the RJR Nabisco takeover, engineered in 1988 and completed in 1990, was the largest takeover in history. The two companies, RJR and Nabisco, were originally merged in order to help RJR diversify away from tobacco. Then KKR spotted the company as one with potential for eventual restructuring. The purchase price paid by RJR was $23 billion, a record. The financing was so large that a host of Wall Street firms and banks were employed. Drexel was working on the deal when its legal problems were first announced.

Many of the mergers of the decade were fueled by the egos of some of the raiders themselves. Many set out to carve themselves empires from relatively small bases. Robert Maxwell in Britain was one, Rupert Murdoch in Australia another. Both assembled a coterie of publishing companies and broadcast media companies (in Murdoch's case) around them. Ted Turner did the same in the United States, expanding rapidly into cable television. Junk bonds figured prominently in the merger trend. Sometimes a company would borrow heavily until its credit rating declined, from which point junk bonds became the only viable means of financing. Without them, much of the economic growth that made the 1980s famous would not have occurred. Almost 20 percent of new corporate bond financings were technically junk by 1985. Companies facing enormous takeover bills also borrowed from banks when the bond market ran dry. Without the bank loans, many takeovers would not have been consummated either. The "junk" loans advanced by the banks also made them very vulnerable if and when the companies ran upon hard times. And the Fed also came in for some extreme criticism. Critics maintained that it should not have allowed banks under its charge to participate in the merger spree. As the money supply began to expand, it was clear that the merger trend was heating up. Some contended that the Fed was "monetizing" the merger trend.

Many junk bonds were also used in management buyouts, where a company's managers leveraged themselves to buy the outstanding stock. The Kohlberg, Kravis, Roberts takeover of RJR Nabisco was actually a buyout, specifically a *leveraged buyout*. All of the borrowed money was used to buy the stock and take the company private. KKR got its start after the conglomerate trend of the 1960s when the trend began to reverse. The conglomerates began to shed some of their acquisitions and were bought by their management. Borrowed money became the tool used to take a company private.

Deficits and the Dollar

Until 1985 the dollar was riding on the crest of a wave. By March the high point of its appreciation against other currencies came. Persistently high interest rates accounted for most of the rise. From the outside, the trend seemed to be the best of both worlds. Imports were cheap and overseas vacations were cheap. But looking beyond consumers, the picture was darker. The boom in imports caused a massive merchandise trade deficit while the budget deficit itself was growing. The two, known as the *twin deficits*, were causing concern all around. Why was no one in an official position tackling the problem? The news was full of deficit stories, but Wall Street did not appear overly concerned. While analysts lamented the deficits, the Street continued its preoccupation with the rally inspired by mergers and acquisitions.

Although the Treasury had to borrow more and more money to fund the deficit, overseas buyers proved to be a voracious source of cash. Japanese, German, and British investors began buying sizable amounts of Treasuries on new issue. Estimates had them buying as much as 50 to 70 percent of new bonds issued. By 1985–86 the trend hit its peak when the British and the Japanese traded $1 trillion worth of Treasuries.[6] Only a fraction of that amount was net buying, but Wall Street benefited because of the overall increase in trading. The Treasury quickly began to rely on this source of buying power. In 1984 it waived the withholding tax that used to be levied against foreigners' interest payments, ensuring that foreign demand would remain high in the future. Quickly, the United States was developing into a borrower nation for the first time since World War I. Although there were reasons to believe that the press reports of the country turning into a debtor nation again were not entirely true, the enormous buying power from abroad made good headlines and further reinforced the image that the country was being bought by foreigners. But Japanese purchases of Treasuries did not make the same sort of intriguing news as foreign purchases of American companies.

The Reagan administration paid lip service to the trade deficit but had other positive benefits of the strong dollar in mind. Martin Feldstein, chairman of Reagan's Council of Economic Advisors, made it very clear that if confronted with a clear choice between a strong dollar and weak dollar, he would choose the strong. He stated, "It is better to reduce exports and increase imports."[7] The strong dollar brought in a torrent of foreign investment, much of which went to Treasury securities. The Treasury was financing the budget deficit with foreign cash. Interest paid on Treasury debt rivaled defense spending as the number one item in the federal budget. If the Treasury or the Fed tried to weaken the dollar, it would be acting against the administration's best interests. The administration had not intervened in the foreign exchange market to influence the dollar since the day Reagan was shot in 1981. By 1982 all pretense to intervention was given up and the dollar was allowed to rise.

Curiously, the strong dollar also attracted foreign direct investment, something that was not anticipated. Many foreign companies began buying property and American companies that would serve their manufacturing and marketing interests in the United States. The lure of the American market and the pent-up consumer demand was too tempting to ignore. This was not a new phenomenon. European interests had been present in the United States for years. Most American thought of Shell or Lever Brothers as American companies when in fact they were British (and Dutch) in origin. But when the Japanese began making inroads into the United States, the situation became more tense. Some of the acquisitions were particularly large. Rockefeller Center in New York and the Pebble Beach Golf course in California were both purchased in the 1980s by Japanese investors. The purchases of such well-known American institutions heightened suspicions that the best the country had to offer was for sale. Stories abounded of Oriental people being hounded, and in one case even killed, because they "appeared" Japanese. The years of industrial deterioration and lack of competitiveness were beginning to show an ugly side.

Congress reacted strongly to the increasing budget deficit, passing the Gramm-Rudman bill in 1985 to force a balanced budget by making mandatory cuts in government spending. Wall Street was almost uniformly behind the bill, which provided support for one of the two major planks the Street always advocated: emphasizing tough anti-inflation policies. But the spectacle of Congress passing a law to hold down its own spending appeared a bit more ridiculous from outside Wall Street than from within. The *Economist* took a jaundiced view of the bill, characterizing the plan to end deficit spending by 1991 as "one of the most desperate acts ever to have come out of Washington. It's like a girl who can't say no, so she puts on a chastity belt and throws away the key."

While the Street applauded Gramm-Rudman, a more serious reform was in the making when the Tax Reform Act of 1986 was passed. The tax system favored deductions and was overhauled to make life simpler for the taxpayer, both corporate and individual. The act reduced the number of tax brackets and eliminated many deductions. Depreciation rules were liberalized. The preferential treatment for long-term capital gains was eliminated, breaking a decades-old tradition. The interest deduction for consumers was also eliminated, making all consumer interest except for mortgage interest nondeductible. This was another old chestnut that had been broken. But the most serious part of the reform for the Street concerned the municipal bond market. Some munis were reclassified, losing their tax-exempt status. Congress suspected that these bonds were really nothing more than corporate bonds disguised as munis. Needless to say, the muni market did not appreciate the interference. The day the new regulations went into effect, the muni market experienced one of the worst days in its history. The prices of many existing industrial revenue bonds fell by as much as ten percent.

The dollar's decline in later 1985 did more to help the trade balance than any other measure. In October, Fed and Treasury officials met with the finance ministers of the industrialized countries at the Plaza Hotel in New York to consider measures to bring down the dollar. They agreed to act in tandem to sell dollars, raising their own currencies in the process. They adopted a common policy to help force the dollar down. A cheaper dollar would hurt their own exports but would reduce U.S. reliance on imports and help defuse some elements in Congress that wanted to impose trade sanctions against foreigners. Farming interests and manufacturers did not have much influence with the Fed, but they could mount substantial political support for trade sanctions in both houses. But the Plaza meeting did the trick. The dollar, already declining, was given substantial help and began to slide on the foreign exchange markets. The effect did not last long, but it got the markets off on the right track. Margaret Thatcher, originally in favor of the policy, later remarked that, in hindsight, she thought it was not sound: "The Plaza Agreement gave finance ministers . . . the mistaken idea that they had it in their power to defy the markets indefinitely. This was to have serious consequences for all of us."[8] Within a few years, the U.S. trade deficit began to decline, but the effect was not long-lasting. Increasing trade deficits made a return in the 1990s after several years of relative decline.

While the markets were making the most of the decline in interest rates and the merger boom, one sector of the economy was in serious financial trouble. Farmers, especially independent farmers, were having difficulty meeting interest payments and were losing their farms as a result. To some this only showed the backwardness of the agricultural sector: everyone else was prospering while farmers languished. Some entrepreneurs earned widespread publicity by "adopting" a farm family and helping them out of their plight by paying off their mortgages or making them loans to help forestall bank foreclosures. The same high interest rates that crippled the financial markets in 1981 and 1982 took slightly longer to hit the farmers. When they did, the results were more severe because the rest of the country was already in a boom.

While consumers enjoyed the benefits of the strong dollar, the farmers suffered. Much of their income came from exports. The strong dollar was killing their businesses as buyers sought cheaper products elsewhere. Making payments on loans and mortgages became difficult. The result was a full-blown farm crisis. The television news was replete with stories of farm families giving up their homesteads after generations of farming. The 1980s version was as severe in some cases as the dust bowl of the 1930s. But the boom-bust cycle in agriculture was just another unfortunate chapter in an unfortunate industry as far as Wall Street was concerned.

Wall Street traditionally had had little to do with farmers since the 1920s with the major exception of the bonds of the Farm Credit System, which were generally well received and popular among investors on the Street. But when a few land banks that were part of the Farm Credit System began to fail in 1985 and 1986, the plight of the farmers started to receive broader attention. The banks were part of the system that was analogous to the Fed for farmers. If their central credit-generating agency became bankrupt, agricultural financing would certainly collapse. In 1987 President Reagan announced a bill to correct the farmer's plight. Congress created a new agency designed to put the finances of the farm system in order. The bonds created for the occasion were sold on the Street with great fanfare, although they did not take long to sell. They were partially guaranteed by the Treasury, the only viable way to sell them. True to form, the new agency got a good ole' boy nickname, "Farmer Mac."

While the farmers suffered, Wall Street continued to take in record profits. But signs of wear were beginning to show. The boom kept the new issues market working overtime. Arbitragers also flourished buying and selling the shares of brides and grooms. The most publicized, Ivan Boesky, would soon plead guilty to charges of insider trading. Not actually the best known of Wall Street's arbitrage contingent, Boesky was perhaps the most visible, a characteristic most "arbs" usually liked to avoid. It would soon be shown that his arbitrage was built more upon receiving tips about impending takeovers from mergers and acquisitions specialists than on doing his homework. The giddy times and the surging stock market made the practice all too common.

The Swap Market

Junk financings and exotic eurobonds created a whole new class of debt in the early 1980s. Bonds and bank loans now had floating (or adjustable) interest rather than the traditional fixed variety. Interest rates were extremely volatile, which presented problems to many companies and made many corporate treasurers nervous. Many companies were already in serious trouble because of spiraling interest rates. Was this problem going to continue for the foreseeable future?

The financial world responded. Out of those bad cases of nerves came a new financial concept that, within a few years, was translated into the largest market ever devised. The challenge to Wall Street was now very clear because the market was not entirely within its grasp. A large derivatives market called the *swap market* sprang up, providing solutions for those with interest payment problems. The potential threat to Wall Street was enormous. The new market developed not at the Chicago futures exchanges or even in the traditional over-the-counter market but among the commercial banks and investment banks seeking new products to brandish among their corporate clients.

Many firms on the Street participated. The idea of what was known as an *interest rate swap* originated on the Street in the late 1970s. Salomon Brothers and other fixed-income specialists began allowing their customers, usually banks and other financial institutions, to change their interest payments with each other. One party would swap with another to assume interest payments based upon a bewildering variety of formulas. If the swapper got it right, money could be made on the swap. If interest rates did not perform, large losses could be incurred.

Wall Street houses and the commercial banks both flocked to the new market. Investment banks seemed better suited for it because trading interest rates was their normal business. But the big banks quickly muscled their way in. Customers required the bank they swapped with to have high levels of capital on its books. The commercial banks, which usually had more capital than the securities houses, began to push the investment banks to the sidelines. The largest of the houses were able to make significant inroads, but it took the capital of Merrill Lynch to compete with the likes of Citibank or J. P. Morgan.

Interest rate swapping was accompanied by other forms of swapping (currencies, commodities futures contracts) but remained the most popular. All major corporations participated in some way or another. Many proved to be novices at trading and eventually began to show substantial losses on their books. But swapping not only represented a new market to conquer; it also marked the beginning of the commercial banks' intrusion into trading, a traditional Wall Street preserve. Swaps were a form of derivative that Wall Street had come to embrace as its own. Now the banks were crowding into the market, showing their muscle at the expense of the smaller securities houses. Firms on the Street found themselves at a significant disadvantage. Customers that wanted to swap certainly would not do business with them precisely because of their size: small did not mean nimble in the swap business.

The new market was lucrative as swaps exploded onto the scene. By the end of the decade, the market was estimated to be in excess of $4 trillion, the size of the total debt of the United States. What began as simple swaps developed into tricky, exotic strategies that often bewildered everyone except those who designed them. The new market also gave the Fed fits of anxiety. The banks broke into the market with this new device, and there appeared to be little the Fed could do to regulate it. Swaps had no written rules. Fortunately, no major scandals or frauds erupted in the swap market, at least in the United States in the early years, but the new market aroused the interest of central banks around the world. Its sheer size suggested it could not go unregulated for long.

Swaps represented a new source of income for the Street. Since securities were not involved, at least initially, the money earned was simply trading income. The bond houses in particular benefited since the new market was closely allied with the bond market. Other products could be designed and sold in conjunction with swaps. But all swap traders risked substantial interest rate exposure because of the positions they swapped with their clients. As a result, they began to devise other financial instruments that would complement the swap market. Large options based upon bonds, foreign exchange, stocks, and preferreds all were designed to help companies and swap dealers lay off risks in the market. Those who designed the entrées on this menu became known as *financial engineers*. Their tools were quantitative methods driven by computers. Many of these new techniques were much more sophisticated than the original portfolio theories of the 1950s and 1960s and were devised by mathematicians hired by the larger houses with large research departments. Wall Street entered a new era of financial design engineered by what quickly became known as *quant jocks*.

Swap trading also reintroduced the commercial banks to trading for their corporate clients. Since Glass-Steagall was passed, most contented themselves with trading Treasury bonds or foreign exchange for their large clients. Swap trading was the first significant inroad they had made into trading in years. As more and more corporate clients showed interest in swapping, the commercial banks were reintroduced to a form of investment banking that had previously eluded them. Swap trading began a revolution that would pave the way for commercial banks' intrusion back into investment banking after decades of separation.

Other innovative products and investments also appeared in the 1980s. One of the most high powered was hedge funds. Many were originally established off-shore. These investment funds set their chosen investment instruments against Treasury bonds or similar securities to try to protect their value while capitalizing on a rise in their value. Some were phenomenally successful. One of the best-known fund managers was the Hungarian born George Soros whose funds made him a legend in the investment community. His fame only increased when he made a massive bet that sterling would drop dramatically during a currency crisis in Europe in 1992. When the pound did fall, he was reputed to have made a profit of over $1 billion. Giving large sums to charities and to projects in eastern Europe insured him a place in investment lore equal to that of some of the nineteenth-century financiers who also gave generously to charity and to public causes.

The Market Collapse

Investment bankers enjoyed some of their best years ever between 1982 and 1987. Companies, municipalities, government agencies, and of course the U.S. Treasury all began issuing new securities, and the markets prospered. Underwriting surged, and trading and sales naturally followed. The bond market exploded. Companies, mortgage assistance agencies, and municipalities all tapped the market for fresh funds at a pace not seen for ten years. Surging corporate profits sparked new capital investments, and funds were raised for expansion. Interest rates were still relatively high, however. Treasury bonds fell by a full 2 percent between 1982 and 1985; yields collapsed by another 2 percent in 1986. The rush was on. Everyone tried to get to market as soon as they could.

Contrary to popular opinion, American industry was on the rebound. Bonds were the most popular form of financing by companies, and manufacturing industries borrowed the most money of any sector in the economy that produced goods rather than services. But all types of businesses went to market. New common stock financing doubled during the 1980s before the market collapse.

After several profitable years, memories of the bad days before 1982 faded quickly. But not all traders and investors were bull market traders. Many remembered the days of high inflation and dwindling corporate profits. In the summer of 1987, many of the old warning signs flashed again. Citicorp announced the largest loss in corporate history because of the third world debt crisis, and it appeared that interest rates were again on the rise. Distressingly, for the Street, Paul Volcker had been replaced at the Fed by Alan Greenspan, well known on the Street as an economic consultant but an unknown quantity compared with Volcker. After years of having an inflation fighter it admired at the Fed, the Street naturally looked askance at anyone new replacing Volcker. Until further notice, it signaled that it preferred to see his policies continued. Greenspan accommodated the Street, but his manner was not appreciated. When he assumed office, he had the discount rate raised in early September. The Japanese and the Germans responded by raising theirs, apparently concerned about the effect the American increase would have on their currencies.

After interest rates bottomed out in 1985, they began to creep up again. Then the market was hit with the 1987 fear that worldwide interest rates would rise. The month of October again proved to be bad luck for the stock market. For the second time in sixty years, a major market collapse was brewing. Politics also intruded. A House committee had recently suggested that the interest rate deduction should be eliminated for junk financings. For several years, much market speculation built up over mergers and rumors of them. Without that element, many stocks were bound to be sold in a panic if the tax treatment of them was threatened. In the middle of October the stock markets began to wobble. The combination of factors came to a head on October 19, 1987. The market started to decline quickly, and pandemonium followed.

The market collapse challenged all the institutions that had been established since the depression. Would the safety net operate as planned, protecting the banking system from a market fall? Would investors panic or remain relatively calm, recognizing that the safety net was in place? And how severe was market speculation in this bull market? No one could be sure of the reaction as the market started to slide during the week of October 12. The one thing that was apparent was that the reaction spread worldwide very quickly. All of the other stock markets would feel the chill as well.

The market rout culminated on October 19. The morning was frantic, with waves of sell orders hitting the markets. The drop in the major indices proved to be the largest in history. The Dow Jones Thirty Industrials fell by six hundred points before finishing more than five hundred off for the day, while the Standard and Poor's 500 stock index fell by fifty-eight points, or 30 percent. The NASDAQ composite was off by fifty points, or 15 percent. Unlike previous crashes and collapses, the problem became international in a matter of hours. Soon London and the other major markets were also feeling the effects. No major stock market was immune. For the second time, the NYSE and the other exchanges had apparently exported a serious market correction to the rest of the world. But the major question remained: How serious was the market rout? The *Wall Street Journal* jumped the gun by dubbing the rout the "Crash of '87." Its lead article read simply, "The stock market crashed today." Other articles took a slightly more positive tone. "Depression in '87 Is Not Expected" ran another.[9]

The U.S. market indices lost about 21 percent of their value in the October rout on what became known as "Black Monday." The NYSE chairman John Phelan called the performance "the worst market I've ever seen, as close to a financial meltdown as I'd ever want to see." For a while, it certainly did look like a meltdown, and it spread quickly. The biggest loser was the Australian stock market, losing about 58 percent of its value. The smaller the market, the worse the damage. Hong Kong was right behind

New York Daily News, L. P. Reprinted with permission.

Australia, followed by Singapore and Mexico.[10] But in terms of total losses, the largest absolute figures were found in the United States. The trends of the 1980s came to a head, and the result was a staggering loss, at least on paper, for investors. But there were no banking collapses as a result and no clear panic once the drop occurred. The Fed announced that it would provide emergency reserves to any bank that needed them. The gesture proved unnecessary, but the effects were chilling and lingered long after the event.

Gerald Corrigan, the president of the New York Fed, noted the market rout's effects on other markets as well. A month after the market collapse he remarked:

> It is important that we learn all we can about exactly what happened on Monday, October 19, when the Dow fell by 500 points, including the answers to such questions as whether programmed trading or highly leveraged positions in stock futures and options played an important role in unleashing those events. . . . let us also keep in mind that stock prices in countries other than the United States . . . have fallen by even greater amounts.[11]

He went on to attribute the rout to psychological fears in the market, world trade imbalances, and problems within the U.S. economy as well. He was not ducking blame. The markets had become so international that blaming the problem on a single factor would not have been accurate. The major culprit behind the fall was what is known in finance circles as *hot money*—high-velocity money that can be quickly shifted from one market to another, always seeking a higher return. But when it becomes nervous, it becomes very nervous. Ample supplies of hot money floating around at the time of the market break caused all the markets to dive together. Much of the money taken out of the stock markets went into Treasury bills and bonds, another flight to quality. As William J. McDonough, Corrigan's successor at the New York Fed, later noted, "The speed at which international investors redirect their capital has greatly shortened the time frame in which global situations have to be identified and agreed upon."[12] The market break occurred so quickly that regulators were caught unaware, but all of the central banks stood by in case of emergency.

Not only the exchanges suffered. Customers' margin money declined precipitously. Many bull market investors had never received a margin call on their holdings. Many others did not know they could actually receive one despite the fact that they traded on margin.[13] Margin money declined almost $7 billion, or 25 percent, after the market rout. The effects were widely felt. Real estate prices began to fall quickly in New York as the suspicion grew that much of the margin money had found its way into the property market.

Underwritings in syndication were badly hit and produced significant losses. The largest equity issue to date was in syndication for British Petroleum when the rout began. New shares were being sold around the world. Buyers quickly disappeared, and the issue price fell significantly. The total issue size of over $12 billion was difficult enough to digest even in a good market. The Conservative government of Margaret Thatcher was selling off British Petroleum as part of its privatization program. Bad markets in London and New York made marketing the huge volume of

shares a difficult job. Although the British government received its money
from the underwriters, it pushed the issue through despite the bad market,
earning it no kudos from the many underwriters who took serious losses
on the issue.

Much suspicion about the rout began to center on program trading.
Sophisticated computer-driven trading was developed in the early 1980s
to allow arbitrage between stocks, options, and financial futures. Programs were designed that would automatically set off buy and sell signals
in the different markets if one appeared cheap or expensive against the
others. Program trading brought a bit of science fiction to the Street.
Computers were now executing orders on behalf of predetermined strategies. Apparently, they were also capable of triggering a significant market
rout. But despite much study and debate, program trading never became
the culprit behind the market collapse, only one of its contributing factors. But it did bring attention to "triple witching hour." On the close of
business on certain Fridays every few months, options and futures contracts expired. Often they had an unsettling effect on the stock markets as
traders closed positions. Suddenly, the derivatives markets had forced
their way onto center stage in the debate about how to prevent another
market collapse.

The Reagan administration quickly moved to tackle the market's problem by setting up a presidential task force to study the market collapse. It
was chaired by Nicholas Brady, co-chairman of Dillon Read. There was
much disagreement about the October event. Was it a crash, a collapse, or
just an enormous price correction? The name finally adopted fell on the
conservative side. Borrowing a term from the 1920s, the event was referred to as the *market break*. In the 1920s that term had clearly been a euphemism. But in 1988, when the commission met, it was more accurate
than *crash* or *collapse*. The financial system was still intact, although a few
beleaguered investors did not know what had hit them.

The task force criticized the markets for being too disjointed. As derivatives became more popular, they began to have an effect upon the stock
markets. Stock, options, and futures exchanges all were self-governing and
had little to do with each other on a day-to-day basis. The task force suggested that a "one-market" concept be used. When events in one market
spilled over into another, procedures should be in place to prevent a rout.
This suggestion struck at the heart of the problem in the financial markets.
Too many exchanges offering too many products had developed over the
years. They were separate but often spilled over into each other's territory.
Circumstances proved that problems in one could easily be magnified in
the others. Brady later wrote, "If we have learned anything from the events
of last October, it's that the nation's financial marketplaces are inextricably
linked. What historically have been considered separate marketplaces for

stocks, stock-index futures and options do in fact function as one market."[14] Wall Street was put on notice: the other markets were significant and could no longer be ignored.

Brady was later named secretary of the treasury by President Reagan. One of his recommendations was quickly taken up by the NYSE. The exchange instituted a "circuit breaker" that would automatically stop trading if prices fell too quickly. Essentially, the idea was to allow back rooms to catch up with delayed orders and also give floor traders some breathing space if prices began to move quickly. The idea came from the Japanese market, where breakers had been used for some time. Commodities futures exchanges also used a type of circuit breaker. Some firms took a cue from the criticism and voluntarily suspended program trading. Shearson Lehman Brothers began the trend and was soon followed by Morgan Stanley, Salomon, Paine Webber, and Kidder Peabody.

The NASDAQ market also needed to improve its image after the break. The NASDAQ fell the least of the major market indicators, although there was a general suspicion about its performance. When prices started to tumble, many NASDAQ market makers refused to answer their phones or trade with customers. That unwillingness became part of basis for trenchant criticism of the market. As a result, the NASD itself proposed reforms to keep its 545 market makers in line and prevent them from walking away from a declining market in the future. The market had always been known as slightly more risky and less efficient than the NYSE, and critics contended that its image had not really changed, as indicated by the October collapse.

The 1987 break scared foreign investors badly. They began selling their American holdings and disappeared for a couple of years, adding to Wall Street's postbreak blues. After the market rout, foreigners began selling stocks. The British were the major sellers, followed by the Swiss. But the British kept their investments in the United States by buying Treasury bonds with the proceeds. For about the next six months, the flight to bonds continued. Foreign investors remained net sellers of stocks.[15] This dampened any enthusiasm the Street may have been able to muster in the months following the market break. Foreign buying of stocks had become a regular feature of many Wall Street news reports over the previous few years. Now there was little to report, and there was little good news to set the tone for the NYSE trading day before it began.

Domestic investors also abandoned the market. Mutual funds became favorites of small investors over the 1980s, more than tripling in the number outstanding since 1982. After the market break, their numbers declined substantially, as did the number of individual investors. As in many earlier bear markets, the small investor was the last to leave the party, and his absence began to have an impact upon the Street. Investment banking

'THINGS AIN'T ALL BAD – THE SHELTER ISSUED ME A WALL STREET YUPPIE TO CARRY MY BAGS.'

Oliphant@Universal Press Syndicate. Reprinted with permission.

and brokerage both contracted as a result of the market break, and unemployment increased as many houses scaled back their staffs. The losses on the British Petroleum syndication alone could have caused unemployment on the Street. When combined with the losses suffered by investors across the board, it also had a strong effect upon New York City's economy, sending housing prices into a tailspin that took several years to finally reverse.

Another serious consequence of the collapse was actually an old issue that flared up in times of trouble. Traders and investment bankers again came to loggerheads at many firms as one blamed the other for losses during the rout. Investment bankers were more conservative, while traders, by their nature, tended to be more aggressive risk takers. "A lot of the tensions do break down to investment banking against trading," said Felix Rohatyn of Lazard Freres. "The two have such different cultures. They are just not compatible in some cases."[16] The tensions produced some defections on the Street. Some investment bankers left their firms to start their own boutiques, worried that their firms were dominated by traders' mentality. The market break temporarily ended the era of trader supremacy on Wall Street.

Consolidation on the Street

Wall Street spent a good part of the late 1980s looking over its collective shoulder. For the past twenty years, commercial banks had been lobbying for the opportunity to get back into the investment banking business. The Glass-Steagall wall had proved too high for the banks to hurdle. Attempts at repealing it never gained much momentum, but pressure was mounting. How long could the investment banks and brokers hold off the challenge? Not long, because the proverbial back door opened and banks entered the realm of investment banking for the first time since 1933.

In the 1970s the banks had some success affiliating with discount brokers, enabling them to buy and sell shares for their customers. But that was hardly a measure of success. Chase Manhattan bought Rose and Company and offered brokerage services from its branches in one of the better-known cases. Banks were arguing that underwriting would be cheaper if they were allowed to perform it along with the investment banks. But repealing Glass-Steagall was not an easy matter. Then the Fed took matters into its own hands. The excesses of the decade were beginning to show. Without serious new banking legislation, the potential for further abuses of the banking–investment banking relationship appeared certain. Most commercial bank activities fell under the Fed's jurisdiction. It allowed what had been forbidden for over fifty years: a limited number of commercial banks began underwriting corporate stocks and bonds on a trial balloon basis.

The balloon would never come back down to earth. Morgan was the first commercial bank to receive the Fed's blessing to engage in investment banking; other banks were included after the initial decision. The original authority came from the Board of Governors of the Federal Reserve System. The relationship between the Fed and Morgan was still strong, as it had been since the 1920s. The two institutions also often shared personnel. Many Morgan officers were former Fed men. Alan Greenspan had been a director of Morgan before becoming Fed chairman, succeeding Paul Volcker. In 1984 Morgan produced an essay entitled "Rethinking Glass Steagall," making a case for repeal of the fifty-year-old law. Greenspan was instrumental in putting together the pamphlet.[17]

In 1983, when Continental Illinois, the country's eighth-largest bank, was on the verge of closing its doors, the Fed provided support for its deposits while Morgan organized a syndicate of banks to raise cash to bolster the failing Chicago bank. Later in the 1980s, Morgan was instrumental in putting together a rescue package for Mexico that included backing Mexican bonds with Treasury securities, dubbed "Brady bonds" after Secretary of the Treasury Nicholas Brady. Of the five banks that applied for permission to underwrite, two—Morgan and Bankers Trust—were wholesale corporate banks that had slowly been acquiring investment banking skills over the years. Bankers Trust was a major dealer in commercial paper. The other three—Citicorp, Chase Manhattan, and Security Pacific—were full-service commercial banks.

The Fed announced that it would allow these banks underwriting privileges because "the introduction of the new competitors into these markets may be expected to reduce concentration levels and correspondingly, to lower customer and financing costs and increase the types and availability of investment banking services."[18] Greenspan abstained from the written decision. Initially, the banks had to form their own syndicates and were not invited into investment banking syndicates. But the ostracism did not last long. Within a couple of years, some of the major commercial banks were legitimate contenders for the top ranks of underwriters. The Fed allowed them into the ranks based upon a technicality in a section of the Glass-Steagall Act.[19] The Fed derived that power from the Bank Holding Company Act, by which it supervised the activities of large bank holding companies. Clearly, it was interpreting the Glass-Steagall Act but was doing so in a manner within its scope. That accomplished something Congress had never done. The banks that quickly jumped at the opportunity were also changing. J. P. Morgan and Bankers Trust, the two most prominent banks to enter the underwriting ranks, were swiftly changing their business away from commercial banking. Both were concentrating on wholesale (corporate) banking, and underwriting was a natural profit center for them. For those who would argue that the Fed had abrogated the intent of the 1933 law, the banks could contend that they were more investment banks than commercial banks so it did not make any difference. The close relationship over the years paid off for Morgan. When the Glass-Steagall Act originally was passed, there was widespread agreement that it was intended to begin dismantling Morgan's empire. Sixty-five years later, part of that empire was given back, less officially than it had been taken away.

The Fall of Drexel Burnham

Many of the junk bonds sold by Drexel Burnham and other junk merchants on the Street landed in the hands of savings and loans. Placing new issues with them had been one of the successes of junk bond marketing. But after the market collapse, many of the junk companies' financing plans went awry. And then the unthinkable began to happen. The economy began to slow down. By the time of the presidential election in 1988, the country had been without a recession for over six years. Although the slowdown did not figure into the election itself, the rumblings were already present in the property market. Real estate prices stopped rising, and the savings and loans began to feel the pinch.

But the junk bonds were difficult to sell. The market for them was spotty, and when thrifts tried to sell them prices were not firm. Then accounting regulations were passed that made thrifts mark the bonds to market prices. Prices tumbled and a full-blown crisis emerged. Well over $200 billion of junk had been issued, a sizable amount of which was in the thrifts' vaults. Junk bonds were blamed for creating a major financial crisis, with Michael Milken and Drexel bearing the brunt of sharp criticism. Then things began to go terribly wrong when some flamboyant thrift operators came to light. They had been using their depositors' funds to finance lavish lifestyles, replete with exotic automobiles, gleaming corporate headquarters, and extraordinarily expensive works of art. The Lincoln Savings and Loan, run by Charles Keating, was an example. Keating was later indicted and found guilty of massive fraud, but in his heyday he was one of the most prominent of the unscrupulous savings and loan operators. His employees sold bonds in the thrift's parent company to unwary investors from its branches, illegally touting them as fully insured just like deposits. When the thrift failed, investors' funds were lost. It did not take long to find some ambitious bond salesmen lurking behind the scenes, many of them specializing in junk.

Then, in 1986, arbitrager Ivan Boesky surrendered to federal authorities on charges of insider trading. Dennis Levine, a Drexel investment banker, confessed to authorities that he had passed tips on takeovers to Boesky, who then traded the stocks for his own gain. Boesky was another of those Wall Street "outsiders" who nevertheless had gained an important foothold on the Street in the 1970s. Coming from relatively obscure origins, and having attended a law school the status-conscious Street never heard of, Boesky used his wife's family money to enter the arbitrage business when he could not find a job on his own. Over the years he had built a reputation for himself as a shrewd operator. By 1986 he decided to close his firm and open an investment arbitrage fund called the Hudson Fund. Drexel agreed to raise over $600 million for him through a junk offering provided that it was paid almost $24 million in fees. The details of the transaction eventually led to the undoing of both Boesky and Milken.

Boesky received a three-and-a-half-year prison sentence after admitting to the charges. He made a plea bargain deal with Rudolph Giuliani, U.S. attorney for the Southern District of New York. He served about half of the actual sentence and paid a $100-million fine. Boesky's treatment by Giuliani drew much criticism. Because he was allowed to unload his Ivan Boesky Limited Partnership before his indictment was officially announced, he realized profits from it before being convicted. Many considered his sentence too light and the fine too small. Wall Streeters suspected that Giuliani harbored larger political ambitions and that messy arrests and prosecutions of alleged inside traders served his purposes. He had been known to say on occasion that the real crooks in New York lived in Westchester County. But authorities were after bigger game, and the treatment was viewed in that light. Boesky turned state's evidence on several other Wall Street figures. One well-known speculator was arrested on charges of threatening to shoot Boesky if he caught up with him. One of the other individuals Boesky rolled over on was Michael Milken.

Milken's empire within Drexel came to an abrupt halt when he was indicted under federal racketeering and fraud laws. In March 1990 he was offered a deal by government prosecutors to plead guilty to two counts of fraud, but he refused and a week later was indicted on almost one hundred counts of racketeering under the Racketeer Influenced and Corrupt Organizations Act (RICO) laws. He was sentenced by federal judge Kimba Wood (later nominated to the Supreme Court by Bill Clinton) to ten years in prison and community service. Milken's supporters contended that his sentencing was as political as it was punitive. "The Judge went out of her way to deny that she was pronouncing a verdict on the decade of greed but that is precisely what she wound up doing," contended one.[20] Milken's total fines amounted to over $1 billion, $200 million of which was exacted at his sentencing. He actually served three years in prison. One of Wall Street's most conspicuous success stories had ended in apparent failure about twenty years after Milken got his start with Drexel.

Milken's contributions to Wall Street remain hotly debated. He is viewed as a financier of predators, a raiser of capital for weak companies, and the ultimate inside trader. But there is no denying that many of the once weak companies that he helped finance became highly successful in the long run. Among them were Duracell, Viacom, and MCI Communications. His relationship with MCI recalled Morgan's relationship as investment banker with AT&T a generation earlier. At the time of his indictment, the *New York Times* summed up by stating:

> Michael Milken is a convicted felon. But he is also a financial genius who transformed high risk bonds—junk bonds—into a lifeline of credit for hundreds of emerging companies. . . . the Milken case presents issues far more important than one person's slide from the financial pinnacle. There is no condoning Mr. Milken's criminality. But if overzealous Government regulators overreact by indiscriminately dismantling his junk bond legacy, they will wind up crushing the most dynamic part of the economy.[21]

Differing courts of opinion maintained that Milken was a visionary, unfairly treated by government bureaucrats much as some financiers had been pursued by Ferdinand Pecora. Others saw him as a twentieth-century version of Jay Gould. He and Gould did share one chacteristic: by the late 1980s Milken had become one of the most hated men in America. But true to recent standards, his notoriety did not last as long as Gould's.

Drexel itself was soon out of business as a result of the Milken affair. Under pressure since the junk bond market began collapsing after the market break in 1987, the firm began to run short of capital in 1990. It had paid several fines to the government for several hundred million dollars and also had a large inventory of unsold junk bonds on its books. The regulators at the Fed and the SEC began to unite against the firm. With junk bonds in serious disarray and with little hope of financial assistance, Drexel announced it was filing for bankruptcy in February 1990. This all occurred before Milken was actually indicted. Within months, Drexel's retail brokerage division was sold to Smith Barney, and many of its other employees went looking for new jobs on the Street. Many felt Rudolph Giuliani was the force that caused the demise of a major investment bank. Others found the end only fitting. But the entire affair hurt the image of the American capital markets, especially abroad. In many countries, notably Japan, investment banks tended to be supported by their governments when they faced financial difficulties. As a result, their costs of doing business were relatively low because investors had faith in them and their regulators. In the case of Drexel, the government had shown it was more than willing to throw a miscreant to the sharks. The Drexel affair was a setback for Wall Street, which realized it was still vulnerable to zealous regulators and the negative public opinion that drove them.

Drexel was not the only major Wall Street house to suffer. The bull market began to take its toll in more ways than one. By the late 1980s, the thrift crisis was causing serious problems for the junk bond market, which already had enough troubles. The boom in Treasury bond trading also caused some serious problems for the usually unpublicized Treasury bond market. Scandal and allegations of wrongdoing were mounting in various quarters. Some of the Street's most famous names were involved and were destined to be banished from the securities business.

Ever since the days of Jay Cooke, Treasury bond financing by Wall Street had come under periodic attack. Since World War I, the Treasury used the Federal Reserve Bank of New York as its agent when selling new issues. The New York Fed served as the government's auctioneer, putting the bonds and bills out for quotes among the dealers. The auctions were conducted cleanly and efficiently. Dealers received no commissions but only profited by the small markup they could charge their clients. This was the same process that had been used for decades. Clients indicated how many bonds they wanted, and the dealers then put in a bid to the Fed. But no dealer was allowed to disproportionately bid for an issue; it had to be spread around the Street. Anyone trying to acquire too much of a new issue would be guilty of trying to corner the market.

Salomon was run by CEO John Gutfreund, who had received considerable notoriety over the years, being dubbed the "king of Wall Street" in a *Business Week* cover story. He also received slightly less sympathetic raves in a well-known 1989 book about Salomon, *Liar's Poker*, by Michael

Lewis. One of New York's best party throwers, Gutfreund fashioned himself a lifestyle worthy of Jay Gatsby, spending millions on his Fifth Avenue apartment. But his reputation did not prove an asset in the long run. After a routine Fed auction of Treasuries in 1990, a staffer made some calls to verify subscriptions to the new issues. Some investment clients whose names appeared on the list, under Salomon's heading, professed that they had no interest in the particular issue, but they were marked down as clients anyway. An investigation revealed that Salomon's traders had used the client names to cover their own oversubscription to the issue. When the smoke cleared, it was discovered that Salomon had violated regulations by taking more of the new issues than legally allowed. It had also used its clients' names in an inappropriate manner. Sixty-five percent of the issue had found its way into Salomon's hands rather than the maximum 35 percent allowed to any single dealer.

True to charges laid against all large organizations, the question at Salomon revolved around who was to blame. The head government trader bore the brunt of the charges because it was he who actually was responsible for submitting the false bids. Rumors circulating that he was paid $23 million in salary and bonuses only helped fuel the publicity surrounding the case. John Gutfreund did not survive the ordeal and was forced out. He had not made the Fed aware of the problems when they were first uncovered at Salomon and was ultimately held responsible for the affair. Investor Warren Buffett's Berkshire Hathaway Company took a larger stake in Salomon and proceeded with new appointments to sort out the mess. The Fed sanctioned the firm but stopped short of withdrawing its primary dealer status. Salomon's punishment was the sternest the Justice Department and the SEC had meted out in some time and was the most significant problem in the Treasury market since the failure of Drysdale Securities ten years earlier. But it would pale in comparison to Milken's problems and did not affect the viability of the firm to do business. The reprimand and $190-million fine still amounted to a serious rebuke for one of the Street's best-known underwriting and trading houses. But the fact that Salomon was not sanctioned more severely testified to its prowess in the bond markets, developed since the 1920s.

Continuing Crises

The dollar remained remarkably stable during the election campaign of 1988, meaning that interest rates would not have to be used to strengthen it. Some of those familiar with the situation called the entire affair a massive conspiracy by the Fed and the major central banks to ensure George Bush's election as president, although Secretary of the Treasury James Baker emphatically denied it.[22] After Bush handily defeated Michael

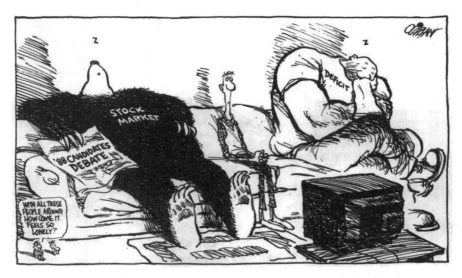

Oliphant@Universal Press Syndicate. Reprinted with permission.

Dukakis, the thrift crisis quickly surfaced. Congress quickly had to provide assistance to the industry, which appeared on its knees and needed a massive infusion of funds to protect depositors. Most, but not all, of its woes could be attributed to the junk bond market, itself not in very good shape. In 1990 and 1991, almost $40 billion worth of bonds defaulted, a record. The debt explosion, beginning in the early 1970s and paralleling much of Michael Milken's career, seemed to be coming to a head.

Congress worked for the first half of 1989 on a rescue plan. The result, finally passed in the summer, was the cumbersomely named Financial Institutions Reconstruction, Recovery and Enforcement Act, or FIRREA. It became the apparatus by which the thrift industry would be infused with enough cash to dispose of the assets of failed savings and loans. It created the Resolution Trust Corporation (RTC) to implement the rescue. Within weeks, the RTC found itself in the position of selling the assets of failed thrifts all over the country. At the same time, money was needed to fund the operation. The RFC would be endowed with Treasury securities in the same way that Mexico had several years earlier. Rescues were becoming more and more sophisticated as time wore on. The RFC borrowed bonds, which were secured by Treasury bonds. Unfortunately, the estimated cost of the bailout increased. The original $50-billion price tag was changed within a year and a half to $300 billion. While the public outcry was great, Wall Street enjoyed the occasion. The RFC bonds were treated much like the Farmer Mac bonds issued a few years earlier; they became hot items because of the government guarantee and sold quickly.

Ironically, the thrift crisis helped the banks become stronger. Fewer and fewer customers did business with thrifts, and the stronger ones that survived the debacle began changing to commercial bank status. This coincided well with the enhanced powers given to the large money center banks by the Fed in underwriting. The financial supermarket never came to fruition, but assuming investment banking functions was becoming more and more of a reality. The Securities Industry Association responded by requesting that the Fed extend some of the privileges normally given to commercial banks to its members as well. Why could the Fed not extend access to its reserve funds to investment banks that may have need of them from time to time? That may have helped Drexel out of difficulties in the past. But the Fed remained firm. Its facilities were for commercial banks only. Helping firms like Drexel Burnham was not in its best interest because of the purported fraud committed by the firm over a number of years.

In their own way, the 1990s proved to be as volatile as the preceding years. The stock market declined between 1990 and 1992 as the first recession in eight years finally brought down interest rates and economic activity. Wall Street was ready for a recession. All but the youngest of the bull market traders realized the economic cycle was ready for a downturn. But accompanying the usual retrenchment on the Street was a small time bomb waiting to explode, caused by the very same drop in interest rates. The complexities of new products were coming back to haunt their designers in ways they had never imagined.

Interest rates declined in 1992 and appeared destined to remain low. But in 1993 they began to rise again as the Fed tightened credit conditions. The worst bond market since the early 1980s followed. Bond investors were stunned as prices declined by 10 percent or more on some issues. But those who were stunned even more were investors who had bought packages of derivatives from banks and securities dealers. Most were sensitive to interest rates and rates were going in the wrong direction. Many of these enormous packages, based upon swaps and other exotica, began to lose value rapidly. When the losses were announced, embarrassment was found all around, from the dealers selling them to the investors who bought them. Many times they were not fully aware of the associated risks.

Soon it became apparent that companies of all sorts were playing with derivatives and were clearly losing on the deals. Proctor and Gamble and Gibson Greeting Cards both sued their derivatives dealer, Bankers Trust, claiming they had been misled about the risks in their derivatives portfolios. But in either case, their losses were measured only in the millions. The time bomb exploded when the municipal government of Orange County, California, announced that it had racked up enormous losses on a huge derivatives portfolio sold to it primarily by Merrill Lynch. Almost immediately, reverberations were felt throughout the country.

The corporate world was not the only place that derivatives packages were being sold. Many municipalities and their treasurers became targets of aggressive Wall Street selling of the hard-to-understand fixed-income portfolios. Bond and derivatives salesmen became so aggressive that "they were like camels, trying to put their nose in our tent," remarked one Idaho municipal investment manager, but "I just said no, no, no."[23] Salesmen targeted the municipal fund managers much as they had targeted savings and loans with junk bonds ten years earlier. The results were much the same. The highly analytical and aggressive impressed the less worldly with their packages of exotic, no-lose instruments. But not everyone was buying.

Orange County was also managing money for other smaller entities around the country, so the losses were not confined to California. Some 180 other municipal entities entrusted part of their investment funds to Orange County, impressed by the gains it had racked up over the previous few years. But Wall Street and the local taxpayers were not prepared for the sorts of losses Orange County claimed. It borrowed over $1 billion of its own debt in the municipal bond market. Payments on those bonds became doubtful almost immediately as the investment portfolio lost. The derivatives fund managed by Orange County and its treasurer Robert Citron totaled about $8 billion. Losses were estimated at around $1.5 billion. Problems arose immediately because even experts called in by the county and its court-appointed monitors found the portfolio difficult to understand. Parts of it revealed that Citron had invested in derivatives tied to foreign interest rates rather than U.S. rates, a position that would be difficult to explain. After the losses were made public, Orange County sued Merrill Lynch, claiming that it had been misled by the investment bank, a pattern that would be repeated many times as more derivatives losses were announced.

Compounding Wall Street's public relations woes were losses attributed to rogue traders at some firms. Kidder, Peabody announced that a Treasury bond trader at the firm had falsified records in order to generate phony profits. When the smoke cleared, the firm had incurred a huge loss of over $350 million. As a result, the firm's owner—GE Capital—put it up for sale. After an illustrious history dating back to the days of Jay Gould and the railroads, Kidder finally shut its doors. But the most serious derivatives loss of all came when a trader in Baring's Singapore office took enormous positions in the options and futures markets and lost several billion dollars. The loss far outweighed Baring's capital of $750 million equivalent at the time. The Bank of England refused to bail out the old bank, which eventually was absorbed by a Dutch insurance company. Dillon Read, which was partially owned by Barings, bought back its share in order to remain independent. After 330 years of a magnificent history, the bank that had served almost all British monarchs since its founding and had arranged the Louisiana Purchase was closed because of the actions of a 28-year-old trader. The finance industry's reputation for sloppy management controls was not enhanced by any of these episodes.

The Orange County problems were only heightened on the Street by an extremely poor year in 1994. Profitability was down, and Wall Street bonuses reflected it. Layoffs began as even the top firms planned to trim their workforces. The trend would swing the other way later in the year, continuing into 1995. The merger trend warmed up substantially, and many large mergers were announced. This trend was somewhat different than previous booms. Many of the mergers, whether between banks (a favorite) or between entertainment companies or manufacturers, were described as prompted by efficiency and downsizing. Two companies professed to merge in order to cut costs. *Corporate downsizing* became a favorite buzzword as many brides and grooms rushed to the altar to save on domestic help. This continued the other emerging trend in the economy that saw well-announced corporate layoffs coupled with simultaneous reports of a strong economy. The major paradox of the 1990s was only being enhanced by the rush to merge. Was the country becoming more efficient through the new synergies, or was Wall Street simply aiding and abetting another megalomaniac movement, hurting workers in pursuit of profits? Probably a bit of both.

Familiar Arguments Again

All of the crises of the 1980s, including the scandals in the securities industry, helped make an even stronger case for the repeal of the Glass-Steagall Act. The implication was that the securities industry was still in a relatively weak position as the financing demands of industry became greater all the time. Commercial banks had whittled away at the wall of separation to the extent that some were effectively in the investment banking business by the mid-1990s. But many of the banks still did not possess the expertise to call themselves full-service banks and remained primarily in commercial and retail lending.

The commercial banks that made the most impact in the securities business were those calling themselves wholesale banks. Their business was corporate, and they continued to argue that full-blown investment banking was a corporate service they needed to provide their customers. The old distinctions and worries were gone as banking entered a new age. What was the difference between underwriting corporate securities and making loans to Mexico, the banks continually asked. The securities business was probably safer for banks, shareholders, and depositors than very risky loans to developing countries. The point was made by bankers from both sides of the industry interested in seeing Glass-Steagall repealed. John Thain, a partner at Goldman Sachs, and Michael Patterson of J. P. Morgan and Company both made the same point before the House Committee on Banking and Financial Services. Patterson argued forcefully for reforming Glass-Steagall when he said that the very point "was repeated by Treasury Secretary Rubin [formerly a Goldman Sachs partner] in his testimony to this committee a month ago when he said 'It is difficult to argue that the security underwriting risk of an investment bank is greater than the loan making risk of a commercial bank.'" In terms of competition, the world of finance was becoming too small to allow distinctions in the banking business. Patterson continued, "As the business of banking and finance continues to evolve rapidly, and as the financial and risk management needs of clients around the world change and grow, U.S. institutions must have the same flexibility as our global competitors to adapt, to innovate, and to lead."[24]

Morgan led the assault on the banking law. Being the first commercial bank allowed into the corporate underwriting ranks gave it an edge that it was able to exploit. Problems in the derivatives markets, such as those encountered by Bankers Trust, the other major wholesale bank, did not necessarily help the argument, however. But Morgan's argument was more than curiously historical. It produced a study entitled *Glass-Steagall: Overdue for Repeal*, which made the point in stronger terms. The study argued that the eurobond market, where commercial banks had always been free to underwrite without restriction, was less dominated by an oligopoly of investment banks. Underwritings therefore were spread more evenly among all sorts of banks. The U.S. market, however, was dominated by top-tier investment banks only. Between 1990 and 1994, well over 90 percent of debt and equity underwritings in the United States were done by the top fifteen firms in the industry. It argued that such domination by the top firms indicated "a concentration unequaled in all but a few U.S. industries." If the wholesale banks were allowed into underwriting on an unrestricted basis, costs would drop as competition increased.

The argument was vaguely familiar. The Temporary National Economic Committee, convened by the Roosevelt administration fifty-five years earlier, had made the very same point in arguing for the breakup of the investment banking monopoly, which had managed to survive the Glass-Steagall Act.[25] Now the argument was being used again by Morgan to show that the business was still dominated by an oligopoly, now of fifteen firms. The argument was turned on its head and aimed back at the same sort of regulators that had forced Morgan out of the private banking business in the past. The long memory of investment bankers was still very much in evidence.

Not only investment bankers possessed long memories. Early in 1994 the German government announced that it was finally going to pay back the remainder of the Dawes loan, originally negotiated in 1924. After Hitler came to power, the balance of the loan had never been paid back. Conscious of the credit markets' penchant for a clean history, the Germans made provisions for new bonds to be issued to replace the old ones, although their good credit standing did not absolutely require it. As part of a postwar settlement in the 1950s, they were required to pay back only if the country was ever united. Investors were finally satisfied after almost seventy years of waiting.

The strong market continued into the mid-1990s and became the largest bull market in Wall Street history. The merger trend continued on the back of low interest rates, a relatively cheap dollar and extraordinary demand for stocks, mostly by mutual funds. Merger activity increased to record amounts. Deals were being struck across the spectrum, from mining and manufacturing companies to transportation companies and utilities. Underwriting of new issues set records in both 1995 and 1996 as all sorts of new securities, from initial public offerings to exotic asset-backed bonds increased in volume. Merrill, Lynch was Wall Street's premier investment banking house, leading underwriting by a large margin over its nearest rivals Lehman Brothers and Goldman Sachs. Profitability for the Street hit record levels in almost every category.

The rosy picture painted by the fundamentals led more and more investors to purchase stocks. The market indices soared as a result and the Dow Jones Industrial Averages broke 6,000 and then 7,000 in relatively quick succession. Investor interest turned into a stampede and mutual funds began to rise in numbers, all seeking to cash in on the trend. By 1996, over 5,000 registered funds were operating, offering investors a varied menu. Mutual fund advertising on television became common and their values were reported in the press on a daily basis. The three largest funds—Fidelity, Vanguard, and Capital Research—between them totaled $850 billion worth of assets by the end of 1996. Many of their fund managers also became well-known and loved on the Street because of the buying power they represented.

Part of the reason for the phenomenal rally was the rise of the dollar during the same period. Foreign investors were attracted while American business benefited from more sluggish economic growth in Europe and Japan. But concern grew that the market rally was unsustainable given the state of the economy. Only the stock and bond markets seemed to boom, not the economy itself. Commentators and analysts began to openly worry about the possibility of a large scale selling spree or even a crash. Henry Kaufman maintained that the Fed would eventually have to take some action to slow the market's growth. "Embarking on such a policy course would not find widespread public acceptance. . . . But preventative action is consistent with the broader mandate to maintain the financial well-being of society, including discouraging financial excesses."[26] Shortly thereafter, Fed Chairman Greenspan also sounded a note of caution which was taken as a warning shot across the market's bow. In comments that badly shook the market temporarily, he questioned "how do we know when irrational exuberance has unduly escalated asset values, which then become subject to unexpected and prolonged contractions as they have in Japan over the past decade?"[27] He was referring to the stock market rout in Japan several years before which forced the Japanese economy into a recession. He made it clear that the Fed could use its powers to steady the markets. Clearly, as the market continued its unabated rise, concern was becoming evident. The collapse of 1987 was still fresh in memory and the Crash of 1929 was never far from mind, although details of it had long since faded from view. But it was becoming apparent that the recent surge in investment was broader based than previous rallies. More households had become involved in the market than ever before.

Part of the concern was that a collapse in the market could also affect the banks. The line of separation between Wall Street and the commercial banks continued to disappear. In the fall of 1996, the Comptroller of the Currency allowed banks to engage in securities underwriting and sell insurance to customers if they did so through subsidiary companies. The only reservation was that they could do so if the new businesses were limited to only 10 percent of the banks' capital. But it was clear that the Glass-Steagall wall was again under pressure although Congress still refused to remove it altogether, allowing the Fed and the Comptroller to chip away at it out of the public eye. The Fed picked up the gauntlet later in the year by extending the amount of investment banking fees allowed to banks from 10 percent to 25 percent. The Fed was not shy in helping to extend banks' ability in investment banking, although "We hope the next move would be up to Congress," remarked Alice Rivlin, the Fed's vice chairman.

A Poke at the Pig

The bull market caused many investors to search for new and different investments, especially as stock prices continued to climb. Many of the investment banks, operating in a liberalized environment, began to dabble in merchant banking activities and in direct ownership of businesses that were sometimes alien to them. The results were not always encouraging.

In the early 1990s, Morgan Stanley invested in a pig farm venture, hoping to cash in on the foods business. The farm was located in Missouri and was home to two million hogs. The firm's merchant banking unit invested millions in the farm and floated junk bonds to raise even more money. Things began to go wrong shortly thereafter. Feed prices rose and a swine virus killed some of the pig population, reducing cash flows. When the smoke cleared several years later, the firm had lost $190 million on the venture, and the $412 million of junk bonds also went into default. Clearly, pig raising was not the company's forte. A Morgan Stanley executive remarked that, "We were not as successful at operating these facilities as expected." The better pork chop would have to be produced by someone else as the firm reduced its interest in the venture substantially.

One of the most remarkable features of the 1990s market rally was the dramatic increase in trading volume on the stock exchanges and NASDAQ. Volume literally exploded from the low hundreds of millions to over a billion shares per day by the end of the decade on both the NYSE and the NASDAQ. In contrast, the record NYSE volume 20 years before was only about 70 million shares per day. Increased activity by individuals and institutions had put the stock markets under increased pressure to update their trading facilities whenever possible. While the latter part of the decade was better known for new issues, especially initial public offerings (IPOs), traders had their best years ever—although the inevitable scandals were never out of sight.

Ever since the over-the-counter market had grown in the late 1960s, prices of OTC issues were suspect. Traditionally, issues trading on the NYSE had smaller bid-offer spreads than OTC stocks. When the NASDAQ marketplace superceded the OTC market in 1975, the spreads were still wider although market makers claimed, with some justification, that their spreads had to be adjusted for the smaller issues they traded. The issue persisted into the 1990s when it came under scrutiny again as a movement for quoting prices in decimals rather than in fractions gained momentum.

Needless to say, quoting prices in decimals had few supporters at the exchanges although the increased trading volume and record number of investors in the marketplace justified closer examination of the issue. Most of the controversy surrounded the size of the average NASDAQ bid, which was 1/4 of a point (25 cents per share). By contrast, the average spread on the NYSE was 1/8 of a point (12.5 cents per share). A considerable amount of fuel was thrown on the fire when two academic researchers, William Christie and Paul Schultz, concluded that a quarter-point spread was indefensible and that the only reason the wide spreads persisted was because of collusion by market makers to keep them wide. The market makers avoided what was called the "odd-eighth" spread by simply raising bids and offers by another quarter point when something less may have been more appropriate.[28] The NASAQ naturally disagreed and vigorously defended itself.

The market hired Merton Miller, an economist who won the Nobel Prize for Economics, to study the findings of Christie and Schultz. Both were previously students of Miller. Miller commented that, "I've read their study. There are problems they are aware of and some they may not be aware of."[29] But a respectable defense would not be enough. Both the Antitrust division of the Justice Department and the SEC began inquiries into the market makers' activities, citing 24 of them for rigging prices. The NASDAQ found few supporters from the investment community since the charges had been suspected for years but never vigorously pursued.

The issue was anything but scholarly. At the time, the average share volume was about 400 million shares per day, and adding extra pennies to a spread could result in considerable amounts of extra money for market makers at the expense of investors. Mindful of the implications, the Justice Department began an antitrust investigation that relied upon tapes subpoenaed from the market makers, amply demonstrating that they did indeed artificially maintain wide spreads. Although the regulators settled the charges too leniently in the opinion of many, the message to the marketplace was clear. Bull markets were not an excuse for predatory behavior.

Unfortunately for NASDAQ, the problem did not end. Critics became even more vocal in their drive for quoting prices in decimals rather than fractions, as had been the marketplace's tradition since the eighteenth century. But the change was still several years away. Of more immediate importance were the class-action lawsuits filed against many of the firms named in the probe. Both investors and regulators fired off charges at the market. But even the bad press could not diminish investors' fervor in their quest for profits. The market continued to rise despite the discouraging news.

After much self-study and denial, the NASDAQ maintained its innocence in the face of the charges and implemented better order-handling protections, demanded by the SEC. Finally, in December 1997, 30 of the best known market-makers settled a class action antitrust civil lawsuit without admitting guilt and paid $910 million in damages. While the settlement seemed stiff, an average of $30 million each was not an undue burden on any of the firms and amounted to small change. Not one of the firms named admitted guilt. One of the largest market-makers agreed to pay the costs but refused to acknowledge any wrongdoing. Its president remarked that, "We remain financially strong and fully engaged in our regular market-making activities and we are committed to serving our clients fairly," adding that the settlement was reached to avoid further costs associated with the problem.[30] The practice of paying lawsuits and fines without admitting guilt was still an accepted strategy on Wall Street, enabling the firms to put the problems behind them and continue to make money as long as the bull market continued.

The affair, which continued into 1998 as the SEC proceeded with its investigation, did have one unanticipated effect that harmed NASDAQ in the long run. The integrity of the market had been questioned and its reputation hurt, despite the denials from the member firms. Investors, especially money managers—many of whom had suspected the market of manipulation in pricing for some time—began to circumvent the market and began directing their orders to the new 1990s version of a stock market called ECNs. These electronic communications networks were markets where institutional investors could cross-buy and sell orders without using the facilities of one of the organized exchanges or NASDAQ, saving themselves commission dollars in the process. These new, upstart markets would capture one-third of the NASDAQ's market-makers trading volume in a short period of time, attesting to the disgruntlement of many of the market's largest traders.[31]

During the 1990s, NASDAQ presented itself as the market of the future, the natural successor to the NYSE. It claimed that the market-maker system was far superior to the specialists used by the organized exchanges and that it would be the wave of the future, when all markets would be fully computerized. When that occurred, there would be little need for central markets, and all trading could be done as firms entered prices through the market-maker system. However, at the same time the NYSE was successfully listing many new companies, while the NASDAQ was actually losing listings. Many new tech companies bypassed the traditional route of seeking a listing on the NASDAQ and went instead directly to the NYSE. This helped give the NYSE a much needed image boost under its aggressive chairman Richard Grasso, especially since the NYSE was having its own problems with trading scandals among its specialists, who were accused of front-running and other unfair floor trading practices.[32]

Aware of the decades-old rivalry between the two that began in the 1970s when NASDAQ was officially launched, replacing the OTC market, the market bought the older American Stock Exchange in 1998, in what NASDAQ chairman Frank Zarb called a fusion into the "market of markets." The new marketplace would eclipse the NYSE and provide a blueprint for the future, according to the NASDAQ. The Amex had become a place where innovation abounded. It traded derivatives on its options floor and did a considerable business trading basket type securities called exchange traded funds, or ETFs. As a pure stock exchange, its days were numbered but as an adjunct of the larger NASDAQ, its future could be more secure. Unfortunately, the marriage did not last long, and NASDAQ began looking for a buyer several years later.

Avuncular

Throughout the 1990s, Wall Street held Fed chairman Alan Greenspan in the highest esteem, crediting him with presiding over the greatest bull market in history. By the middle of the decade, the hagiography began, anointing him as the most powerful man in the country and one of its most recognizable figures. As the market indices continued to rise, silence from the Fed was considered tacit approval of the market's direction. Wall Street owed him much, since it was he who spearheaded the dismantling of Glass-Steagall and oversaw the deregulation of the banking industry. As stock prices continued to rise, Wall Street felt secure since the Fed seemed to be in control of the market and committed to deregulating the financial services industry.

Then Greenspan stunned Wall Street and the world stock markets by suggesting that the markets were a bit overdone. In a 1996 speech at the American Enterprise Institute in Washington, Greenspan posed a question: "But how do we know when irrational exuberance has unduly escalated asset values, which then become subject to unexpected and prolonged contractions as they have in Japan over the past decade? And how do we factor that assessment into monetary policy?"[33] The Street was well aware of the problems encountered in Japan after its property bubble burst, and the stock market indices collapsed after a highly speculative borrowing binge in the late 1980s and early 1990s. Was Greenspan suggesting the same could happen in the United States? After the initial shock, Wall Street was even more intrigued by his lack of an answer. The chairman posed a question but provided no clear view of the road ahead. Other Fed chairmen in the past had been accused of thwarting the markets in an attempt to put the brakes on stock prices. Would Greenspan do the same?

The markets took the speech badly and temporarily retreated. The Fed chairman was practicing the softest form of monetary policy at his disposal, called jawboning. Instead of using the one tool available to the Fed to stop rampant speculation—raising the margin rate—he chose instead to suggest the market was too highly priced. Once the market concluded that he had chosen the soft option, it regained its upward course, and "irrational exuberance" became the fashionable term to describe the stock market as it rose higher and higher. All Greenspan had been able to accomplish was to contribute to the folklore of the period. He inadvertently had named the 1990s the decade of irrational exuberance much as the 1980s had been the decade of greed.

Similar signs were appearing on the regulatory front. While the Fed chairman was in favor of deregulation, the chairman of the SEC was confronted by burgeoning problems all signaling greater regulation. In 1993 Arthur Levitt succeeded Richard Breeden, who was chairman during the conclusion of the Milken affair at Drexel Burnham Lambert. Levitt was a native New Yorker who had once been a partner of Sanford Weill of Citigroup in a small brokerage firm when both were new to the securities business decades before. During his first term in office, he became a vocal champion for small investors who were encountering increasing fraud in the markets, especially at small brokerage houses that often bilked them. However, when Congress passed the Private Securities Litigation Reform Act in 1995, limiting the ability of shareholders to file class-action lawsuits alleging securities fraud, Levitt supported the legislation, appearing to counter his previously stated intentions. But in his second term in office, he continued to fight for the small investor, often calling conferences with brokerage firms at the SEC to discuss the continuing problem of small investor fraud.

During the SEC investigation of NASDAQ, Levitt was able to proclaim that "We've probably done more to reform the structure of financial markets than any commission in history," when assessing his own performance.[34] As a result of the pricing scandal, NASDAQ was forced to separate into market and enforcement divisions to avoid any further conflict of interest. The suggestion originally was made by former Senator Warren Rudman, who chaired a commission advocating NASDAQ reform. The SEC was quick to enforce change at the over-the-counter market but would be slower to enforce it at the NYSE, which also had its share of trading scandals and problems in the later 1990s.

One other point being raised during the 1990s bull market was the matter of accounting practices. Some accountants contended that new accounting rules set down by the Financial Accounting Standards Board (FASB) were too strict and were actually hurting the competitiveness of American industry. With the economy booming and the markets soaring, many did not want to hear naysayers claim that accounting rules were being stretched, ultimately putting shareholders at risk. Levitt came down on the side of strict enforcement. In a speech to the Economic Club of Detroit, he stated that, "In an era of global securities markets, it has never been more important for the United States to have a strong and independent body [FASB] standing guard over our accounting standards."[35] And he did not confine his worries to stocks alone, also citing the meteoric increase in the volume of derivatives trading. Four years later, the sentiment would win many more converts.

Increased activity in all of the markets put many established Wall Street firms under pressure. The bull market in stocks was attracting more and more small investors every year, and many firms that eschewed retail business in the past were regretting past neglect. Some of the largest firms began quietly searching for merger partners that could aid in diversification. But arranged marriages were becoming harder to accomplish in the late 1990s because many of the firms that were previously single had already found partners. Any mergers on the Street would have to be large ones.

One of the largest, and most discussed, came when Morgan Stanley and Dean Witter announced their plans to merge. The news did not entirely startle Wall Street since Morgan Stanley had been discussing the matter with Dean Witter for several years, but many thought that the two corporate cultures could never successfully be combined. Morgan Stanley previously had been investment banker to Dean Witter's rebirth after Sears. In early 1997, the two surprised many by announcing their intention to join, in what they billed as a "merger of equals."

The marriage crossed two distinct cultures established in the earlier part of the century. For years, Dean Witter had been a wire house, dealing mainly with retail customers and had been a subsidiary of Sears Roebuck since 1981 when the giant retailer bought it, hoping to gain entry into the world of financial services. Sears originally hoped to station some of those brokers in its stores so that its customers could purchase securities in addition to traditional Sears products. But the experiment did not work as well as hoped. After 12 unsuccessful years, the firm was spun off and Morgan Stanley managed its public offering. Dean Witter had a solid, volume retail business but was not a trendsetter in any respect. However, it took with it a valuable asset when it became independent again, notably the Discover credit card business. The card business earned over $500 million per year on a pre-tax basis and, when combined with the firm's 9,000 stockbrokers, proved to be just the sort of firm that would help Morgan Stanley cash in on the retail side of the business.

Morgan Stanley did not seem to be a good fit at first glance because of its heritage and its preeminent position in investment banking services. When combined, however, the two would be the major presence on Wall Street, eclipsing Merrill Lynch as the top broker in market capitalization. The proposed deal was worth $23 billion in market cap, versus only $14 billion for Merrill at the time. The actual terms of the $10 billion merger called for a stock swap, with Morgan Stanley shareholders receiving 1.65 shares of Dean Witter for each share they held. Wall Street was impressed by the size and breadth of the new company but wary of the difference in their corporate cultures. "One firm is white shoe and the other is white socks," commented one Wall Streeter, "they may both have the same philosophy but they are very different."[36] The cultural differences between the two would resurface for a few years after the merger, but the firm took great strides to accommodate them. In order to have a fresh start, the new Morgan Stanley Dean Witter moved into new headquarters in Times Square, a long emotional distance from Morgan Stanley's origins downtown.

The motivation for the merger came from the changing face of investors in the 1990s. Retail investors were increasing rapidly during the bull market, and Morgan Stanley had almost no entrée to them without linking up with a retail-oriented firm. Since the late 1980s, when 401K pension plans became the rage, the number of investors owning stocks and mutual funds literally exploded. Between 1990 and 1997, the amount of money invested in mutual funds increased ten times over, and the number of investors buying them almost doubled. The 401K accounts increased 15 times since the mid-1980s and the defined contribution industry as a whole totaled almost $1.5 trillion. Numbers of that sort were too strong to be ignored. And the Morgan Stanley name still proved a strong allure. Several years after the merger, Dean Witter was dropped from the letterhead. The merger of equals came to an end.

The exuberant market and the occasional lack of policy direction was aided on the psychological front by all sorts of books claiming that the New Economy had finally arrived and that prudence was an archaic term. Not since the 1920s had books appeared extolling the virtues of Jesus as a chief executive officer or the executive traits of such well-known management types as Attila the Hun or Elizabeth I of England. The Dow Jones Industrial Average was purportedly capable of reaching 36,000 (as the NIKKEI in Japan had done earlier in the decade before dropping precipitously), and traditional trading techniques such as quick buys and sells now became known as "momentum trading." As in the 1920s, the entire market revolved around the term "growth," and "growing" a company's earnings in the double digits was as natural as selling radios and Model-T Fords 70 years before.

The anecdotal evidence was beginning to show disturbing parallels with the years preceding the 1929 Crash. In addition to the hyperbole surrounding the market, the Comptroller of the Currency's actions in 1996 were oddly similar to those actions taken in 1927, also allowing banks to underwrite stocks. Arthur Levitt's concern about corporate disclosure was also a problem in the 1920s, before the SEC was created. And Alan Greenspan's somewhat benign view of the market bubble was similar to the Fed's indecisive action in the spring of 1929, before the October Crash. The pressing question became whether this was all purely anecdotal evidence or whether the past was bound to repeat itself. The answer was not long in coming.

CHAPTER TWELVE

Running Out of Steam (1998 -)

The rules had become so ambiguous and the lack of enforcement of rules of fiduciary duty and integrity had become so pervasive that everybody was playing improperly. The rules themselves needed to be changed.

— Eliot Spitzer

Throughout the late 1990s, some market commentators began preaching restraint, especially as the stock indices continued to climb. Investors heard cautionary tales about previous bull markets but watched in amazement as the exuberance continued, forcing even the levelheaded to begin accepting new valuation models for stocks that made little sense. No one seemed to mind if some investment bankers reportedly were being paid $100 million and stock analysts not old enough to remember the last bear market were acting as cheerleaders for the New Economy, recommending stocks with no earnings history and questionable prospects.

The New Economy provided a smokescreen behind which many untried and untested concepts flourished. Reports began circulating that stocks that once were known for dividends and potential capital gain were now passé since their prices were high and dividend levels did not rise to match them. In such cases, many of these stocks, considered growth stocks in times past, were supplanted by newer concept stocks, many from the dot.com sector. The market was constantly in quest of the "new, new thing," and anything smacking of the old economy did not merit investors' attention. A new method of doing business had arrived, differing markedly from the old. Alan Greenspan helped the industry indirectly by suggesting that Internet trading between companies probably helped keep inflation low during the latter 1990s. When companies traded B to B (business to business) on the Internet, they were often able to avoid the costs of traditional middlemen, keeping the costs of production low as a result. The market did not wait for the actual facts to be proved, however. Internet trading was accepted as the greatest thing since the development of the railroads 150 years before.

Many Internet and other concept stocks were aided by a large number of venture capital firms that sprang up after the recession of 1991. These privately owned firms funneled hundreds of millions of dollars into New Economy companies with acceptable business plans and highly marketable ideas, even if many of them did not survive the rigors of the marketplace. The IPO market often seized upon these new companies after they had been in business only a short time, having limited track records and no tangible proof of success. As the venture capitalists cashed out of their holdings and the companies became full-fledged IPOs, returns were often calculated on a cash basis, meaning that returns of 20 percent or more could be achieved by the venture capitalists in less than a year. It certainly seemed that the New Economy differed from the old in the way newfound riches were recorded.

The stock markets proved to be amazingly resilient, even in the face of bad news, and that underlying strength helped investors throw caution to the wind. Each time bad news appeared the markets naturally stepped back but then began again their inexorable climb.

Each year seemed to bring a new milestone. In 1990, in the wake of the Gulf War, the Dow Jones 30 Industrials almost touched 3,000. Then the upward march began. In 1994, it barely touched 4,000 but within two years it cracked 6,000, 8,000 a year later, and 10,000 in early 1999. The same year it reached 11,700 and appeared poised to continue. Television business news programs celebrated each new milestone although skepticism began to build as the 12,000 mark was approached.

Although the bull market news was dominated by stock exchange trading, the primary markets also witnessed a bonanza not seen in years. The run-up in stock prices and low interest rates produced a boom in raising new capital that kept investment bankers busy. In the second half of the 1990s, new corporate underwritings doubled, total capital raised tripled, and the market capitalization of the NYSE doubled while the NASDAQ index increased almost fivefold over the earlier part of the decade. The long rally was fueled by the merger trend, which also continued unabated. Merger bankers were perhaps the busiest of all. In 1995, $613 billion worth of mergers were accomplished. By 1998, the record was reached, at $1.40 trillion. After the markets began to drop in 2001, the number fell by 50 percent but not before the face of corporate America had been changed by the urge to merge.[1]

The phenomenal increase in trading was propelled by retail investors, either trading individual stocks or in mutual funds in which they were investing their retirement savings. The Internet was used more for information than it was for stock transactions, however. Although almost one half of equity investors used the Internet for checking stock prices or doing on-line banking, only 20 percent actually traded stocks using a computer and even fewer used the Internet for mutual fund transactions.[2] The news reports about home-based day traders moving stocks with the click of their mouse was vastly overdone although the number of people trying to make a living like a professional trader using on-line services did increase as the 1990s moved closer to the millennium.

Even more ironic was that the markets would record their record climb during a Democratic administration in Washington. The New Democrats led by Bill Clinton proved friendly to investors and the usual worries about free-spending Democrats did not bother the markets, but the administration still had its tense financial moments with Congress nevertheless. In 1995, Congress came to one of its occasional impasses over the size of the federal debt ceiling. Without appropriate action, the Treasury would have been forced to default on its debts, in the middle of a rising market. Clinton treasury secretary Robert Rubin, widely admired on Wall Street since his days as a partner at Goldman Sachs, averted a crisis by borrowing over $60 billion from some government retiree trust funds and then borrowing against it, avoiding the debt ceiling in the process. The adroit move made some Republicans in Congress furious. "If he goes much further, without a doubt, that's an impeachable act," snorted Representative Gerald Solomon, a New York Republican.[3] The threat of impeachment initially startled the markets, but then it was accepted as just another case of political backbiting and the markets resumed their upward course. Over the next several years, the issue receded because borrowing declined as the budget deficit of previous years began to shrink quickly.

Since the fall of Soviet Communism, the term "globalization" has been increasingly used to describe the world's markets, which were moving closer as time progressed. The stock market collapse in 1987 made traders and investors painfully aware how quickly bad news could be transmitted from one market to another. Beginning in 1997, another version of global strife appeared under the banner of the "Asian contagion." The expanding economies of the Pacific Rim countries began to suffer as their rapid growth proved unsustainable. Many American mutual funds had holdings in their stock markets and began selling, only helping to exacerbate the situation. Capital flight began in earnest and many of the funds sustained serious losses both in stocks and currency values. After the fact it was discovered that several of the Asian stock markets did not provide the same sort of protection that the American markets did, allowing practices such as short selling on down-ticks.[4] Lack of basic protections only exacerbated the situation further, and it appeared that the Asian problem was poised to infect the domestic American market as well.

While the stock markets grappled with the problem, the Asian contagion never became quite the problem feared until the following summer of 1998. The Russian economy also began to suffer as a result of the Far

Eastern problem, and the government called a moratorium on its debts—effectively instigating a default. Most of the foreign investment planned for Russia came abruptly to a halt, especially in the oil and natural resource industries. But the problem was not confined to investments with Russia. Investors had been avid buyers of Russian government bonds, which suddenly were no longer paying interest, while the currency situation deteriorated as well. And then the situation most feared abruptly appeared. A large American institutional investor was exposed to Russian bonds and was suffering as a result.

Apples and Oranges

During the 1990s, large offshore hedge funds had become popular with institutional and wealthy retail investors. When they first appeared in the 1970s, they were committed to exactly what their name implied—hedging. They would be both long and short securities or currencies at the same time, hoping to benefit from a spread between the positions, which would eventually narrow. As the years passed, many funds began to drift from the original concept, but many made substantial amounts for their investors because they usually traded in large volume. George Soros's currency funds became particularly well known, especially after taking a short position against the British pound when Britain abandoned the common European currency peg in the early 1990s. Hedge funds gained a reputation for presenting the well-heeled with above-average market gains in a market already known for above-average gains.

During the same period, a new hedge fund was started with headquarters in Connecticut. Long-Term Capital Management (LTCM) was founded by John Merriwether, a former Salomon Brothers bond trader who had presided over the firm's government bond department during the 1991 bond trading scandal when the firm cornered the market for some Treasury issues. Ironically, Salomon was suspected, and found guilty, of cornering Treasury notes after some hedge funds complained that they could not find enough notes in the marketplace with which to hedge their positions. After leaving the firm, he began LTCM to practice, at least initially, long-term bond arbitrage. The firm would take both long and short of positions in certain bonds deemed to be a good arbitrage match. Only their yields differed. If the bet proved correct, the yield spread would narrow and the hedge fund would be presented with a profit.

Merriwether put in place a unique team to run the fund. He included two economists who subsequently won Nobel Prizes for their previous work on options pricing models and the capital asset pricing model. Myron Scholes originally teamed with Fisher Black (since deceased) to develop the Black-Scholes model, which was universally used to price puts and calls. Robert Merton was a Harvard economist who also worked with Black and Scholes and did most of his original work on the efficient market hypothesis, another well-known and accepted finance theory. The two were teamed with David Mullins, a former member of the Federal Reserve, in a star-studded lineup of investment professionals. Unlike other hedge funds, this group appeared to be the best of the best and also understood how to mitigate risk, a continuing concern among investors since hedge funds were notoriously secretive and did not divulge their positions to investors.

Investors needed a minimum of $10 million to invest in the fund, and LTCM had no shortage as many lined up to subscribe. Many banks and investment banks also invested in the fund as well as senior Wall Street officials. Long-Term's client roster was as impressive as its partners, and the program soon became very successful. Scores of celebrities, universities, pension funds, and insurance companies signed up for what appeared to be the most sophisticated and highly regarded investment institution to develop in years.

Long-Term was still a relatively small institution despite all of the interest. It had eleven partners and about two dozen traders to oversee its enormous positions. Within a few years, its capital had increased to over $5 billion through successful bond arbitrage. The success began to bring unanticipated problems, however. Many other funds and investment firms began imitating LTCM, seeking to make similar sorts of arbitrage profits in the bond markets. As a result, arbitrage opportunities began to disappear. Consequently, the fund began making investments outside its original sphere of expertise. It began trading derivatives on equity investments, called equity swaps. This was nothing more than a disguised way of avoiding the Fed's margin requirements on common stocks.[5] Although LTCM understood derivatives well, equity swaps required knowledge of the companies involved, and the fund was weaker in that respect than it was with yield curves and bonds.

The fund engaged in all sorts of derivatives trading. By 1997, its derivative book doubled from the year before and was valued at a nominal $1.3 trillion.[6] Extraordinary numbers of that nature put it in the category of a financial institution like a bank, not simply an investment fund. The big banks often accumulated swaps worth that much as off-balance sheet liabilities, but their individual capital was more than $5 billion. Generous loans from the banks and the large investments made by investors had given the fund the aura of a bank in its own right. Long-Term was emerging as the 1990s' bull market version of a New Economy financial institution. Simply put, it did not do much for a living. No customers were served and no traditional banking functions were performed. All it did was borrow and make money by taking advantage of esoteric yield spreads and arbitrage opportunities in equities. The only question was how long could it last?

As events unfolded, the answer was not for long. Arbitrage spreads narrowed and LTCM was faced with a dilemma. At the end of 1997, it decided to start returning profits and all money invested after 1994 to its investors. It returned $2.7 billion at the end of 1997 while recording a 25 percent rate of return that year, the worst year in its short history. Investors still realized over an 80 percent profit on their investment.[7] Since the firm charged a hefty annual fee to investors along with a substantial portion of the annual profit as part of its return, its own profit was also quite healthy. In the same year, the fund's public relations were bolstered again when Merton and Scholes were awarded the Nobel Prize in Economics for their previous academic work. Clearly, LTCM was riding the crest of the wave. Unfortunately, the crest of this wave and the tip of the yield curve were not the same.

The hedge fund overlooked one basic axiom in the bond markets that ultimately proved to be its undoing. When market conditions become uncertain, investors quickly sell risky investments and buy U.S. Treasury securities instead. The Treasury market becomes a haven for "flight to quality" investors seeking safety. Such occurrences were relatively rare and usually unfolded during times of international financial crises or stock market collapses. The flight may be short, but it cannot be interrupted and attempting to disregard it or stand in its way is futile.

Long-Term's problems began in 1998 when credit market conditions began to change, forcing the Russian debt and currency crisis. The situation was catastrophic for the fund because it had bought Russian government securities while selling short U.S. Treasury bonds of comparable maturities. The idea of converging yields evaporated overnight as the Russian obligations fell precipitously in price and the Treasuries gained as a result of the flight to quality. The fund was on the wrong end of both sides of the trade.

Merriwether and his partners found themselves between a rock and a hard place. One of their main problems was their assumption about the behavior of markets. The efficient market theory for which Merton was best known held that knowledge of the past was no indicator of future price performance of securities. Many of LTCM's models were based upon what were considered to be ineluctable forces that caused yields to converge over time. Flights to quality and the subsequent illiquidity found in poor quality bonds were not part of the consideration.

The distortions in the marketplace were exacerbated only by the disclosure that LTCM was in bad financial shape as a result. The solution to the problem was somewhat unique by Wall Street standards. Although a private investment fund, LTCM was bailed out by a consortium of 50 banks and investment banks in a deal orchestrated by Alan Greenspan at the Fed. The Fed had to step in to prevent damage to the banks themselves rather

6/28

than to the fund. The commercial banks in particular had loaned it so much money that if an arrangement were not worked out their own capital could have been jeopardized by the losses. The intervention was in keeping with the Fed's avowed policy of reacting to situations in the credit markets on a case-by-case basis but was still viewed as unusual by most market observers who did not expect the central bank to intervene on behalf on a nonbanking institution.

Former Salomon Brothers' partner Henry Kaufman, an erstwhile colleague of Merriwether, later commented that, "LTCM nevertheless got into deep trouble. Surprisingly the firm's analytical wizards apparently did not take into account some financial market fundamentals . . . that sizeable positions in individual securities cannot always be liquidated quickly, especially when the obligations are of weaker credit quality. And they misconstrued the complexities of convergence trade."[8] Although arbitrage assumptions often proved correct, LTCM had bet so much money on the outcome that it was acting as a gambler. The combination of strong analytics and the traders' penchant for gambling proved too combustible, however. The cocky attitude for which the fund had become known cast long shadows over the markets.

Larger investors who insisted on remaining after the fund began returning money also suffered, at least temporarily. Over 100 Merrill Lynch executives had a total of $22 million invested in the fund at the time of the bailout package. The news hit Goldman Sachs so hard that its highly publicized initial public offering had to be postponed so that investors could assess the impact of the losses on the bank's bottom line. Repercussions were heard long after the crisis and the subsequent bailout. The fund itself continued in business on a diminished basis, subject to limits on its positions and activities. Critics naturally questioned the role of the Fed in the affair. Many failed to recognize that LTCM had created a major problem for the banks that would require a strong regulatory hand to correct.

The initial public offering from Goldman Sachs had to be postponed as a result of the affair since Goldman was one of the main counterparties to LTCM. The issue was subsequently sold the next year in an extremely popular IPO. Lazard Frères was left as the only major Wall Street house to remain a partnership although the firm was much smaller than Goldman. The trend begun in the early 1970s by Donaldson, Lufkin & Jenrette and Merrill Lynch had come full circle. All the major securities dealers were now public companies. The increasing size of underwriting deals and the increased trading capacities of market makers required amounts of capital beyond the reach of traditional partnerships. As a result, Wall Street firms had all finally taken the advice that they had so often given to clients: go public. The only firms that could remain private were those with niche (or boutique) businesses like Lazard.

The travails at LTCM helped underscore a new phenomenon in the markets. The hedge funds were having a serious impact on the markets because of their private, and secretive, nature. Few conclusions could immediately be drawn about their impact. But it was clear that they traded enormous volume in the instruments they borrowed to buy or sell, and that resulted in very sharp market movements, especially in 2001 when the market began to decline precipitously. But as far as the stock markets were concerned, heavy volume in equities was a blessing, leading to increased rivalry between the NYSE and its nemesis, the NASDAQ.

Anything You Can Do . . .

During the late 1990s, the traditional rivalry between the NASDAQ and the NYSE continued to motivate both markets. They fought for new listings, especially of recent IPOs, and marketed themselves as the future of the marketplace, touting their own respective trading systems as the best. The NASDAQ even ventured into foreign markets in order to open "foreign sites," but they did not prove as successful as initially advertised. And both markets continued to have their share of internal problems. While the NASDAQ had the market makers scandal to contend with, the NYSE had a front-running scandal, in which floor traders were accused of trading before customer orders in order to take advantage of subsequent price movements. The technique was proscribed but occasionally raised its head in both the stock and (especially) the commodities futures markets where a major scandal in the late 1980s on the Chicago Board of Trade and the International Monetary Market had given both of those markets a black eye. In all cases, traders disavowed any knowledge of the practice, leading market followers to wonder if the practice was so prevalent that most floor traders had no second thoughts about it.

One major change in market practices came as a result of the NASDAQ market-makers scandal and the subsequent fines and lawsuits. The stock markets began moving toward decimal pricing rather than using fractions, as had been the custom since the eighteenth century. Pointing to the wide spreads used by NASDAQ, critics maintained that dropping fractions and adopting decimals would provide cleaner pricing and save the investing public a good deal of money. Using fractions was only unnecessarily adding pennies and fractions of pennies to the price of a trade, which naturally went into the traders' pockets.

The NASDAQ entered the fray before the NYSE, using the 1997 scandal as an example of how to turn bad news into good future public relations. The NASD chairman, Frank Zarb, told a congressional committee in 2000 that, "NASD's commitment to decimals was early and strong. As you are aware, the NASD was the first U.S. market to support decimal pricing, beginning with our testimony before this Subcommittee on April 16, 1997. The NASD Board on August 7, 1997 voted to begin operating NASDAQ systems using decimals."[9] Not to be outdone by his archrival, Richard Grasso announced that the NYSE would introduce decimal trading ahead of the NASDAQ by several months, in a clear attempt to embarrass the NASDAQ, which had been billing itself as the stock market of the future in its advertising. Both markets had decimal trading in place by 2001.

While the two stock markets engaged in some healthy competition, the electronic communications networks, or ECNs, continued to develop, providing their own competition for the major markets. Dedicated to making markets in select stocks using streamlined order placing procedures mandated by the SEC, the ECNs continued to drain volume away from both the NASDAQ and the NYSE, especially for large block trades in well-traded issues. The private networks were favored by large traders because the procedures were streamlined and could get an execution for a stock very quickly, better than the traditional order placing routes in place. And by extending trading hours into the evening, the ECNs provided an additional service to institutional investors. For the most part, their services remained out of the realm of the small investor unless he or she was a day trader, buying and selling quickly using online Internet services instead of a traditional telephone broker. Crossing trades between buyer and seller without the aid of a market-maker or specialist required a trader's skills, something the average investor did not possess. After the bull market subsided, the idea of after-hours trading lost some of its allure, however; but the ECNs remained favorites of some institutional investors. The decline of the small day trader after the market's serious decline hurt some of the ECNs' volume but they remained firmly in place among professionals.

Like many of the firms that were members of the exchange, the NYSE seriously began considering going public itself, through an IPO, in order to raise capital to maintain its place as the premier stock market. The expansion of NASDAQ, and its short-lived merger with the American Stock Exchange, demonstrated that even the marketplaces needed to expand to maintain their competitiveness. But those plans were put in abeyance when the market began to drop precipitously. Few successful IPOS would be launched in 2001 and 2002 as investors retreated to the sidelines, wary of anything being sold to them by Wall Street.

Tearing Down the Wall

One of the most memorable images of the early part of the 1990s was the dismantling of the Berlin wall by ordinary citizens armed with hammers. Equally memorable but less visible was the image of the Glass-Steagall wall being dismantled by Sanford Weill of Travelers Insurance with Alan Greenspan giving encouragement from ground level. After decades of false starts, the end was in sight for the act that had kept investment banking and commercial banking separated since 1934.

Despite the liberalization of the traditional lines of demarcation between commercial and investment banking, dismantling the Glass-Steagall Act legally proved to be difficult. Congress was divided on the issue since it touched many other areas of banking by implication and was still considered one of the basic parts of the safety net erected during the Depression to protect investors and savers. However, the Fed's gradual nudging of the process since 1989 finally gave dealmakers an opportunity to test the limits of Congressional resolve and pull off one of the most astounding deals of the postwar years.

Since 1989, commercial banks had gradually been buying smaller investment banks following guidelines laid down by the Fed, limiting the amount of total revenue the combined entities could derive from the securities business. The mergers were still significant. Alex Brown, the oldest of the investment banks based in Baltimore, was bought in 1997 by Bankers Trust. Smith Barney was purchased by Travelers Insurance, run by Sanford Weill, and later was merged again with Salomon Brothers when Weill purchased that firm in 1997. Dillon Read was bought by British merchant bank S.G. Warburg & Co., and Robertson, Stephens was absorbed by Bank of America, also in 1997. The mergers created some strange historical bedfellows. Salomon Brothers was considered the strongest bond house on Wall Street, at least until the Treasury auction scandal in 1991. When it merged with Smith Barney to create Salomon Smith Barney, it inadvertently became the successor to Jay Cooke & Co., the strongest Treasury bond house during the Civil War. The "Barney" in Smith Barney was Charles Barney, Jay Cooke's son-in-law and successor, whose name was still on the masthead.

Although Travelers's acquisition combined insurance and securities houses, it still did not include a commercial bank, staying clear of the Glass-Steagall Act. Matters changed in 1997 when Weill and Citigroup chairman John Reed astonished Wall Street with their merger announcement, combining Citibank and its parent Citicorp with Travelers. But the two were not stumbling in the dark because they had the full blessing of the Federal Reserve, which regulated the activities of bank holding companies through the Bank Holding Company Act. The Fed gave its blessing despite Congress's lack of action in repealing Glass-Steagall. Only a year before, it appeared that banking reform was dead in Congress, prompting the regulators to act alone. The Comptroller of the Currency already reacted by allowing banks to underwrite equities. After years of trying, banking, investment banking, and insurance were all again under one roof. Pierpont Morgan would have smiled on the union.

There was ample reason to smile. The combined institution created by the merger was huge by any standard. The newly created Citigroup had assets in excess of $1.5 trillion, 250,000 employees, and revenues of $84 billion. The deal also helped bring Weill's personal wealth close to the $1 billion mark, but the union itself was still at risk. While it conformed to the Fed's interim measures for merging banks with other financial companies, deregulatory legislation was needed if the deal was to stand. The Fed did its part by approving the merger in October 1998, but the ink was not entirely dry. The Fed approved the deal on the condition that Travelers and Citi conform to all the requirements of the Holding Company Act within two years of approval. That was not the difficult part. It also stated that, "The [Federal Reserve] Board's approval is also subject to the condition that [Citigroup] conform the activities of its companies to the requirements of the Glass-Steagall Act. . . . "[10] The only way to hurdle that barrier was to get Glass-Steagall effectively repealed. Time was ticking, but there was hope in Congress, where a bill, HR 10, had been milling around for some time that would roll back the 1933 act.

A year later HR 10 passed Congress, and it was clear that the Financial Services Modernization Act (Gramm-Leach-Bliley Act) was ready to be signed. Citigroup then announced the hiring of Robert Rubin, former treasury secretary in the Clinton administration who resigned from his post in 1999. While in office, Rubin favored the dismantling of Glass-Steagall. Rumblings were heard from consumers' groups almost immediately after the announcement. They only became louder when Rubin's first year compensation, including salary, bonuses, and stock options, were reported to be around $45 million. In another move that would have left muckrakers from an earlier era running for their pens, Weill was named to a three-year term on the Board of Directors of the Federal Reserve Bank of New York beginning in 2001. It was natural that the CEO of the country's largest financial institution would sit on the board, but it seemed to critics that the gamekeepers and the poachers had all joined the same club.

The demise of Glass-Stegall and the official opening of a new era occurred in the late fall of 1999. As President Clinton signed the new law, he stated that, "This legislation is truly historic, we have done right by the American people." Senator Phil Gramm, chairman of the Senate banking committee, added a note of progress by adding that, "the world changes, and Congress and the laws have to change with it."[11] Gramm was not only a staunch supporter of HR 10 but also one of the authors of the Financial Services Modernization Act that eventually passed. Like Rubin, he benefited from the new legislation when he was offered a job with the investment banking unit of UBS Warburg as its vice chairman in 2002. The job was seen by many as payback because it was the new modernization legislation that allowed UBS to buy securities house Paine Webber for $12 billion in 2000 in a smaller, yet significant, deal in the new deregulated environment.

Gramm later joked about his new job, commenting that he would have to take the appropriate securities licensing tests despite his age and experience. Critics were not in so jovial a mood, however. A writer at the ever-watchful *San Francisco Chronicle* commented that he was "glad to see Wall Street is serious about cleaning up its act . . . the man holds a doctorate in economics from the University of Georgia, awarded during the Harding administration, I believe."[12] It seemed that memories of the Teapot Dome scandal, like many other financial scandals, died hard.

The formation of Citigroup allowed many other bank mergers that, ten years before, would have been considered marginal at best. In a more traditional sort of horizontal merger, Chase Manhattan and the venerable J.P. Morgan & Co. began talks to merge. Originally the Chase National Bank, John Thompson founded the bank after the Civil War and named it after Salmon Chase, the Secretary of the Treasury who employed Jay Cooke to successfully market Treasury bonds during the conflict. Chase had previously grown into a full-scale money-center bank through merger, while Morgan remained independent through the years.

The deal was announced in 2000 in the wake of the Citicorp/Travelers merger, creating a full-service bank roughly equal to the Bank of America in terms of assets. The new J.P. Morgan Chase Bank had assets of $660 billion, presence in almost two dozen foreign countries, and a substantial retail banking operation, including the Chase branch network and extensive credit card services. The combined operation had over 30 million customers. The deal itself was worth $36 billion, paid for by a stock swap of Chase shares for Morgan shares. The Chase name became affiliated with the retail side of the merger, while the Morgan name was used for investment banking purposes.

Although Chase Manhattan's investment banking capabilities were much weaker than those of Morgan, the deal also created the world's sixth largest investment manager. Both banks had extensive money management capabilities, and bringing together the two buy side managers was widely viewed as the best part of the deal. As it turned out, the deal came just in time before the merger mania of the 1980s and 1990s finally abated. The cause was not a dampening of enthusiasm but a change in accounting rules that crept up on Wall Street, unknown to anyone except the merger specialists themselves. While accounting changes would bring an abrupt end to merger mania, the close ties between analysts and their investment banking employers would be the straw that broke the proverbial camel's back of investor exuberance.

Pay the Piper

The latter years of the bull market witnessed some remarkable IPOs, remembered more for their quick price appreciation than for the durability of their business models. Many recorded price appreciation unseen before in the markets, including recorded gains of 500 percent within the first days of release. Many prices remained firm until the downturn in 2001. At first glance, they seemed to be the products of more irrational exuberance, but events subsequently showed that there was more to their appreciation than just investor enthusiasm. History was about to repeat itself, showing the dark underbelly of the market.

Investigations by the SEC later showed that many of these "hot issues" had been allocated by major brokerage houses to influential clients, many of whom were corporate executives. In a flagrant attempt to ingratiate themselves to them, the brokers often allocated them large blocks of new issues. They were then free to sell them in the market for disproportionate gains. Other large investors were also granted the same privilege, but there was often an unwritten stipulation. In return for the allocation, some of these investors had to buy more stock, ensuring that its price would hold up in the market. These relationships were known as tie-ins. The investment bankers selling the issue were using investors to run up the prices of many new stocks, with gratifying short-term results. But once the bubble burst and smaller investors became aware of the practice, it resulted in a number of lawsuits against the brokers managing the original offerings. And many of them were also supported by analysts employed by the same brokers who touted the issues as sound when investigations later proved that just the opposite was true. Small investors, once referred to as "lambs" in Pierpont Morgan's heyday, were again being led to slaughter while believing that they were protected by securities laws.

The technique was not unlike the preferred lists kept by the major securities houses in the late 1920s. While investors did not remember Morgan and others handing out shares at below-market prices to cronies, they still realized they had been duped by the most recent version of the same practice. The question naturally arose about the protections supposedly written to protect investors in the Securities Act of 1933. But as *Business Week* noted, "Clearly, there's enough ambiguity in the rules to make enforcement cases shaky."[13] Proving that a securities firm purposely defrauded or misled its small investors was difficult under normal conditions, but in the frenzy of a bull market it was even more so because many record-keeping procedures by the securities houses were often minimized in favor of speed. But the nagging question remained of how such an old problem could resurface after 70 years despite the Securities Act of 1933, written and amended over the years to prevent such abuses.

The analyst/investment banking relationship became front-page business news in the early 2000s. Ever since Benjamin Graham and David Dodd published their classic book on investment analysis in 1934, securities analysis had grown to become a respected art.[14] In the post–World War II bull market, analysts had assumed a position of importance on the Street as many new companies came to market and older companies raised more and more equity through additional stock issues. But beginning in the 1990s, the role of analysts was questioned more than at any time in the past.

Investors came to expect that analysts reports on companies were objective, even if they were written under the auspices of a Wall Street firm rather than a private analytical company. The Street then institutionalized the reputation of the gurus. Professional magazines like *Institutional Investor* regularly published league tables for analysts in various sectors. The all-star team represented the best analysts in their respective industry or sector, and the rankings depended upon their reputations. But often the reputation was based upon the ability to move a stock price. An analyst's prowess was measured by how quickly institutional investors reacted to his or her recommendations, often severely affecting prices. Frequently the price movements had little to do with objective investment analysis. Appearing in the league tables of most influential analysts meant generous paydays, sometimes in the millions, for those who showed they could hold sway over stock prices. Occasionally, conflicts of interest could place analysts in a difficult position.

In 1992, an analyst at Janney Montgomery Scott—Marvin Roffman— wrote a report predicting the failure of Donald Trump's Taj Mahal casino complex in Atlantic City, New Jersey. The prediction was widely circulated in the press, offending Trump in the process. As a result, he demanded that Janney either fire Roffman or have him apologize, something the analyst did. But the next day he recanted and was summarily fired. Apparently, Roffman failed to recognize a basic Wall Street proposition that "he who pays the piper plays the tune." But that did not change the outcome for Trump. The casino went bankrupt as predicted, and Roffman successfully sued his former employer and Trump for reparations.

Another skirmish with Wall Street in 1994 provided more unwanted publicity and raised some ethical questions that would resonate within several years. In 1994, Conseco, a rapidly growing insurance company, attempted a takeover bid for much better known Kemper Insurance. It was in the process of raising a large convertible bond issue to help finance the deal through Merrill Lynch when, unexpectedly, a Merrill analyst issued an unfavorable report on Conseco. As a result, the company immediately fired Merrill as its lead underwriter and instead installed Morgan Stanley to run the deal. Its chief executive officer claimed that Morgan

Stanley was better for the deal than Merrill and that the two incidents were unrelated. Merrill lost a potential $1 million in fees in the fiasco, but questions were being raised about Conseco that the company tried to quash. The incident shed some light into the close relationship analysts maintained with investment bankers. The bankers were in the driver's seat in most of the arrangements because it was they who produced fee revenue for their firms, not the analysts.

Ten years after his problems, Roffman was asked whether the investment banking/analyst relationship was any different from the way it was in 1992. His response was characteristically frank. "It's worse," he replied, "the whole investment picture is worse; it's a disaster out there. In corporate America, greed and avarice are running amok."[15] He did not need the benefit of hindsight. Both predictions proved correct in the end. Trump fell into financial trouble relatively quickly while Conseco eventually filed for bankruptcy some years later in 2002.

But those problems seemed simple when compared with the close relationships that investment bankers and analysts forged in the late 1990s. Only reinforcing the notion that in a bull market the only remarks anyone wants to hear are bullish, the two major cheerleaders of the New Economy tailored their comments to attract business, pure and simple. Unknown to the investing public at the time, analysts and the investment banks for which they worked were forging relationships that would produce exceptional strong buy recommendations for stocks whose prospects were relatively weak or even poor. The aura of objectiveness, always suspect in the best of times, was now seriously strained by the desire to make money.

The two best-known and most publicized examples of analysts acting in consort with their investing banking colleagues came from very different ends of the business. One was from a purely New Economy business model, while the other was in a more traditional line of business. Of all the New Economy companies, Amazon.com was the epitome of a new age retailer, selling books from its web site. At the other end of the spectrum was AT&T, the slimmer version of the old telephone giant, trying to compete in a business with many new rivals. While a potentially inviting prospect for investors, Amazon had yet to turn a profit and absorbed millions in start-up costs. The telephone company was in the throes of a revolution in the telecom industry since long-distance rates were falling and competition increasing, especially from wireless services. Both were in need of some extracurricular help and both received it in grand fashion.

In the late 1990s, a Merrill Lynch analyst and a CIBC Oppenheimer analyst, Henry Blodget, argued publicly over the value of Amazon. Its stock price was trading very high, not on any traditional valuation but as a multiple of sales dollars per share, the new version of the PE ratio for those more concerned with the future than past performance. The Merrill analyst was bearish on Amazon.com when it was trading at $250 in late 1998. Henry Blodget, the CIBC analyst, was extremely bullish and set an even higher price target of $400 per share. Amazon soon reached that price as a result. Realizing his potential, Merrill fired its less enthusiastic analyst and hired Blodget in his place.

The term most analysts used to describe the business model employed by these new companies flocking to market was "new paradigm." The companies could not be evaluated in the same manner as old companies so a new model was needed, and a new buzzword was created. The ideas were inherited from venture capitalists, who often used such terms to describe in optimistic terms their risky, and usually short-lived, investments. Everyone was searching for the New Thing, and it began to appear with greater frequency from month to month as the market forged ahead. In general terms, the New Thing was Internet trading and Amazon was the preeminent company of its type.

Despite the hyperbole, there were still objections to the notion that all Internet companies were winners. It was not possible to simply invest in these companies with spotty records and become rich. In an interview, Blodget demonstrated some common-sense restraint, stating that, "we do think this is still a paradigm shift. We think the Internet is tremendously profound. It will continue to have an effect on the global economy over the next five to 10 years. But there's no way that it is a large enough opportunity to support the 400 companies that have gone public." His advice sounded sensible although it eventually rang hollow as the market turned sour in late 2000 and 2001. "So one of the things that we've always tried to recommend is: do try to buy the companies with underlying fundamentals that are very strong, and even that unfortunately in recent weeks has not protected you at all; you're still down quite a bit."[16] It was identifying companies as sound when they were not that eventually cost him his job and got him banned from working in the securities industry.

Events later revealed that many analysts were willingly making false statements about the companies under review so that their investment banking divisions could reap fees by underwriting their stocks. Traditionally, securities analysts earn their keep by making recommendations that institutional investors valued. But as the bull market wore on, it was painfully clear that no one was making "sell" recommendations any more, only "buy" or perhaps "hold" recommendations. During 2001, some 7,500 recommendations were made on stocks in the Standard & Poor's 500 index and only 1.2 percent were "sell" recommendations. When the survey was made public, a warning went with it. "When something is given to you free, it's usually worth what you pay for it," wrote *Pensions and Investments*.[17]

Analysts were paid based upon the amount of "soft dollars" they generated for their securities firms. The actual securities analysis was free, but the firms were rewarded by increased trading volume in the stocks in question. The increased revenues compensated the firms for producing the research in the first place. During the bull market, a respected analyst could expect to receive several million dollars in compensation if he or she was generating hard trading dollars. But the $20 million made by one analyst was difficult to justify unless the revenue he generated was based upon something other than trading.

The unofficial Wall Street title of "King of Telecom" in the 1990s belonged to Jack Grubman, an analyst employed by Salomon Smith Barney, a subsidiary of Travelers and later Citigroup, after their merger. He became the most respected and widely sought guru of the telecommunications industry. Performing duties that went well beyond the traditional analyst role, he advised telecommunications companies on mergers and acquisitions and strategic policy, an especially alien role in the traditional sense. He was called to advise SBC Telecommunications on its purchase of Ameritech in 1998 for over $70 billion and helped Salomon to underwrite 18 public offerings of telecom stocks in the late 1990s. But it was an apparent flip-flop on a recommendation concerning AT&T stock that raised eyebrows and led to further problems with regulatory authorities.

After being relatively negative on AT&T for several years, Grubman wrote a favorable research report about the company months before it sold off its wireless division in an IPO. The report helped Salomon Smith Barney win a mandate to underwrite the issue. Several years before, Grubman had written a negative report on AT&T that cost Salomon key underwriting business when AT&T spun off Lucent Technologies in an IPO. The second time around, the timing was more political. After the underwriting of AT&T Wireless, he again slashed his ratings and AT&T's price plummeted. Eyebrows were raised around Wall Street at the time although his association with Weill made him somewhat immune to the criticism. Weill defended Grubman, at one time stating that, "Jack probably knows more about the business [telecommunications] than anybody I've ever met." But the relationships forged by Grubman and other analysts would not weather the fallout from the crumbling market.

Grubman and Citgroup were also closely involved with another telecom giant, WorldCom. The company got its start when AT&T originally was broken up in the early 1980s. Grubman worked closely with the chief executive officer and founder Bernard Ebbers as the company continued to grow rapidly through acquisition in the late 1980s and 1990s. At one point, it absorbed MCI Communications, the company that originally challenged the original AT&T monopoly. Grubman and Citigroup played an integral role in the merger and benefited on both sides of the new banking business from the relationship, by loaning the company money and underwriting its securities. WorldCom quickly supplanted AT&T as the favorite of many investors, based heavily on Grubman's recommendations. The investment world quickly sang WorldCom's praises as a result. A technology magazine, *Network World*, named it one of the ten most powerful companies, behind only Cisco and Microsoft. After listing its virtues, the magazine went on to conclude that, "MCI WorldCom will probably be a keeper on this list."[18] As for its investment virtues, Grubman claimed that it was a traditional "widows and orphans" stock, to be held for the long-term. Based partially upon his recommendations, *Fortune* listed WorldCom as one of its ten "safe harbor" stocks; those that should reward its investors' faith in good times and bad. "There are few, if any, companies anywhere in the S+P 500 that are as large as WorldCom . . . that have [its] growth potential . . . this company remains the must-own large-cap stock for anyone's portfolio," Grubman stated unequivocally.[19] Within three years, it would file the largest Chapter 11 proceeding in corporate history after being involved in a massive accounting scandal.

The role of analysts in the latter stages of the bull market became known after many of the large securities houses were sued by irate investors when many speculative stock prices collapsed. In the various SEC and state investigations that followed, many of the analysts' recommendations were shown to be purely tendentious. Their real opinions of the companies they reviewed were far less enthusiastic than their public utterances. In Blodget's case, several e-mails found on his computer at Merrill Lynch proved his recommendations to be mostly hyperbole. In an ironic twist, analysts were undone by the Internet, the same New Thing they had recommended so strongly to investors. E-mail became a major weapon in uncovering fraud and deceit by regulatory authorities, something the bullish analysts never anticipated.

The impact on investors was devastating, but Wall Street minimized the results. A study by the Securities Industry Association, the post–World War II successor to the Investment Banking Association, showed that around the turn of the millennium the highest proportion of individual investors (20 to 24 percent) had between $25,000 and $50,000 invested in the stock market. Only 3 percent of all individual investors had $1 million or more invested. Many first-time purchasers during these years bought equity mutual funds rather than stocks directly,[20] but they were still angry. Hundreds of suits were filed against securities houses for losses alleged to have been caused by their analysts' misrepresentations. Merrill Lynch agreed to a $100 million fine without admitting guilt to settle the issue although other legal action was to follow. Although several trillion had been wiped off the market's value by the bear market, the small investor still was heard, if only to a small extent.

Restraint

The basic component of a bull market—merger mania—was in full swing in the late 1980s. One of its key forces was an esoteric accounting method used to account for the costs of two companies joining together. Virtually unknown outside of accounting circles, the rules used for mergers had been unchanged for decades. Any change would probably go unnoticed as well except in the investment banks that acted as marriage counselors to corporate America.

Since the 1950s, mergers had been booked through what was known as the pool accounting method. In contrast to the other accepted method—the purchase method—pool accounting did not require acquiring companies to write off premiums paid for their acquisitions. As a result, companies could buy others, sometimes paying outrageous premiums without having to suffer the consequences of opening their checkbooks so wide because many of the purchases were made in stock of the acquiring company.

In response to continuing complaints about accounting methods used in takeovers and mergers, the Financial Accounting Standards Board (FASB) issued a new statement known as FAS 141. Critics maintained that the large premiums were being paid for with diluted stock and the market was well aware of this fact. Usually, when a merger was announced, the stock of the buyer declined in the market. The hotter the market, the greater the urge to pay high premiums so that a competitor would not enter a bidding war, which would only drive the price of a stock even higher. The FASB was well aware of the controversy since both methods had been used for several decades.

The new ruling confronted the decades-old debate over which method of accounting should be used for merged entities. The issue had been hotly debated with no resolution. Finally, the FASB acted, and M&A specialists did not like the outcome. The new rule required the use of the purchase method only after June 30, 2001. The older, softer way of pooling interests finally was put to sleep in favor of a more stringent method of accounting for the premiums paid by companies acquiring others. The results were dramatic.

Now companies were required to record the premiums paid for acquisitions as goodwill above market value and the difference was to be amortized, resulting in losses to income in many cases. Many companies accustomed to paying premiums, such as the 1990s stock market favorite, the Cisco Corporation, felt the reverberations from the new method quickly. But none suffered a more dramatic outcome than the newly formed AOL Time Warner, whose merger was completed just as the new rule went into effect. As a result, its subsequent financial statements struck the market like a thunderbolt. The accumulated loss for 2001 was $100 billion. The merger itself was valued at slightly more than that, making it the largest of all time, although most commentators agreed it was not a marriage made in heaven, even from the beginning.

Even more mature, diversified international companies could not escape the new ruling. Not since the FASB changed its rules to account for overseas assets and liabilities of U.S. companies in the mid-1980s had such a potential mess hit the stock market. But one implication already was clear. Future M&A activity had to take the new rule into account because pool accounting was no longer permitted. And the notion that the problem was ephemeral because it was only an accounting technicality was no longer valid. It was not valid because the rule recognized that too many high prices paid for acquisitions were being ignored in the original pool accounting method, seeking to incorporate earnings immediately into the acquiring company while ignoring the write-off problem. Now, premiums had to be booked as goodwill and written off over time. The *Economist* remarked that, "the Financial Accounting Standards Board new rule concerning goodwill in business combinations is having an impact on deal making."[21]

Mergers dropped off quickly after FAS 141 was implemented, although most on Wall Street attributed the slowdown to a poor stock market. In reality, it was the new rule that caused the market to begin slowing substantially after the turn of the new millennium. Companies that had relied on mergers as the major route to recording high growth rates in the 1990s now saw their stock prices begin to turn downward. Market darlings such as Cisco, Microsoft, and Conseco all watched their prices collapse. The driving force behind the prolonged bull market that began during the early days of the Reagan presidency had dissipated. The adoption of FAS 141 caused more uncertainty among merger specialists than any other single factor; once the potential implications of the new rule became clear, the market was poised for a new bear phase. Irrational exuberance was at an end, but it took a dose of esoteric medicine to end the bull market. One company could not buy another for an exorbitant price and then pretend that the price was justified because of the potential gain for earnings growth. Now future earnings would have to absorb purchase prices, an untenable proposition in many cases. The party was over as the Dow approached 11,800.

The word spread quickly down through the ranks on Wall Street, but it was that traditional group normally associated with objectiveness that provided the link between the mergers specialists and other investment bankers and investors, and they were not about to spoil the party. Securities analysts were about to come under more scrutiny than at any time in the relatively brief time they occupied places of importance on Wall Street. The scrutiny only created more skepticism among investors about whether anyone on Wall Street had anything except their own interests at heart during the 1990s.

Catastrophe

Terrorist attacks had been a sporadic part of Wall Street history in the twentieth century. In 1916, a bomb exploded in Jersey City across the Hudson River at a government munitions site, which shattered windows along the Street. Another attack in 1920 at the corner of Broad and Wall killed dozens of people when a car bomb exploded outside the offices of J.P. Morgan & Co. In neither case were the perpetrators apprehended.

Years later in 1975, a bomb exploded in the well-known watering hole the Fraunces Tavern on lower Broad Street, killing several lunchtime diners. While Wall Street was not unfamiliar with the occasional episode of terrorism, the impact of September 11 was much more serious. On September 11, 2001, the effects on firms based in the World Trade Center towers were devastating. Cantor Fitzgerald, primarily a bond broking firm, had offices high atop the towers and lost over two-thirds of its 900 employees. Keefe, Bruyette & Woods, a smaller boutique firm specializing in financial services company stocks also lost heavily. The effects spilled over onto the Street itself. The NYSE and the Amex closed their doors for several days after the attacks, experiencing their longest closings since the bank holiday of the 1930s. Communications were interrupted and transportation came to a standstill in lower Manhattan in what proved to be the most serious catastrophe ever to affect the area.

As a result, the exchanges and many of the financial firms located in the immediate vicinity deployed plans to diversify their operations by moving employees away from the area to protect themselves against potential future problems. The exchanges developed back-up trading floors at undisclosed locations designed to continue trading in the event that the main facilities were closed again. Even securities firms that had moved out of lower Manhattan into other parts of the city decided to split their operations into parts so that similar incidents in the future would not leave them crippled. Developments in computers and telecommunications since the 1970s allowed Wall Street to become more physically diversified over the years. In the new century the diversification became more than just an attempt to escape lower Manhattan property costs and space restrictions.

Adding to the sinister nature of September 11 were reports that unknown short sellers had established large positions in certain stocks prior to the attacks. After the attacks, the stocks naturally declined substantially along with the market, suggesting that someone with inside knowledge of the attacks sought to profit by them. The shares of several airlines were heavily shorted, and the positions quickly became news almost immediately after the attacks. But discovering who sold short was a different matter. The Justice Department and the SEC quickly began investigations, which proved inconclusive at the time. The best that investigators could report was that they were tracking down the financial trail of potential terrorist supporters.

The reports sparked another round of criticism of short selling. The complaints had been heard since the War of 1812, to no avail. Critics stated that short selling at crucial periods in history was unpatriotic. In times of difficulty, it was a trader's patriotic duty to buy, supporting the market. Both the stock and futures markets had heard the criticism at crucial junctures in their histories. Fortunately for them, no action had ever been taken to ban the activity. The financial community continued to believe that critics did not really understand the process, much as Richard Whitney believed about Herbert Hoover in 1932. For their part, short sellers pointed out that the activity was temporary at best and aided the markets rather than hindered them. George Soros added that he was, "at a loss to understand what is unpatriotic about [shorting]. It probably helps the market reach whatever level it is going to go to."[22]

The attacks had the worst one-day effect on the major indices of any national security event in Wall Street history. The Dow 30 declined by 7 percent when it finally reopened several days later—despite calls for restraint. Investors remained calmer than they had during times of skittishness in the past however, with the decline in October 1987 and decline in October 1929 still remaining the largest ever recorded. Investors quickly realized that the attacks targeted capitalism as much as the United States and that the New York targets were apparently chosen for that reason. The stock markets all made strong statements affirming their resolve to overcome their logistical problems and not be intimidated. The bear market that continued in late 2001 and early 2002 was seen as a natural consequence of past exuberance rather than of the attacks.

Child of Deregulation

During the merger mania of the 1980s and 1990s, many companies opted for growth through merger and acquisition. In many cases, it was cheaper to acquire a company than it was to develop one from the ground up. Restructuring of American business became a continual process that reaped large rewards for securities houses with strong merger departments. But the process had assistance from Washington, which aided other industries besides banking and Wall Street.

Of the many industries deregulated in the 1990s, utilities companies were among the last. The Public Utility Holding Company Act had held sway since the 1930s and usually stayed in the background while other industries took the limelight. But by the mid-1990s, energy had become a hot topic in Washington and the time was ripe for deregulation in the utilities business. The industry was part of a larger picture, however. Energy was a new buzzword in the New Economy. Traditionally, that meant energy as part of the oil business, but it was no longer confined to the oil industry. The crucial part of the Energy Policy Act of 1992 allowed sales of power between utility companies and liberalized the rules for mergers between holding companies. Excess energy had been sold between power companies for some time and was often imported via Canada as well. As a result of the law, mergers also began to occur between energy companies and utilities. The industry was being shaken by the new competitive environment. At the same time, many states were threatening to allow consumers to choose their own utility suppliers. In this environment, merger appeared to be a valid way to achieve economies of scale and produce cheaper prices.

One of the most aggressive energy companies in the 1990s was Houston-based Enron Corporation. Originally a natural gas producing company, it began to expand into electrical utilities in 1997 with the acquisition of the Portland General Corporation, the Oregon-based electrical utility. The merger was the first of it kind although it was almost blocked by Oregon regulators. It also introduced the Texas company to electricity trading in addition to its traditional gas trading. "The proposed merger with Portland General represents an outstanding opportunity for us to create the leading energy company of the future in the North American energy markets," said Kenneth Lay, its chairman and CEO.[23]

Enron was one of the most aggressive companies in the merger market in the 1990s. One management consulting company referred to the company, along with other rapid growth companies, as "serial acquirers." Their growth was achieved through acquisition. They used merger as their chief method of research and development, preferring to buy the expertise they needed rather than develop it internally. The company embarked on its more aggressive business model with gusto. Soon, it acquired the knack of performing its own financial services as well. It hired its own mergers specialists from Wall Street and employed them rather than pay fat fees to the usual merger houses. In a remark that was characteristic of investment banks 20 years before, the company described its new strategy: "The company is one of the most transaction-oriented non-investment bank companies in the world," one of its directors remarked; "acquisitions are a part of the daily life of the company."[24] Within a short time, Enron would be more of a trading company than a traditional energy supplier.

Operating like an investment bank, the company began moving away from its core businesses toward the end of the 1990s and began shopping for a buyer for Portland. The utility was not returning the 20 percent annual return that Enron required. The quest for higher and higher returns finally led to fraud and the demise of the company in 2002. But it was not alone. Both WorldCom and Conseco, two other serial acquirers, also found themselves in bankruptcy at the same time, providing a chilling final chapter to the strategy that made them grow exponentially in the previous decade.

Caught up in the New Economy growth model, Enron decided to take the low road to profitability. It created offshore entities through special purpose vehicles that held relatively small amounts of assets and liabilities. But the offshore entities could be used to hide poorly performing assets or mask assets as revenue, giving the misleading impression that the company was more profitable than it actually was. Then the stock market began to decline, and the company's earnings and offshore vehicles began to implode. Once the seventh largest company in the country (measured by assets), Enron and its accounting firm Arthur Anderson did not survive the scandal. When the entire house of cards collapsed, Enron became the largest bankruptcy filing in American history. Unfortunately, it would not retain the distinction for long. A widespread accounting fraud allowed WorldCom to eclipse it for that distinction, finally leading to new legislation to tighten financial control of accountants and corporate boards.

Arthur Anderson also became a victim of the fraud and was prosecuted for helping Enron destroy documents that it had been ordered to surrender as part of the SEC investigation following the losses. The firm began losing clients and finally disintegrated. Many questioned why the SEC held Anderson to such a high standard and pursued that firm when the real culprits worked at Enron, but the securities laws clearly mentioned the role of accountants in the process of assisting SEC-registered public companies. But the real question was larger than the fate of the parties involved. How had such a massive fraud been committed at a public company almost 70 years after the original securities laws had been passed? If such large-scale fraud could be committed, how would the investing public ever come to trust corporate America and Wall Street again? Many voted with the rights at their disposal. Lawsuits against Wall Street firms intensified after the market collapse, with the majority of them filed over the allocation of IPO shares.

The collapse of Enron and WorldCom also had a severe effect on the newly merged banking institutions. Many of the large money center banks, notably J.P. Morgan Chase and Citigroup, lost substantial amounts of money because the two companies had collapsed. They loaned money to them as part of their commercial banking function while seeking investment banking business at the same time, something that the old Glass-Steagall rules prohibited. When losses came, they hit from both sides. Until the losses were incurred, however, the investment banking side was particularly rewarding. Despite its internal investment banking operations, Enron was still a major source of fees for Wall Street until its collapse, as was WorldCom.

The question was clearly on the mind of Congress when it passed the Sarbanes-Oxley Act in the summer of 2002. The bill was sponsored by Senator Paul Sarbanes, a Democrat from Maryland, and Representative Mike Oxley, a Republican from Ohio. Officially known as the Public Company Accounting Reform & Investor Protection Act, the law addressed the problem of accounting by public corporations and the responsibility of auditors to investors. The law created the Public Accounting Oversight Board, which has the broad responsibility of administering the act. Its passing demonstrated the progress made over the years in financial engineering and the uses to which it could be put by those intent on breaking the existing securities laws. Simply, the act put the onus on accountants to spot difficulties before they occurred, and it also put attorneys on the spot by requiring them to inform regulators if they spotted illegalities being committed by their clients regarding financial disclosure. Wall Street was not fond of new regulation, but publicly criticizing the new law was not political given the climate of investor unrest and potential political backlash.

In the wake of the market decline and the destruction of many investors' wealth, Wall Street naturally retrenched and waited for the stock market to rise again. As in the 1930s, strong leadership from the Street itself was lacking as most investment banks appeared to hope that investors would forget the most recent debacle before returning to business as usual. The prospects for a vigorous market remained questionable because demographics seemed to be militating against it. The greatest bull market in American history had been fueled by the postwar baby-boom generation, which had poured more retirement savings and speculative funds into the markets than at any other time. By the mid-2000s, many of those investors were due to become eligible for retirement. If the destruction of wealth had been as great as many feared, the prospects for the stock market were not healthy because net withdrawals rather than net investment would be the order of the day.

Epilogue

The bear market that burst the stock market bubble was a product of the deregulated environment of the 1990s. Many of the leading companies that helped fuel the boom, and those that capitalized on it by engaging in mergers, would not have existed without legislation that enabled them to grow exponentially. Enron was the result of the Energy Policy Act; WorldCom was the product of the Telecommunications Act. Contemporary Wall Street was the product of the relaxation of the banking laws since the late 1980s and the Financial Services Modernization Act. Naturally, not all companies in these industries were to blame for the excesses of the few, but the unraveling of the market and the substantial blow to asset values owed much to the deregulation trend. When added to the effects of the new accounting rules, it became clear that the financial markets had received a substantial boost from Washington and regulators only to overplay its hand, leading to its own collapse.

Not everyone agreed. The architects of deregulation continued to argue that they did their best to modernize an antiquated banking system and that human nature was responsible for the mess, as it had been so many times before on Wall Street. Representative Jim Leach, Republican from Iowa, remarked that, "It has nothing to do with Gramm-Leach-Bliley," when questioned on whether the 1999 financial reform law led to the financial industry's entanglement with Enron.[25] Critics remained unconvinced that Wall Street was capable of reforming itself any more than it had been in the past. Even those who normally favored regulation began to realize that the liberalized environment of the 1990s bore the seeds of its own destruction and the destruction of investors' wealth.

In the nineteenth century, Wall Street was often depicted as a place where a constant battle between bulls and bears occurred. Artists depicted the stock exchange as a battleground between the two factions, one bent on cornering the market, and the other equally intent on selling short. Over the years, Wall Street made extraordinary progress in becoming a legitimate marketplace that investors began to trust. But the battleground impression never disappeared entirely, as the 1930s Senate hearings and the ensuing securities and banking legislation demonstrated. In the 1990s boom, history and caution were thrown to the wind again—and the result was calamitous.

Despite scandals after World War II, Wall Street managed to grow into the most dynamic marketplace in the world, and the market indices assumed their position as the leading economic indicator in a growing, and changing, economy. Equity investments became trusted and millions of investors poured their retirement money into the market in the late 1980s, creating a wash of liquidity never seen before in the markets. The greatest bull market was bound to follow in the 1990s. When the market indices finally began to crumble, the contemporary marketplace came into clearer view. Precipitous market crashes like that of 1929 and drastic falls like 1987 were less likely to occur because of a more diversified investor base. But serious bear markets could never be prevented because some old Wall Street practices never really died. Cheating investors, rewarding friends with cheap stock, and self-serving investment research still existed after decades of attempts to clean up the marketplace. Wall Street made giant gains in its 210-year history but was still capable of taking giant steps backward at the same time, destroying investor confidence and clouding its own future in the process.

Notes

Chapter 1

1. Alexander Hamilton, James Madison, and John Jay, *The Federalist Papers*, (New York: New American Library, 1961) 54.

2. William Parker Cutler and Julia Cutler, *Life, Journals and Correspondence of Rev. Manasseh Cutler*, vol. 1 (Cincinnati: R. Clarke, 1888), p. 240.

3. This was the beginning of a long and often acrimonious tradition whereby state banking interests prevailed upon the federal government and Congress to prevent out-of-state banks from obtaining access to other states by branching. Since many of the commercial banks would also practice merchant and investment banking services over the years, it had the net effect of keeping much of the securities business primarily in New York, where it originated.

4. Edmund C. Stedman, ed. *The New York Stock Exchange* (1905; reprint, New York: Greenwood Press, 1969), p. 53.

5. Ibid.

6. Mira Wilkins, *The History of Foreign Investment in the United States to 1914* (Cambridge, Mass: Harvard University Press, 1989), p. 54.

7. Vincent Carosso, *Investment Banking in America: A History*. (Cambridge, Mass: Harvard University Press, 1970), p. 2.

8. This name was kept until 1863, when the organization became known as the New York Stock Exchange.

9. *Daily Record*, New York Stock and Exchange Board, October 16, 1818.

10. Vera Smith, *The Rationale of Central Banking and the Free Banking Alternative*. (1936; reprint, Indianapolis: Liberty Press, 1990), p. 47.

11. *McCulloch v. Maryland*, 4 Wheat. 316, 4 L.Ed. 579 (1819).

12. T. F. Gordon, *The War on the Bank of the United States* (Philadelphia: Key and Biddle, 1834), p. 13.

13. Quoted in Herman Krooss, ed., *Documentary History of Money and Currency in the United States* (New York: Chelsea House, 1969), vol. 1, p. 703.

14. J. T. Holdsworth and D. R. Dewey, *The First and Second Banks of the United States*. (Washington, D.C.: 61st Cong., 2nd Sess. S. Doc. 571, 1910), p. 302.

15. Stedman, *New York Stock Exchange*, p. 91.

16. Gustavus Myers, *History of the Great American Fortunes* (New York: Modern Library, 1936).

17. Wilkins, *History of Foreign Investment*, p. 55.

18. Short sellers benefit from a stock's price fall. They borrow stock to deliver to their buyers and later buy it back at a lower price, delivering it to the lender.

19. Time deliveries were common on the London Stock Exchange, where they were broken into periods of one month or less, called *accounts*. Buyers could purchase a stock at the beginning of an account period and not pay for it in full until the end.

20. A Reformed Stock Gambler (Anonymous), *Stocks and Stock-Jobbing in Wall Street with Sketches of Brokers and Fancy Stocks* (New York: New York Publishing Co., 1848), p. 12ff.

21. These fraudulent practices were all finally proscribed in Article 9 of the Securities Exchange Act of 1934. Until that time they were considered a normal part of doing business on the exchange.

22. A Reformed Stock Gambler, *Stocks and Stock-Jobbing*, p. 21.

Chapter 2

1. Carosso, *Investment Banking in America*, p. 12.

2. Matthew Josephson, *The Robber Barons: The Great American Capitalists 1861–1901* (New York: Harcourt Brace, 1934), chap. 9.

3. Stephen Birmingham, *"Our Crowd": The Great Jewish Families of New York* (New York: Harper and Row, 1967), chap. 1.

4. U.S. Senate, "Report of the Secretary of the Treasury in Answer to a Resolution of the Senate Calling for the Amount of American Securities Held in Europe and Other Foreign Countries, on 30th June 1853," Executive Document No. 42, 33rd Congress, 1st sess., 1854.

5. Birmingham, *"Our Crowd,"* p. 32.

6. Quoted in Wilkens, *History of Foreign Investment*, p. 70.

7. Stedman, *New York Stock Exchange*, p. 100.

8. Alastair Burnet, *America 1843–1993: One Hundred Fifty Years of Reporting the American Connection* (London: The Economist, 1993), p. 16.

9. Ibid., p. 18

10. Wilkins, *History of Foreign Investment*, p. 96.

11. Quoted in Stedman, *New York Stock Exchange*, p. 115; italics added.

12. Henry Clews, *Twenty Eight Years in Wall Street* (New York: Irving Publishing, 1887), p. 10.

13. Quoted in Henrietta M. Larson, *Jay Cooke: Private Banker* (Cambridge, Mass.: Harvard University Press, 1936), p. 69.

14. Ibid., p. 106.

15. Ibid., p. 108.

16. Burnet, *America 1843–1993*, p. 30.

17. *Philadelphia Press*, April 8, 1863.

18. Larson, *Jay Cooke*, p. 165.

19. Ibid., p. 177.

20. A national bank was one that registered as such with the Comptroller of the Currency and received the designation "national." The smaller banks that did not register continued to be called state banks.

21. The term *robber baron* was first used by a New York journalist, Matthew Josephson, in a book with that title published in 1934.

22. Richard O'Connor, *Gould's Millions* (New York: Doubleday, 1962), p. 86.

23. Quoted in ibid., p. 129.

Chapter 3

1. Myers, *History of the Great American Fortunes*, p. 309.

2. Margaret G. Meyers, *A Financial History of the United States* (New York: Columbia University Press, 1970), p. 182.

3. "The Ticker," December 1907.

4. The idea that economic downturns were "panics," caused by lack of confidence, became a dominant theme of many politicians who refused to recognize the need for changes in economic policy. As late as 1932, Herbert Hoover still insisted that the Great Depression could be overcome only if investors began to have more faith in the marketplace. Workers would have to work harder to overcome falling incomes, and the lazy would simply have to find new jobs if their old employment ceased.

5. Clews, *Twenty Eight Years in Wall Street*, p. 247.

6. Quoted in Vincent Carosso, *More Than a Century of Investment Banking: The Kidder, Peabody and Co. Story* (New York: McGraw-Hill, 1979), p. 24.

7. *Harper's Weekly*, February 24, 1872, p. 165.

8. Myers, *History of the Great American Fortunes*, p. 475.

9. Ibid., p. 477.

10. Andrew Carnegie, *Autobiography* (Boston: Houghton Mifflin, 1920), p. 115.

11. The deplorable state of the rails also led George Westinghouse to invent the air braking system for railway rolling stock, using compressed air as the heart of its mechanism. Westinghouse began working on the project in 1868, and it took almost four years to perfect.

12. Carnegie, *Autobiography*, p. 152.

13. Ibid.

14. Ibid., p. 156.

15. Ibid., p. 157.

16. Burnet, *America 1853–1993*, p. 57.

17. Quoted in Alan Nevins, *John D. Rockefeller*, abridged by William Greenleaf (New York: Scribner, 1959), p. 48.

18. Philanthropy became a major preoccupation with many of the financiers and industrialists of the period. Most visibly, Rockefeller endowed the University of Chicago and Carnegie endowed the Carnegie Institute in Pittsburgh in addition to hundreds of public libraries across the country. Each contributed in excess

of $250 million. Vanderbilt contributed to the Central University in Tennessee, which changed its name to Vanderbilt University to honor him. Even Daniel Drew helped endow a college by pledging money to the Methodist Seminary in New Jersey, which was later to become Drew University. Russell Sage endowed a college bearing his name in Troy, New York. Less visibly, the Seligmans supported Mary Todd Lincoln in later life after her husband was assassinated and she was left almost destitute. She spent most of her later years living in Germany.

19. Josephson, *Robber Barons*, p. 184.

20. Myers, *History of the Great American Fortunes*, p. 340. Vanderbilt eventually accumulated over $50 million in Treasury bonds but was forced to liquidate some of the proceeds in 1884 to bail out his two sons, who had lost millions on the New York Stock Exchange.

21. Carosso, *Investment Banking in America*, p. 31.

22. Clews, *Twenty Eight Years in Wall Street*, p. 65.

23. Josephson, *Robber Barons*, p. 210. Although Field was a party to the operation, he was subsequently ruined by Gould in the process.

24. O'Connor, *Gould's Millions*, p. 188.

Chapter 4

1. Edward Bellamy, *Looking Backward, 2000–1887* (Boston: Houghton Mifflin), pp. 55–56.

2. Named after Charles Ponzi, who opened an investment scheme in Boston, mostly among Italian immigrants. Promising huge gains, Ponzi was able to pay old shareholders in his scheme enormous gains, using newer shareholders' funds to do so. He was finally exposed after the *Wall Street Journal* reported on the plan and showed that no investment at the time was mathematically capable of producing the returns that Ponzi guaranteed.

3. Clews, *Twenty Eight Years in Wall Street*, p. 591.

4. Burnet, *America 1843–1993*, p. 58.

5. Lloyd Wendt, *The Wall Street Journal: The Story of Dow Jones and the Nation's Business Newspaper* (Chicago: Rand McNally, 1982), p. 38.

6. Nevins, *John D. Rockefeller*, p. 156.

7. Ron Chernow, *The House of Morgan: An American Banking Dynasty and the Rise of Modern Finance* (New York: Simon and Schuster, 1990), p. 76.

8. Henry Adams, *Letters of Henry Adams*, vol. 2, (Boston, Houghton Mifflin, 1930), p. 103.

9. Forrest McDonald, *Insull* (Chicago: University of Chicago Press, 1962), p. 40.

10. Carnegie, *Autobiography*, p. 253.

11. Chernow, *House of Morgan*, p. 84.

12. Carnegie, *Autobiography*, p. 256.

13. Edwin Lefevre, *Reminiscences of a Stock Operator* (New York: George H. Doran, 1923), p. 241.

14. Chernow, *House of Morgan*, p. 123.

15. Myers, *History of the Great American Fortunes*, p. 623 ff.

16. Chernow, *House of Morgan*, p. 125.

17. Myers, *History of the Great American Fortunes*, p. 624.

18. Dow tracked the prices of American Cotton Oil; American Sugar; American Tobacco; Chicago Gas; Distilling and Cattle Feeding; General Electric; Laclede Gas; National Lead; North American; Tennessee Coal and Iron; US Leather; and US Rubber. See Wendt, *Wall Street Journal*, pp. 66–70.

Chapter 5

1. Quoted in Louis D. Brandeis, *Other People's Money and How the Bankers Use It* (New York: Frederick A. Stokes, 1914), p. 223.

2. Myers, *History of the Great American Fortunes*, p. 594.

3. Quoted in Krooss, *Documentary History of Banking and Currency in the United States*, vol. 3, p. 2112.

4. Ibid., p. 2123.

5. Brandeis, *Other People's Money*, pp. 32–33.

6. *New York Sun*, January 11, 1913.

7. Birmingham, *"Our Crowd,"* p. 354.

8. Paul Warburg, *The Federal Reserve System* (New York: Macmillan, 1930), pp. 16–19. See also William Greider, *Secrets of the Temple: How the Federal Reserve Runs the Country* (New York: Simon and Schuster, 1987), p. 286 ff., for an account of the Jekyll Island meeting and the conspiracy theories that surrounded it.

9. [Clinton Gilbert], *Mirrors of Wall Street* (New York: Putnam, 1933), p. 262.

10. Quoted in J. A. Livingston, *The American Stockholder* (New York: Lippincott, 1958), p. 190.

11. Carter Glass, *An Adventure in Constructive Finance* (Garden City, N.Y.: Doubleday, Page, 1927), p. 116.

12. Alpheus Thomas Mason, *Brandeis: A Free Man's Life* (New York: Viking, 1946), p. 202.

13. Ibid., pp. 203–4. Pamphlets and special-purpose magazines and books would become a favorite method used by industrialists and Wall Street bankers in later decades to attack political opponents. This would be true especially in the 1920s and early 1930s. See Chapters 6 and 7.

14. John Morton Blum, ed. *Public Philosopher: Selected Letters of Walter Lippmann* (New York: Ticknor and Fields, 1985), p. 63.

15. Brandeis, *Other People's Money*, p. 7.

16. Ibid., pp. 82–83.

17. Ibid., p. 62.

18. Ferdinand Pecora, *Wall Street Under Oath: The Story of Our Modern Moneychangers* (New York: Simon and Schuster, 1939), p. 39.

19. Austin Chamberlain of Britain shared the prize with Dawes for his work in helping form the Locarno Pact.

20. Chernow, *House of Morgan*, p. 207.

21. Carosso, *Investment Banking in America*, p. 226.

22. Josephson, *Robber Barons*, p. 452.

Chapter 6

1. Glass, *Adventure in Constructive Finance*, p. 275.

2. Joseph Stagg Lawrence, *Wall Street and Washington* (Princeton, N.J.: Princeton University Press, 1929), p. 14.

3. U.S. Department of the Treasury, *Annual Report*, 1918, p. 70.

4. *The Magazine of Wall Street*, June 9, 1917.

5. Lefevre, *Reminiscences of a Stock Operator*, p. 11 ff.

6. John Maynard Keynes, "The Economic Consequences of Mr. Churchill," in *Essays in Persuasion* (New York: Norton, 1963), pp. 248–49.

7. Chernow, *House of Morgan*, p. 276.

8. Harold van B. Cleveland and Thomas Huertas, *Citibank, 1812–1970* (Cambridge, Mass.: Harvard University Press, 1985), p. 136.

9. Ibid., p. 139.

10. Fletcher Dobyns, *The Amazing Story of Repeal: An Expose of the Power of Propaganda* (Chicago: Willett, Clark, 1940), p. ix.

11. Another wealthy investor of the period was Walter Chrysler, who announced plans to build the world's tallest office building in midtown Manhattan. Unknown to everyone at the time, Raskob had been secretly planning to build the Empire State Building at Fifth Avenue and Thirty-fourth Street for some time with the assistance of architect William Lamb.

12. Dobyns, *Amazing Story of Repeal*, p. 18.

13. Blum, *Public Philosopher*, p. 186.

14. Dobyns, *Amazing Story of Repeal*, p. 249.

15. Quoted in Dobyns, *Amazing Story of Repeal*, p. 255.

16. At the low end of the income scale, tax rates started at about 4 percent and fell to around 1.5 percent by 1929.

17. John Kenneth Galbraith, *The Great Crash 1929* (London: Penguin, 1975), p. 172.

18. House Committee on Banking and Currency, 70th Congress, 1st sess., H.R. 11806. On January 17, 1928, the Senate passed what was known as the La Follette resolution, sponsored by Senator Robert La Follette of Wisconsin. It stated that the Senate should suggest the Federal Reserve Board take steps to advise against further expansion of loans by member banks for purely speculative purposes and to encourage contraction of the loans in the near future.

19. *New York Times*, April 2, 1929.

20. *New York Times*, April 19, 1929.

21. Ibid.

22. The McFadden Act was better known for prohibiting commercial banks from establishing new branches across state lines. It was finally rolled back when the Interstate Banking Act of 1994 was passed.

23. *Wall Street Journal*, December 8, 1928.

24. Burnet, *America 1843–1993*, p. 109.

25. The term *market break* was also used to describe the stock market collapse of October 1987. The term appeared in the official Republican administration's response to the market drop and recommendations of how to prevent future precipitous market falls.

26. February 7, 1929; quoted in Lawrence, *Wall Street and Washington*, p. 437.

27. Quoted in the *New York Times*, March 31, 1929.

28. Gordon Thomas and Max Morgan-Witts, *The Day the Bubble Burst: A Social History of the Wall Street Crash of 1929* (Garden City, N.Y.: Doubleday, 1979), p. 136.

29. Sheridan A. Logan, *George F. Baker and His Bank: 1840–1955* (Privately published, 1981), p. 263.

30. One abuse found during the Senate hearings in 1933 concerned investment banks' underwriting techniques. It was traditional for underwriters to allocate more bonds to the underwriting syndicate than were actually in existence. This created a demand among investors that helped prop up the price of the bonds. Some underwriters took this to an extreme and used funds from the bond issuer to prop up the bond price in the secondary market after the syndicate had finished its business. The process was objectionable because it gave investors a false feeling of confidence that the bonds would behave well in the future, which may not have been the case.

31. *New York Times*, April 15, 1929.

32. Lefevre, *Reminiscences of a Stock Operator*, p. 233. This book was dedicated to Jesse Livermore, one of the best-known stock manipulators of his day, whose antics on the exchange extended well into the 1920s.

33. Thomas and Morgan-Witts, *Day the Bubble Burst*, p. 122.

34. Galbraith, *Great Crash 1929*, p. 50f.

35. Chernow, *House of Morgan*, p. 309.

36. Mason, *Brandeis*, p. 598.

37. February 12, 1929; quoted in Lawrence, *Wall Street and Washington*, p. 447. Brookhart was quoting from a U.S. Department of Agriculture publication.

38. Bernard Baruch, *My Own Story* (New York: Holt, Rinehart and Winston, 1957), p. 241.

39. Barrie Wigmore, *The Crash and Its Aftermath: A History of Securities Markets in the United States, 1929–1933* (Westport, Conn.: Greenwood Press, 1985), p. 28.

40. Pecora, *Wall Street Under Oath*, pp. 154–57.

41. Apart from a few well-known suicides, the rate did not actually increase in New York, as Galbraith points out (*Great Crash 1929*, chap. 8). The newspapers created the illusion after some well-known traders, including James Riordan of the County Trust Company and a close colleague of Al Smith, took their own lives. But the postcrash period became known as one of suicides nevertheless.

42. Wigmore, *The Crash and Its Aftermath*, pp. 32–33.

Chapter 7

1. [Gilbert], *Mirrors of Wall Street*, p. 268.

2. *New York Times*, March 18, 1933.

3. *New York Times*, December 14, 1929.

4. Jesse Jones, with Edward Angly, *Fifty Billion Dollars: My Thirteen Years with the RFC* (New York: Macmillan, 1951), p. 72 ff.

5. Morgan was accused more than once of involving the United States in the war unofficially, eventually causing Woodrow Wilson to be dragged into the con-

flict. In a 1935 book about Morrow, Harold Nicholson suggested that Morgan's actions helped involve the United States in the war militarily. Thomas Lamont wrote to the *New York Times* (October 18, 1935) to refute the charge.

6. Matthew Josephson, *Infidel in the Temple: A Memoir of the Nineteen Thirties* (New York: Knopf, 1967), chap. 5.

7. Herbert Hoover, *The Memoirs of Herbert Hoover* (New York: Macmillan, 1952), p. 115.

8. Gilbert, *Mirrors of Wall Street*, p. 255. Gilbert died a year before the book was published. Several other of his books were also published anonymously, notably *The Mirrors of Washington* and *Behind the Mirrors*.

9. Baruch, *My Own Story*, p. 51.

10. *New York Times*, April 9, 1932.

11. Pecora, *Wall Street Under Oath*, p. 52.

12. U.S. Senate "Stock Exchange Practices Report." Senate Report 1455, Senate Banking Committee, 73rd Cong., 2nd Sess. (1934), p. 339.

13. Ibid., p. 6. Underwriting had a different meaning in the period prior to the passage of the Securities Act and the Securities and Exchange Act. As the Fletcher Report showed, underwriting technically meant that investment bankers would buy any unsold stock from the issuer and dispose of it in point of time (Chapter 2, part 3). What is known as underwriting today (the purchase of an entire issue of securities by an investment banker from an issuer with the intention of selling them to investors) was also practiced at that time but was not properly underwriting as such. Agreeing to buy the unsold portion was actually underwriting.

14. Quoted in ibid., p. 87.

15. Pecora, *Wall Street Under Oath*, p. 86.

16. Chernow, *House of Morgan*, pp. 352–53.

17. Eliot Rosen, *Hoover, Roosevelt and the Brains Trust* (New York: Columbia University Press, 1977), chap. 9.

18. *Barron's*, February 13, 1933.

19. McDonald, *Insull*, p. 316.

20. Pecora, *Wall Street Under Oath*, p. 13.

21. Ibid., pp. 32–33.

22. Mason, *Brandeis*, p. 615.

23. Pecora, *Wall Street Under Oath*, p. 82.

24. *New York Times*, February 28, 1933.

25. *New York Times*, February 28, 1933.

26. Quoted in Joel Seligman, *The Transformation of Wall Street: A History of the Securities and Exchange Commission and Modern Corporate Finance* (Boston: Houghton Mifflin, 1982), p. 53.

27. The Securities Act required new issues of securities to be subject to a twenty-one-day "cooling-off" period. The FTC and then the SEC would not allow the securities to be sold to the public during that time.

28. A mandate is given by an issuer of securities to an investment banker, who then puts together the deal and arranges for it to be sold.

29. Quoted in Pecora, *Wall Street Under Oath*, p. 285. Technically, the Banking Act did not prohibit commercial banks from underwriting and trading corporate

securities outright. A specific section (20) prohibited a commercial bank from earning more than 10 percent of its profits from the securities markets. That particular bit provided for the actual separation. Most commercial banks realized how much of a restraint it was and decided to remain commercial banks.

30. *New York Times*, June 1, 1934.

31. Chernow, *House of Morgan*, p. 380.

32. Ibid., p. 379.

33. Bruce Allen Murphy, *The Brandeis/Frankfurter Connection* (New York: Oxford University Press, 1982), p. 133.

34. Arthur M. Schlesinger Jr., *The Coming of the New Deal* (Boston: Houghton Mifflin, 1959), p. 463.

35. *Stock Exchange Practices*, p. 113.

36. Printed in the *New York Times*, July 26, 1934.

37. Seligman, *Transformation of Wall Street*, p. 122.

38. George Wolfskill, *The Revolt of the Conservatives: A History of the American Liberty League, 1934–1940* (Boston: Houghton Mifflin, 1962), p. 29.

39. Quoted in Charles Geisst, *Visionary Capitalism: Financial Markets and the American Dream in the Twentieth Century* (New York: Praeger, 1990), p. 165.

40. *Schecter Poultry Corporation v. United States*, 295 U.S. 495, 55 S.Ct. 837, 79 L.Ed. 1570 (1935).

41. Quoted in Wolfskill, *Revolt of the Conservatives*, p. 73.

42. Quoted in ibid., p. 152.

43. Murphy, *Brandeis/Frankfurter Connection*, p. 164.

44. Quoted in Carosso, *Investment Banking in America*, p. 436.

Chapter 8

1. Quoted in Harold Gosnell, *Truman's Crises: A Political Biography of Harry S. Truman* (Westport, Conn.: Greenwood Press, 1980), p. 130.

2. Harry S. Truman, *Memoirs*, vol. 2 (Garden City, N.Y.: Doubleday, 1956), p. 45.

3. Gallup polls of October 20, October 27, and November 11, 1935, respectively. See George H. Gallup, *The Gallup Poll: Public Opinion 1935–1971* (New York: Random House, 1972).

4. Floor members included the specialists who dominated trading in their respective stocks. Commission brokers were those who operated for customers rather than for their own accounts.

5. Carosso, *Investment Banking in America*, p. 385.

6. William O. Douglas, *Democracy and Finance* (New Haven, Conn.: Yale University Press, 1940), p. 8 ff.

7. Ibid., p. 82.

8. *New York Times*, August 3, 1937.

9. Carosso, *Investment Banking in America*, p. 397.

10. Gallup poll, April 13, 1938.

11. Douglas, *Democracy and Finance*, p. 89.

12. Quoted in Geisst, *Visionary Capitalism*, p. 87.

13. Jones, *Fifty Billion Dollars*, p. 24.

14. Ibid., p. 151.

15. *New York Times*, May 1, 1938.

16. Temporary National Economic Committee, "Hearings before Temporary National Economic Committee." 75th Congress, 3rd Sess, pt. 24, p. 12991.

17. Chernow, *House of Morgan*, p. 471.

18. David Lynch, *The Concentration of Economic Power* (New York: Columbia University Press, 1946), p. 118.

19. Quoted in Carosso, *Investment Banking in America*, p. 432.

20. Harold Stanley, "Competitive Bidding for New Issues of Corporate Securities," (New York: Morgan Stanley & Co., 1939).

21. Otis and Co., "Investors, Dealers and Issuers Would Benefit by Competitive Bidding for the Securities of Public Utilities: A Reply to the Opponents of Competitive Bidding." Cleveland: Otis and Co., 1941.

22. Quoted in Seligman, *Transformation of Wall Street*, p. 218.

23. *New York Times*, January 2, 1942.

24. *New York Times*, January 3, 1943.

25. Jones, *Fifty Billion Dollars*, p. 460.

26. U.S. Department of Commerce, *Historical Statistics of the United States: Colonial times to 1957.* (Washington, DC: U.S. Department of Commerce, 1961), p. 720.

27. Margin requirements on loans by brokers to customers were governed by Regulation T of the Federal Reserve, giving the central bank the power to change the percentage requirements in order to ward off speculation in the stock markets.

28. Truman, *Memoirs*, vol. 2, p. 45.

29. In addition to Morgan Stanley, the codefendants were Kuhn, Loeb & Co., Smith, Barney & Co.; Lehman Brothers; Glore Forgan & Co.; Kidder Peabody; Goldman, Sachs; White Weld & Co.; Eastman Dillon & Co.; Drexel & Co.; The First Boston Corporation; Dillon Read & Co.; Blyth & Co.; Harriman Ripley & Co.; Union Securities Corporation; Stone & Webster Securities Corp.; Harris, Hall & Co.; and the Investment Bankers Association as well.

30. *Corrected Opinion of Harold R. Medina United States Circuit Judge, in United States of America v. Henry S. Morgan et al.*, February 4, 1954, p. 2.

31. Ibid., p. 9.

32. Ibid., p. 48.

33. Carosso, *Investment Banking in America*, p. 466.

34. *US v. Henry S. Morgan*, vol. 1, p. 29.

35. *Corrected Opinion*, p. 416.

Chapter 9

1. By a ratio of five or six to one on average until the mid-1970s.

2. The NYSE listed eight stocks that had paid dividends for the previous one hundred years, led by the Pennsylvania Railroad, paying since 1848. Another seventeen had paid for at least seventy-five years, and 113 for at least fifty years. NYSE *Year Book, 1963*.

3. Blum, *Public Philosopher*, p. 594.

4. Mutual fund investment is counted as an individual's investment, not an institutional one.

5. Cited in Vance Packard, *The Status Seekers* (New York: Pocket Books, 1961), p. 99.

6. Dwight D. Eisenhower, *The White House Years: Waging Peace 1956–1961* (Garden City, N.Y.: Doubleday, 1965), p. 661.

7. Quoted in Seligman, *Transformation of Wall Street*, p. 417.

8. LTV went into bankruptcy proceedings partly because of the Employees Retirement Income Security Act (ERISA), passed by Congress in 1974. It was later found to owe a substantial amount of pension money to its employees, finally forcing it to file for protection under the bankruptcy act.

9. Anthony Sampson, *The Sovereign State of ITT* (New York: Stein and Day, 1973), p. 18.

10. Seligman, *Transformation of Wall Street*, p. 422.

11. *Consumer Reports*, November, 1967.

12. *New York Times*, June 7, 1969.

13. *New York Times*, May 22, 1969; italics added.

14. *New York Times*, May 20, 1969.

15. *New York Times*, May 17, 1969.

16. Quoted in Seligman, *Transformation of Wall Street*, p. 361.

17. Raymond L. Dirks and Leonard Gross, *The Great Wall Street Scandal* (New York: McGraw-Hill, 1974), p. 6.

18. First-market trading referred to the NYSE, the second market to the other exchanges (Amex and the regionals), and the third market to the over-the-counter market for stocks.

19. A link still existed between banks and brokers in the form of call money, loaned by banks to brokers for margin lending. SEC regulations existed to monitor the amounts.

Chapter 10

1. Robert Solomon, *The International Monetary System, 1945–76* (New York: Harper and Row, 1977), p. 191.

2. *New York Times*, August 16, 1971.

3. *Wall Street Journal*, November 18, 1970.

4. The SEC, which had jurisdiction over the options markets for stocks, was slow in allowing new puts (options to sell) to be created on many stocks. Short sellers could force down the price of a stock by buying puts, a technique that had been practiced since the previous century.

5. Interest rates on deposits were regulated by Federal Reserve Regulation Q, in effect since the Glass-Steagall Act was passed in 1933.

6. Paul Einzig, *The Eurobond Market* (London: Macmillan, 1969), p. 13.

7. By avoiding the Yankee bond market, the company did not have to file with the SEC or pay the required premium in the Yankee market, which would have been taxed at the investors' level in any event.

8. *New York Times*, July 22, 1975.

9. Freddie Mac is short for the Federal Home Loan Mortgage Corporation. It functions in a similar manner to Ginnie and Fannie Mae but buys predominantly mortgages originated by savings and loan associations.

10. Connie Bruck, *The Predators' Ball: The Junk Bond Raiders and the Man Who Staked Them* (New York: American Lawyer/Simon and Schuster, 1988), p. 65.

11. Quoted in Greider, *Secrets of the Temple*, p. 47.

12. "The Contributions and Limitations of 'Monetary Analysis'" (meeting of the American Economic Association, Atlantic City, NJ, September 16, 1976).

13. *New York Times*, October 8, 1979.

14. A week after the bond deal was announced and syndicated, IBM announced a third-quarter loss of 18 percent over the previous quarter on a revenue increase of only 2 percent.

15. *Wall Street Journal*, January 30, 1981.

16. Donald Regan, *For the Record: From Wall Street to Washington* (New York: Harcourt Brace, 1988), p. 142.

17. *Wall Street Journal*, December 12, 1980.

18. The Open Market Committee was a group of Fed officials who were responsible for implementing the board's decisions in the market. Its minutes were never released at the time of the meeting but only before the next meeting, usually five weeks later, which added an element of intrigue to the Fed's actions.

19. *International Herald Tribune*, May 10, 1981.

20. Regan, *For the Record*, p. 172.

Chapter 11

1. *Wall Street Journal*, November 3, 1982.

2. *New York Times*, November 7, 1982.

3. Ibid.

4. Mary Zey, *Banking on Fraud: Drexel, Junk Bonds, and Buyouts* (New York: Aldine de Gruyter, 1993), p. 16.

5. *Business Week*, November 11, 1985.

6. Securities Industries Association, *The International Market: Growth in Primary and Secondary Activity* (New York: Securities Industries Association, 1987), p. 2.

7. Quoted in I. M. Destler and C. Randall Henning, *Dollar Politics: Exchange Rate Policymaking in the United States* (Washington, D.C.: Institute for International Economics, 1989), p. 27.

8. Margaret Thatcher, *The Downing Street Years* (New York: HarperCollins, 1993), p. 694.

9. *Wall Street Journal*, October 20, 1987.

10. Charles Geisst, *Exchange Rate Chaos: Twenty Five Years of Finance and Consumer Democracy* (London: Routledge, 1995), p. 137.

11. Speech to the Canadian Club of Toronto, November 16, 1987.

12. "International Economic Cooperation," in Federal Reserve Bank of New York, *Annual Report*, 1994.

13. Margin trading means buying a stock on borrowed money. If the stock declines, additional funds can be required by the broker. If the investor does not have the money, the broker sells his holdings.

14. *New York Times*, February 17, 1988.

15. Securities Industry Association, "Foreign Activity," October 21, 1988, p. 10.

16. *New York Times*, February 4, 1988.

17. Chernow, *House of Morgan*, p. 716.

18. Board of Governors of the Federal Reserve System, "Order Conditionally Approving Applications to Engage, to a Limited Extent, in Underwriting and Dealing in Certain Securities," Press Release, January 18, 1989, p. 29.

19. Specifically, Section 20, known as the 10 percent rule. This prohibited commercial banks from ever earning more than 10 percent of their revenue from underwriting. That was the provision that had forced many of the banks from the securities business almost sixty years earlier. The rule was waived for those banks that made substantial profits dealing Treasury securities.

20. Robert Sobel, *Dangerous Dreamers: The Financial Innovators from Charles Merrill to Michael Milken* (New York: Wiley, 1993), p. 209.

21. *New York Times*, May 1, 1990.

22. Destler and Henning, *Dollar Politics*, pp. 69–70.

23. *New York Times*, December 20, 1994.

24. "Reforming Glass-Steagall in the Public Interest," JP Morgan & Co., April 1995.

25. See Chapter 8.

26. *Wall Street Journal*, November 25, 1996.

27. *New York Times*, December 7, 1996.

28. Christie, William G. and Paul Schultz, "Why Do NASDAQ Market Makers Avoid Odd-Eighth Quotes?" *The Journal of Finance*, December 1994, Vol. 49, Issue 5, p. 1813 ff.

29. *Los Angeles Times*, March 14, 1995.

30. *Wall Street Journal*, June 9, 1997.

31. Mark Ingebretsen, *NASDAQ: A History of the Market That Changed the World* (New York: Forum Books, 2002), p. 154.

32. Front running was a practice also found on the futures exchanges where a trader would enter his own order having already seen a customer's order, hoping to profit from the ensuing price movement.

33. *New York Times*, December 7, 1996.

34. *Washington Post*, September 28, 1997.

35. *Journal of Accountancy*, August 1997.

36. *Washington Post*, February 6, 1997.

Chapter 12

1. Securities Industry Association, *Securities Industry Fact Book* (New York, 2002).

2. Investment Company Institute & Securities Industry Association, *Equity Ownership in America* (New York, 2002).

3. *Wall Street Journal*, January 5, 1996.

4. Selling short on a down-tick means that a short seller can sell a stock that is on a steady downward trend. In the Securities Exchange Act of 1934, short selling was only allowed on an up-tick, meaning that someone must have bought the stock before a short sell order could be executed.

5. Roger Lowenstein, *When Genius Failed* (New York: Random House, 2000) p. 103.

6. Ibid., p. 104.

7. Ibid., p. 120.

8. Henry Kaufman, *On Money & Markets: A Wall Street Memoir* (New York: McGraw-Hill, 2000), p. 283.

9. Federal Document Clearing House, June 13, 2000.

10. Federal Reserve, *Press Release*, September 23, 1998.

11. *New York Times*, November 12, 1999.

12. Alan T. Saracevic, "So Much for Wall Street Cleaning Up Its Act," *San Francisco Chronicle*, October 13, 2002.

13. *Business Week*, June 18, 2001.

14. In addition to the Graham and Dodd book, *Security Analysis*, the period also produced one of the best-known analytical bond techniques, known as duration analysis. In a paper produced for the National Bureau of Economic Research in 1938, Frederick Macaulay described the technique that would later become widely used on Wall Street, especially on the buy side, and in academic circles.

15. *On Wall Street*, July 1, 2002.

16. Interview on CNNfn, "Before Hours," June 30, 2000.

17. *Pensions and Investments*, June 25, 2001.

18. *Network World*, December 28, 1998.

19. *Fortune*, December 21, 1998.

20. Investment Company Institute & the Securities Industry Association, *Equity Ownership in America*, 2002.

21. *Economist Intelligence Unit*, December 13, 2001.

22. *Fortune*, October 15, 2001.

23. *Financial Times*, July 23, 1996.

24. *Merger & Acquisitions Report*, September 9, 1996.

25. *American Banker*, January 22, 2002.

Bibliography

Primary Sources

Adams, Henry. *Letters of Henry Adams*. Boston: Houghton Mifflin, 1930.

Anonymous. *Stocks and Stock-Jobbing in Wall Street with Sketches of Brokers and Fancy Stocks*. New York: New York Publishing Co., 1848.

Baruch, Bernard. *My Own Story*. New York: Holt, Rinehart and Winston, 1957.

Bellamy, Edward. *Looking Backward, 2000–1887*. Boston: Houghton Mifflin, 1926.

Berle, Adolph, and Gardiner Means. *The Modern Corporation and Private Property*. New York: Macmillan, 1933.

Blum, John Morton, ed. *Public Philosopher: Selected Letters of Walter Lippmann*. New York: Ticknor and Fields, 1985.

Brandeis, Louis D. *Other People's Money and How the Bankers Use It*. New York: Frederick D. Stokes, 1914.

Carnegie, Andrew. *Autobiography*. Boston: Houghton Mifflin, 1920.

Clews, Henry. *Fifty Years in Wall Street*. New York: Irving Publishing, 1908.

Cutler, William Parker, and Julia Cutler. *The Life, Journals and Correspondence of Rev. Manassah Cutler*. Cincinnati: R. Clarke, 1888.

Dobyns, Fletcher. *The Amazing Story of Repeal: An Expose of the Power of Propaganda*. Chicago: Willett, Clark, 1940.

Douglas, William O. *Finance and Democracy*. New Haven, Conn.: Yale University Press, 1940.

Eisenhower, Dwight D. *Mandate for Change, 1953–1956*. Garden City, N.Y.: Doubleday, 1963.

———. *The White House Years: Waging Peace, 1965–1961*. Garden City, N.Y.: Doubleday, 1965.

Fowler, William Worthington. *Twenty Years of Inside Life in Wall Street*. New York: Orange Judd, 1880.

Gallup, George H. *The Gallup Poll: Public Opinion 1935–1971.* New York: Random House, 1972.

Hoover, Herbert. *American Individualism.* Garden City, N.Y.: Doubleday Page, 1922.

———. *The Challenge to Liberty.* New York: Scribner, 1934.

———. *The Memoirs of Herbert Hoover.* New York: Macmillan, 1952.

Investment Company Institute and the Securities Industry Association. *Equity Ownership in America.* New York: Securities Industry Association, 2002.

Johnson, Lyndon Baines. *The Vantage Point: Perspectives on the Presidency 1963–1968.* New York: Holt, Rinehart and Winston, 1971.

Jones, Jesse, with Edward Angly. *Fifty Billion Dollars: My Thirteen Years with the RFC.* New York: Macmillan, 1952.

Keynes, John Maynard. "The Economic Consequences of Mr. Churchill." In *Essays in Persuasion.* New York: Norton, 1928.

Krooss, Herman, ed. *Documentary History of Money and Banking in the United States.* 3 vols. New York: Chelsea House, 1969.

Lefevre, Edmund. *Reminiscences of a Stock Manipulator.* New York: George H. Doran, 1923.

Levine, Dennis. *Inside Out: An Insider's Account of Wall Street.* New York: Putnam, 1991.

Lewis, Michael. *Liar's Poker.* New York: Norton, 1989.

Moley, Raymond. *After Seven Years.* 1939. Reprint, Lincoln: University of Nebraska Press, 1971.

Morgan, J. P., and Company. *Rethinking Glass-Steagall.* New York: Privately published, 1984.

———. *Glass-Steagall: Overdue for Repeal.* New York: Privately published, 1995.

New York Stock Exchange. *Fact Book.* Various issues.

New York Stock and Exchange Board. *Report of the Committee of the Gold Board.* June 3, 1865.

Otis and Company. "Investors, Dealers and Issuers Would Benefit by Competitive Bidding for the Securities of Public Utilities." Cleveland: Privately published, 1941.

Pecora, Ferdinand. *Wall Street Under Oath: The Story of Our Modern Moneychangers.* New York: Simon and Schuster, 1939.

Regan, Donald. *For the Record: From Wall Street to Washington.* New York: Harcourt Brace, 1988.

Solomon, Robert. *The International Monetary System, 1945–76.* New York: Harper and Row, 1977.

Stanley, Harold. "Competitive Bidding for New Issues of Corporate Securities." New York: Morgan Stanley & Co., 1939.

Stockman, David. *The Triumph of Politics: The Inside Story of the Regan Revolution.* New York: Avon Books, 1987.

Thatcher, Margaret. *The Downing Street Years.* New York: HarperCollins, 1993.

Truman, Harry S. *Memoirs.* 3 vols. Garden City, N.Y.: Doubleday, 1956.

Secondary Sources

Allen, Frederick Lewis. *Only Yesterday: An Informal History of the 1920s*. New York: Harper and Row, 1931.

———. *The Lords of Creation*. New York: Harper, 1935.

Ambrose, Stephen E. *Nixon: The Triumph of a Politician, 1962–1972*. New York: Simon and Schuster, 1989.

Anders, George. *Merchants of Debt: KKR and the Mortgaging of American Business*. New York: Basic Books, 1992.

Anderson, Clay. *A Half Century of Federal Reserve Policymaking*. Philadelphia: Federal Reserve Bank of Philadelphia, 1965.

Anderson, Gordon. "The Effect of the War on New Security Issues in the United States." *Annals of the American Academy of Political and Social Sciences* 68 (November 1916): 115–27.

Atwood, Albert W. *The Stock and Produce Exchanges*. New York: Alexander Hamilton Institute, 1921.

Auletta, Ken. *Greed and Glory on Wall Street: The Fall of the House of Lehman*. New York: Random House, 1986.

Barron, Clarence W. *They Told Barron*. New York: Harper, 1930.

Baskin, Johnathan B., and Paul J. Miranti. *A History of Corporate Finance*. New York: Cambridge University Press, 1997.

Birmingham, Stephen. *"Our Crowd": The Great Jewish Families of New York*. New York: Harper and Row, 1967.

Black, David. *The King of Fifth Avenue: The Fortunes of August Belmont*. New York: Dial Press, 1981.

Brandes, Joseph. *Herbert Hoover and Economic Diplomacy*. Pittsburgh: University of Pittsburgh Press, 1962.

Brooks, John. *The Seven Fat Years: Chronicles of Wall Street*. New York: Harper and Row, 1958.

———. *Once in Golconda: A True Drama of Wall Street 1920–1938*. New York: Harper and Row, 1969.

———. *The Go-Go Years*. New York: Weybright and Talley, 1973.

———. *The Takeover Game*. New York: Dutton, 1987.

Bruck, Connie. *The Predator's Ball: The Junk Bond Raiders and the Man Who Staked Them*. New York: American Lawyer/Simon and Schuster, 1988.

Burrough, Bryan, and John Helyar. *Barbarians at the Gate: The Fall of RJR Nabisco*. New York: Harper and Row, 1990.

Carosso, Vincent. *Investment Banking in America: A History*. Cambridge, Mass.: Harvard University Press, 1970.

———. *More Than a Century of Investment Banking: The Kidder, Peabody and Co. Story*. New York: McGraw-Hill, 1979.

———. *The Morgans: Private International Bankers*. Cambridge, Mass.: Harvard University Press, 1987.

Chernow, Ron. *The House of Morgan: An American Banking Dynasty and the Rise of Modern Finance*. New York: Simon and Schuster, 1990.

Cleveland, Harold van B., and Thomas Huertas. *Citibank, 1812–1970*. Cambridge, Mass.: Harvard University Press, 1985.

Coit, Margaret L. *Mr. Baruch*. Boston: Houghton Mifflin, 1957.

Congdon, Don, ed. *The Thirties: A Time to Remember*. New York: Simon and Schuster, 1962.

Cowing, Cedric B. *Populists, Plungers, and Progressives: A Social History of Stock and Commodity Speculation 1890–1936*. Princeton: Princeton University Press, 1965.

Davis, Forrest. *What Price Wall Street?* New York: W. Goodwin, 1932.

DeBorchgrave, Alexandra Villard, and John Cullen. *Villard: The Life and Times of an American Titan*. New York: Doubleday, 2001.

Dies, Edward. *Behind the Wall Street Curtain*. Washington, D.C.: Public Affairs Press, 1952.

Dirks, Raymond L., and Leonard Gross. *The Great Wall Street Scandal*. New York: McGraw-Hill, 1974.

Eames, Francis L. *The New York Stock Exchange*. New York: Thomas G. Hall, 1984.

Einzig, Paul. *The Eurobond Market*. London: Macmillan, 1960.

Emery, Henry C. *Speculation on the Stock and Produce Markets*. New York: Columbia University Press, 1986.

Endlich, Lisa. *Goldman Sachs: The Culture of Success*. New York: Knopf, 1999.

Fisher, Irving. "The Rate of Interest After the War." *Annals of the American Academy of Political and Social Sciences* 68 (November 1916): 245–56.

Fowler, William W. *Ten Years in Wall Street*. New York: J. D. Denison, 1870.

Friedman, Milton, and Anna Schwartz. *A Monetary History of the United States*. Princeton, N.J.: Princeton University Press, 1963.

Galbraith, John Kenneth. *The Great Crash 1929*. London: Penguin, 1954.

Geisst, Charles R. *Monopolies in America: Empire Builders and Their Enemies from Jay Gould to Bill Gates*. New York: Oxford University Press, 2000.

———. *The Last Partnerships: Inside the Great Wall Street Money Dynasties*. New York: McGraw-Hill, 2001.

———. *Wheels of Fortune: The History of Speculation from Scandal to Respectability*. New York: John Wiley, 2002.

———. *Deals of the Century: Wall Street, Mergers, and the Making of Modern America*. New York: John Wiley, 2003.

[Gilbert, Clinton]. *Mirrors of Wall Street*. New York: Putnam, 1933.

Gordon, John Steele. *The Scarlet Woman of Wall Street*. New York: Weidenfield and Nicholson, 1988.

Gordon, T. F. *The War on the Bank of the United States*. Philadelphia: Key and Biddle, 1834.

Gosnell, Harold. *Truman's Crises: A Political Biography of Harry S. Truman*. Westport, Conn.: Greenwood Press, 1980.

Govan, Thomas Payne. *Nicholas Biddle: Nationalist and Public Banker, 1786–1884*. Chicago: University of Chicago Press, 1959.

Greider, William. *Secrets of the Temple: How the Federal Reserve Runs the Country*. New York: Simon and Schuster, 1987.

Henriques, Diana. *The White Sharks of Wall Street: Thomas Mellon Evans and the Original Corporate Raiders*. New York: Scribners, 2000.

Hodgson, James. *Wall Street, Asset or Liability?* New York: H. W. Wilson, 1934.

Homer, Sidney. *A History of Interest Rates.* New Brunswick, N.J.: Rutgers University Press, 1963.

Hutchinson, Robert A. *Vesco.* New York: Praeger, 1974.

Ingebretsen, Mark. *NASDAQ: The History of the Market that Changed the World.* New York: Forum Books, 2002.

Josephson, Matthew. *The Robber Barons: The Great American Capitalists 1861–1901.* New York: Harcourt Brace, 1934.

———. *Infidel in the Temple: A Memoir of the Nineteen Thirties.* New York: Knopf, 1967.

Kador, John. *Charles Schwab.* New York: John Wiley, 2002.

Kaufman, Henry. *On Money and Markets: A Wall Street Memoir.* New York: McGraw-Hill, 2000.

Kennedy, David M. *Freedom from Fear: The American People in Depression and War, 1929–1945.* New York: Oxford University Press, 1999.

Kennedy, Susan Estabrook. *The Banking Crisis of 1933.* Lexington: University Press of Kentucky, 1973.

Klein, Maury. *Rainbow's End: The Crash of 1929.* New York: Oxford University Press, 2001.

Kuczynski, Robert. *Banker's Profits from German Loans.* Washington, D.C.: Brookings Institution, 1932.

Larson, Henrietta M. *Jay Cooke, Private Banker.* Cambridge, Mass.: Harvard University Press, 1936.

Lawrence, Joseph Stagg. *Wall Street and Washington.* Princeton, N.J.: Princeton University Press, 1929.

Leuchtenberg, William. *Franklin D. Roosevelt and the New Deal.* New York: Harper and Row, 1963.

Levitt, Arthur. *Take on the Street.* New York: Pantheon Books, 2002.

Logan, Sheridan A. *George F. Baker and His Bank, 1840–1955.* Privately published, 1981.

Lowenstein, Roger. *When Genius Failed: The Rise and Fall of Long-Term Capital Management.* New York: Random House, 2000.

Lundberg, Ferdinand. *America's 60 Families.* New York: Citadel Press, 1937.

———. *The Rich and the Super Rich.* New York: Bantam Books, 1969.

Lynch, David. *The Concentration of Economic Power.* New York: Columbia University Press, 1946.

McCraw, Thomas K. *Prophets of Regulation.* Cambridge, Mass.: Harvard University Press, 1984.

McCusker, John J. *Money and Exchange in Europe and America, 1600–1775.* London: Macmillan, 1978.

McDonald, Forrest. *Insull.* Chicago: University of Chicago Press, 1962.

Mackay, Charles. *Extraordinary Popular Delusions and the Madness of Crowds.* London, 1841. Reprint, New York: Three Rivers Press, 1980.

Mason, Alpheus Thomas. *Brandeis: A Free Man's Life.* New York: Viking, 1946.

Mayer, Martin. *Wall Street: Men and Money.* New York: Harper and Row, 1959.

———. *Nightmare on Wall Street: Salomon Brothers and the Corruption of the Marketplace.* New York: Simon and Schuster, 1993.

————. *Stealing the Market: How the Giant Brokerage Firms, with Help from the SEC, Stole the Market from Investors*. New York: Basic Books, 1992.

Medbury, James Knowles. *Men and Mysteries of Wall Street*. Boston: Fields, Osgood, 1870.

Meyer, Charles H. *The Securities Exchange Act of 1934 Analyzed and Explained*. New York: Francis Emory Fitch, 1934.

Meyers, Margaret G. *A Financial History of the United States*. New York: Columbia University Press, 1970.

Murphy, Bruce Allen. *The Brandeis/Frankfurter Connection*. New York: Oxford University Press, 1982.

Myers, Gustavus. *History of the Great American Fortunes*. 3 vols. Chicago: Charles H. Kerr and Co., 1911.

Moody, John. *Masters of Capital: A Chronicle of Wall Street*. New Haven, Conn.: Yale University Press, 1921.

Neikirk, William. *Volcker: Portrait of the Money Man*. Congdon and Weed, 1987.

Nevins, Allan. *John D. Rockefeller*, Abridged by William Greenleaf. New York: Scribner, 1959.

Noyes, Alexander Dana. *The Marketplace: Reminiscences of a Financial Editor*. Boston: Little, Brown, 1938.

Oberholtzer, Ellis Paxson. *Jay Cooke: Financier of the Civil War*. Philadelphia: George W. Jacobs and Co., 1907.

O'Connor, Harvey. *Mellon's Millons: The Biography of a Fortune*. New York: John Day Co., 1933.

O'Connor, Richard. *Gould's Millons*. New York: Doubleday, 1962.

Packard, Vance. *The Status Seekers*. New York: Pocket Books, 1961.

Partnoy, Frank. *FIASCO: The Inside Story of a Wall Street Trader*. New York: Penguin Putnam, 1999.

Peach, W. Nelson. *The Securities Affiliates of National Banks*. Baltimore, Md.: Johns Hopkins University Press, 1941.

Perez, Robert C., and Edward F. Willett. *Clarence Dillon: Wall Street Enigma*. Lanham, Md.: Madison Books, 1995.

Regan, Donald T. *A View from the Street*. New York: New American Library, 1972.

Ripley, William Z. *Main Street and Wall Street*. Boston: Little, Brown, 1927.

Robbins, Lionel. *The Great Depression*. London: Macmillan, 1934.

Rosen, Eliot. *Hoover, Roosevelt and the Brains Trust*. New York: Columbia University Press, 1977.

Rottenberg, Dan. *The Man Who Made Wall Street: Anthony J. Drexel and the Rise of Modern Finance*. Philadelphia: University of Pennsylvania Press, 2001.

Sampson, Anthony. *The Sovereign State of ITT*. New York: Stein and Day, 1973.

Schlesinger, Arthur M., Jr. *The Coming of the New Deal*. Boston: Houghton Mifflin, 1959.

Seligman, Joel. *The Transformation of Wall Street: A History of the Securities and Exchange Commission and Modern Corporate Finance*. Boston: Houghton Mifflin, 1982.

Siebert, Muriel. *Changing the Rules: Adventures of a Wall Street Maverick*. New York: Free Press, 2002.

Smith, B. Mark. *Toward Rational Exuberance: The Evolution of the Modern Stock Market*. New York: Farar Straus and Giroux, 2001.

Smith, Matthew H. *Bulls and Bears of New York*. Hartford: J. B. Burr, 1875.

Smith, Vera. *Central Banking and the Free Banking Alternative*. 1936. Reprint, Indianapolis: Liberty Press, 1990.

Sobel, Robert. *The Curbstone Brokers: The Origins of the American Stock Exchange*. New York: Macmillan, 1970.

———. *Amex: A History of the American Stock Exchange, 1921–1971*. New York: Weybright and Talley, 1972.

———. *The Big Board: A History of the New York Stock Exchange, 1935–1975*. New York: Weybright and Talley, 1975.

———. *Dangerous Dreamers: The Financial Innovators from Charles Merrill to Michael Milken*. New York: Wiley, 1993.

Sparling, Karl. *Mystery Men of Wall Street*. New York: Blue Ribbon Books, 1930.

Staley, Eugene. *War and the Private Investor*. Chicago: University of Chicago Press, 1935.

Stedman, Edmund Clarence, ed. *The New York Stock Exchange*. 1905. Reprint, New York: Greenwood Press, 1969.

Stewart, James B. *Den of Thieves*. New York: Simon and Schuster, 1991.

Stone, Amey, and Mike Brewster. *King of Capital: Sandy Weill and the Making of Citigroup*. New York: John Wiley and Sons, 2002.

Stone, Dan. *April's Fools: An Insider's Account of the Rise and Collapse of Drexel Burnham*. New York: Donald I. Fine, Inc., 1990.

Strouse, Jean. *Morgan: American Financier*. New York: Random House, 1999.

Thomas, Gordon, and Max Morgan-Witts. *The Day the Bubble Burst: A Social History of the Wall Street Crash of 1929*. Garden City, N.Y.: Doubleday, 1979.

Warburg, Paul. *The Federal Reserve System*. New York: Macmillan, 1930.

Wasserstein, Bruce. *Big Deal: The Battle for Control of America's Leading Corporations*. New York: Warner Books, 1998.

Wendt, Lloyd. *The Wall Street Journal: The Story of Dow Jones and the Nation's Business Newspaper*. Chicago: Rand McNally, 1982.

Werner, M. R. *Little Napoleons and Dummy Directors: Being the Narrative of the Bank of United States*. New York: Harper and Bros., 1933.

Werner, Walter, and Steven T. Smith. *Wall Street*. New York: Columbia University Press, 1991.

White, Brouck. *The Book of Daniel Drew*. Reprint, New York: Citadel Press, 1980.

White, Lawrence J. *The S and L Debacle: Public Policy Lessons for Bank and Thrift Regulation*. New York: Oxford University Press, 1991.

Wicker, Elmus. *The Banking Panics of the Great Depression*. New York: Cambridge University Press, 1996.

Wigmore, Barrie. *The Crash and Its Aftermath: A History of Securities Markets in the United States, 1929–1933*. Westport, Conn.: Greenwood Press, 1985.

———. *Securities Markets in the 1980s: The New Regime, 1979–1984*. New York: Oxford University Press, 1997.

Wilkins, Mira. *A History of Foreign Investment in the United States to 1914*. Cambridge, Mass.: Harvard University Press, 1989.

Willis, Henry Parker. *Investment Banking*. New York: Harper, 1929.

Wilson, John David. *The Chase*. Boston: Harvard Business School Press, 1986.

Wolfskill, George. *The Revolt of the Conservatives: A History of the American Liberty League*. Boston: Houghton Mifflin, 1962.

Zey, Mary. *Banking on Fraud: Drexel, Junk Bonds, and Buyouts*. New York: Aldine de Gruyter, 1993.

Government Documents

Board of Governors of the Federal Reserve System. "Order Conditionally Approving Applications to Engage, to a Limited Extent, in Underwriting and Dealing in Certain Securities." January 18, 1989.

Brady, Nicholas, et al. *Report of the Presidential Task Force on Market Mechanisms*. Washington, D.C.: U.S. Government Printing Office, 1988.

Corrected Opinion of Harold R. Medina, United States Circuit Judge, in United States of America v. Henry S. Morgan, Harold Stanley, et al. February 4, 1954.

Federal Reserve System. *Bulletin*. Various issues.

Interim Report of the Working Group on Financial Markets. Washington, D.C.: U.S. Government Printing Office, 1988.

Holdsworth, J. T., and D. R. Dewey. *The First and Second Banks of the United States*. Washington, D.C.: 61st Cong., 2nd Sess., S. Doc. 571, 1910.

United States v. Henry S. Morgan et al. Civil No. 43–757. United States District Court for the Southern District of New York.

United States v. Michael Milken. D.N.Y. S89. October 18, 1990.

United States. Temporary National Economic Committee. Hearings before Temporary National Economic Committee. Congress of the United States. 75th Congress, 3d sess. pursuant to Public Resolution No. 113.

U.S. Department of Commerce. "The Balance of International Payments of the United States in 1927." Washington, D.C.: U.S. Department of Commerce, 1927.

———. "The Balance of International Payments of the United States in 1929." Washington, D.C.: U.S. Department of Commerce, 1929.

———. *Historical Statistics of the United States: Colonial Times to 1957*. Washington, D.C.: U.S. Department of Commerce, 1961.

U.S. Department of the Treasury. *Annual Report*, various years.

U.S. House of Representatives. "Report to the Special Commissioner of the Revenue upon the Industry, Trade, Commerce &c. or the United States for the Year 1869." Executive Document No. 47. 41st Congress, 2d sess., 1869.

Index

Boldfaced numerals provide the reader with the best explanation of the term.